INSECT CELLS

Their Structure and Function

To
UNA

INSECT CELLS

Their Structure and Function

David S. Smith PhD

*The School of Medicine and
Department of Biology
The University of Miami*

OLIVER AND BOYD · EDINBURGH

OLIVER AND BOYD LTD
Tweeddale Court   Edinburgh 1

First published 1968
© 1968 David S. Smith
05 001699 7

Printed in Great Britain by
R. & R. Clark Ltd   Edinburgh

Contents

'For you must not think that in Man only the Art of the great Artificer is so great, . . . but what creature soever you would dissect, you shall finde the like art and wisdome to appear in it. And such creatures as you cannot possibly dissect, will make you admire the more, the smaller they are.'

THOMAS MOUFFET, *The Theater of Insects* (translated by Edward Topsel, 1658).

That insects are represented by some seven hundred thousand described species out of the million or so in the entire animal catalogue[1] is a tribute not only to the zeal of taxonomists, but also to the great biological success of these arthropods.

Insects have colonised in a spectacular manner the land, air and fresh water, in fact all available habitats except the sea and the extreme polar regions, and within each general environment they have achieved a great range of structural adaptation to meet varying ecological and physiological needs. A study of their form and function is largely a study of these adaptations, viewed in the light of fundamental physiological and biochemical principles shared by animals in general. All animals, regardless of their level of organisation, are faced with certain common functional problems—sensory perception, locomotion, feeding and digestion, excretion, water and ionic balance, respiration, reproduction and so on. The anatomical variations with which these problems are met are virtually limitless: one may think of the modes of locomotion—walking, swimming, jumping, flying—in insects and in vertebrates, equipped respectively with an endoskeleton and a cuticular exoskeleton, or of the anatomical differences between the eyes of these animals. The complex glomerular capsule of many vertebrate kidneys may be contrasted with the anatomically simpler urine-producing Malpighian tubules of insects, or the respiratory function of the vertebrate circulatory system may be contrasted with the tracheal supply which brings molecular oxygen to the tissues of insects without the involvement of a respiratory pigment, such as haemoglobin.

However striking such anatomical differences may be, they sometimes mask close similarities occurring at the level of cellular design and function. Thus the chief differences between the nervous and muscular systems of an insect and a mammal lie in the distribution of excitable cells rather than in fundamental dissimilarities in the mechanisms of impulse conduction and synaptic transfer of excitation from one cell to the next. Again, urine secretion in insects is accomplished without the aid of glomerular filtration from a capillary circulation, but involves a balance between elimination of waste and conservation of useful materials, very similar to that of the vertebrate glomerular kidney. Together with points of resemblance such as these, of course, must be considered the special features in design of each Phylum which represent novel solutions to functional problems. The integument of insects, for example, is quite unlike the vertebrate skin in its physical properties, its function and its cellular and extracellular composition: the cuticle provides the support for skeletal muscles, endows the insect with resistance to desiccation and where it overlies various sensory nerve cells is modified in a number of ways to permit the insect to perceive its environment by means of senses analogous to those of the vertebrate. In short, from the physiological standpoint, an animal may be thought of as presenting a blend of the general and the particular, in the construction and disposition of its functional parts.

It has long been recognised that, at the cellular level, details of structure and function are closely interrelated. Light microscopic studies suggested that cellular specialisation over the range of animal Phyla has been attained conservatively, by permutations of the shape and interrelations of cells and by variation in the number and distribution of a rather small complement of subcellular structures—mitochondria, the ergastoplasm, Golgi bodies, cilia and so on. This general conclusion has been amply confirmed by studies on cellular architecture that make use of the greatly enhanced resolution and magnification provided by the electron microscope. Observations on a wide variety of cells, tissues and organs made over the last fifteen or so years, since the introduction of adequate methods of fixing, embedding and sectioning biological material for electron microscopic study, have brought into sharper focus the interplay between general function and special adaptation.

The value of insects as a medium for the study of many aspects of physiology is becoming increasingly realised, and this collection of electron micrographs is intended to illustrate some of the fine structural details upon which the function of the insect body is based. Sometimes interpretation of these details must rely on previous work carried out on other animals, particularly on the usual laboratory vertebrates, but it is clear that, in turn, the study of insect material provides a useful contribution to the general field of cell biology.

The electron micrographs have been prepared from a small number of insect species, generally on such readily available animals as cockroaches, stick insects and blowflies, and should be regarded as exemplifying rather than typifying the organisation of cells in various parts of the body. Corresponding tissues may differ in their construction from one insect to the next: Malpighian tubules are sometimes made up of one type of cell or they may include several distinct regions; salivary glands may be modified for silk production; cuticular structures vary widely in their form and function; the hind-gut is often modified locally to carry out water absorption—these and a wealth of other examples are a measure of the adaptive success of the group, and underline many interesting problems that invite further study at the fine structural level.

The text of this book includes brief background sketches of the basic anatomy and physiology of the parts of the insect body illustrated. A general reference may be made to the textbook by Sir Vincent B. Wigglesworth[2] for detailed information and an extensive bibliography on the range of functional and histological diversity met with in insect tissues. Reference to each of the micrographs is made in the text, and the main features contained in these illustrations are mentioned in the captions. Some of the more important papers on the fine structure of insect material are cited after each section of the text: these are marked with an asterisk to distinguish them from references that are not primarily concerned with insects or which deal with aspects other than fine structure. Growth of the literature on insect fine structure is rapid, and doubtless present gaps in this work will be filled, and corrections supplied, before the manuscript goes to press. A selected list of references to papers published after June 1967 is added as an appendix.

The author's task has been greatly eased by the generosity of several colleagues who have contributed electron micrographs to this collection or have collaborated in their preparation. Acknowledgements are given with the appropriate captions, but the author would like to offer his thanks at this point to J. V. Collins, K. Compher, E. Copeland, M. Berridge, B. L. Gupta, H. E. Hinton, M. Janners, J. Lai-Fook, M. Locke, M. A. Message, M. Moses, J. Ross, M. Rothschild, C. Scola, U. Smith, A. Tombes and W. Wittle. Thanks are also due to the National Science Foundation for their generous support to the author (Grants GB-1291 and GB-5635) for work on the fine structure of the insect muscular and nervous systems.

It is a pleasure to thank Miss Ulla Järlfors for reading the manuscript and making many helpful suggestions, and Mrs Ruth McClenaghan for her patient assistance in the final stages of production.

D. S. SMITH

Miami
July 1967

REFERENCES

1. ROTHSCHILD, LORD 1965. *A Classification of Living Animals*, 2nd edn. Longmans Green, London.
2. WIGGLESWORTH, V. B. 1965. *The Principles of Insect Physiology*, 6th edn. Methuen, London.

Notes on the preparation of the electron micrographs

Towards the end of the last century, a great expansion in the study of the architecture of organisms was initiated by the development of the microtome, which, in conjunction with progressively refined techniques of fixation, embedding and staining, has told us much, within the limits of resolution of the light microscope, of the ways in which cells are constructed and are knit together into the tissues and organs of the body. In a similar way, the potential value of the electron microscope, with its greatly enhanced resolving power (less than ten, instead of several thousand Ångstrom units), in revealing further levels of cellular structure, was realised through parallel advances in specimen preparation, necessitated by the physical characteristics of the instrument. While many useful fixatives for light microscopy preserve only some components of a cell, which may then be accentuated by suitable stains, fixation for electron microscopy aims to preserve the very complex framework of all parts of the cell, with the least possible change from its arrangement in life. At the new level of resolution and magnification, imperfections in preservation, acceptable or undetectable in the light microscope, become all too evident. Until recently, the most widely used fixative for animal cells prepared for examination in the electron microscope has been osmium tetroxide—a molecule that not only stabilises cellular membranes and other constituents but has the additional advantage that the heavy osmium atoms greatly enhance the definition and contrast of subcellular structures, aiding photography and interpretation of the sectioned material. Another fixative, glutaraldehyde, has been found to preserve subcellular detail even more faithfully, but this small organic molecule adds little to the low intrinsic contrast of a tissue section, and for this reason material treated in this way is generally 'stained', after fixation and prior to embedding and sectioning, in a solution of osmium tetroxide.

Technical problems other than fixation had to be solved before the electron microscope could successfully be brought to bear on cellular structure. The thickness of sections generally prepared for study in the light microscope, two micra or more, is too great to allow transmission of the electron beam and formation of an image, and several microtomes capable of cutting thinner sections, within the useful range of 1000 Å (0·1 micron) or less, have been developed. These instruments are used in conjunction with diamond or plate-glass cutting edges, in preference to the conventional steel blades of histology. Furthermore, the histological wax in which fixed and dehydrated tissues are usually embedded is too soft to support the much thinner sections required for the electron microscope, and for this is substituted polymerised methacrylate (Perspex) or, more usually in recent years, synthetic resins such as Epon or Araldite.

The majority of the plates included in this book, and unless otherwise stated in the captions, represent thin sections of material fixed in glutaraldehyde, then 'stained' with osmium, dehydrated in ethanol and embedded in Araldite. Sections were in most cases cut by means of glass knives on a Huxley microtome (Cambridge Instrument Company), mounted on copper specimen grids bearing a thin supporting film of collodion and carbon, and examined in a Philips EM 200 microscope after further staining with salts of uranium and lead. Detailed accounts of the methods that are at present available for preparing biological and other specimens for electron microscopy have been given in the recent book edited by Kaye.[1]

Five of the plates in this collection (Plate Nos. 7, 8, 10, 11 and 113) represent micrographs produced by another instrument, for which thin sections are not required —the electron scanning microscope—a general account of which has recently been included by Cosslett[2] in an introduction to the principles and instrumentation of light, X-ray and electron microscopy. In this type of microscope, the surface of the specimen is scanned with a 'flying spot' of electrons, a few hundred Ångstrom units in diameter, and electrons reflected from the surface as the spot passes are collected by a scintillation counter, emitting light in proportion to the number of electrons received. This number will fluctuate if the scanned surface is uneven; regions tilted towards the counter will reflect more electrons than will regions tilted away from it. This variation in the reflecting power of different parts of the specimen is ultimately recorded as a pattern of varying degrees of brightness on a cathode-ray display tube. The resolution so far attained with this type of microscope is usually a few hundred and at best 100 Ångstrom units, at least ten times poorer, that is, than the resolving power of the usual transmission electron microscopes. Nevertheless, the resolution of the scanning instrument lies beyond the limits of light microscopy, and this fact, together with the great depth of focus of this microscope, has already afforded very detailed images, with a remarkably three-dimensional appearance, of such biological specimens as the minutely sculptured shells of insect eggs and of the cuticle of the body surface.

REFERENCES

1. KAYE, D. H. 1965. *Techniques for Electron Microscopy*, 2nd edn. Blackwell, Oxford.
2. COSSLETT, V. 1966. *Modern Microscopy*. Bell, London.

Abbreviations

A	A-band		Mt	Microtubule
Ax	Axon		MF	Muscle fibre
			MFl	Moulting fluid
Ba	Bacteroid		Mv	Microvilli
BB	Basal body			
BM	Basement membrane		N	Nucleus
			ND	Neurosecretory droplet
CC	Crystalline cone		NF	Nerve fibre
Ce	Centriole		NL	Neural lamella
CJ	Intercellular junction		Nt	Neurotubule
Cl	Cytolysome			
Co	Collagen		O	Oocyte
Cy	Cytoplasm			
Cu	Cuticle		P	Pigment granule
			PC	Pigment cell
D	Desmosome		pc	Pore canal
DD	Duct of duct cell		Ptm	Peritrophic membrane
DS	Duct of secretory cell		Pr	Protein granule
			Pk	Perikaryon
Ep	Epithelium			
ER	Endoplasmic reticulum		R	Rhabdom
ES	Extracellular space		Re	Retinular cell
			Rb	Ribosome
F	Fibril			
Fl	Flagellum		S	Secretory material
			SER	Smooth endoplasmic reticulum
G	Golgi body		Sh	Sheath
Gl	Glia		Sp	Spermatozoa
Gy	Glycogen		SR	Sarcoplasmic reticulum
			SV	Synaptic vesicle
H	H-band		SD	Septate desmosome
He	Haemolymph			
			T	Transverse tubule
I	I-band		TJ	Tight junction
IS	Intercellular space		Tr	Tracheole
			TR	Trachea
L	Lipid droplet			
Lu	Lumen		V	Vacuole
			VS	Vacuole containing secretory material
M	Mitochondrion			
Ma	Mesaxon		Z	Z-band
Mtr	Mestracheon			

Introduction

General studies on the structure of cells are often introduced or augmented by a diagram showing the features of a 'generalised cell'—a composite unit, constructed from a wide variety of tissues. This unit, in classical cytology, is defined with an emphasis on the form of cell components resolved in the light microscope, occasionally their observed behaviour in living material, and especially their response to a variety of fixation and staining techniques.

A corresponding diagram drawn from electron micrographs takes into account the structure and disposition of the cell membrane and of the intracellular membranes defining many of the most important constituents of the cell, together with other components, at a level of resolution far surpassing the limits imposed by light optics.

The conservatism of cellular evolution is such that this illustration could apply to representatives of any animal Phylum, but the electron micrographs illustrating the selected features included in the drawing have been prepared from insect material, and may help the reader in his interpretation of the tissues described later.

The static image of an electron micrograph has been enlivened in a variety of ways, which have played an important part in the functional interpretation of subcellular details. Changes in cell organisation, such as occur in cyclic secretory events, may be monitored by physiological and biochemical methods and referred to the fine structural level by judicious selection of material for electron microscopic 'stills'. An ever-increasing number of methods are available for the localisation of sites of enzyme activity in intact cells and in cell fractions, at the level of the electron microscope. These, together with micro-autoradiographic studies, are able to reveal biochemical and functional details of cellular organisation that are hidden in conventional preparations. Specialised techniques, together with continuing light microscopic observations, serve to bring electron micrographs closer to the minutely integrated activities of the living cell.

See over ▷

1 Unlike most other animals, insects do not posses *scilia* or *flagella* in their somatic tissues, such as those occurring in the flame cells of platyhelminths, the gill epithelia of molluscs, or the ciliated olfactory and tracheal epithelia of mammals. The well-known ring configuration of nine doublet microtubules surrounding an inner separated pair (the 9+2 pattern) of cilia and flagella is seen in the tails of developing insect male gametes (spermatids), illustrated here in transverse section. As maturation proceeds, the simple 9+2 pattern is complicated in these cells by the addition of accessory microtubules, which join the outer doublets.

2 At the base of the sperm tail flagellum, as in other cilia and flagella, is situated a short *basal body*, seen here in longitudinal section [arrow]. Transverse sections show that this organelle comprises a ring of nine triplet microtubules, lacking the inner microtubules present in the motile shaft. This arrangement is also found in the basal bodies of specialised sensory neurones and in the centrioles associated with the spindle apparatus of dividing cells.

3 *Multivesicular bodies* have been found in a wide variety of animal cells, and are characterised by a variable number of small vesicles contained within an enveloping membrane. This structure probably represents a type of lysosome containing hydrolytic enzymes, and appears to be concerned with the digestion of materials brought into the cell by pinocytosis—the internal vesicles being contributed by the Golgi complex.

4 A special type of pinocytic uptake into the cell is carried out by '*coated vesicles*'. Here, the crypts pinched off from the cell membrane bear, on their cytoplasmic side, a coat of fine fibrils [arrow]. The role of these vesicles is thought to be the selective uptake of proteins, represented by the amorphous material [*] clumped alongside the outer surface of the crypt.

5 The *agranular* or *smooth-surfaced endoplasmic reticulum* is devoid of the ribosomes characterising the granular reticulum, and unlike the latter generally consists of irregular tubules rather than flat cisternae. In vertebrates this system has been implicated in such varied functions as lipid metabolism, steroid hormone synthesis and detoxification of experimentally administered drugs. Amongst insect cells, this organelle is highly developed in the prothoracic gland, responsible for synthesising the steroid moulting hormone, and in oenocytes which may include the manufacturing of cuticular lipids amongst their functions.

6 This micrograph includes the plasma membranes of adjoining cells, illustrating the triple-layered organisation of each *unit membrane*. Arrows indicate the two plasma membranes,

each about 75Å in width, separated by an intercellular gap of about 150Å.

7 *Microtubules* about 200Å in diameter are common in many types of cell. Specialised microtubules are associated with the flagellar system (1), centrioles, the spindle apparatus of dividing cells and in the general cytoplasm of many animal and plant cells. At least some cytoplasmic microtubules appear to perform a cytoskeletal function, supporting elongated cell processes—as in the example illustrated here in glial cells surrounding insect peripheral nerve axons.

8 Within the *mitochondria* are situated the enzymes responsible for making available the energy of food molecules—the cytochrome system and associated phosphorylating enzymes, linked to the Krebs citric acid cycle. Structurally, mitochondria adhere to a common plan: they possess an outer membrane, defining the spherical or elongated form of the organelle. Beneath this lies an inner membrane, generally folded into more or less tightly packed 'cristae' which may be transversely arranged or disposed in irregular or whorled patterns. The cytochromes and phosphorylating enzymes are thought to be situated on the crista membranes and the enzymes of the Krebs cycle within the intervening mitochondrial matrix.

9 The outer membrane of the nuclear envelope is studded with ribosomes, and is often confluent with the cisternae of the rough surfaced endoplasmic reticulum, as indicated here by asterisks. The envelope is thus sometimes termed the '*perinuclear cisterna*'.

10 Arrays of *cytoplasmic filaments* are most highly ordered in striated muscle cells, as in insect flight muscle illustrated here, where thick (150Å) myosin filaments are associated in a double hexagonal array with thin (50Å) actin filaments. Less ordered and less well characterised cytoplasmic filaments occur in a variety of cells and include the 'neurofilaments' of axons and the 'tonofilaments' associated with certain vertebrate desmosomes.

11 The *granular* or *rough-surfaced endoplasmic reticulum* is represented by an intracellular membrane system of vesicles, tubules and flattened sacs or cisternae. This organelle is demarcated from the agranular reticulum (5) primarily by the presence of ribosomes—small dense RNA-rich particles, attached to the cytoplasmic face of the membranes. In certain secretory cells, the intracellular compartment provided by the reticulum membranes receives proteins synthesised in association with the ribosomes, prior to their transport to the Golgi cisternae (15), where they are concentrated as droplets and later discharged from the cell. Unattached ribosomes are abundant in the cytoplasm of differentiating cells, engaged in rapid synthesis of proteins for growth of the cell rather than for secretory export.

12 Cells are rarely simple cubes, although they may appear to be so in the light microscope. Cell surfaces engaged in absorption of materials may be increased by the presence of *microvilli*—minute finger-like projections of the apical cell border. Transverse sections of microvilli are seen in the left half of this electron micrograph. The micrograph on the right shows mitochondria extending into similar microvilli, a situation comparable with the close association between mitochondria and infoldings of the basal cell membrane (20); a feature that in each case probably points to the existence of ATP-dependent movement of ions or molecules across the cell surface.

13 The *septate desmosome* is a type of cell-to-cell attachment that occurs commonly in insect and other invertebrate tissues. Here, the narrow intercellular gap between adjoining cells is bridged by regularly placed bars of opaque material, presenting a ladder-like appearance when seen in transverse section.

14 *Pinocytosis* represents an important mechanism by which droplets of the external medium may be taken into a cell. This ingestion may occur on a scale readily observed in the light microscope, ranging down to the formation of minute pinocytic vesicles pinched off into the cytoplasm and detectable only in electron micrographs. A similar mechanism, operating in the reverse direction (reverse pinocytosis or 'exocytosis'), accomplished by momentary fusion between the plasma membrane and the membrane surrounding an intracellular vesicle or secretion droplet, has been noted in many cell types. The micrograph shown here represents the latter situation, but from the morphological standpoint the omega-shaped configuration could equally well represent pinocytic intake —the direction of movement in each instance must be judged on other information about the cell under consideration.

15 The *Golgi complex* typically consists of a series of parallel agranular cisternae and numerous small vesicles. The best known role of this organelle is the sequestration and concentration of protein-rich products synthesised in association with the granular endoplasmic reticulum (11). Opaque secretory droplets may accumulate within the cisternae, as in this field selected from an insect neurosecretory cell. The presence of Golgi bodies in functionally diverse cells suggests that other functions may be performed by this intracellular system.

16 *Desmosomes* of the macula adhaerens type, illustrated here, are local cell-to-cell attach-ment points. These structures vary in complexity, particularly in epithelia of vertebrates, but in insect tissues are generally represented by pairs of dense plaques, flanking the adjoining lateral cell membranes. Other forms of attachment are illustrated in (13) and (17).

17 The lateral surfaces of epithelial cells may be linked by a variety of specialised attachment regions (cf. 13, 16). The most intimate of these, illustrated here, is the *tight junction* or zonula occludens, where the pair of adjoining unit membranes (6) become partially fused [arrow], obliterating the intercellular gap.

18 In a *cytolysome* or 'isolation body' a portion of the cytoplasm is isolated by agranular membranes from the rest of the cell, and is subsequently digested by hydrolytic enzymes. In this instance, a small mitochondrion [*] and a cisterna of the endoplasmic reticulum [arrow] are included within the body, but have not yet been broken down within this special type of lysosome.

19 The nuclear envelope consists of two 75Å membranes, separated by a space of several hundred Ångstrom units. The envelope is interrupted, frequently in some cells and less so in others, by circular *nuclear pores*, each about 500Å in diameter. These may well provide sites for exchange of materials between the nucleus and the cytoplasm. As seen in this micrograph, each pore is traversed by a diaphragm or septum [arrow], and it is probable that passage of materials through the pores is controlled, rather than free.

20 Just as the apical surface area of cells engaged in solute transport may be enhanced by the presence of microvilli (12), the basal cell surface may be greatly increased by the development of *basal infoldings* or *pleats*. Mitochondria may be closely associated with these folds, as in the proximal convoluted tubule of the vertebrate kidney or the insect Malpighian tubule, and presumably provide energy for trans-membrane active transport.

21 Deposits of stored *glycogen* seen in electron micrographs of suitably fixed and stained thin sections of animal cells have been identified as small opaque particles. While their lower size limit of 150Å is similar to that of ribosomes, glycogen particles may reach a diameter of over 300Å. They may occur singly or often, as in this illustration, clustered into 'rosettes'. In addition to glycogen, food reserves, identified in electron micrographs of many cells, include lipid droplets.

The Integument

The form of insects, their success as terrestrial animals in resisting desiccation and in breathing atmospheric air, and their diverse modes of locomotion are among the many features of the group that are directly related to the properties of their integument. In essence, the integument is simple in construction—it consists of an epithelial layer, the epidermis, which has the capacity of secreting and maintaining an extracellular matrix, the cuticle, which is periodically moulted and replaced as the insect passes through its immature stages. One of the most remarkable aspects of insect anatomy is the great variation in physical and mechanical properties of the cuticle produced in different parts of the body.

The cuticular exoskeleton provides the superstructure of the body and its appendages; the articulating plates and tubes, and the thin arthrodial membranes that link them and permit their movements. The sensory cells associated with the surface of the body lie beneath a variety of specialised regions of the cuticle: over the photo-receptors, the cuticle is transparent, and in the compound eye forms the array of 'corneal lenses' overlying the ommatidia, while the tactile sense is often met by displaceable cuticular bristles and hairs, linked to sensory neurones. Auditory organs involve cuticular tympani, while chemoreceptors require some form of perforation of the cuticle to permit access to the sampled molecules to the receptive cells. Furthermore, a very important feature of insect construction is that the epidermis is by no means restricted to the outer surfaces of the body, but is invaginated to form the muscle apodemes, the walls of the tracheal system, the fore- and hind-gut, the lower genital ducts and a wide variety of 'integumentary glands', all of which reveal their origin by possessing a cuticular lining (e.g. Plates 43, 71, 87, 117).

Some of the general aspects of cuticular organisation have been established by light microscopic studies, while electron micrographs have provided further information on its macromolecular structure, on the finely detailed sculpturing that its surface may exhibit, and on the functional *rapport* that it retains, despite its extracellular nature, with the epidermal cells that secrete it. The electron micrographs accompanying this section (Plates 1 to 11) cannot do more than provide an introduction to a very complex field of insect structure and function.

The light microscope revealed three principal regions in many cuticles: a very thin outermost 'epicuticle', a more or less darkly coloured and hard layer of 'exocuticle' and, between the latter and the epidermal cells, a less hard colourless 'endocuticle', usually comprising a closely packed series of fine lamellae. The chemical composition of insect cuticles has recently been reviewed by Hackman (1964) and it is sufficient to mention here that the exo- and endocuticular layers are composed of molecules of the polysaccharide chitin (unbranched chains of N-acetyl D-glucosamine residues), associated with a number of proteins, and that the hardness of the exocuticle is the result

B   1 of cross-linkage stabilisation of the cuticular proteins by quinones produced by oxidation of dihydric phenols supplied by the epidermal cells.

A remarkable almost perfectly elastic protein, resilin, is present in certain regions of the cuticle, notably in some tendons and wing-hinge ligaments but also in small patches elsewhere in the body. The occurrence of resilin, its mechanical properties, molecular organisation and biochemistry have recently been reviewed by Anderson and Weis-Fogh (1964). This protein occasionally occurs in virtually pure form, as in an elastic tendon of adult dragonflies, but elsewhere, in rubber-like regions of the cuticle, it may be laminated with separate thin layers cf chitin and may adjoin resilin-free exo- and endocuticle (Anderson and Weis-Fogh, 1964; Neville, 1967). Electron micrographs of thin sections of resilin, which is not stabilised by the usual chemical fixatives, reveal no trace of fine structure, and its amorphous appearance, together with the absence of X-ray reflections indicative of molecular orientation, are consistent with its physical rubber-like properties (Elliott, Huxley and Weis-Fogh, 1965).

A good deal of our knowledge of the fine structure of various regions of the cuticle at the body surface and along the invaginated tracheal system stems from the studies of Locke, who has included both structural and functional features of the integument in a recent review (1964). Neville (1967) has stressed the fact that the fabric of the cuticle provides one example of a wide range of instances in which macromolecular polymers are laid down in an oriented fashion in animal skeletons and plant cell walls, and has considered in detail the ways in which chitin deposition may be carried out and controlled in insects.

The lamellar nature of the endocuticle, resolved in the light microscope, is immediately obvious in electron micrographs of thin sections, as, for example, in the larva of the mealworm beetle *Tenebrio* (Plate 1) and in the adult milkweed bug *Oncopeltus* (Plates 2 and 3). Each lamella appears to include a tightly packed series of parabolic fibrils, and a similar arrangement is found, for example, in the thin cuticular lining of the crop (Plate 41) and the hind-gut (Plate 87). Recent work by Bouligand (1965) on the fine structure of crustacean cuticle, discussed by Neville (1967) and Noble-Nesbitt (1967), has suggested that cuticular lamellae do not, in fact, contain parabolic fibrils, but rather that these arise as an optical artefact, based on an entirely different macromolecular structure. According to this interpretation, each lamella is built up of many layers or laminae of chitin-protein microfibrils, arranged parallel with the surface of the cuticle, the direction of orientation of successive laminae changing slightly and progressively, through a total of 180° from one side of the lamella to the other, and so on in helicoid fashion throughout the fabric of the endocuticle. Even slightly oblique sections through these ranks of fibrils will give rise to a parabolic pattern. As is evident from the survey made by Neville, parabolic patterns occur not only in insect cuticle, at all stages of development including (Slifer and Sekhon, 1963) the egg, but also in the cuticle of other arthropods and in a variety of other biological systems. However, endocuticle is not always uniformly lamellate: Neville has found, for example, that locust endocuticle is deposited according to a circadian rhythm—layers formed at night containing several lamellae resulting from chitin orientation changes as described above, while layers formed by day are non-lamellate and presumably contain chitin-protein microfibrils oriented in one direction only.

In the more rigid cross-linked exocuticle, on the other hand, patterns arising from chitin orientation are not seen in electron micrographs (Plate 1), perhaps, as Noble-Nesbitt has suggested, either because the three-dimensional fabric of the cross-linked proteins masks the original lamellate structure established before tanning occurred, or through actual disruption of the lamellae during this process.

Neville (1967) has described other ways in which chitin-protein chains may be built into the cuticle. The chains may be grouped together into parallel fibres in such special cuticular structures as apodemes providing attachments for muscles, tendons, and in the sometimes very long and slender ovipositors. In other instances, the chains may be likewise arranged into fibres but disposed in layers, in each of which the orientation of the fibres changes to form a cross-ply fabric, readily seen in the light microscope, that perhaps adds strength to the cuticle.

The outermost region of the cuticle, termed the epicuticle, contains no chitin, and has for some time been recognised as possessing a complex organisation, consisting of up to four layers. Locke (1964, 1966) has examined the structure, mode of formation and probable function of this part of the integument, and his conclusions may briefly be summarised. The most general, indeed almost universal component of the epicuticle, is the cuticulin layer, extending over the surface of the body and over cuticular projections such as bristles and scales, as well as along the tracheal and tracheolar branches (p. 136) and over the cuticle lining the fore- and hind-gut, the ducts of integumentary glands and other epidermal invaginations. The cuticulin has a total thickness of up to 175 Å, and has been resolved into three dense laminae, the outermost of which is thought to represent a lipid monolayer. Beneath the cuticulin is often found a thicker dense layer, probably containing protein, while outside it over the surface of the body lies a wax layer of variable thickness, in turn covered by a varnish-like protective coat of 'cement', secreted by dermal glands associated with the epidermis.

The surface cuticle is usually penetrated by more or less numerous pore canals, extending from the base of the endocuticle and ending beneath the epicuticle (Plates 1, 2 and 3). When these canals pass through lamellate regions of the cuticle, they follow a helical course, apparently imposed by the oriented laminae of chitin and protein (Neville, Thomas and Zelazny, 1968). Locke (1961) has studied the fine structure of these canals in insect cuticles, and has suggested that they play a vital role in maintaining a functional link between the cuticle and the cells that secreted it. The cuticle is, of course, entirely extracellular, but it nevertheless is in some respects still within the metabolic sphere of influence of the epidermis. The pore canals may provide a pathway along which, for example, phenolic substances involved in tanning of the exocuticle may travel, and along which wax precursors may pass to effect the deposition and repair of the epicuticular wax layer; a crucial factor in the insect's resistance to water loss. Each pore canal generally contains one or more 'filaments' or tubules (Plate 3), which may maintain the form of the canal, and which arise within the epidermal cells. In addition, the canals contain more slender filaments, 60–130 Å in diameter, which are especially abundant in regions of cuticle that are surfaced with a thick wax layer. These filaments extend beyond the outer end of the canals into the epicuticle, and Locke has suggested that they represent lipid-water liquid crystals *en route* for the surface of the body.

During postembryonic development, the insect passes through several stadia or instars, each marked by the moulting of the old cuticle and its replacement by a newly secreted cuticle. Locke (1966) has contrasted the insect integument with the vertebrate epidermis, and has pointed out that whereas the keratins secreted by the latter are irretrievably lost, the insect cuticle, by virtue of a remarkably economic device, remains largely within the metabolic pool of the body. The progression from one instar to the next involves not only the formation of a new cuticle, but also the digestion and absorption of the greater part of the old—only the epicuticle and tanned exocuticle of which are cast off at the moult. Details of the sequence of events taking place before, during and after moulting have been described by Locke (1964, 1966), Rinterknecht and Levi (1966) and Noble-Nesbitt (1967). The first stage in the sequence is marked by the separation of the epidermal cells from the inner surface of the endocuticle, followed by the secretion of a moulting fluid into the resulting subcuticular space. This fluid contains enzymes (protease and chitinase), initially in inactive form and sometimes contained in opaque granules (Noble-Nesbitt, 1963), which will in due course commence the digestion of the old cuticle. The first portion of the new covering to be formed outside the epidermal cells is the cuticulin, which appears first as discrete patches which grow in area and ultimately coalesce into a continuous sheet. Beneath the cuticulin is laid down the protein layer of the new epicuticle. When formation of the cuticulin is complete, the enzymes of the moulting fluid are activated, and begin to break down the untanned portion of the old cuticle. Before moulting takes place, the cuticulin has a dual responsibility—it must protect the epidermal cells and the new endocuticle they are forming from the enzymic action of the moulting fluid, but must also be permeable to small molecules produced by its digestive action, perhaps as Locke (1966) has suggested, by virtue of the presence of fine 30 Å pores. Plate 2 illustrates a section of the integument of a fourth instar larva of the milkweed bug *Oncopeltus*, at a stage when formation of the adult cuticle has commenced. The moulting fluid has started to digest the innermost lamellae of the old endocuticle; as is more clearly seen at higher magnification (Plate 3), the precise parabolic pattern resulting from the oriented disposition of the chitin and protein microfibrils is becoming lost.

Throughout development, epidermal cells may divide and differentiate to produce such specialised structures as sensory hairs and bristles. These include a cuticular shaft secreted by an elongated process of a trichogen cell, articulating with a rigid socket provided by the cuticle of a tormogen cell. A forming hair sensillum of this type, within the epidermis of *Oncopeltus*, is shown in Plate 4: the surface of the trichogen and tormogen cells are already covered with a thin epicuticular layer, prior to the deposition of chitin and protein which, after shedding of the old cuticle, will become hardened by tanning. The cytoplasmic components present within epidermal bristles show a high degree of orientation parallel with the long axis of the trichogen cell outgrowth: as is seen in Plate 5, precisely oriented microtubules and bundles of cytoplasmic fibrils are abundant within a bristle of *Calpodes*. The cytoplasm of the general epidermis, as well as of specialised processes of the epidermal cells, is well supplied with mitochondria and cisternae of the rough- and smooth-surfaced endoplasmic reticulum, while pigment granules are a conspicuous addition in the epidermis of some insects (Plate 2).

The details of external cuticular structure vary in an almost limitless fashion over the range of insect species. Indeed, most of the characters used by taxonomists in classifying this enormous class of arthropods—the general form of the body, the shape and proportions of the segments and appendages together with their surface sculpturing, the distribution of hairs and bristles, the form and venation of the wings, the structural and pigmentary colours of the body surface and scales and the complex arrangement of the external genitalia—rest on the minutely precise genetically controlled deposition of the cuticle. While the techniques of electron microscopy have no immediate or obvious part to play in insect taxonomy, they are able to reveal in great detail just how minutely precise this deposition can be, and the micrographs shown in

Plates 6 to 11 are included to illustrate this fact. The details of fine structure within the depth of the cuticle can only be resolved at present by polarising microscopy, X-ray diffraction or by examination of thin sections by transmission electron microscopy. However, information about the cuticular surface may be gained in two ways: firstly, by examination of thin carbon or plastic replicas of the surface in the conventional transmission microscope, or secondly, by direct observation in the scanning or reflecting electron microscope (p. xii). Examples of epicuticular sculpturing displayed by the first of these methods are illustrated in Plate 6A and B, while examples of the results obtained by scanning microscopy are shown in Plates 7, 8, 10 and 11.

Locke (1964, 1966) has shown that increase in the area of the newly formed cuticulin sheet of the epicuticle coincides with, and apparently determines, the formation of the detailed surface pattern of the cuticle. This is true not only of the tracheal system, where cuticulin expansion results in the appearance of the characteristic taenidial folds (p. 136), but also of the external cuticular covering. Plate 6A represents a transmission electron micrograph of a carbon replica stripped from the surface cuticle of the larva of a butterfly *Calpodes*, showing a series of irregular tubercles. Locke found that each of these tubercles lies over a single epidermal cell, and that they form because cuticulin deposition takes place most rapidly outside the centre of each cell, resulting in the formation of an outward bulge and smaller pleats and folds. The plasma membrane follows the contours of this cuticulin sculpturing, and in due course fixes the pattern by consolidating the cuticulin with the rest of the epicuticle. The larvae of *Calpodes* possess two areas of the integument that are specialised for the production of a large amount of wax shortly before pupation, which is smeared round the inside of the cocoon. Replicas of the surface of the cuticle in these regions show an entirely different pattern, as is illustrated in Plate 6B. The surface is divided into polygonal areas with raised edges, corresponding to the limits of the cells that secreted the epicuticle, and within each of these areas lie many small crater-like tubercles, each about 0·5 micron in diameter. From the rim of each tubercle is extruded a fine tubule of wax (Locke, 1960, 1966) which may reach a length of half a millimetre, before being broken off and wiped onto the fabric of the cocoon.

Two examples of special cuticular formations are shown in Plates 7 and 8. The first of these illustrates some details of the highly ordered surface of a haltere, the greatly modified hind-wing of a fly which acts as a vibratile gyroscopic balancing organ. The organisation and function of halteres has been investigated by Pringle (1948) and it is sufficient to note here that the batteries of sensory nerve cells leading from the organ are associated with exactly positioned, domed projections of the cuticle, the deformation of which permits the perception of inertial forces set up in the cuticle of the oscillating haltere. The second of these plates of scanning electron micrographs shows the contouring of the cuticle covering the labellar lobes of a blowfly—the pliant terminal expansions of the proboscis, surrounding the opening of the mouth. The function of these lobes during feeding, together with their very complex structure, has been described in detail by Graham-Smith (1930), and the micrographs shown here display with added clarity some of the cuticular features previously recognised with the aid of the light microscope. These include the prestomal teeth, which filter the liquid food sucked into the proboscis, together with the regular rows of cuticular plates running across the lower surface of the labella, between which food passes into collecting tubules that empty into the mouth between the cuticular teeth.

Scales borne on the body surface, and most conspicuously on the wings of butterflies, moths and certain other insects, provide a final example of specialised cuticular structures. A scale is a thin flattened cuticular sac produced by a single cell that differentiates, together with an anchoring socket-forming cell, within the surface epidermal sheet. The formation of scales involves a remarkable series of events. The epidermal cell first produces an outgrowth, the scale rudiment, which changes radically in form, becoming broad and flat; this secretes a cuticular covering that may be sculptured in an astonishingly intricate fashion, and afterwards degenerates leaving an air-filled space within the mature scale. These structures are coloured either by contained pigments, or by interference effects resulting from the fine structure of their cuticle; the patterns arising from the distribution of different types of scale are under very precise genetic control.

Pawaletz and Schlote (1964) and more recently Overton (1966) have followed the development of wing scales of the flour moth *Ephestia*, with the aid of thin sections. A portion of a scale that is structurally similar to those of the flour moth is shown in Plate 9 as a whole mount, viewed by conventional transmission electron microscopy. The upper of the two surfaces of this scale exhibits a striking herringbone pattern, with longitudinal ridges linked by transverse ribs that are interrupted by numerous holes. In *Ephestia* it has been shown that surface and intracellular changes in the rudiment determine this type of pattern: in the flat rudiment, bundles of longitudinally running cytoplasmic fibrils become spaced out just beneath the cell membrane and between these the membrane bulges out to form the template of the ridges. Between the ridges, the membrane forms minute regular pleats, yielding the pattern of the ribs. Cuticulin is secreted over the rudiment, preserving the pattern determined by the cell. The upper surface of the mature scale becomes perforated, as in Plate 9, and is linked with the smooth lower surface by struts or trabeculae.

Many scales are a good deal more elaborate in their construction, particularly those which show physical interference colours. These were among the first biological objects examined in the electron microscope, and early reports on their structure were published by Anderson and Richards (1942), Gentil (1942) and Kinder and Süffert (1943). Later, Lippert and Gentil (1959) followed up this work with a study of sections of such iridescent scales. These observations brought to light new details of scale architecture, and supported earlier conclusions (Refs. in Wigglesworth, 1965) that physical colours in lepidopteran scales arise in two main ways: in one type, exemplified by moths of the genus *Urania*, colours appear to be due to the presence of multiple thin films of cuticle built into the thickened upper or lower surface of the scale. Iridescent colours in butterflies of the genus *Morpho* are seen when the scales are viewed along their long axis, and are caused by deep laminated ridges that run longitudinally along the upper surface of each scale. The control that results in the formation of these extracellular structures must be exact; a fascinating exercise in the expression of genetic information. Examples of scanning electron micrographs of wing scales of *Urania* and *Morpho* are shown in Plates 10 and 11: these display some details of surface sculpturing, but in particular clearly illustrate the cuticular sockets arising from the wing membrane, and the narrow necks of the scales that are inserted into them.

Not all metallic colours in insects are attributable to the presence of multiple thin cuticular films, however. A few iridescent beetles, including the rosechafer *Cetonia*, are known to reflect circularly polarised light from the surface of the coloured elytra and other parts of the body (Refs. in Robinson, 1966)—a property apparently due to some helical molecular organisation residing in the outer part of the cuticle.

6

REFERENCES

In each chapter, references dealing primarily with the fine structure of insect cells are marked with asterisks.

ANDERSEN, S. O., and WEIS-FOGH, T. 1964. Resilin. A rubber-like protein in arthropod cuticle. In *Advances in Insect Physiology* (J. W. L. Beament, J. E. Treherne and V. B. Wigglesworth, eds.), Vol. 2, pp. 1-65. Academic Press, London and New York.

★ANDERSON, T. F., and RICHARDS, A. G. 1942. An electron microscope study of some structural colors of insects. *J. appl. Phys.*, **13**, 748-758.

BOULIGAND, Y. 1965. Sur une architecture torsadée répandue dans de nombreuses cuticules d'arthropodes. *C.r. hebd. Séanc. Acad. Sci., Paris*, **261**, 3665-3668.

★ELLIOTT, G. F., HUXLEY, A. F., and WEIS-FOGH, T. 1965. On the structure of resilin. *J. molec. Biol.*, **13**, 791-795.

★GENTIL, K. 1942. Elektronenmikroskopische Untersuchungen des Einbaues schillernder Leisten von Morpho-Schuppen. *Z. Morph. Ökol. Tiere*, **38**, 344-355.

GRAHAM-SMITH, G. S. 1930. Further observations on the anatomy and function of the proboscis of the blow-fly, *Calliphora erythrocephala* L. *Parasitology*, **22**, 47-115.

HACKMAN, R. H. 1964. Chemistry of the insect cuticle. In *Physiology of Insecta* (M. Rockstein, ed.), Vol. 1, pp. 471-506. Academic Press, New York and London.

★KINDER, E., and SÜFFERT, F. 1943. Über den Feinbau schillernder Schmetterlingsschuppen vom Morpho-Typ. *Biol. Zbl.*, **63**, 268-288.

★LIPPERT, W., and GENTIL, K. 1959. Über lamellare Feinstrukturen bei den Schillerschuppen der Schmetterlinge vom Urania- und Morpho-Typ. *Z. Morph. Ökol. Tiere*, **48**, 115-122.

★LOCKE, M. 1960. The cuticle and wax secretion in *Calpodes ethlius* (Lepidoptera, Hesperiidae). *Q. Jl microsc. Sci.*, **101**, 333-338.

★LOCKE, M. 1961. Pore canals and related structures in insect cuticle. *J. biophys. biochem. Cytol.*, **10**, 589-618.

★LOCKE, M. 1964. The structure and formation of the integument in insects. In *Physiology of Insecta* (M. Rockstein, ed.), Vol. 3, pp. 379-470. Academic Press, New York and London.

★LOCKE, M. 1966. The structure and formation of the cuticulin layer in the epicuticle of an insect, *Calpodes ethlius* (Lepidoptera, Hesperiidae). *J. Morph.*, **118**, 461-494.

NEVILLE, A. C. 1967. Chitin orientation in cuticle and its control. In *Advances in Insect Physiology* (J. W. L. Beament, J. E. Treherne and V. B. Wigglesworth, eds.), Vol. 4, pp. 213-286, Academic Press, London and New York.

NEVILLE, A. C., THOMAS, M. G., and ZELAZNY, B. 1968. Pore canal shape related to molecular architecture of arthropod cuticle. *Tissue & Cell*, **1**, 183-200.

★NOBLE-NESBITT, J. 1963. The cuticle and associated structures of *Podura aquatica* at the moult. *Q. Jl microsc. Sci.*, **104**, 369-391.

★NOBLE-NESBITT, J. 1967. Aspects of the structure, formation and function of some insect cuticles. In *Insects and Physiology* (J. W. L. Beament and J. E. Treherne, eds.). Oliver and Boyd, Edinburgh.

★OVERTON, J. 1966. Microtubules and microfibrils in morphogenesis of the scale cells in *Ephestia kühniella*. *J. Cell Biol.*, **29**, 293-305.

★PAWALETZ, N., and SCHLOTE, F.-W. 1964. Die Entwicklung der Schmetterlingsschuppe bei *Ephestia kühniella* Zeller. *Z. Zellforsch. mikrosk. Anat.*, **63**, 840-870.

PRINGLE, J. W. S. 1948. The gyroscopic mechanism of the halteres of Diptera. *Phil. Trans. R. Soc.* B, **233**, 347-384.

★RINTERKNECHT, E., and LEVI, P. 1966. Étude au microscope électronique du cycle cuticulaire au cours du 4e stade larvaire chez *Locusta migratoria*. *Z. Zellforsch. mikrosk. Anat.*, **72**, 390-407.

ROBINSON, C. 1966. The cholesteric phase in polypeptide solutions and biological structures. *Molec. Crystals*, **1**, 467-494.

★SLIFER, E. H., and SEKHON, S. S. 1963. The fine structure of the membranes which cover the egg of the grasshopper, *Melanoplus differentialis*, with special reference to the hydropyle. *Q. Jl microsc. Sci.*, **104**, 321-324.

WIGGLESWORTH, V. B. 1965. *The Principles of Insect Physiology*, 6th edn., Ch. 2. Methuen, London.

Plates 1–11 ▷

Plate 1 ▷

An electron micrograph of an approximately transverse section
through the abdominal surface cuticle of a larva of the mealworm
beetle *Tenebrio molitor*. The bulk of the field is occupied by the
endocuticle, disposed in parallel lamellae [between arrows]. Each
lamella is believed to be made up of a number of superimposed
laminae of chitin-protein microfibrils, each parallel with the surface of
the cuticle, but with the direction of orientation of the microfibrils
changing slightly from one sheet to the next, over a full 180° across
the thickness of the lamella. Following this model, the parabolic
pattern within each lamella apparently arises as an optical artefact,
resulting from juxtaposition of slightly oblique profiles of microfibrils
of successive laminae. Towards the outer surface of the cuticle [black
asterisk] the lamellae disappear; probably this region represents the
tanned exocuticle, in which the protein molecules associated with the
chitin are cross-linked by quinones. The outermost layer is represented
by the thin epicuticle, seen in the upper right of the micrograph
[white asterisk]. Pore canals [pc] traverse the greater part of the
cuticle; they run a helical course through the lamellae, and are here
seen in transverse and oblique profile.

(×8000.)

*(RCA EMU 3. From Locke (1964). Micrograph reproduced by
courtesy of Dr M. J. Locke and Academic Press.)*

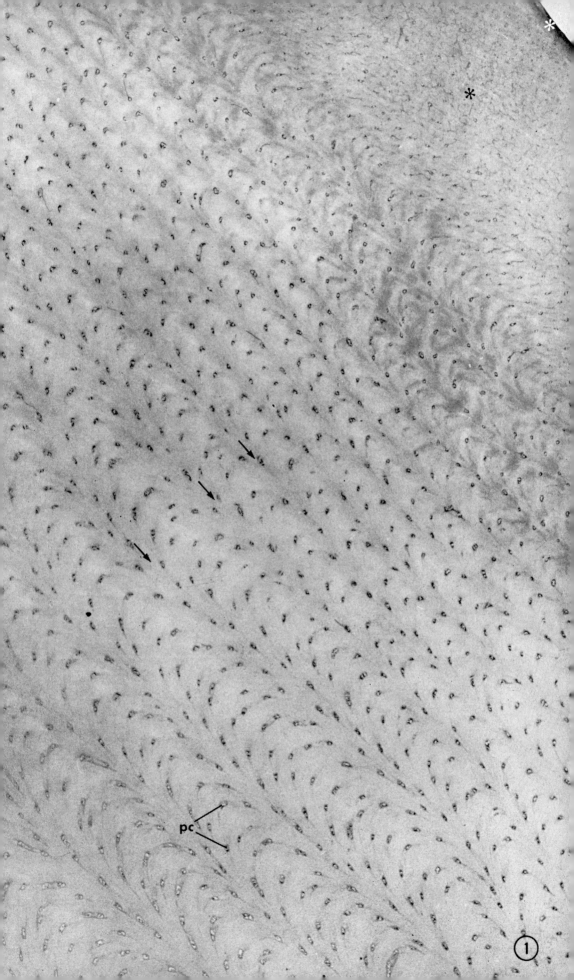

Plate 2 ▷

A micrograph of a section through the integument of a larva of the
milkweed bug *Oncopeltus fasciatus*, shortly before the moult to the
adult. The upper part of the field is occupied by the old endocuticle
[Cu], showing regularly spaced lamellae [between white asterisks]
and wide pore canals [pc]. At this time, formation of the new
cuticle [Cu_2] has started, and this is visible as a narrow sheet over
the outer surface of the epidermal cell. Outside this lies a space
containing granular material—presumably the precipitated proteins of
the enzymatically active moulting fluid [MFI], under the action of which
the inner lamellae of the old cuticle are already becoming disorganised
[Cu′]—a feature further illustrated, at higher magnification, in Plate 3.
The gap [black asterisks] adjoining the surface of the new cuticle is
an artefact due to shrinkage. These epidermal cells are rich in cisternae
of the rough-surfaced endoplasmic reticulum, and also contain
numerous pigment granules [P], and deposits of glycogen [Gy]. Part
of a cell nucleus is included at N.

Beyond this point, laying down of the new cuticle and breakdown
of the old continue; eventually the moulting fluid breaks down the
latter except for the epicuticle and the hardened exocuticle, and
products of this digestion are absorbed by the epidermal cells. After
moulting has occurred, further endocuticle may be added, and the
outer lamellae tanned by quinones.

($\times$ 13,000.)

*(Philips EM 200. Micrograph reproduced by courtesy of
Dr P. A. Lawrence.)*

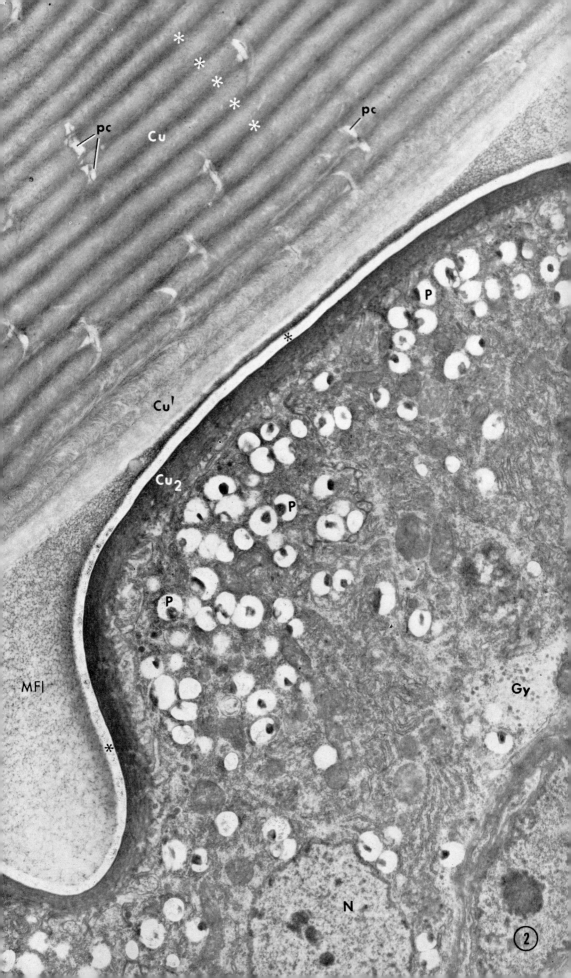

Plate 3 ▷

A micrograph of the same material as that shown in Plate 2, at higher magnification. On the left-hand side of the field, the parabolic pattern of chitin-protein microfibrils is clearly seen. Two wide pore canals [pc] containing filaments traverse the lamellae. The moulting fluid, secreted by the epidermal cells, lies on the right of the field [MFl], and the chitinase and protease activity of this solution has started the digestion of the innermost cuticular lamellae [Cu′] in which the parabolic pattern resulting from the precise orientation of multiple laminae of microfibrils (p. 2) is undergoing disruption.

($\times$ 42,000.)

(*Philips EM 200. Micrograph reproduced by courtesy of Dr P. A. Lawrence.*)

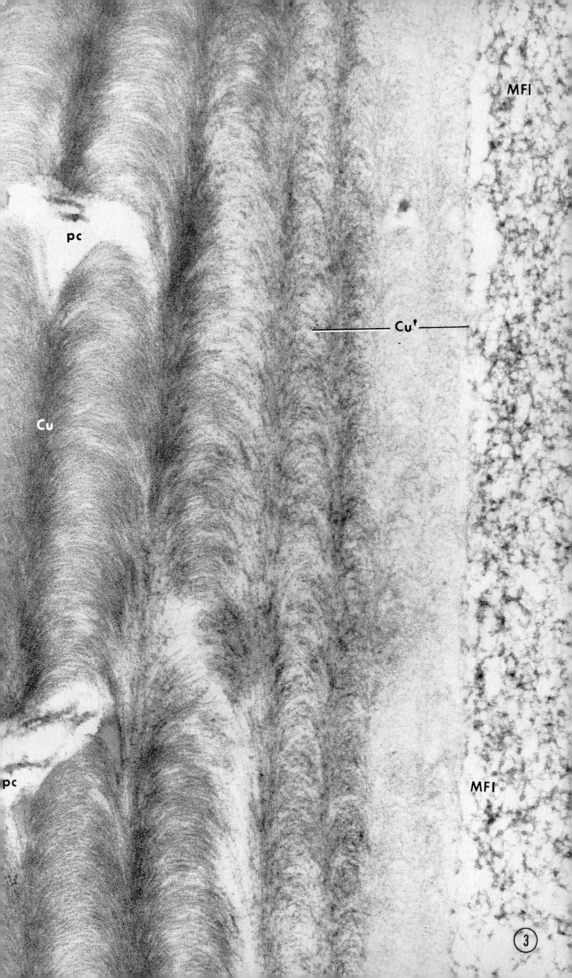

Plate 4 ▷

A section through the epidermis of the milkweed bug *Oncopeltus fasciatus* at a region where a tactile bristle and associated cells have differentiated. At the upper right of the field, the old cuticle [Cu] is about to be digested by the moulting fluid [MFl] secreted by the epidermal cells (cf. Plate 3). The very thin epicuticle [arrows] which defines the outer surface of the cuticle of the next instar has already been laid down. Each of these sensilla develops from four daughter cells produced by two divisions from a single epidermal cell: of the four, the trichogen cell gives rise to an elongated process which forms the shaft of the bristle [1], a tormogen cell produces a socket at the base of the bristle [2], while the remaining pair differentiate into a sensory nerve cell [3] linked with the base of the moveable bristle, and an accompanying sheath cell. Portions of three of these are seen in this micrograph. Before moulting occurs, further deposition of cuticle strengthens the bristle and its socket. Around this specialised structure lie the pigmented cells [*] of the general epidermis, further illustrated in Plate 2.

These sensilla provide one example of a very wide variety of special regions of the integument, each produced by the controlled differentiation of cells within the general epidermal sheet. Other examples illustrated here include mechanoreceptors that do not make use of an articulated bristle (Plate 7), and wing scales (Plates 9 to 11).

(× 13,000.)

(Philips EM 200. Micrograph reproduced by courtesy of Dr P. A. Lawrence.)

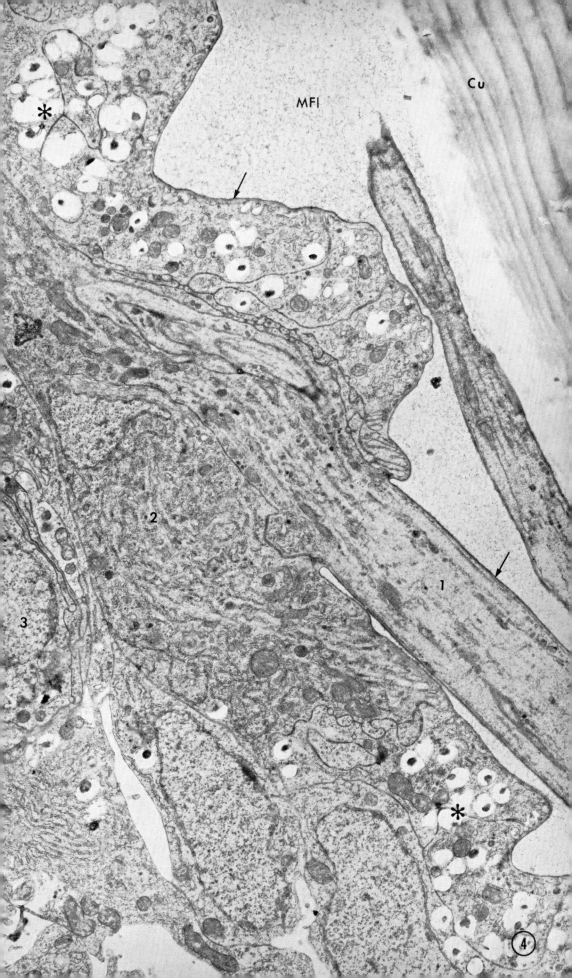

Plate 5 ▷

The epidermal cells of an insect are responsible for laying down not
only the general cuticle of the body surface, but also the cuticular
covering of a variety of specialised sensory receptors including
campaniform sensillae (Plate 7) and articulated bristles which function
as tactile organs. This micrograph represents a transversely sectioned
bristle of this type, from the proleg of a larva of the butterfly *Calpodes
ethlius*. A thin cylinder of cuticle [Cu] surrounds the elongated process
of the bristle-forming epidermal cell. The cytoplasm of this process
shows some special features that may be associated with its elongated
form: abundant microtubules [Mt] and bundles of fibrils [*] are
oriented with precision along the long axis of the cell extension.
Many profiles of mitochondria [M] and cisternae of the smooth-
[SER] and rough-surfaced [ER] endoplasmic reticulum are also seen.
Bristles of this type, together with their sockets and associated sensory
nerve cells, are differentiated from the products of division of 'typical'
epidermal cells, and a newly formed sensillum within the epidermis of
the milkweed bug is illustrated in Plate 4.

(× 38,000.)

(RCA EMU 3. Micrograph reproduced by courtesy of Dr M. J. Locke.)

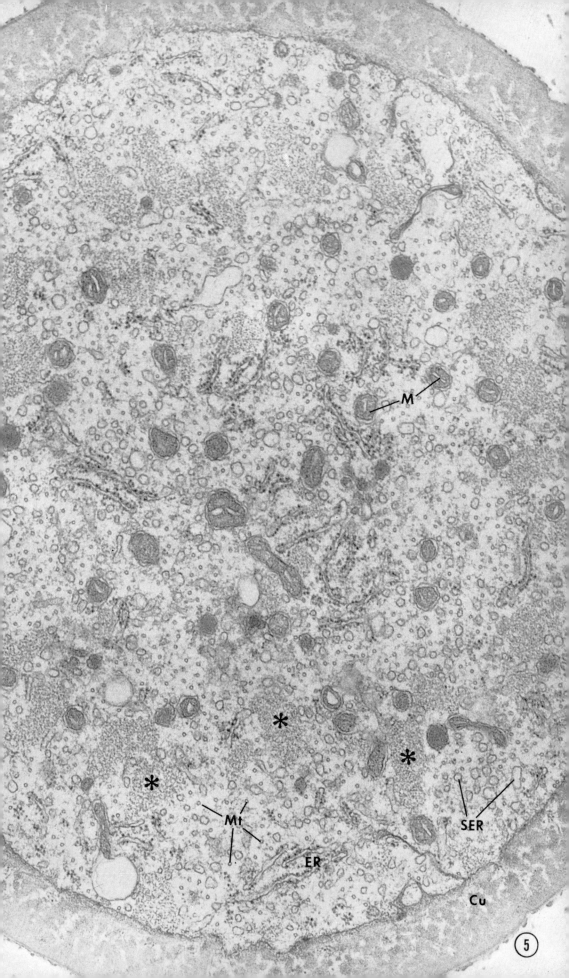

Plate 6 ▷

A. A transmission electron micrograph of a thin carbon replica that
has been stripped from the cuticle of a larva of the butterfly *Calpodes
ethlius.* This technique makes possible the examination of the surface
form and sculpturing of a specimen, and involves none of the usual
procedures of fixation, embedding and section cutting. During
development of this cuticle, the newly secreted cuticulin is formed
into irregular domes, one over the centre of each cell. This pattern is
fixed by the subsequent deposition of the rest of the epicuticle and
the chitin-protein layers, and is preserved unchanged throughout the
instar. This replica shows the domes [*] and the pleats and folds that
lie between them. An entirely different pattern is found, however, on
the surface of patches of cuticle in the larva which are responsible for
producing copious amounts of wax—a pattern illustrated in the second
micrograph of this plate.

B. A replica prepared as in the previous micrograph, but taken from
the surface of the wax-secreting cuticle of the caterpillar. The
epicuticle preserves a pattern of raised ridges [*] which outline the
polygonal limits of the epidermal cells that secreted it. Each of the
areas defined in this way bear many minute crater-like tubercles
[arrows], from the rims of which are extruded wax cylinders, smeared
by the larva around the inside of its cocoon.

(*A*: × 3500. *B*: × 3500.)

(*RCA EMU 3. From Locke (1966). Micrographs reproduced by courtesy
of Dr M. J. Locke and the* Journal of Morphology.)

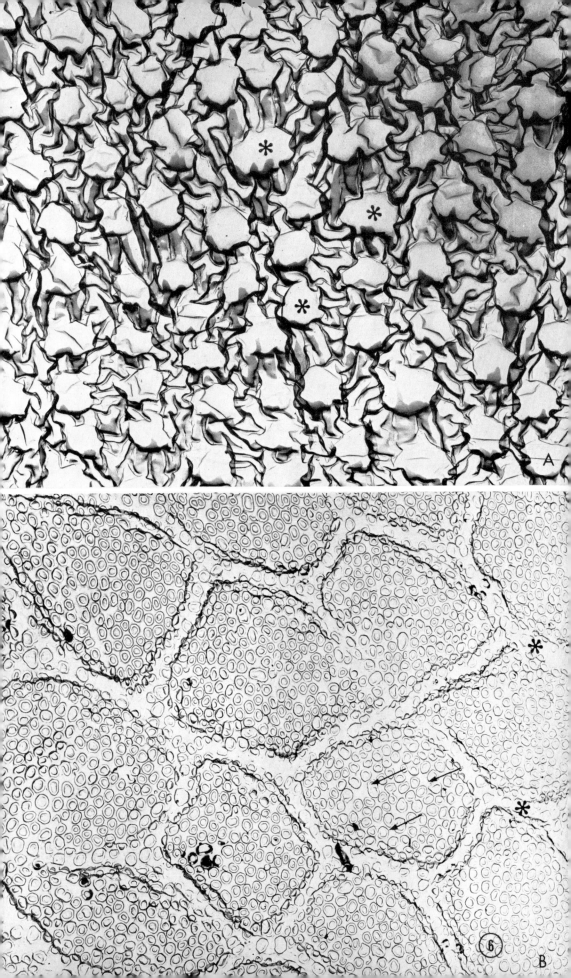

Plate 7 ▷

A pair of scanning electron micrographs, illustrating some features of the complex cuticular structures that are found over the highly modified hind wings, or halteres, of flies. The cuticle of the basal region of each haltere is associated with a large number of sensory nerve cells, stimulated by stresses in the cuticle set up when the haltere oscillates rapidly during flight. Some of these sensilla are thought to be activated by the forces set up by the 'normal' oscillation but others respond to the deforming effect on the cuticle of gyroscopic torques set up when the fly rolls or yaws, and the analysis of this sensory information within the central nervous system permits the fly to make the necessary balancing corrections.

A. A low-power micrograph of the dorsal surface of the basal region of a haltere from the blowfly *Calliphora erythrocephala*. Sculptured cuticle overlying two main groups of sensilla is resolved: each group of sensilla is arranged in several rows, as in the region marked with an asterisk. Less than one-third of the entire haltere is visible here—a long stalk and a swollen end-knob extend beyond the right-hand margin of the field.

B. A micrograph showing at higher magnification the precisely repeating domed arrangement of the cuticle present over the right-hand group of sensilla in the low-power survey field. Many minute cuticular hairs arise from the troughs between the rows of domes.

Full details of the experimental evidence concerning the stabilising function of the haltere sensilla are given by Pringle (1948). The chief reasons for the inclusion of these micrographs and those shown in Plates 8 to 11 are twofold: firstly, they provide examples of the enormously wide range of special cuticular formations over the surface of the insect body, and, moreover, they illustrate the value of scanning electron microscopy as a technique for studying directly the three-dimensional structure of biological specimens, beyond the limits of resolution imposed by light microscopy.

($A : \times 600.$ $B : \times 5500.$)

(Micrographs taken on a scanning electron microscope in the Department of Engineering, Cambridge, by Mr L. Peters. Material prepared in collaboration with Dr M. A. Message.)

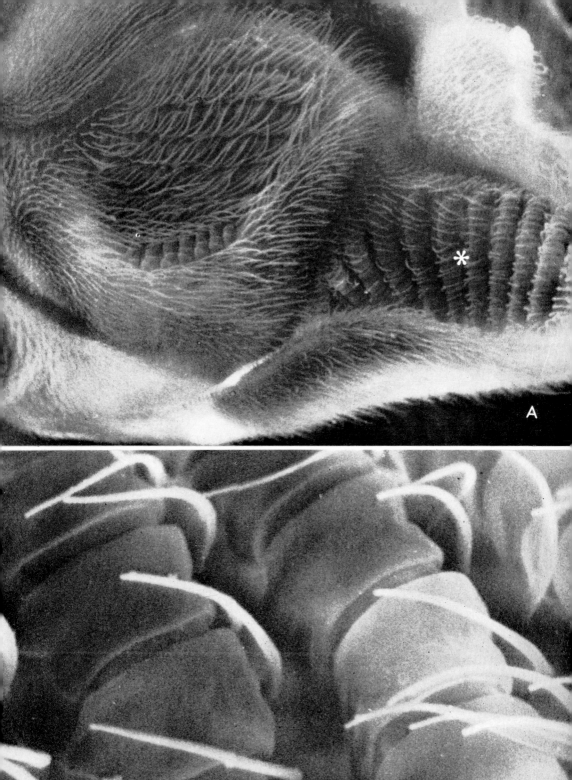

Plate 8 ▷

A pair of scanning electron micrographs illustrating some features of the lower surface of the oral disc of an adult blowfly, *Calliphora erythrocephala*. The disc is borne on the end of the proboscis and consists of two labellar lobes, surrounding the aperture of the mouth. which are pressed closely against the surface upon which the fly is feeding.

A. This micrograph includes the opening of the mouth, which is ringed by cuticular teeth [*], which serve to filter solid particles from the fluid food sucked into the proboscis. Details of the sculptured surface of the labellum [arrow] are illustrated in the next micrograph.

B. The cuticle of the oral surface of each labellar lobe is arranged in a very complex fashion. Each lobe bears several parallel series of double rows of separate but closely apposed cuticular plates [arrows]. Beneath each of these rows lies a cuticle-lined tubular 'pseudo-trachea' open to the exterior through narrow gaps between the plates, through which fluid food is sucked by movements of the muscular pharynx. The pseudotracheae unite to form common ducts, which eventually open into the mouth between the cuticular teeth shown in *A*.

(*A* : × 600. *B* : × 1500.)

(*Micrographs taken on a scanning electron microscope in the Department of Engineering, Cambridge, by Mr L. Peters. Material prepared in collaboration with Dr M. A. Message.*)

22

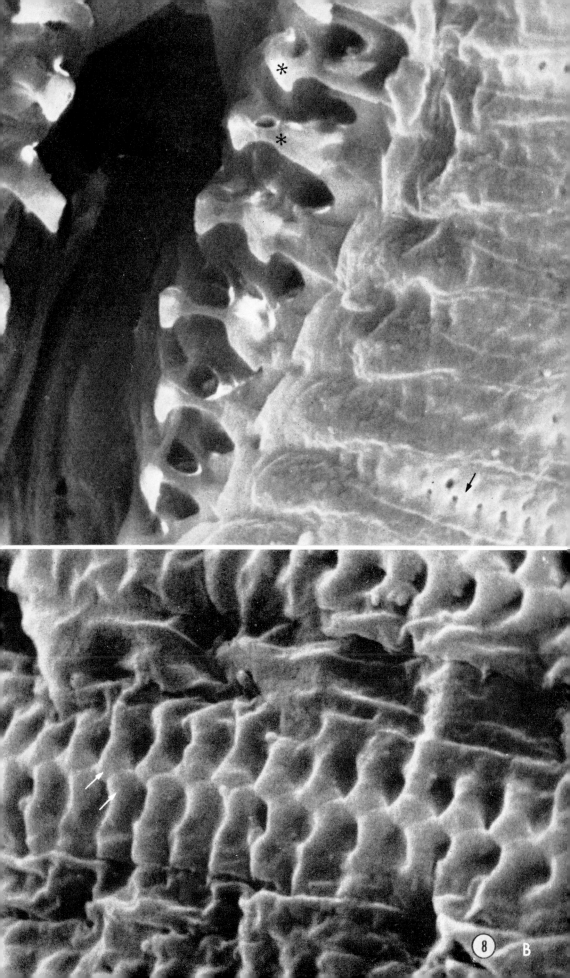

Plate 9 ▷

A transmission electron micrograph of part of an unfixed, unstained
scale, taken from the under surface of a wing of the butterfly
Morpho helena, and viewed as a whole mount. This is an example of a
non-iridescent scale, and its structure is relatively simple compared
with that of scales whose cuticular arrangement is reponsible for
iridescent interference colours, but nevertheless strikingly complex
and highly ordered. In a mature scale such as this, the formative
epidermal cell has degenerated and only the cuticular shell that it
secreted remains. The upper surface of the scale, producing the
herringbone pattern seen here, bears parallel longitudinal ridges about
2 micra apart, running obliquely across the field; the troughs
between the ridges are evenly ribbed at intervals of about 1800 Å
and are perforated by rows of holes. The lower surface of the scale is
a smooth cuticular membrane and does not contribute to the pattern
in this picture. The upper and lower surfaces are joined by struts
lying roughly perpendicular to the plane of this micrograph, and the
interior of the scale is filled with air. The base of each scale, whether
borne on the wings or on the surface of the body, is anchored by a
cuticular socket secreted by another specialised epidermal cell, a
feature illustrated in the scanning electron micrographs shown in
Plates 10 and 11.

($\times$ 10,000.)

(*Philips EM 200.*)

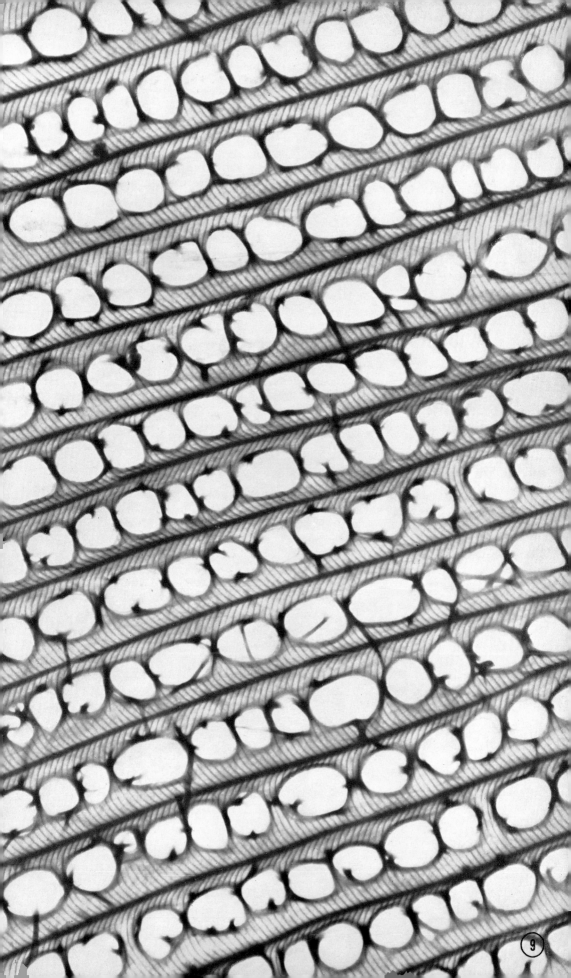

Plate 10 ▷

A pair of scanning electron micrographs of wing scales of the tropical moth *Urania ripheus*.

A. A low magnification field, including portions of several overlapping scales. A row of cuticular sockets arising from the wing membrane are visible [arrow]; into each of these is inserted the narrow neck of a scale, which soon broadens into a flattened sac. The upper surface of these scales is formed into a grating [*] of longitudinal ridges and transverse partitions, but the iridescent colours they display are believed to arise not as a diffraction grating effect, but by interference produced by multiple thin films of cuticle present beneath the surface of the scale.

B. A higher magnification field of the same material, illustrating the insertion of the neck of a scale into its cuticular socket, together with the overlapping tip [*] of a scale in the adjoining rank.

(*A* : × 1300. *B* : × 11,000.)

(Micrographs taken on a scanning electron microscope in the Department of Engineering, Cambridge, by Mr L. Peters and prepared in collaboration with Dr M. A. Message. The material was provided by Dr J. Smart.)

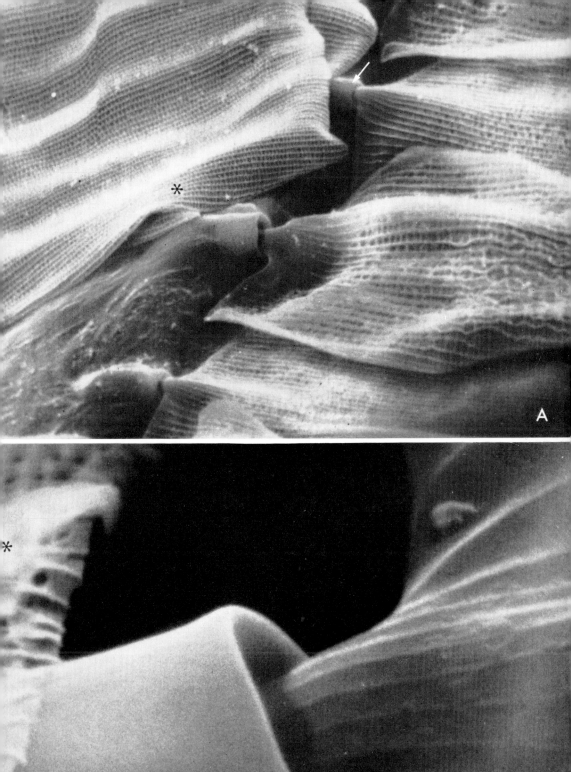

Plate 11 ▷

A pair of scanning electron micrographs of iridescent wing scales of the tropical butterfly *Morpho cypris*.

A. A micrograph showing the insertion of a scale into the annular cavity provided by its accompanying socket cell. The depth of focus and the striking three-dimensional effect are valuable features achieved by this type of electron microscope.

B. A micrograph similar to that shown above, but viewing the insertion of a scale from behind, and illustrating the confluence between the socket and the general cuticle of the wing surface. These micrographs resolve the closely-packed longitudinal ribs that traverse the scale: each of these ribs bears several laminae arranged obliquely to the scale surface—presenting a 'Christmas tree' pattern in cross-section—and the interference effects resulting from these laminae produce the iridescent colour of the scale, when viewed along its long axis. The colour produced in this way adorned many Victorian rings and tea trays, and the sight of a *Morpho* in flight is memorable.

These micrographs illustrate very well the stability of insect cuticle; the wing fragments used here were taken from a museum specimen collected in Brazil over a century ago.

($A : \times 9000.$ $B : \times 3500.$)

(Micrographs taken on a scanning electron microscope in the Department of Engineering, Cambridge, by Mr L. Peters and prepared in collaboration with Dr M. A. Message. The material was provided by Dr J. Smart.)

28

While many types of cell show some degree of cytoplasmic contractility, or bear specialised contractile processes such as cilia and flagella, muscle cells stand apart in possessing a greatly hypertrophied system of contractile proteins, representing their main synthetic output and often virtually filling the cell. During the latter half of the last century, striated muscles received a great deal of attention from light microscopists, as a result of their mechanical properties and the striking change in striation pattern that occurs as the cell changes in length during contraction and elongation. These early studies formed the basis of a wide spectrum of hypotheses on the nature of the contractile system, but the most successful of these studies were based on the belief that the cell is built up of a striated contractile apparatus, often divided into discrete fibrils, lying in a cytoplasmic (or 'sarcoplasmic') matrix containing nuclei and organelles similar to those present in other cell types.

More recently, our understanding of the architecture and mode of function of the muscle cell, and of the way in which excitation is transferred from nerve to muscle, has been greatly enhanced by studies using the electron microscope, and techniques of biochemical and X-ray analysis.

In insects, as in vertebrates and other animals, it is often convenient to classify the muscular system into general categories on the basis of their location in the body. Thus muscle fibres in insects are often grouped into skeletal, visceral and cardiac components, but it should be stressed that while these may perform roles analagous to those in higher animals, this correspondence is by no means precisely reflected in similarity of physiology and structure. Thus skeletal fibres in insects are inserted directly onto the cuticular exoskeleton or onto apodemes derived from it, and act by deforming or moving the articulated cuticular plates. Visceral fibres invest the gut and other organs within the body cavity, but are always striated, whereas their functional counterparts in vertebrates are smooth or unstriated cells. Both vertebrate and insect heart muscle is striated, but the cells of the insect heart or dorsal vessel are arranged to form a simple tube (p. 153). Perhaps the most convenient way to consider the fine structure of insect muscles is not according to their situation and function, but rather through the variations that they display in the disposition of the contractile system, membranes and cellular organelles.

(a) *The contractile system*

Insect muscle fibres are largely filled with the fibrillar proteins of the contractile system, and vary greatly in diameter from a few micra to several hundred micra. In the slenderest visceral fibres (Plates 12, 48) the contractile proteins extend with little interruption throughout the cell, but in larger visceral muscle cells (Plate 13) are

31

to some extent broken up into separate fibrils. In skeletal fibres, which are generally of larger diameter than those of the visceral system, this division into fibrils is more pronounced, and the geometry of this division is very variable. In some instances the fibrils are polygonal in cross-section (Plate 14); they may be precisely cylindrical, as in some flight muscles (Plate 15), or, as in leg muscles and flight muscle fibres of dragonflies and damselflies, the fibrils may be lamellar, extending radially from the centre of the cell to the periphery (Plate 16).

The striation pattern of the successive sarcomeres is seen when the fibre is sectioned longitudinally. In visceral and intersegmental muscles (Plate 17) the bands may zigzag irregularly across the cell, but in flight muscles the striation pattern is well aligned from one myofibril to the next (Plates 18 and 19). The divisions of each sarcomere, extending between adjacent Z bands of the fibril, appear to be basically similar in insect and vertebrate cells: the Z band is flanked by the light I bands, and the greater part of the sarcomere is occupied by the denser A band traversed by a medial light H band. The electron microscope has revealed that this sequence of bands reflects the manner in which the subunits of the fibril, the myofilaments, are fitted together. An array of thin filaments, 50 Å in diameter and containing the protein actin, extend from the Z band to the edge of the H band in a relaxed sarcomere, while thicker filaments, about 150 Å in diameter and containing the protein myosin, extend through the A band and end at the edge of the I regions. These two sets of filaments are connected, throughout the A band, by periodic 'cross bridges' extending laterally from the myosin molecules within the thick filaments, and are believed to represent enzymatically active (adenosine triphosphatase) sites at which chemical energy is used to carry out mechanical work during contraction. Huxley and Hanson proposed the now familiar 'sliding filament' hypothesis to account for the cyclic length changes of striated muscle, according to which neither set of filaments changes in length as the sarcomere shortens but rather they move with respect to each other—the I band (actin) filaments passing further into the A band towards the centre of the sarcomere, while at the same time the ends of the myosin filaments approach the Z bands, a movement reversed during relaxation. During contraction, the cross bridges are pictured as performing rapid cycles of attachment and detachment between the interdigitating filaments (as a crude model, by a ratchet mechanism), as the filaments slide past each other. This hypothesis, in the light of our present knowledge of the structure and biochemistry of striated muscle cells, has been reviewed by Huxley and Hanson (1960), and Huxley (1960), and accounts in a very satisfactory way for many aspects of muscle function.

Despite the general resemblance between the sarcomeres of insect and vertebrate fibres, closer examination shows that evolution of striated muscle has not produced an entirely standard pattern in the arrangement of actin and myosin within the A band. In vertebrate skeletal muscle, each actin filament is 'shared' by three myosin filaments (Huxley, 1957), whereas in most insect flight muscle (Plate 15) and in the sound-producing tymbal muscle of cicadas (Plate 14) each actin filament in the A band array lies midway between two myosin filaments; a configuration first described in adult blowfly flight muscle by Huxley and Hanson (1957), and in the developing pupal muscle of this insect by Auber (1965). This pattern is met with in almost all flight muscles that have been examined in the electron miscroscope: it occurs, for example, in Drosophila (Shafiq, 1963), in dragonflies and damselflies (Smith, 1966a), in aphids (Smith, 1965), and in Lepidoptera that have a relatively high rate of wing beat—in a skipper butterfly (Reger and Cooper, 1967) and in several moths (Auber, 1967). In other insect muscles, however, the ratio of actin and myosin filaments is increased. In the flight muscles of slow-flying butterflies, from seven to nine actin filaments surround each myosin filament (Auber, 1967), and a similar arrangement is found in the leg muscle of a butterfly whose flight muscles possess an exact double hexagonal array of myofilaments (Reger and Cooper, 1967). In intersegmental and visceral fibres (Smith, 1966c; Hagopian, 1966; Smith et al., 1966), the myosin filaments are surrounded by orbitals of up to twelve actin filaments (Plate 12). The reason for this variation has not yet been clearly established, but the evidence that has been collected so far suggests that the departure from the double hexagonal array of myofilaments shown by most flight muscles, by an increase in the number of actin filaments relative to the myosin of each fibril, is correlated with slower or more infrequent activity.

Amongst insect muscle fibres, the contractile system has been most extensively studied in examples of 'asynchronous' flight muscles. This special type of muscle has been evolved in the Diptera, Hymenoptera, Coleoptera and in most Hemiptera, and is characterised physiologically by the fact that the contraction frequency of the fibre exceeds that of the motor nerve impulses reaching the neuromuscular junctions at the fibre surface. The fibrils possess very narrow I bands (Plate 18), reflecting the shortness of the distance over which length changes of this type of muscle take place. Unlike vertebrate skeletal fibres, in which the myosin filaments end sharply at the edge of the I band, these insect flight muscles possess tapering threads (of unknown composition), extending from the ends of the myosin filaments into the Z band (Auber and Couteaux, 1963); an interesting structural feature, the significance of which is not at present clear. Detailed attention has also been given to the cross bridges of this type of muscle, and Reedy and his colleagues (1965) have described changes in their orientation, induced by experimental conditions, but perhaps corresponding to the movements the bridges may perform in a living active fibre. The structure and physiology of this tissue, and its relationship with more conventional striated muscles in insects and vertebrates has recently been fully reviewed by Pringle (1967).

(b) *The mitochondria*

Mitochondria, for long identified by their staining properties as an almost universal constituent of cells, were recognised in earlier light microscopic studies as lying in abundance within the cytoplasm of many striated muscles. As in other cells, these organelles provide an energy source by synthesis of ATP utilised by the muscle, notably by the myofibrils as they contract. As might be expected, the richness or paucity of a fibre's mitochondrial supply reflects its activity and oxidative requirements.

Mitochondria are more or less sparsely distributed in the smaller insect visceral muscles (Plate 12) as in the functionally comparable smooth visceral muscles of the vertebrate body, and also in intersegmental fibres (Plate 17) which are called into play infrequently. At the other end of the scale, the very high rate of oxygen consumption of insect flight muscles is matched by a greatly increased complement of mitochondria which, in both synchronous and asynchronous fibres alike, may account for about 40 per cent of the total cell volume. The richness of the mitochondrial supply of these muscles was revealed by early electron microscopic studies (Chapman, 1954; Edwards and Ruska, 1955), and has been described in detail in many subsequent reports. This feature is illustrated in Plates 18 and 19. The development of functional flight muscles is an important part of metamorphosis in most insects, and this involves not only the production of the contractile fibrils, but also the elaboration of the required mitochondrial system, providing energy for contraction through ATP synthesis. Brosemer and his colleagues (1963), for example, have traced in electron micrographs, and in biochemical assays, the spectacular increase in the mitochondrial content of locust flight muscle from the last larval instar to the final burst of differentiation, taking place soon after the emergence of the adult. It is thought that the cytochromes and associated phosphorylating enzymes, grouped into 'respiratory assemblies' (Lehninger, 1964), are bound to the internal membrane folds or cristae of the mitochondrion, and the respiratory equipment of flight muscles appears even more impressive when it is realised that each of these organelles may be so constructed as to contain a considerable membrane area. The cristae may be arranged in irregular or whorled patterns, or sometimes, as in the blowfly (Smith, 1963), these may be disposed in parallel arrays, separated by spaces of the mitochondrial matrix (believed to contain the Krebs cycle enzymes) only about 100 Å in width. In this case, the close packing of cristae achieves a membrane area of about 50 square micra per cubic micron of mitochondrion, and the cristae are fenestrated, perhaps to facilitate movement of metabolites within the congested interior of the organelle.

The mitochondria of insect muscles may be scattered randomly through the cell, but often they are arranged within the sarcoplasm in register with the striations of the adjoining myofibrils. In the intersegmental muscle shown in Plate 17, for example, small mitochondria lie opposite the I bands, and larger ones occur more sparsely at other levels of the sarcomere. In the flight muscle of Hymenoptera (Plate 18) pairs of large mitochondria generally surround each sarcomere of the cylindrical myofibrils; in the Odonata (Plate 19) large slab-like mitochondria are inserted between the Z band levels of each sarcomere of the lamellar fibrils, while Lepidoptera have adopted a triplet arrangement (Smith, 1962). This sort of variation certainly poses a fascinating problem concerning the morphogenetic *rapport* between the developing contractile material and the surrounding cytoplasm and its contents, but its physiological significance is obscure, and indeed perhaps merely represents an evolutionary quirk that accompanied the emergence of the various insect Orders.

(c) *The tracheal supply*

Tracheal twigs and smaller tracheoles invest the muscle fibres throughout the insect body, but with varying richness in different types of muscle. Visceral fibres, for example, are generally sparsely tracheated in their own right, but often apparently share the tracheal supply of the cells they invest, as in the mid-gut and salivary glands, illustrated in Plates 45, 48 and 72. Many skeletal muscles, on the other hand, enjoy a very intimate respiratory supply by possessing tracheoles closely applied to the fibre surface (Plate 16), or invaginated into the depths of the cell (Plates 14 and 18). The latter device ensures a great reduction in the distance over which oxygen must diffuse to reach the respiratory sites of the cell. Whether or not a particular muscle fibre will be invaded by tracheolar processes is a developmental decision that is constant for a given species. Brosemer and his colleagues (1963) have described the progressive invagination of tracheoblast processes into developing locust flight muscles, which eventually equips the mature fibres with a rich respiratory supply.

(d) *The membranes of the fibre*

The importance of the part played by various membrane systems of striated muscles has in recent years been underlined by physiological, biochemical and electron microscopic approaches, which have complemented each other in a very encouraging manner. Before the detailed structure of the fibre was understood in detail, it was recognised that the sarcoplasm and its fibrillar contents are contained within a membrane which, as in a nerve axon, maintains a potential difference between the inside and outside of the cell, and can support transient waves of depolarisation. This depolarisation, initiated beneath synapses between motor nerve terminals and the muscle, is followed after a very brief delay by contraction. The electron microscope showed that the fibre is limited by a plasma membrane about 75 Å in thickness, similar in appearance to the 'unit membrane' investing other cells. At the same time, a hitherto almost unknown part of the muscle fibre was brought to light. Perhaps only Veratti (1902) had previously seen, in silver-impregnated sections, a delicate network of threads running within the sarcoplasm, the transverse elements of which were often arrayed in register with the striations. The reticulum of Veratti proved to consist of tubules and cisternae, closely applied to the fibrils and forming two quite separate systems. The transversely oriented members are tubular invaginations of the cell membrane traversing the sarcoplasm opposite the Z bands or the junction between the A and I bands in vertebrate skeletal muscles, or midway between the Z bands and the centre of the sarcomere in many insect fibres. Passing close by these tubules are longitudinally disposed cisternae. These two sets of membranes are usually known, respectively, as the T- (or transverse) system and the sarcoplasmic reticulum, and they are believed to play an important role in muscular contraction and relaxation. Studies on the arrangement of these membranes in vertebrate skeletal fibres include those of Franzini-Armstrong and Porter (1964) on fish swim bladder muscle, Peachey (1965) on the frog sartorius and Revel (1962) on the cricothyroid muscle of the bat, and their distribution in representative muscles from the chief insect Orders has been reviewed by Smith (1966b).

It is probable that the T-system tubules make possible the very rapid onset of contraction following nervous stimulation by channelling into the fibre an electrical signal, that is initiated as the wave of depolarisation sweeps over the surface membrane, and that in some ways leads to triggering of the contractile mechanism. Studies on muscle homogenates have shown that vesicles derived from the sarcoplasmic reticulum cisternae are able to withdraw calcium ions very efficiently from their surroundings. The importance of this property lies in the biochemistry of contraction: without an adequate supply of calcium ions, the splitting of ATP by myosin, releasing energy used in contraction, is inhibited, and it may well be that the efficacy of the T-system signals lies in their ability to induce the sudden release of a surge of these ions from the cisternae permitting the splitting of ATP within the fibril, the interaction of actin and myosin, and filament sliding. On this model, relaxation promptly ensues when the calcium ions are pumped back into the reticulum cisternae to await further cycling as the next wave of excitation is initiated and spreads over the cell. The part played by these membranes in the functioning of striated muscles in insects, vertebrates and other animals has been discussed by Franzini-Armstrong and Porter (1964), Peachey (1965), and Smith (1966b).

It is interesting to view the internal membranes possessed by various types of insect muscle against the background provided by this physiological model.

(i) *Skeletal fibres.* Most of the muscle fibres operating the leg and wing mechanisms and the intersegmental fibres of the abdomen resemble vertebrate fast or 'twitch' muscles in possessing a well-ordered array of transverse tubules, together with a well-developed sarcoplasmic reticulum. These features have been described, for example, in cockroach femoral muscle (Hagopian, 1966), intersegmental muscle (Smith, 1966c), and in flight muscles of Odonata and Lepidoptera (Smith, 1966a; Reger and Cooper, 1967; Auber, 1967), and they are illustrated here in electron micrographs of dragonfly flight muscle (Plates 19 and 20) and in the tymbal muscle of the cicada (Plate 14). Plate 19 shows the appearance of a longitudinal section of part of a fibre and includes in cross-section the T-system tubules, two of which pass alongside each surface of every sarcomere. These tubules are very closely associated with the adjoining portion of the sarcoplasmic reticulum to form two-membered 'dyads'. In vertebrate muscles, the geometry of these membranes is somewhat different, and each transverse tubule usually lies between two 'terminal cisternae' of the reticulum to constitute a three-membered 'triad'. The transverse section of a fibre, shown in Plate 20, passes through a series of transverse tubules, and in several places the plane of section includes the point where these open-mouthed invaginations arise from the plasma membrane of the cell. These skeletal muscles share with vertebrate twitch fibres the ability to respond synchronously to a volley of motor nerve impulses. However, in the flight muscles of the four Orders that have evolved asynchronous oscillatory capacity, the transverse tubules are retained, but the sarcoplasmic reticulum is markedly reduced in volume and indeed is generally restricted to small vesicles lying alongside the tubules (Smith, 1961; Shafiq, 1964; Ashhurst, 1967, and Further Refs. in Smith, 1966b). The absence of a sheath of cisternae around the fibrils is clearly seen in Plates 15 and 18 taken from the flight muscle of an aphid and a wasp. These asynchronous fibres move the wings at very high frequencies (sometimes several hundred cycles per second), and at first sight the reduction of the reticulum might seem paradoxical. Actually, it appears to be an exception that proves the rule. Whereas calcium movements synchronised with the motor impulse train may control contraction and relaxation in most muscles, the frequency of oscillatory length changes in asynchronous fibres is determined quite differently (Pringle, 1965)—by the mechanical properties of the wings and thorax, and an intrinsic oscillatory mechanism residing in the myofibrils. The development of asynchronous muscle is not only of great physiological interest, but has also had a profound effect upon the evolution of body form, notably in such insects as flies, bees, wasps and some beetles in which the relatively bulky body may be moved with great manoeuvrability by small heavily loaded wings, operating at high frequency.

(ii) *Visceral fibres.* Visceral muscles of insects, although striated, perform slow contractions resembling those of vertebrate smooth muscles. Furthermore, these cells are in each case generally much smaller in diameter than skeletal fibres. Vertebrate smooth muscles lack T-system invaginations and an organised sarcoplasmic reticulum, and contraction is probably triggered by calcium ions entering the cell across the surface membrane and leaving by the same route during relaxation. In synchronous striated muscles, despite their large diameter, the transverse tubules carry excitation to within a micron or so of every sarcomere of each fibril, whereas the activating ions of smooth muscles must actually diffuse further (and thereby elicit contraction more slowly) than in the larger skeletal fibres. With this comparison in mind, it is interesting to discover that in the smaller visceral muscle cells in insects (Plate 12), transverse tubules and cisternae of the sarcoplasmic reticulum are poorly developed, but become more prominent as the diameter of the fibre increases (Plate 13). While little is known of the physiology and biochemistry of these muscle cells investing the gut and other tissues within the insect body cavity, their membrane organisation invites speculation about the way in which they function. Perhaps the smallest fibres, like vertebrate smooth muscle, rely on slow activation by ions passing in from the haemolymph, but larger fibres increasingly rely on ion movements between the sarcoplasm and the internal compartments provided by the membranes of the sarcoplasmic reticulum, so well developed in the faster-acting synchronous skeletal muscles.

The development of a cuticle resisting desiccation and the acquisition of a tracheal system for respiration of atmospheric oxygen opened up the terrestrial environment to the insects; an evolutionary opportunity that they exploited to the full. During the elaboration of novel methods of walking and feeding, and the development and refinement of flight mechanisms, they presumably adapted the musculature of their ancestral arthropods and also introduced various muscular innovations of their own. The mechanical requirements of these various muscles are quite different from those controlling, for example, the circulation of the haemolymph and the passage of food along the gut. All these requirements have been met by muscles in which the contractile proteins are organised into repeating sarcomeres. The electron microscope has already brought to light many of the structural features of these cells, contributing to our knowledge of comparative aspects of muscle form and function.

Insect cardiac muscle fibres are also striated, and are arranged into a tubular dorsal vessel which is principally responsible for the circulation of the haemolymph in the body cavity. The fine structure of the cockroach heart and the cells that are associated with it are described separately, on p. 153.

REFERENCES

*AUBER, J. 1965. Sur le mécanisme de la formation des filaments primaires au cours de l'accroissement des myofibrilles chez *Calliphora erythrocephala* (Mg.) (Insecte Diptère). *C.r. hebd. Séanc. Acad. Sci.*, Paris, **260**, 668–670.

*AUBER, J. 1967. Particularités ultrastructurales des myofibrilles des muscles du vol chez des Lépidoptères. *C.r. hebd. Séanc. Acad. Sci.*, Paris, **264**, 621–624.

*AUBER, J., and COUTEAUX, R. 1963. Ultrastructure de la strie Z dans des muscles de Diptères. *J. micr.*, **2**, 309–324.

*ASHHURST, D. E. 1967. The flight muscle of giant water bugs: an electron microscope study. *J. Cell Sci.*, **2**, 435–444.

*BROSEMER, R. W., VOGELL, W., and BÜCHER, T. 1963. Morphologische und enzymatische Muster bei der Entwicklung indirekter Flugmuskeln von *Locusta migratoria*. *Biochem. Z.*, **338**, 854–910.

*CHAPMAN, G. B. 1954. Electron microscopy of ultra-thin sections of insect flight muscle. *J. Morph.*, **95**, 237–262.

*EDWARDS, G. A., and RUSKA, H. 1955. The function and metabolism of certain insect muscles in relation to their structure. *Q. Jl microsc. Sci.*, **96**, 151–159.

FRANZINI-ARMSTRONG, C., and PORTER, K. R. 1964. Sarcolemmal invaginations constituting the T-system in fish muscle fibers. *J. Cell Biol.*, **22**, 675–696.

*HAGOPIAN, M. 1966. The myofilament arrangement in the femoral muscle of the cockroach, *Leucophaea maderae* Fabricius. *J. Cell Biol.*, **28**, 545–562.

*HAGOPIAN, M., and SPIRO, D. 1967. The sarcoplasmic reticulum and its association with the T system in an insect. *J. Cell Biol.*, **32**, 535–545.

HUXLEY, H. E. 1957. The double array of filaments in cross-striated muscle. *J. biophys. biochem. Cytol.*, **7**, 255–318.

HUXLEY, H. E. 1960. Muscle cells. In *The Cell* (J. Brachet and A. E. Mirsky, eds.), Vol. 4, pp. 365–481. Academic Press, New York and London.

*HUXLEY, H. E., and HANSON, J. 1957. Preliminary observations on the structure of insect flight muscle. In *Electron Microscopy, Proceedings of the Stockholm Conference*, 1956, pp. 202–203. Almqvist and Wiksell, Stockholm.

HUXLEY, H. E., and HANSON, J. 1960. The molecular basis of contraction in cross-striated muscles. In *The Structure and Function of Muscle* (G. H. Bourne, ed.), Vol. 1, pp. 183–227. Academic Press, New York.

LEHNINGER, A. L. 1964. *The Mitochondrion. Molecular Basis of Structure and Function.* W. A. Benjamin, New York and Amsterdam.

PEACHEY, L. D. 1965. The sarcoplasmic reticulum and transverse tubules of the frog's sartorius. *J. Cell Biol.*, **25**, 209–232.

PRINGLE, J. W. S. 1965. Locomotion: flight. In *The Physiology of Insecta* (M. Rockstein, ed.), Vol. 2, pp. 283–329. Academic Press, New York and London.

PRINGLE, J. W. S. 1967. The contractile mechanism of insect fibrillar muscle. *Prog. biophys. molec. Biol.*, **17**, 3–60.

*REEDY, M. K., HOLMES, K. C., and TREGEAR, R. T. 1965. Induced changes in orientation of the cross-bridges of glycerinated insect flight muscle. *Nature, Lond.*, **207**, 1276–1280.

*REGER, J. F. 1967. The organization of the sarcoplasmic reticulum in direct flight muscle of the lepidopteran *Achalarus lyciades*. *J. Ultrastruct. Res.*, **18**, 595–599.

*REGER, J. F., and COOPER, D. P. 1967. A comparative study on the fine structure of the basalar muscle of the wing and the tibial extensor muscle of the leg of the lepidopteran *Achalarus lyciades*. *J. Cell Biol.*, **33**, 531–542.

REVEL, J. P. 1962. The sarcoplasmic reticulum of the bat cricothyroid muscle. *J. Cell Biol.*, **12**, 571–588.

*SHAFIQ, S. A. 1963. Electron microscopic studies on the indirect flight muscles of *Drosophila melanogaster*. I. Structure of the myofibrils. *J. Cell Biol.*, **17**, 351–362.

*SHAFIQ, S. A. 1964. An electron microscopical study of the innervation and sarcoplasmic reticulum of the fibrillar flight muscle of *Drosophila melanogaster*. *Q. Jl microsc. Sci.*, **105**, 1–6.

*SMITH, D. S. 1961. The structure of insect fibrillar flight muscle. A study made with special reference to the membrane systems of the fiber. *J. biophys. biochem. Cytol.*, **10** suppl., 123–158.

*SMITH, D. S. 1962. Cytological studies on some insect muscles. *Rev. Can. Biol.*, **21**, 279–301.

*SMITH, D. S. 1963. The structure of flight muscle sarcosomes in the blowfly *Calliphora erythrocephala* (Diptera). *J. Cell Biol.*, **19**, 115–138.

*SMITH, D. S. 1965. The organization of flight muscle in an aphid, *Megoura viciae* (Homoptera). *J. Cell Biol.*, **27**, 379–393.

SMITH, D. S. 1966a. The organization of flight muscle fibers in the Odonata. *J. Cell Biol.*, **28**, 109–126.

*SMITH, D. S. 1966b. The organization and function of the sarcoplasmic reticulum and T-system of muscle cells. *Prog. biophys. molec. Biol.*, **16**, 107–142.

*SMITH, D. S. 1966c. The structure of intersegmental muscle fibers in an insect, *Periplaneta americana* L., *J. Cell Biol.*, **29**, 449–459.

SMITH, D. S., GUPTA, B. L., and SMITH, U. 1966. The organization and myofilament array of insect visceral muscles. *J. Cell Sci.*, **1**, 49–57.

VERATTI, E. 1902. Ricerche sulla fine struttura della fibra muscolare striata. *Memorie Ist. lomb. Sci. Lett.*, **19**, 87–133. [English translation: *J. biophys. biochem. Cytol.*, 1961, **10** suppl., 3–59.)

Plates 12–20 ▷

Plate 12 ▷

A transversely sectioned visceral muscle fibre from the sheath
surrounding the testis of a stick insect, *Carausius morosus*. Much of
the volume of the cell is taken up by the contractile material, which
is not divided up into separate fibrils. In the A band [A], each of
the thick (myosin) filaments is surrounded by a ring of up to twelve
thin (actin) filaments—a pattern that contrasts with the regular
double hexagonal array found in tymbal and flight muscles, illustrated
in Plates 14 and 15. Short irregular transverse tubules [T] are
invaginated from the cell membrane, and the sarcoplasmic reticulum
is extremely sparse. In the upper and left parts of the field only thin
filaments are present, where the section passes through I-band
regions. Mitochondria are very infrequent in this muscle, but one of
these organelles is seen at M. Microtubules [Mt] are found in the
sarcoplasm, particularly beneath the cell membrane. The fibre is
ensheathed in a sarcolemma of basement membrane-like material [BM]

($\times$ 90,000.)

(*Philips EM 200. From Smith* et al. (*1966*). *Reproduced by courtesy
of the* Journal of Cell Science.)

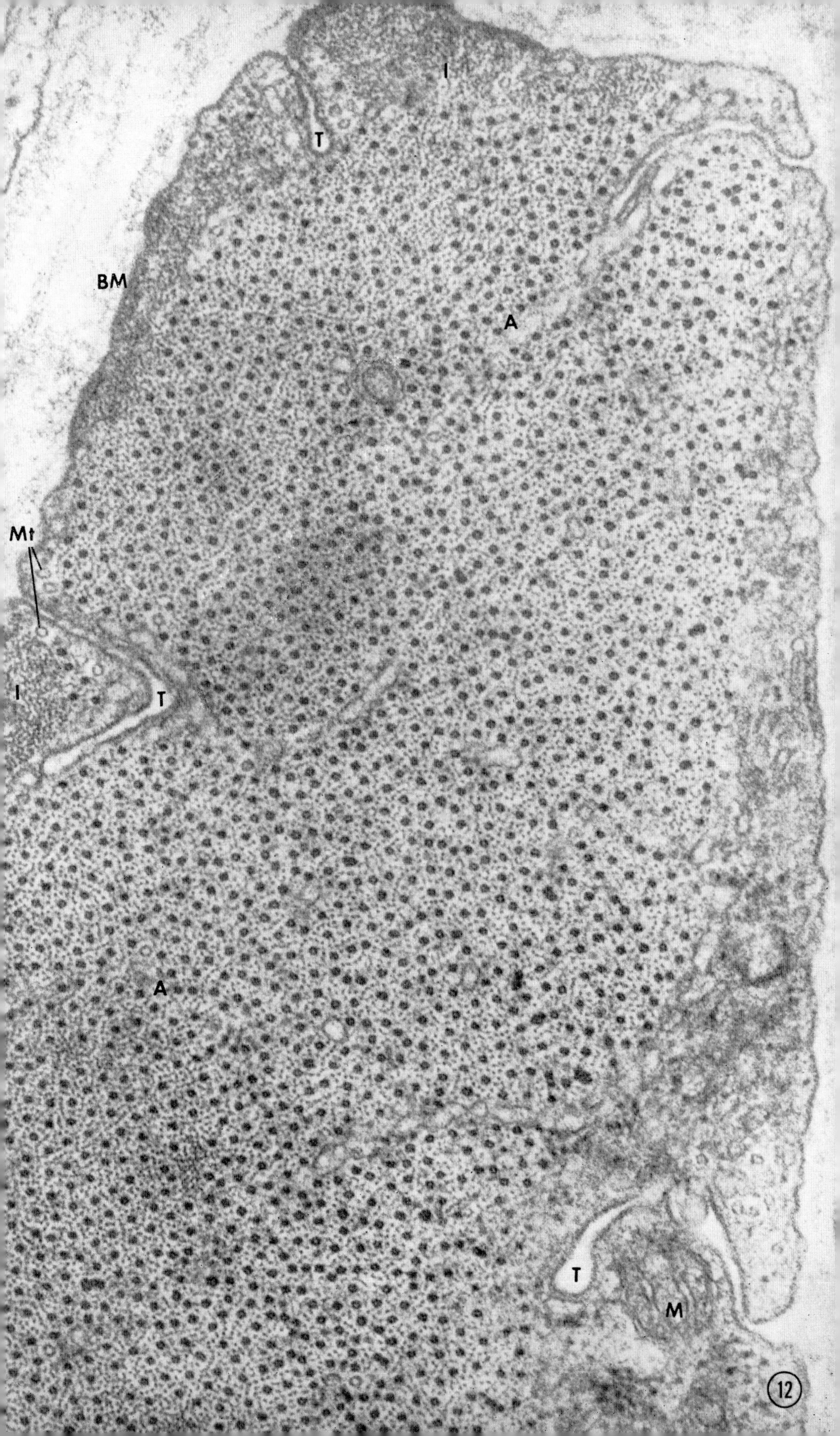
I
T
BM
A
Mt
I
T
A
T
M
12

Plate 13 ▷

A micrograph of a transversely sectioned visceral muscle fibre associated with the spermatheca of the cockroach *Periplaneta americana*. In this muscle, the nuclei are centrally placed [N]. The contractile material is incompletely divided into irregular fibrils [F]. The plasma membrane is frequently invaginated into the fibre to form T-system or transverse tubules [T] which form dyads with the limited number of sarcoplasmic reticulum cisternae with which the cell is equipped [arrows]. It should be mentioned that many insect visceral fibres are much smaller in diameter than that shown here (cf. Plate 12) and show great reduction of these internal membranes, the probable function of which is mentioned in the text. Mitochondria [M] are scattered throughout the cell, but are less abundant than in flight muscle fibres (Plates 15, 18 and 20). The cell is ensheathed by a layered basement membrane [BM]. Nerve axons approaching the surface of the muscle are seen at Ax, and a tracheole at Tr.

(× 22,000.)

(*Philips EM 200.*)

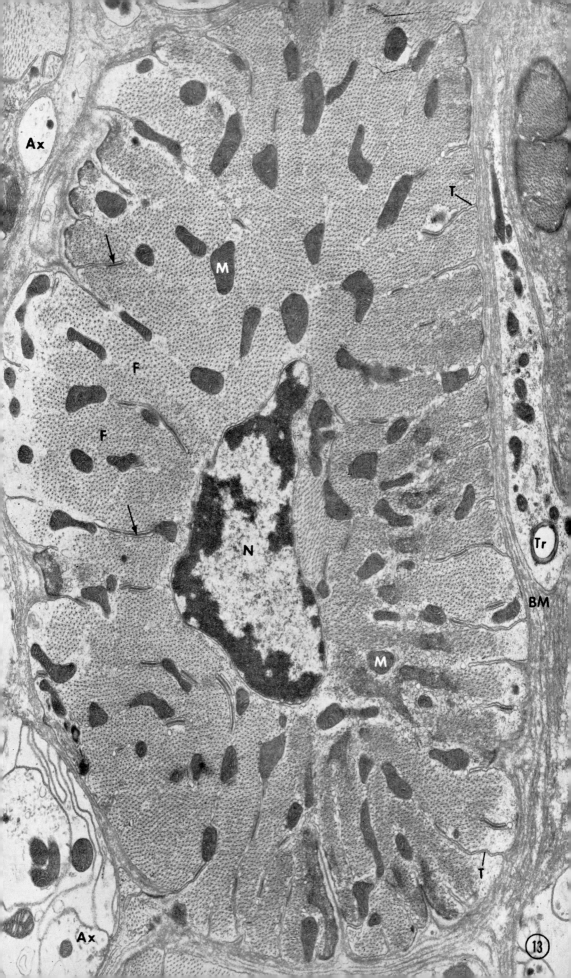

Plate 14 ▷

A field at the periphery of a transversely sectioned sound-producing
(tymbal) muscle of the cicada *Tibicen*. In this muscle the
fibrils [F] are circular or polygonal in profile, and in the A region is
resolved the characteristic regular double hexagonal array of
overlapping actin and myosin filaments. The fibrils are ensheathed by
closely packed cisternae of the sarcoplasmic reticulum [SR] or, when
the plane of section passes midway between the Z band and the
centre of the sarcomere (cf. Plate 20), they are instead encircled by
the invaginated tubules of the T-system [T] believed to conduct an
excitatory signal from the depolarised surface membrane into the cell.
Fitting between the fibrils, and conforming to their shape, are many
large mitochondria [M] containing closely packed internal membranes
or cristae. The cell nuclei in this muscle lie beneath the cell surface
[N]. Profiles of tracheae are seen outside the fibre [TR]: small
traceoles are invaginated into the fibre [Tr], increasing the efficiency
of the respiratory supply.

(× 35,000.)

(*Philips EM 200.*)

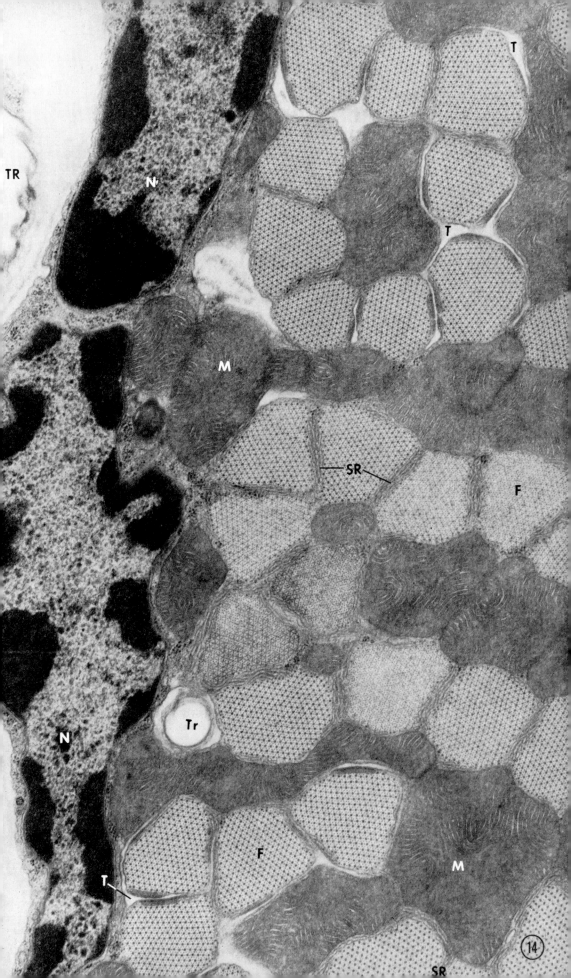

Plate 15 ▷

This transverse section of a fibril within a flight muscle fibre of the
aphid *Megoura viciae* passes through the A band and the double
hexagonal array of interdigitating actin and myosin filaments. The
latter (about 150 Å in diameter) are each surrounded by an orbital of
six thin (50 Å) actin filaments. Each actin filament is shared by two
myosin filaments, in contrast to the trigonal disposition occurring in
vertebrate skeletal muscle in which each actin is shared by three
myosin filaments. In this very exact pattern, the outermost myosin
filaments at the periphery of the fibril complete their orbital [arrows].
Other insect muscles (notably leg, intersegmental and visceral fibres)
have adopted a different array (Plate 12) in which the actin orbitals
number up to twelve. As in other asynchronous flight muscles, the
sarcoplasmic reticulum is much reduced, but tubules of the T-system
permeate the cell, and a portion of one of these is seen at T. As in
other very active muscles, the mitochondria [M] are large and
abundant, and contain many cristae. Deposits of glycogen [Gy] are
stored within the sarcoplasm surrounding the fibril.

(× 70,000.)

(*Philips EM 200. From Smith (1965). Reproduced by courtesy of*
The Journal of Cell Biology.)

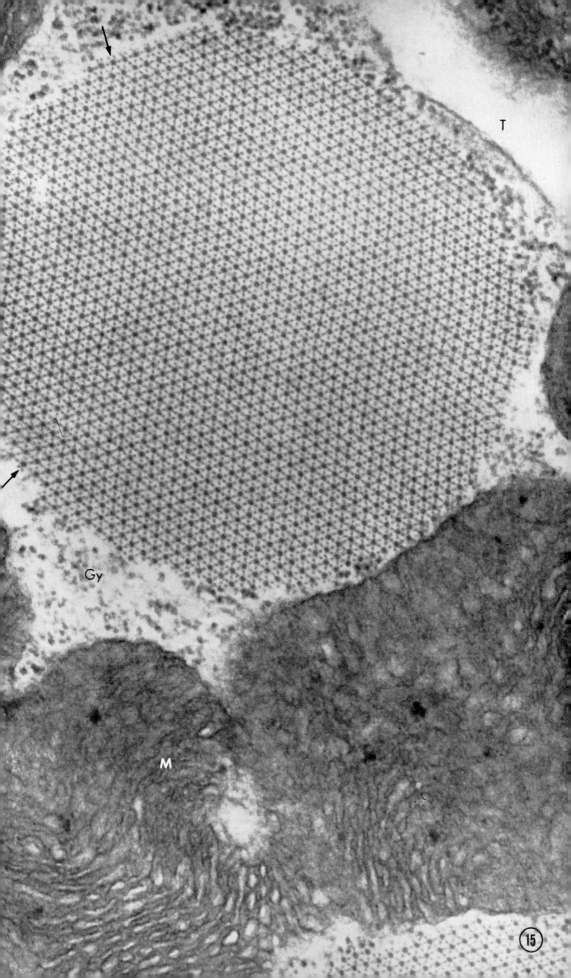

Plate 16 ▷

Striated muscles in insects, as well as in other animals, vary strikingly
in the disposition of their contractile material. This micrograph
illustrates, at low magnification, the radial organisation of transversely
sectioned flight muscle of a damselfly, *Enallagma* sp. The fibres are
polygonal and their cell membranes adjoin each other [arrows] across
a narrow intercellular gap which in life is filled with circulating
haemolymph. The myofilaments are arranged in lamellar fibrils [F],
whereas in other cells the fibrils may be cylindrical (Plate 15) or
poorly demarcated (Plate 13). Between the fibrils in this flight muscle
are situated large wedge-shaped mitochondria [M]: the precise
placing of these with respect to the myofibrillar striations is seen when
the fibre is sectioned in the longitudinal plane (Plate 19). Note the
nuclei [N] lying along the axis of the cell; in other muscles these may
be placed beneath the surface (Plate 14) or scattered throughout
the sarcoplasm. Small tracheoles [Tr] penetrate along the intercellular
spaces between the fibres.

(× 8000.)

(*Philips EM 200.*)

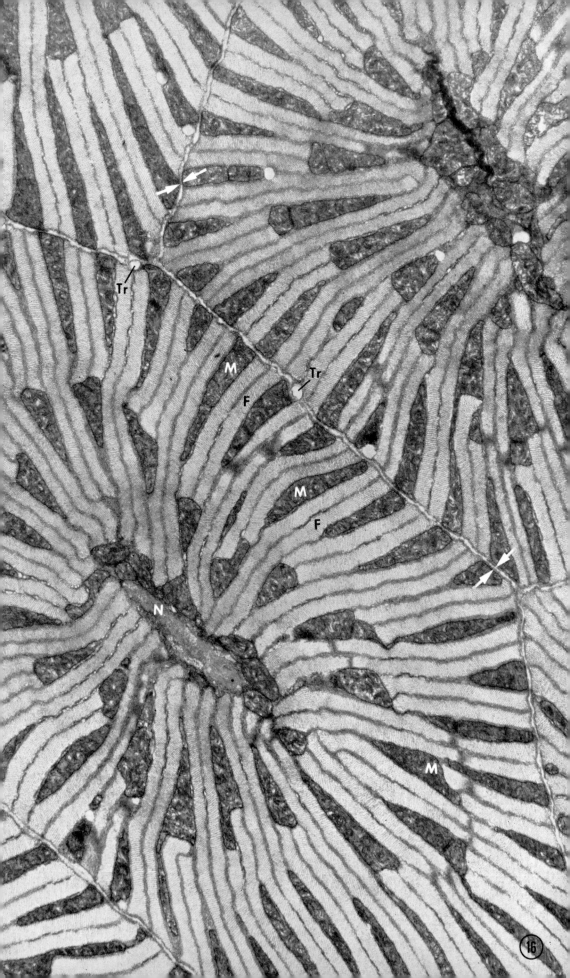

Plate 17 ▷

While the bands of the sarcomere made familiar by studies on striated muscles of vertebrates are present in insect fibres the proportions of these vary considerably between different types of cell. Many flight muscles, for example, which shorten only a few per cent of their resting or relaxed length during activity, possess very narrow I bands (Plate 18). Other fibres may shorten more considerably and, as in the intersegmental muscle of the cockroach shown here, display a band pattern more closely corresponding to that of vertebrate skeletal fibres. The sarcomeres lack the precise transverse alignment shown by flight muscles (Plates 18 and 19) but comprise dense Z bands, A bands and wide I bands [Z, A, I] adjacent to the last of which lie small mitochondria [M]. A nucleus has been caught in grazing section at N.

(× 8000.)

(*Philips EM 200.*)

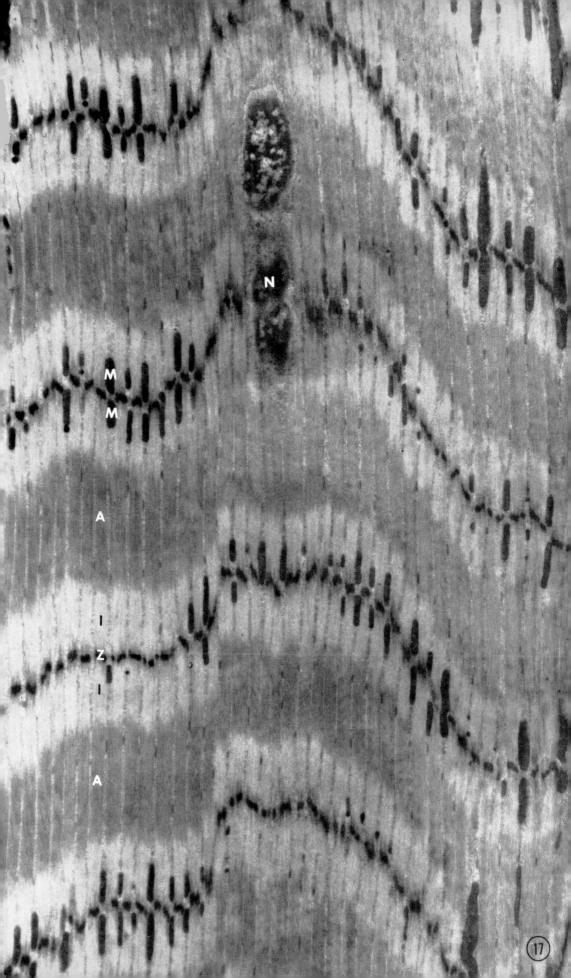

Plate 18 ▷

All insect flight muscles are profusely supplied with mitochondria, and these are often accurately positioned in the sarcoplasm with respect to the striations of the adjoining myofibrils. In the asynchronous muscle of the wasp *Polistes* shown here, each of these organelles [M] generally straddles half a sarcomere, between the Z and H bands. The striations of the myofibrils are well aligned across the cell [Z, I, A, H, M′], and the I bands are narrow as in other flight muscles that change but little in length during activity. The most obvious structural peculiarity of oscillatory asynchronous muscle such as this is that the sarcoplasmic reticulum, extensive and spacious in most synchronous skeletal fibres (Plates 14 and 19), is very reduced. However, the transverse tubules derived from the cell membrane are retained [T] and in this instance lie opposite the H bands at the centre of the sarcomere. This difference between the two physiologically distinct groups of flight muscles is discussed in the text. A small tracheole, invaginated into the cell, is included at the upper left [Tr].

(× 18,000.)

(*Philips EM 200.*)

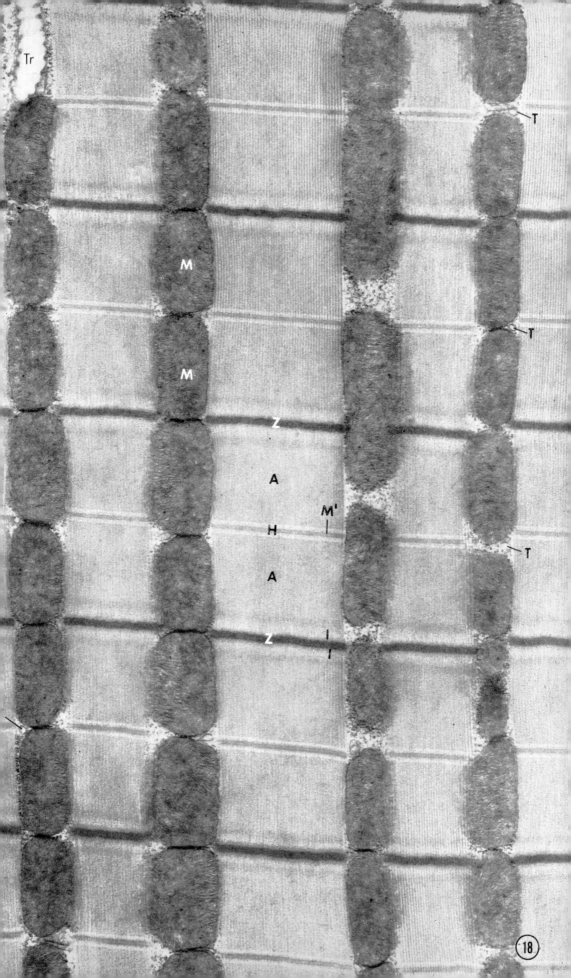

Tr

T

M

M

Z

A

M'

H

A

Z

I

T

T

18

Plate 19 ▷

A longitudinal section of flight muscle of a dragonfly *Sympetrum* sp.
In this very regularly organised fibre, the bands of the sarcomeres
[Z, I, A, H] are aligned across the fibrils, which are separated by very
large mitochondria [M] generally placed singly alongside each
sarcomere. Indenting the mitochondria roughly midway between the
Z and H levels lie the transversely oriented T-system tubules, seen
here in cross-section [T], while the fibril surface is covered by sheet-
like cisternae of the sarcoplasmic reticulum [SR]. The transverse
tubules are closely attached to these cisternae to form two-membered
'dyads'. As is mentioned more fully in the text, it is thought that an
electrical signal, coupled with depolarisation of the surface cell
membrane, reaches the sarcoplasmic reticulum at the dyads via the
transverse tubules, and initiates contraction by triggering the sudden
release of calcium ions from the cisternae and thus activating the
myosin ATP-ase activity of the myofibrils, operating during contraction
It is further supposed that the reticulum cisternae next rapidly take
back the calcium ions from the fibrils by active transport, curtailing
contraction and thus inducing relaxation. The clear areas [L]
adjoining the Z bands perhaps represent lipid droplets that have been
extracted during preparation of the muscle for electron microscopy.

(× 34,000.)

(*Philips EM 200.*)

54

Plate 20 ▷

A field of dragonfly flight muscle similar to that shown in Plate 19, but sectioned transversely. The fibrils [F] are lamellar, and extend from beneath the cell surface to the centre of the cell, and between them lie large slab-like mitochondria [M], in which the cristae are closely packed and arranged in irregular and whorled arrays. The plane of this section lies at the level of the transverse (or T-system) tubules [T], midway between the Z-band level and the middle of the sarcomere (cf. Plate 19). In several places [arrows] the open orifices, linking the tubules with the outside of the fibre, are seen, and the continuity between the tubules and the cell membrane is believed to be of great importance in enabling them to conduct excitation into the depths of the fibre. Cisternae of the sarcoplasmic reticulum [SR] adjoin the tubules to make up the two-membered 'dyads' (cf. Plate 19). The cavity [*] seen in this field may represent the site of a lipid droplet, lost during preparation of the specimen.

($\times$ 28,000.)

(*Philips EM 200.*)

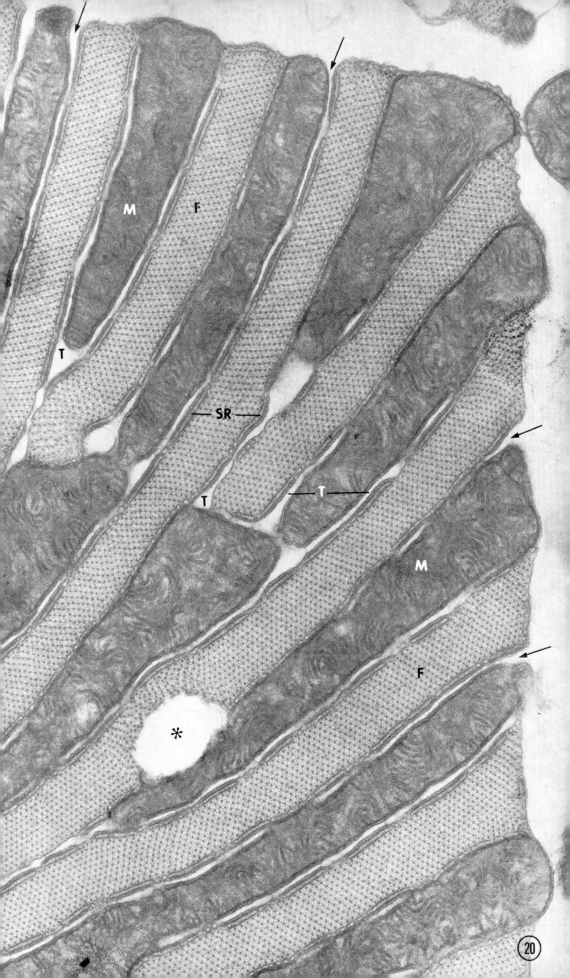

Every skeletal muscle fibre in the insect body, as in the vertebrate, is closely approached by one or more fine endings of motor axons stemming from the central ganglia. These endings establish functional links with the muscle cells—neuromuscular junctions—across which excitation can be transferred to elicit contraction. The arrival of an action potential at an axon terminal triggers depolarisation of the adjacent muscle cell membrane, and this is followed, after a short delay, by a rapid cycle of contraction and relaxation (a 'twitch') or by slower enhancement of the degree of contraction already established by previous nerve impulses. In 'fast' fibres of the vertebrate, and in the flight muscles of insects other than Hymenoptera, Diptera, Coleoptera and most Hemiptera, a volley of nerve impulses produces a synchronised succession of twitches in the innervated muscle. Flight muscles of the insects mentioned above, on the other hand, possess the unusual capacity of undergoing oscillatory length changes at a frequency greater than that of the arriving nerve impulses. In the vertebrate body, fast and slow muscle fibres differing in their fine structure have been recognised, and as in the frog (Peachey and Huxley, 1962), these may sometimes be grouped together within a single anatomical muscle. In insects, however, this type of variation does not seem to occur; instead, individual fibres (e.g. in leg muscles) are able to give either slow or fast contractions by virtue of the presence of separate and physiologically different fast and slow axons, at the neuromuscular junctions. The physiology of neuromuscular synapses on insect skeletal fibres has recently been reviewed in detail by Hoyle (1965).

The appearance and distribution of neuromuscular junctions is quite variable over the range of vertebrate and invertebrate skeletal fibres. Vertebrate twitch fibres bear only a single junction, the motor end-plate, which presents a palmate form in light microscopic preparations. Arthropod skeletal fibres, however, in common with those of slow vertebrate muscles, each possess several junctions—the 'multiterminal' pattern. These may be fairly compact, not unlike vertebrate end plates, but often the slenderest nerve terminals meander for some distance over the surface of the muscle cell (Refs. in Hoyle, 1965). Despite topographical differences between various junctions, the electron microscope has revealed certain structural features shared by all; features that may indicate common aspects of function. Plates 21 and 22 illustrate the appearance of neuromuscular synapses borne by fibres of cockroach intersegmental muscle.

The first important feature of all junctions is that the sheath of glial cells that accompanies the axons on their outward course from the central ganglia is absent or incomplete at the terminal, allowing the plasma membranes of muscle and nerve cells to lie very close together, separated only by a narrow 'synaptic gap'. In vertebrates, this gap may be up to 500 Å in width, but in insect junctions it is often only about 100 Å wide. It is into this gap that molecules of a chemical transmitter (acetylcholine in vertebrate muscles) are released from the nerve ending upon arrival of the action potential; the transmitter alters the permeability of the underlying muscle cell membrane to produce a local depolarisation or end-plate potential, which gives rise to a spreading depolarisation of the muscle membrane that is followed by a contractile response. A second universal feature of these neuromuscular synapses is the presence of large numbers of small vesicles, about 250–450 Å in diameter, within the axoplasm of the terminating nerves. These 'synaptic vesicles' were first noted in vertebrate end-plates by Palade (1954), and subsequently have been described by other investigators: moreover, vesicles similar in appearance to these have been found to occur in association with chemically mediated nerve-to-nerve synapses in the vertebrate central nervous system. Likewise, they are found at neuromuscular junctions on synchronous and asynchronous flight muscles and other skeletal fibres in insects (Edwards, 1959; Edwards and co-workers, 1958a, 1958b; Smith, 1960; Smith and Treherne, 1963; and others) and are abundant, in addition, in regions of the central ganglia that are thought to be rich in synaptic sites (p. 73).

Katz and his colleagues, working with vertebrate material, have drawn together the results of electron microscopy of motor end-plates, and pharmacological and physiological data, in support of an attractive hypothesis on the way in which excitation is transferred from nerve to muscle; an hypothesis first put forward by Palay and de Robertis (Refs. in Smith and Treherne, 1963) to account for the presence of small axoplasmic vesicles in central nervous tissue. This hypothesis is fully discussed by Katz (1962), but in essence it proposes that the synaptic vesicles contain molecules of the transmitter which can be released into the synaptic gap by momentary fusion between the membrane of the vesicle and that of the axon surface, and that the small amplitude blips of depolarisation that occur with low frequency in the region of the end-plate in a resting nerve-muscle preparation are caused by the random discharge of vesicles. The arrival of an action potential at the terminal is pictured as greatly speeding up this process, so that perhaps several hundred vesicles release their contents in less than a millisecond to set up a large end-plate potential and thence a propagated depolarisation of the muscle surface, before the action of the transmitter is curtailed by its rapid hydrolysis—by acetylcholinesterase in vertebrate fibres.

The structural similarity between insect and vertebrate neuromuscular junctions is striking, and the hypothesis described above requires only a qualification concerning the chemical nature of the transmitter, before it can be applied to insect junctions. The physiological events at the synapse seem to be quite comparable in each case; in insects and vertebrates alike, the first response elicited in the muscle by the arrival of a motor nerve impulse is an end-plate potential, and, furthermore, miniature end-plate potentials similar in amplitude and frequency to those of vertebrate material have been detected in resting nerve-muscle preparations in insects (Usherwood, 1963). However, acetylcholine does not appear to play a part in the stimulation of insect muscle, and the molecules released from the terminating axons have not been identified with certainty. No criteria are yet known whereby fast, slow and inhibitory axons may be identified in electron micrographs, but there is physiological evidence that glutamate and γ-amino butyric acid may function respectively as excitatory and inhibitory transmitters in some insect neuromuscular junctions (Refs. in Treherne, 1966).

Although all the muscles in the insect body are striated, a useful functional distinction can be made between the skeletal or voluntary, and the visceral or involuntary fibres—the latter corresponding to the smooth muscles of vertebrates. In a recent review of the control of the insect heart and visceral musculature, Davey (1964) has pointed out that these fibres generally contract in a rhythmic fashion, and are under a complex control which involves a visceral nervous system that is structurally and pharmacologically distinct from the general central nervous system, though connected with it at certain points.

The regulation of heart beat by a myogenic rhythm, direct innervation of the cardiac fibres and also by an active substance released from the pericardial cells is mentioned on p. 154. Electron micrographs have shown that opaque neurosecretory droplets may be distributed to various visceral muscles (amongst other target organs) by nerves leaving the corpora cardiaca (Johnson and Bowers, 1963) and it seems likely that pharmacologically active substances within these droplets, released from the nerve endings, may act as transmitters or local hormones, playing a part in initiating and/or regulating the function of these muscles. Examples of such axons are illustrated in Plate 23. Neurosecretory droplets, together with synaptic vesicles, are also found within the axoplasm of nerves, ending within the luminescent organs of fireflies (Plate 46).

REFERENCES

DAVEY, K. G. 1964. The control of visceral muscles in insects. In *Advances in Insect Physiology* (J. W. L. Beament, J. E. Treherne and V. B. Wigglesworth, eds.), Vol. 2, pp. 219–245. Academic Press, London and New York.

*EDWARDS, G. A. 1959. The fine structure of a multiterminal innervation of an insect muscle. *J. biophys. biochem. Cytol.*, **5**, 241–244.

*EDWARDS, G. A., RUSKA, H., and HARVEN, E. DE. 1958a. Electron microscopy of peripheral nerves and neuromuscular junctions in the wasp leg. *J. biophys. biochem. Cytol.*, **4**, 107–114.

*EDWARDS, G. A., RUSKA, H., and HARVEN, E. DE. 1958b. Neuromuscular junctions in the flight and tymbal muscles of the cicada. *J. biophys. biochem. Cytol.*, **4**, 251–256.

HOYLE, G. 1965. Neural control of skeletal muscle. In *The Physiology of Insecta* (M. Rockstein, ed.), Vol. 2, pp. 407–449. Academic Press, New York and London.

*JOHNSON, B., and BOWERS, B. 1963. Transport of neurohormones from the corpora cardiaca in insects. *Science*, **141**, 244–246.

KATZ, B. 1962. The Croonian Lecture: The transmission of impulses from nerve to muscle and the subcellular unit of synaptic action. *Proc. R. Soc. B*, **155**, 455–477.

PALADE, G. E. 1954. Electron microscope observation of interneuronal and neuromuscular synapses. *Anat. Rec.*, **118**, 335–336.

PEACHEY, L. D., and HUXLEY, A. F. 1962. Structural identification of twitch and slow striated muscle fibres of the frog. *J. Cell Biol.*, **13**, 177–180.

*SMITH, D. S. 1960. Innervation of the fibrillar flight muscle of an insect: *Tenebrio molitor* (Coleoptera). *J. biophys. biochem. Cytol.*, **8**, 447–466.

*SMITH, D. S., and TREHERNE, J. E. 1963. Functional aspects of the organization of the insect nervous system. In *Advances in Insect Physiology* (J. W. L. Beament, J. E. Treherne and V. B. Wigglesworth, eds.), Vol. 1, pp. 401–484. Academic Press, London and New York,

TREHERNE, J. E. 1966. *The Neurochemistry of Arthropods*. Cambridge University Press.

USHERWOOD, P. N. R. 1963. Spontaneous miniature potentials from insect muscle fibres. *J. Physiol., Lond.*, **169**, 149–160.

Plates 21–22 ▷

Plate 21 ▷

While the fast skeletal muscle fibres of a vertebrate each receive only
a single motor nerve terminal, synapsing with the fibre at a restricted
neuromuscular junction, arthropodan skeletal muscle fibres share
with vertebrate slow fibres the feature of multiterminal innervation.
In this case, terminating nerve branches contact each fibre at several
points along its surface, and in arthropods the situation is further
complicated by the fact that branches of more than one axon often
reach a single fibre, eliciting different types of muscular response.
The separate elements of such polyneuronal innervation may initiate
a fast or slow response and sometimes include branches that inhibit
contraction.

   This electron micrograph illustrates some of the features of a
neuromuscular junction on the surface of an abdominal intersegmental
muscle fibre from the cockroach, *Periplaneta americana*. The plane of
section has just grazed the fibre surface, and has passed through
several slender axon branches that splay out across it. This is probably
a polyneuronal junction, but functionally different endings cannot yet
be distinguished on structural grounds. Some of the fibrils [F] have
been cut into, a Z band is distinguishable [Z], and a tracheole
[Tr] adjoining the fibre surface appears in longitudinal section. The
most striking feature of the junctional region is the presence of great
numbers of small synaptic vesicles, clustered within the axon
terminals [Ax]: these perhaps contain chemical transmitter molecules,
released into the narrow synaptic gap between nerve and muscle
(Plate 22) upon arrival of an action potential at the ending. At upper
left is seen the thin basement membrane [BM] covering the glial
sheath that surrounds the axons along their course from the central
nervous system.

($\times$ 14,000.)

(*Philips EM 200.*)

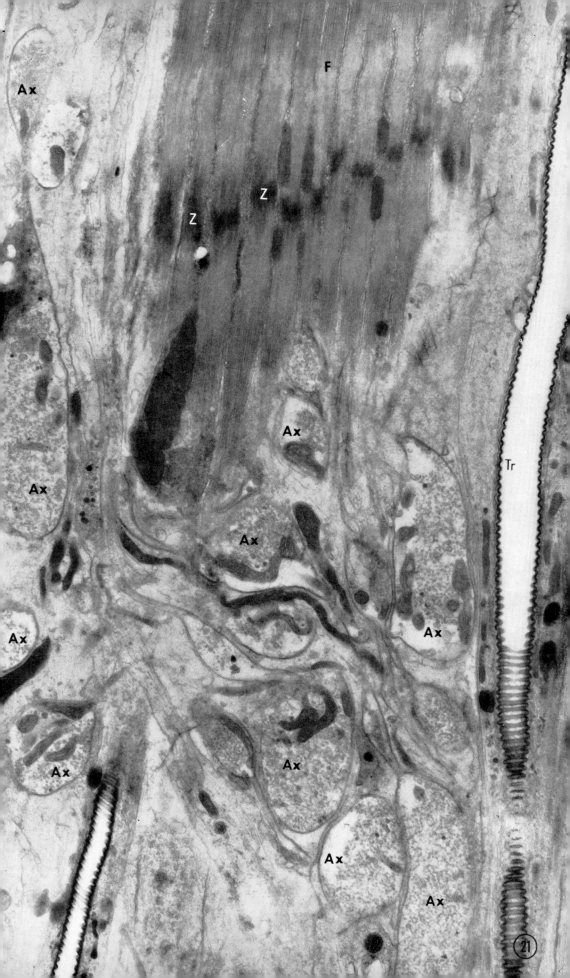

Plate 22 ▷

A micrograph of the same material as that shown in Plate 21,
illustrating further the very close relationship between nerve and
muscle at a neuromuscular synapse. The small nerve in the centre of
this field contains three axons, seen in transverse section. Two of
these [Ax'] are entirely surrounded by the glial sheath [Gl] of the
nerve, but this sheath only partially envelops the third axon [Ax]:
over about half of its surface [between the arrows], this axon lacks the
glial sheath, and is pressed closely against the plasma membrane of
the adjoining muscle fibre [MF] leaving a synaptic gap only
100–150 Å in width between the two. In some vertebrate
neuromuscular junctions, the muscle membrane beneath the
synapsing axon is tightly folded to form a series of parallel gutters,
but in insects the situation is simpler—sometimes the axon lies within
a groove in the fibre surface or often, as here, the muscle provides a
raised trough to accommodate the axon. The axons Ax' have not yet
arrived at their point of synapse and contain hardly any synaptic
vesicles; these are present in large numbers in the third, synapsing,
axon [SV], where they tend to form clusters [*] adjoining the axon
membrane. These clusters have been termed 'synaptic foci' and are
thought to represent special sites where transmitter molecules are
released into the synaptic gap. A mitochondrion [M] accompanies
the vesicles within the axoplasm.

The muscle fibrils on the right are sectioned through the I band [I]
and contain only thin actin filaments, while on the left, in the
adjacent fibre, both I and A bands lie within the plane of section, and
transverse tubules [T] formed by invagination of the plasma
membrane are seen. A small tracheole [Tr] lies in the extracellular
space between the nerve and the right-hand fibre.

(× 55,000.)

(*Philips EM 200.*)

64

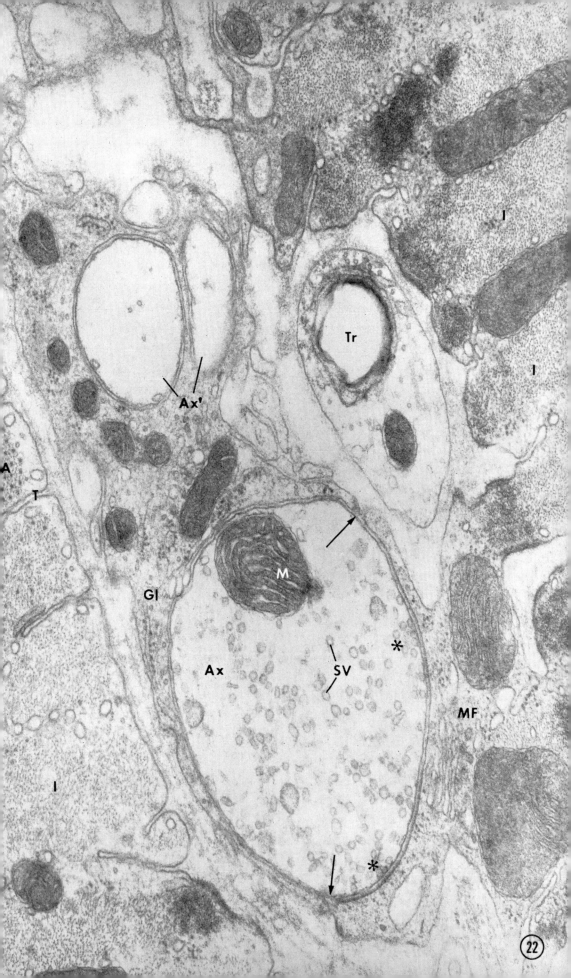

The Nervous System

Despite the obvious topographical differences between the nervous system of an insect and a vertebrate, these employ the same basic plan of construction. In each, sensory information is relayed to the central nervous system along axons whose cell bodies are closely associated with sense organs at the body surface, or with proprioceptive organs within the body. Within the central nervous system are housed the cell bodies of association (or inter-)neurones and motor neurones, the former acting as integrative links between sensory and motor cells and the latter conveying efferent signals to the muscles and other effector cells of the body. Within this simple framework, indeed a triumph of classificatory simplicity, is included a very large number of cells, structurally and functionally linked in an extremely complex manner.

Our present understanding of the function of the nervous system provides an excellent example of the cumulative value of complementary approaches to a single problem, via different techniques. Ultimately, the function of the nervous system becomes the province of the behaviourist (or of the psychologist) concerned with the ways in which the animal responds to its environment. Our understanding of the anatomy of the nervous system, at different levels, is based on the findings of light- and electron microscopy: the former provides us with a necessary overall view of the distribution of nerve cells and their grouping into tracts within the central nervous system, while the electron microscope has been used to resolve details of neurone structure that throw new light on the mode of function of these specialised cells. In particular, the fine structure of the synapse, where excitation is transmitted from one cell to the next, has contributed to an interesting hypothesis concerning the mechanism by which this transmission is brought about. The physicochemical basis of impulse conduction and transmission has been revealed by the techniques of electrophysiology and by study of the effects of drugs that interfere with the normal functioning of nerves and synapses.

The fine structure of the insect compound eye will be considered later, as one example of the adaptation of neurones to perform a sensory function. The electron micrographs accompanying the present section illustrate some of the structural features of the cells making up the central ganglia and the peripheral nerves within the insect body, while the organisation and function of neuromuscular junctions is discussed on pp. 59-61.

The peripheral nerves of insects contain the axons of sensory and motor neurones, ensheathed by neuroglial cells. While the smaller branches may include purely sensory or purely motor populations, the larger trunks close to the ganglia are generally mixed. Electron micrographs have shown that the relationship between the axons and their sheath is morphologically intermediate between that seen in myelinated and unmyelinated nerves of vertebrates. An unmyelinated axon is more or less superficially accommodated by the glial cell, and either merely lies within a groove along the glial surface or, at most, lies within an invagination that is linked to the surface of the glial cell by a very short mesaxon. Myelin, on the other hand, is the product of a very extensive mesaxon invagination of the glial or Schwann cell plasma membrane, initially arranged in a tight spiral around an axon, and which becomes fused into a compact cylinder in which lipid and protein layers alternate, and from which all traces of cytoplasm are excluded. In the insect peripheral nerve, on the other hand, mesaxons are prominent (Plates 23 and 24) and often coil around the axons, but these membranes never become fused into myelin and their coils are always separated by cytoplasm of the glial cell. Nerves showing this type of organisation, which also occur in the Crustacea, are sometimes termed 'tunicated', and their glial cells are often referred to as 'lemnoblasts' to distinguish them from myelin-producing Schwann cells. Whereas myelinated axons achieve a rapid rate of impulse conduction by the restriction of current flow to the 'nodes of Ranvier' at which the insulating myelin sheath is interrupted and the axon membrane thus exposed directly to the milieu outside the nerve, conduction in un-myelinated and tunicated nerves must involve the entire axon surface and is, by comparison, relatively slow.

The glial cells of the peripheral nerves are very elongated, and are covered with an extracellular collagen-containing sheath continuous with the more robust 'neural lamella' surrounding the central ganglia (Plates 24, 26 and 27). The cell nuclei are often indented to conform to the contours of the nearby axon cylinders (Plate 24). The glial cytoplasm is sparsely equipped with mitochondria and membranous cisternae, but may contain impressive numbers of microtubules, ca. 200 Å in diameter (Plate 25), precisely oriented parallel with the axons. Microtubules similar in appearance to these have been recognised in a wide variety of cell types, though whether or not they share a common function is not yet clear. They occur in other elongated cells in the insect; for example, in tracheal cells (Plate 43), in duct cells associated with glands (Plate 117) and in addition to the flagellar microtubules in the spermatid (Plate 102). In these instances, the microtubules perhaps play a 'cytoskeletal' role in maintaining the form of the cell, but it should be noted that they occur, albeit in smaller numbers, in many cells that are not elongate in form.

The cytoplasm within the peripheral axons of insects and vertebrates alike is, for the most part, very simply constructed. The most obvious, and in many sections the only axoplasmic structures visible in the electron microscope are the 'neurotubules', which resemble in size and appearance the microtubules of the adjoining glial cells (Plate 25). These neurotubules are sometimes accompanied by small mitochondria, but other cell organelles are lacking, except for the generally opaque droplets passed out from the perikarya of neurosecretory cells. Most cells, when examined in the electron microscope, have proved to possess a more complex structure, and indeed this is true of the cell bodies of all the neurones making up the nervous system (e.g. Plate 29). The neurone cell body, containing the nucleus, maintains the life and function of the entire cell. However, except in the case of 'neurosecretory cells', des-cribed further below, the electron microscopic structure of the axoplasm gives us little clue to the part perhaps played by the cell body in the synthesis and transport of chemical transmitters or other active molecules, released from the terminals of the axons. Within a few micra of a chemically mediated synapse, the axoplasm suddenly becomes crowded with small vesicles, ca. 250–400 Å in diameter, which are thought to contain transmitter molecules. It has been suggested (see p. 59) that upon the arrival of an impulse at a terminal, large numbers of these 'synaptic vesicles' discharge their contents very rapidly into the narrow synaptic gap interposed between most excitable cells, and that the transmitter molecules trigger excitation in the next cell in line. This may be another neurone (within the central nervous system) or, if the presynaptic member is a motor neurone, a muscle fibre or some other effector unit. Whatever control the cell body may exert upon the synaptic terminal, it is clear that the synaptic vesicles are restricted to the vicinity of the synapse; if they were manufactured within the cell body and passed out along the axon, they would be detected, in transit, throughout the axoplasm.

Within the central nervous system of vertebrates and most invertebrates occur cells that have the form, and in some cases at least, the conducting function of neurones, but which in addition play a glandular or secretory role. These 'neurosecretory cells' are engaged in the synthesis and release of neurohormones and, in contrast with 'typical' nerve cells, the passage of secreted materials from the cell body along the axon may readily be followed in the light- and electron microscope. The most familiar cells of this type in insects are the neurosecretory units whose cell bodies lie within the brain and pass axons back to the corpora cardiaca and corpora allata, and to visceral muscles and other tissues within the body cavity (p. 93). The occurrence of these cells in invertebrate nervous systems has been reviewed by Bern and Hagadorn (1965). In vertebrates, neurosecretory cell bodies are present, for example, within the supraoptic and paraventricular nuclei of the hypothalamus, and synthesise a number of important hormones including oxytocin and vasopressin which are released into the circulatory system from the axon terminals within the neurohypophysis. In the light microscope, neurosecretory material is generally detected through its uptake of fuchsin dye, and in the electron microscope is resolved as droplets ranging in diameter from about 1000–3000 Å which, after 'staining' with heavy metal salts, are generally, though not always, more or less opaque to the electron beam. In peripheral axons, they accompany the neurotubules, as is illustrated in sections of the nerves leading to the corpus cardiacum (Plate 32), to the heart (Plate 24), to the spermatheca (Plate 23) and to the medulla of the rectal papilla (Plate 92). The secretory droplets first appear within the cisternae of the Golgi bodies, from which they are pinched off, enclosed by smooth membranes, and extruded from the cell body and along the axon process.

The ganglia

The insect central nervous system is built on the segmental plan, modified to a greater or lesser extent by fusion of the primitively segmental ganglia. This fusion is most extreme in the head region, where the ganglia of several segments are amalgamated to form the 'brain' and suboesophageal ganglion, but may also occur to varying degrees within the thorax and abdomen. The successive ganglia of the ventral nerve cord are linked by paired connectives, which contain axons but no neurone cell bodies. Within the ganglia, sensory information is passed on to motor units via synapses: generally, this transfer may take place through interposed internuncial neurones, but it is possible that some synaptic links take place between sensory and motor units directly as in local reflex pathways in the vertebrate central nervous system.

Within a ganglion, whether of a vertebrate or an insect, neurones and non-nervous (glial) cells and their processes are knit together into a compact and extremely complex tissue. Much of our knowledge of the neuronal connections upon which the integrative function of the central nervous system is based, has been derived from studies carried out with the light microscope. In particular, the Golgi technique of silver impregnation employed by Cajal and his colleagues (e.g. Cajal and Sánchez, 1915) which relied on the capacity of a small proportion of neurones within a population to take up the stain, revealed many details of the intricate tracery of axonal and dendritic extensions. The electron microscope has brought to light many previously unrecognised structural features of the central nervous system of vertebrates, insects and other animals, and has clarified several important points concerning, for example, the fine structure of the cell bodies and processes of nerve cells, the morphology of synapses and the distribution of glial elements. At the same time, the enhanced resolution of this instrument has underlined the fact that the central nervous system is even more formidably complex in construction than was earlier supposed.

The electron micrographs shown in Plates 26 to 30 have been prepared from sections of the brain and of the hypocerebral ganglion of the sympathetic or stomatogastric system of the stick insect. Each insect ganglion is surrounded by an extracellular sheath, often termed the 'neural lamella', continuous with the sheath extending out along the peripheral nerves. The neural lamella (Plates 26 and 27) consists of an amorphous or finely filamentous matrix containing mucopolysaccharide, in which is embedded a feltwork of periodically cross-banded fibrils. These fibrils of the connective tissue sheath of the nervous system have been described in several accounts, including those of Hess (1958), Gray (1959), Baccetti (1961), Ashhurst and Chapman (1961), Smith and Treherne (1963), and Ashhurst (1965), and their collagenous nature has recently been confirmed biochemically by Harper and others (1967). Ashhurst (1967) has reviewed the occurrence and structure of connective tissue throughout the insect body, and has pointed out that while the distribution of collagen is more limited than in the vertebrate, it is not restricted to the nervous system and is present, for example, in the basement membrane of the locust hypodermis (Rinterknecht and Levi, 1966) and in the thick cartilage-like sheath of the locust ejaculatory canal (Martoja and Bassot, 1965).

The neural lamella doubtless plays a mechanical role in maintaining the form of the ganglion, but must also be taken into account when the nutrition of the ganglion is considered. The insect body does not possess a capillary endothelial system, and nutrients must reach the tissues directly from the haemolymph. Wigglesworth (1960) has pointed out that this simple mechanism is adequate for most tissues, which are made up of single cell layers, but that special provision must be made for the passage of nutrients to the thick, compact cell aggregates of the ganglia, and furthermore, that all nutrient molecules or other substances must first traverse the neural lamella before they reach the outermost ganglion cells.

The ganglion is clearly demarcated into two zones—a cortical region containing the cell bodies of neurones together with glial cell bodies and their processes, and a central 'neuropile', made up of axons and their branches, accompanied by slender glial extensions. Immediately beneath the neural lamella lies a layer of glial cells, often termed the 'perineurium' (Plate 26). The fine structure of these cells has been described by Hess (1958), Trujillo-Cenóz (1962), Smith and Treherne (1963), Rehberg (1966), and most recently by Maddrell and Treherne (1967) and Smith (1967). In the stick insect and cockroach, at least, the lateral cell membranes of the perineurium follow a very tortuous course, often diverging to establish wide intercellular spaces between the outer portions of the cells, but becoming closely linked by septate desmosomes and tight junctions further from the neural lamella (Maddrell and Treherne, 1967). These authors suggest that the perineurium cells may include among their functions a role in maintaining within the ganglion an extracellular ionic balance that permits normal axonal conduction, and which may be very different from that of the haemolymph surrounding the ganglion. In addition, however, the perineurium certainly acts as a storage depot for glycogen, lipids and perhaps other nutrients (Plate 26), and as has been shown histochemically by Wigglesworth (1960), these cells take up nutrient precursors that diffuse through the neural lamella from the haemolymph, and also are able to pass these on to underlying glial cells. These last in turn transfer the food reserves to the neurones.

Beneath the perineurium cells, and very closely applied to them, lie other glial elements. The cytoplasm of the latter is dissected into thin leaflets or sheets which (Plates 28 and 29) are applied, often in concentric stacks, over the cell bodies of the neurones. The innermost of these glial sheets send numerous finger-like invaginations into the neurone cell bodies (Plate 29). These invaginations have for long been thought to have a trophic function (and were termed the 'trophospongium' in early light microscopic accounts), and Wigglesworth found evidence that they indeed appear to transfer to the neurone glycogen and lipid, presumably mobilised from the perineurium. We know little of the cellular mechanisms by which food reserves may be synthesised and mobilised by the glial cells of the ganglion, but it is interesting to note that their agranular endoplasmic reticulum is well represented (Plate 29), a feature of vertebrate cells engaged in the production of lipids and steroids, and perhaps in some way concerned in the synthesis of glycogen in liver cells (Refs. in Smith, 1967).

The fact that the surface of the neurone cell bodies is provided with a continuous glial covering has an important bearing on the location of synapses within the insect ganglion. Synapses between axon terminals and the cell body or dendritic processes such as occur within the central nervous system of vertebrates are not present, so far as is known, in insects. Consequently, central synaptic connections in these animals appear to be entirely restricted to the neuropile region of the ganglion, which thus contains axons and fine terminal branches of sensory and internunciary cells, together with similar branches of collaterals arising from motor neurones.

As is always the case, the cell bodies of the neurones within the insect ganglion contain a variety of cytoplasmic structures that are excluded from their axon processes. Their fine structure had been described by Trujillo-Cenóz (1962), Smith and Treherne (1963), Rehberg (1966), Smith (1967) and others. Typical profiles of the neurone nucleus and surrounding cytoplasm (the perikaryon) are shown in Plates 28 and 29. The crescentic 'dictyosomes' described in light microscopic studies on a variety of invertebrate nerve cells are resolved as ordered arrays of smooth membranes corresponding to the Golgi bodies of other cell types. 'Nissl bodies' comparable with those of vertebrate neurones are absent or poorly defined, and in their place are large numbers of generally distributed ribosomes, both unattached and studding the surface of many of the scattered cisternae of the endoplasmic reticulum. Smooth-surfaced cisternae are also plentiful, and often closely adjoin the neurone cell membrane where this is pushed in by the invaginated glial fingers; a configuration that is perhaps concerned with the uptake of nutrient molecules transferred from the trophic glial processes (Smith, 1967). Mitochondria are usually evenly distributed throughout the perikaryon. The microtubules present in this part of the nerve cell are perhaps continuous with the 'neurotubules' of the axon (Plates 25 and 29). The presence of a well-developed endoplasmic reticulum, of which the Golgi bodies may be regarded as

71

a specialised part, is consistent with the belief that the cell body is engaged in synthesising materials that are passed into the axon. However, only in neurones that manufacture opaque hormone-containing neurosecretory droplets (cf. Plate 34) within the perikaryon has such synthesis been followed in electron micrographs, as described by Nishiitsutsuji-Uwo (1961), and Bloch *et al.* (1966).

From each cell body of the central neurones, an axon process extends inwards into the neuropile. The main axon generally branches within the neuropile, giving off one or more collaterals, and both these and the main axon cylinder may further branch into fine terminal aborisations. Axons of internunciary or association neurones stemming from cell bodies in one ganglion frequently pass along the connectives before terminating in the neuropile of a ganglion elsewhere in the nerve cord. Terminations of sensory axons entering the neuropile complete the framework enabling the insect to respond in a coordinated manner to its environment. The structural basis of this coordination ultimately lies in the myriad synapses between the axon branches within each neuropile. Electron micrographs have proved of great value in clarifying the relationship between axon branches in this part of the ganglion and have revealed morphological details of probable sites of synapse, but from the point of view of a three-dimensional analysis of the neuropile, they possess an inherent limitation. The very thin sections employed are ill-suited to reveal the ramifications of individual nerve cells, and while regions of the neuropile could perhaps be mapped by reconstruction of the axon profiles in many serial sections, this represents an arduous task that has yet to be undertaken.

Hess (1958), Trujillo-Cenóz (1959; 1962), Smith and Treherne (1963) and others have described some of the structural features of the neuropile of thoracic and abdominal ganglia, while those of optic ganglia have been investigated by Trujillo-Cenóz (1965) and Smith (1967a). Each sectioned field of neuropile contains large numbers of closely packed axons and their branches, ranging in diameter from several micra to a few hundred Ångstrom units (Plate 30). Many of these contain neurotubules similar to those found in the axoplasm of peripheral nerves, while others are more or less filled with small 'synaptic vesicles' identical in appearance with those crowding the terminal axoplasm at nerve-muscle junctions (Plate 21). In addition, the neuropile often contains axons charged with electron-opaque structures, larger than the synaptic vesicles, representing neurosecretory droplets that have been extruded from the perikarya of secretory neurones, and are on their way to target organs throughout the body, which they reach after their release into the circulating haemolymph (p. 93) or via peripheral neuroeffector junctions.

In addition to the above, the neuropile also contains narrow processes of glial cells, arising from cell bodies lying in the cortex of the ganglion. As elsewhere, these glial elements may convey nutrients to the axons of the neuropile, but they also appear to play an important role in defining the synaptic pathways within this central region of the ganglion. Electron micrographs of various central and peripheral nervous systems have indicated that at points of synapse the plasma membranes of the two cells involved are very closely apposed across a synaptic gap which may be as narrow as 100 Å (and indeed may even be fused together, as in 'electrical' synapses such as the median-giant synapse of the crayfish (Robertson, 1961)).

The glial 'insulation' and the absence of axo-dendritic and axo-somatic synapses around the perikarya of insect neurones has already been mentioned, and the glial processes ramifying throughout the neuropile appear to insulate many otherwise closely adjoining axon branches (Smith and Treherne, 1963; Smith, 1967). At the same time, as Trujillo-Cenóz pointed out, mere close apposition of axon surfaces is of such general occurrence that this alone cannot be indicative of regions of synapse. De Robertis and Palay first described the synaptic vesicles within the mammalian acoustic ganglion and cerebellar cortex, and found that these often occur in compact clusters or foci adjoining special areas of the cell membrane of the presynaptic member marked by a layer of dense material, sometimes mirrored by similar patches along the surface of the nearby postsynaptic member. In summary, Palay (1958) proposed that 'the complex of a cluster of synaptic vesicles, associated with a focalised area of presynaptic plasma-lemma, and the synaptic cleft may be considered as a morphological subunit' of the synapse and that 'these synaptic complexes may represent the actual sites of impulse transmission across the synapse'. This proposal has received support from physio-logical studies on a more accessible synapse than those within the central nervous system—the neuromuscular junction (p. 60). Synaptic 'foci', similar to those found in vertebrate nerve cells, are associated with axo-axonic junctions within the insect neuro-pile. They have been described, for example, in the last abdominal ganglion of the cockroach (Smith and Treherne, 1963), where the diameter of the foci (about 0·15–0·5 micron) is in the range of those in the vertebrate system. More elaborate synapses which include dense structures within the axoplasm of the presynaptic terminal have been found in sections of the second optic ganglion of the blowfly (Trujillo-Cenóz, 1965; Smith, 1967) while other variations in the morphology of central synapses are reviewed by Eccles (1964).

The fine structural evidence at present suggests that a synaptic apparatus, designed to deliver transmitter molecules from a nerve terminal by momentary fusion between the membranes limiting synaptic vesicles and that of the axon surface, has been adopted as the basis of much of the central and peripheral excitation in the nervous system of insects, vertebrates and probably other animal groups. It should be pointed out, how-ever, that structurally similar synapses may employ chemically different transmitters. Thus, the excitatory transmitter present within motor axons ending on vertebrate skeletal muscle fibres, acetylcholine, is replaced in insect neuromuscular junctions by a functional analogue, perhaps glutamate, while other axons at the same junction may release γ-aminobutyric acid, performing an inhibitory function (Refs. in Treherne, 1966). On the other hand, acetylcholinesterase, the enzyme that hydrolyses acetyl-choline after its release at a synapse, has been identified cytochemically in electron micrographs of the insect neuropile, distributed locally along axon surfaces, providing evidence that this transmitter mediates at least some of the central synapses of insect ganglia (Smith and Treherne, 1965).

REFERENCES

*ASHHURST, D. E. 1965. The connective tissue sheath of the locust nervous system: its develop-ment in the embryo. Q. Jl microsc. Sci., 106, 61–73.
*ASHHURST, D. E. 1967. The connective tissues of insects. A. Rev. Ent., in press.
*ASHHURST, D. E., and CHAPMAN, J. A. 1961. The connective-tissue sheath of the nervous system of Locusta migratoria: an electron microscope study. Q. Jl microsc. Sci., 102, 463–467.
*BACCETTI, B. 1961. Indagini comparative sulla ultrastruttura della fibrilla collagene nei diversi ordini degli insetti. Redia, 46, 1–7.
BERN, H. A., and HAGADORN, I. R. 1965. Neurosecretion. In Structure and Function in the Nervous Systems of Invertebrates by T. H. Bullock and G. A. Horridge, Vol. 1, pp. 353–429. W. H. Freeman, San Francisco and London.

*BLOCH, B., THOMSEN, E., and THOMSEN, M. 1966. The neurosecretory system of the adult *Calliphora erythrocephala*. III. Electron microscopy of the medial neurosecretory cells of the brain and some adjacent cells. *Z. Zellforsch. mikrosk. Anat.*, **70**, 185–208.

CAJAL, S. R., and SÁNCHEZ, D. S. 1915. Contribución al conocimiento de los centros nerviosos de los insectos. Parte 1. Retina y centros ópticos. *Trab. Lab. Invest. biol. Univ. Madr.*, **13**, 1–164.

ECCLES, J. C. 1964. *The Physiology of Synapses*. Springer-Verlag, Berlin.

*GRAY, E. G. 1959. Electron microscopy of collagen-like connective tissue fibrils of an insect. *Proc. R. Soc. B*, **150**, 233–239.

*HARPER, E., SEIFTER, S., and SCHARRER, B. 1967. Electron microscopic and biochemical characterization of collagen in blattarian insects. *J. Cell Biol.*, **33**, 385–393.

*HESS, A. 1958. The fine structure of nerve cells and fibers, neuroglia, and sheaths of the ganglion chain in the cockroach (*Periplaneta americana*). *J. biophys. biochem. Cytol.*, **4**, 731–742.

*LANDOLT, A. M. 1965. Elektronenmikroskopische Untersuchungen an der Perikaryenschicht der Corpora Pedunculata der Waldameise (*Formica lugubris* Zett) mit besonderer Berücksichtigung der Neuron-Glia-Beziehung. *Z. Zellforsch. mikrosk. Anat.*, **66**, 701–736.

*MADDRELL, S. H. P., and TREHERNE, J. E. 1967. The ultrastructure of the perineurium in two insect species, *Carausius morosus* and *Periplaneta americana*. *J. Cell Sci.*, **2**, 119–128.

*MARTOJA, R., and BASSOT, J-M. 1965. Existence d'un tissu conjonctif de type cartilagineux chez certains insectes orthoptères. *C.r. hebd. Séanc. Acad. Sci., Paris*, **261**, 2954–2957.

*NISHIITSUTSUJI-UWO, J. 1961. Electron microscope studies on the neurosecretory system in Lepidoptera. *Z. Zellforsch. mikrosk. Anat.*, **54**, 613–630.

PALAY, S. L. 1958. The morphology of synapses in the central nervous system. *Expl Cell Res.*, **5**, suppl., 275–293.

*REHBERG, S. 1966. Über den Feinbau der Abdominalganglien von *Leucophaea maderae* mit besonderer Berücksichtigung der Transportwege und der Organellen des Stoffwechsels. *Z. Zellforsch. mikrosk. Anat.*, **72**, 370–389.

*RINTERKNECHT, E., and LEVI, P. 1966. Étude au microscope électronique du cycle cuticulaire au cours de 4ᵉ stade larvaire chez *Locusta migratoria*. *Z. Zellforsch. mikrosk. Anat.*, **72**, 390–407.

ROBERTSON, J. D. 1961. Ultrastructure of excitable membranes and the crayfish median-giant synapse. *Ann. N.Y. Acad. Sci.*, **94**, 339–389.

*SMITH, D. S. 1965. Synapses in the insect nervous system. In *The Physiology of the Insect Central Nervous System* (J. E. Treherne and J. W. L. Beament, eds.), pp. 39–57. Academic Press, London and New York.

*SMITH, D. S. 1967. The trophic role of glial cells in insect ganglia. In *Insects and Physiology* (J. W. L. Beament and J. E. Treherne, eds.). Oliver and Boyd, Edinburgh.

*SMITH, D. S., and TREHERNE, J. E. 1963. Functional aspects of the organization of the insect nervous system. In *Advances in Insect Physiology* (J. W. L. Beament, J. E. Treherne, and V. B. Wigglesworth, eds.), Vol. 1, pp. 401–484. Academic Press, London and New York.

*SMITH, D. S., and TREHERNE, J. E. 1965. Electron microscopic localization of acetylcholinesterase activity in the central nervous system of an insect (*Periplaneta americana*). *J. Cell Biol.*, **26**, 445–465.

TREHERNE, J. E. 1966. *The Neurochemistry of Arthropods*. Cambridge University Press.

*TRUJILLO-CENÓZ, O. 1959. Study on the fine structure of the central nervous system of *Pholus labruscoe* (Lepidoptera). *Z. Zellforsch. mikrosk. Anat.*, **49**, 432–446.

*TRUJILLO-CENÓZ, O. 1962. Some aspects of the structural organization of the arthropod ganglia. *Z. Zellforsch. mikrosk. Anat.*, **56**, 649–682.

*TRUJILLO-CENÓZ, O. 1965. Some aspects of the structural organization of the intermediate retina of dipterans. *J. Ultrastruct. Res.*, **13**, 1–33.

WIGGLESWORTH, V. B. 1960. The nutrition of the central nervous system of the cockroach, *Periplaneta americana*. The mobilization of reserves. *J. exp. Biol.*, **37**, 500–512.

Plates 23–30 ▷

Plate 23 ▷

As in the nerves of vertebrates, the peripheral axons of insects are accompanied by glial sheaths, but do not fall into either of the familiar categories of 'myelinated' or 'unmyelinated'. The arrangement occurring in arthropods is illustrated by this transversely sectioned nerve branch, approaching the muscular investment [MF] of the spermatheca of the cockroach *Periplaneta americana*. From the surface glial cell membrane arise mesaxon invaginations [arrows], and these mesaxons [Ma] follow an irregular, often branching, course while coiling loosely around the axons [1–8]. In a vertebrate myelinated fibre, on the other hand, the membranes of the mesaxon become compacted into a solid insulating cylinder from which all trace of cytoplasm is excluded, while in unmyelinated fibres the axons may merely lie in a depression along the glial surface. The morphologically intermediate situation shown here is often referred to as 'tunicated'.

The glial cytoplasm is relatively simple, and contains sparsely scattered Golgi bodies [G] generally lying near the nucleus [N], mitochondria and endoplasmic reticulum cisternae, together with large numbers of oriented microtubules (Plate 25) lying parallel with the axons. The nerve branch is encompassed by a basement membrane [BM] which in this field has become confluent with the corresponding sheath of the nearby muscle fibre, presumably as the region of neuromuscular synapse is approached.

Over much of the course of most peripheral axons, neurotubules and small mitochondria are the most obvious axoplasmic structures, as in axons 1–5. Many of the axons reaching the tissues within the body cavity, however, contain opaque neurosecretory droplets (for example, axons 6–8; ND) perhaps controlling the activity of some of the visceral muscle fibres and/or certain glandular functions including the synthesis of spermathecal secretion.

(× 40,000.)

(Philips EM 200. Micrograph produced in collaboration with Dr B. L. Gupta.)

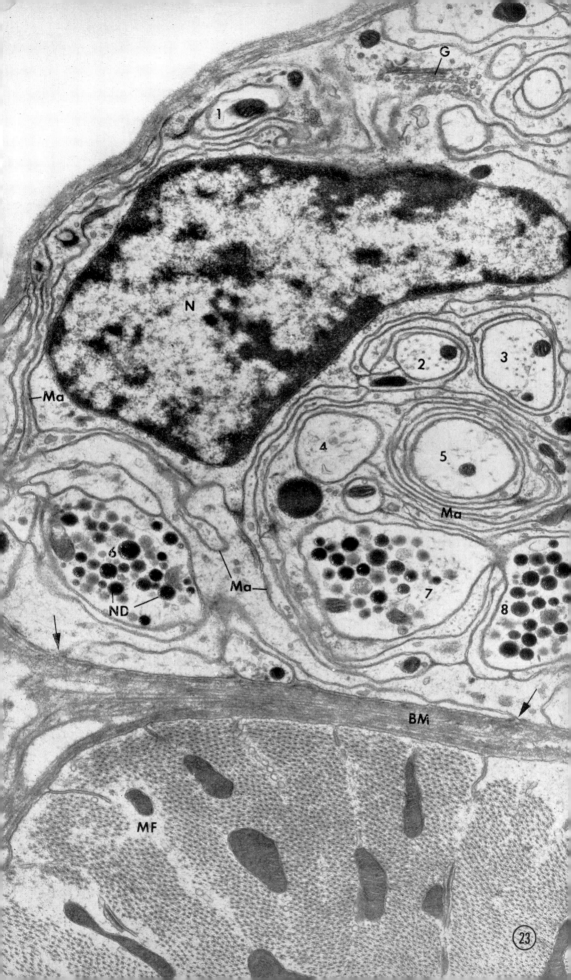

Plate 24 ▷

A transverse section of the aortal nerve of the cockroach *Periplaneta americana*, which innervates the dorsal vessel and other regions of the abdominal body cavity. Many axons [Ax] are included in the composite nerve. These contain large numbers of neurotubules [Nt] accompanied, in some instances, by opaque neurosecretory droplets [ND]. The axons are encompassed by glial cells or lemnoblasts [Gl], the mesaxons of which [Ma] are wrapped loosely and irregularly around the cylindrical axons, in the tunicated configuration more clearly seen in Plate 23. Profiles of glial nuclei, conforming to the shape of nearby axons, are seen at N. The glial cells enclosing the groups of axons within the nerve are each invested with a fibrous sheath which contains collagen-like fibrils. Incorporated into the nerve at upper right is a tracheole or small trachea [Tr], the cuticular tube of which is surrounded by a tracheal cell nucleus [N].

(× 24,000.)

(*Philips EM 200.*)

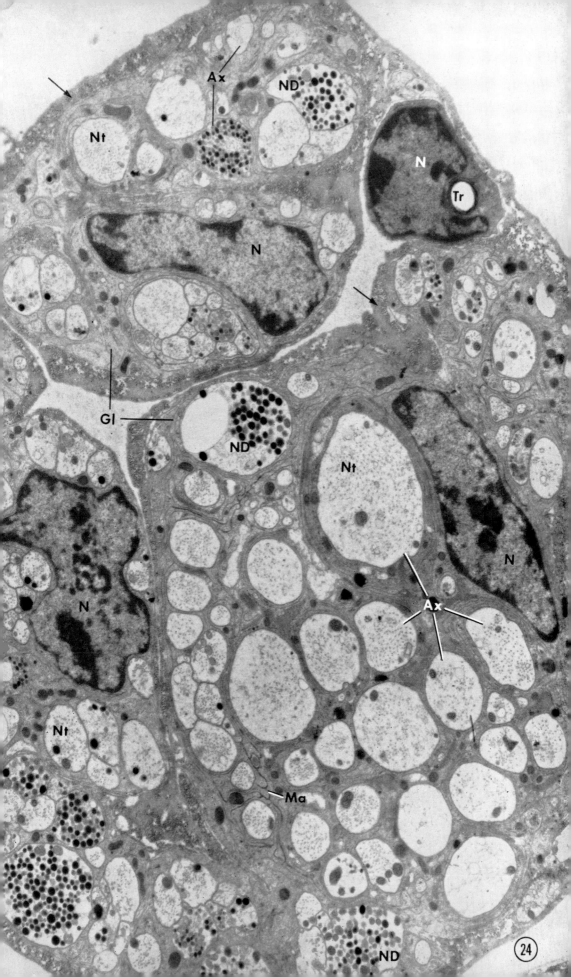

Plate 25 ▷

With the recent introduction of glutaraldehyde as a fixative for electron microscopy, fine tubular structures, *ca*. 200–250 Å in diameter, have been recognised in the cytoplasm of a wide range of animal and plant cells. It has been suggested that these 'microtubules' may perform a supporting function in maintaining the form of the cell, and that they may in some instances either alternatively or additionally be concerned in the movement of materials within the cell.

Microtubules are generally abundant in the cytoplasm of insect glial cells ensheathing peripheral axons, as is shown here in sections prepared from the larva of a butterfly, *Calpodes ethlius*.

In *A*, several axons [Ax] are included, each containing many neurotubules [Nt]. Mesaxon profiles [Ma] invaginated from the surface of the glial cell are arranged spirally around the axons and in the intervening glial cytoplasm lie microtubules [Mt] aligned with the axons and here seen predominantly in transverse section.

In *B*, a field from the same material displays the glial microtubules in longitudinal section.

(*A* : × 90,000. *B* : × 90,000.)

(RCA EMU 4. Reproduced by courtesy of Dr J. Lai Fook.)

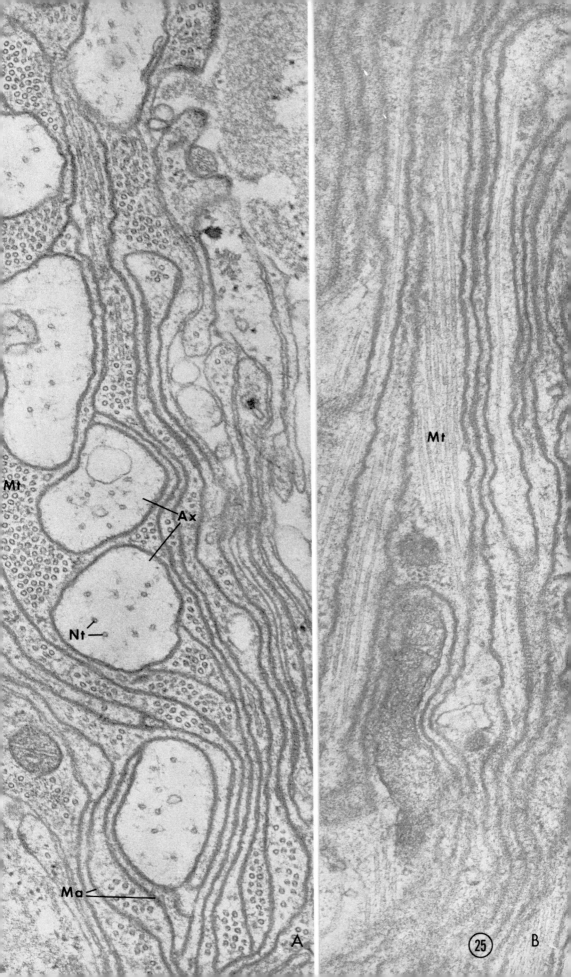

Mt

Ax

Nt

Ma

A

Mt

㉕ B

Plate 26 ▷

A micrograph that includes a peripheral region of the hypocerebral ganglion of the stick insect *Carausius morosus*, together with a closely adjoining fat body cell. The ganglion is surrounded by a thick extracellular sheath or neural lamella [NL] in which collagen-like fibrils are present (cf. Plate 27). Beneath this sheath lie the outermost glial cells [Gl] of the ganglion, sometimes distinguished as the 'perineurium'; these form an irregular spongework, since the lateral cell membranes frequently diverge to form wide intercellular spaces [*]. These cells contain numerous mitochondria [M], lipid droplets [L] and abundant deeply 'stained' granules of stored glycogen [Gy], while similar food stores, together with cisternae of the endoplasmic reticulum [ER] also occur in the fat body. The transfer of small diffusible nutrient molecules into the ganglion (including precursors of lipid and glycogen) represents a crucial feature of the metabolism of the insect central nervous system. When these materials are mobilised from the fat body, they must first traverse the basement membrane surrounding this tissue [BM], then the extracellular space around the ganglion which in life is filled with the haemolymph [He], before passing through the neural lamella to the perineurium cells.

(×11,000.)

(*Philips EM 200. From Smith (1967).*)

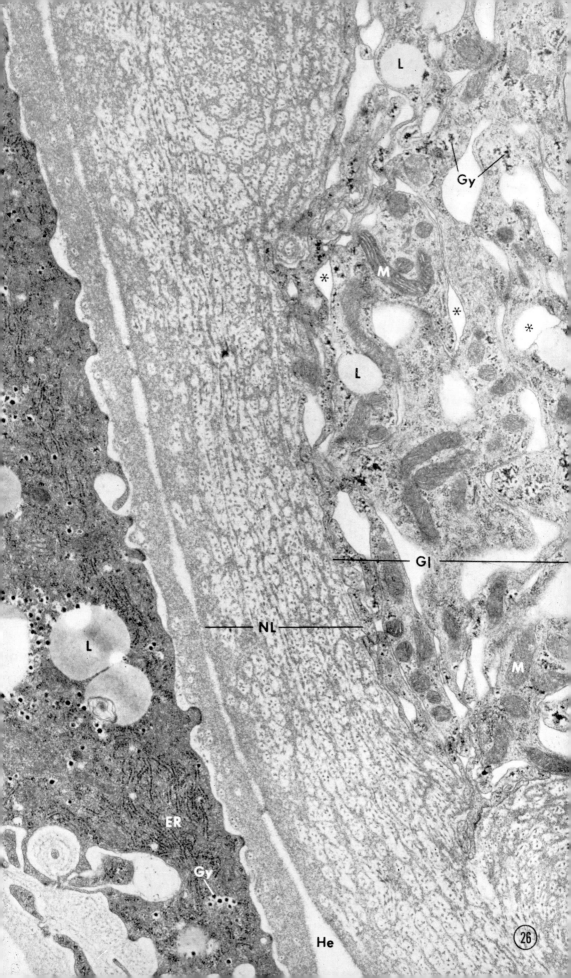

He

Plate 27 ▷

A micrograph illustrating, at higher magnification than in Plate 26, the organisation of the thick extracellular sheath or neural lamella surrounding an insect ganglion. This sheath consists of a fabric of variously oriented fibrils [Co] showing a transverse periodicity resembling that of vertebrate collagen, seen here in longitudinal, oblique and transverse section. These fibrils are embedded in an amorphous or finely granular matrix containing mucopolysaccharide[*]. Immediately beneath the sheath lie the outermost glial cells of the ganglion. These, which are often termed the perineurium cells, are thought to play an important part in the uptake of nutrients diffusing through the neural lamella and in their transfer to the nerve cells situated beneath them in the cortex of the ganglion.

(× 40,000.)

(*Philips EM 200.*)

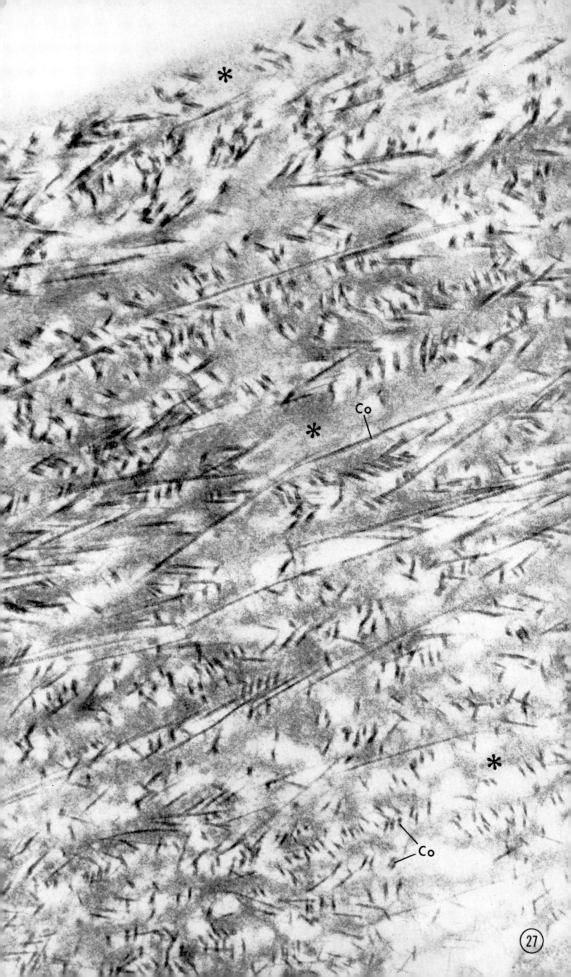

Plate 28 ▷

This micrograph, from the cortical region of the stick insect hypocerebral ganglion, illustrates the relationship between glial elements and a neurone cell body. At the upper left are included wide intercellular spaces [*] lying between the outer glial cells of the perineurium (cf. Plate 26).   Beneath the latter are present other glial cells [Gl] from which extend narrow closely packed processes that tightly ensheath the underlying nerve cell bodies. Glial and neuronal nuclei are seen at N respectively on the left and right of the field, and the arrows mark the limits of a neurone perikaryon. This characteristic association between nervous and glial structures is further illustrated in the next field.

($\times$ 19,000.)

(*Philips EM 200.*)

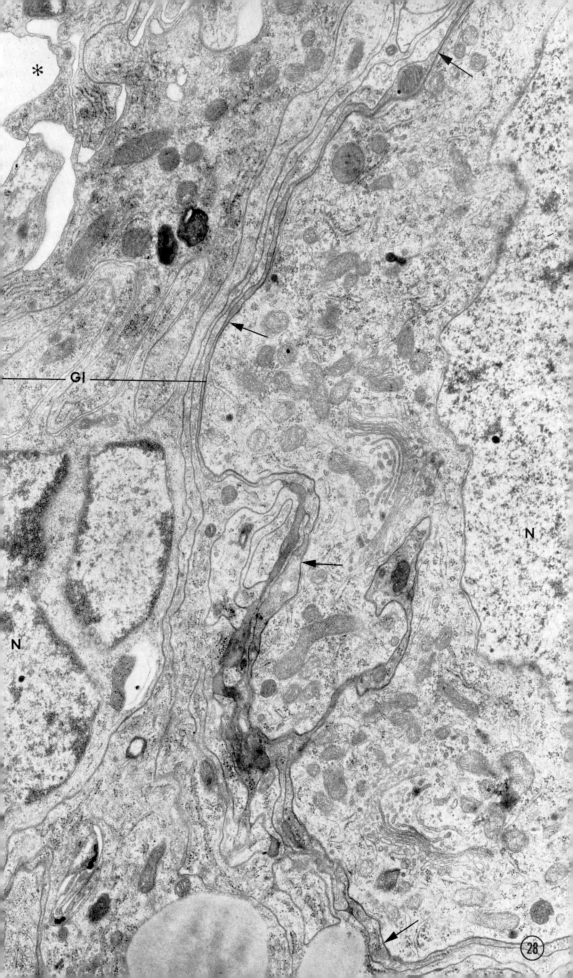

Plate 29 ▷

A field similar to Plate 28, at higher magnification. A portion of
a neurone nucleus appears at lower right [N], limited by the usual
double nuclear envelope. The surrounding cytoplasm (or perikaryon)
of the neurone contains a variety of membranes and other
structures that do not extend along the axon process. The most
prominent of these are the crescentic smooth-membraned cisternae of
the Golgi bodies [G], which correspond to the 'dictyosomes'
recognised in the light microscope. In neurosecretory cells, these
contain opaque intracisternal granules or droplets (Plate 34) and in
other neurones are presumably concerned in the synthesis and/or
sequestration of less readily identifiable materials. The compact Nissl
bodies of vertebrate neurones are absent, and in their place appear
dispersed endoplasmic reticulum cisternae [ER] often partially studded
with ribosomes, together with numerous unattached ribosomes. The
microtubules of the perikaryon [Mt] are perhaps continuous with the
'neurotubules' of the axon (Plates 25 and 32). Small mitochondria
[M] are numerous.

   The surface of the perikarya of the insect central nervous system is
uniformly ensheathed by glial cells. The apposed cell membranes are
separated by a gap of only 100 Å. Dendrites are absent, and no
synaptic endings reach the cell body. In the field shown in this
micrograph, the glial investment [Gl] comprises several narrow sheets,
the cell membranes of which are tightly apposed [*]. From the
innermost sheet, slender processes (Gl') are invaginated into the
perikaryon, forming the 'trophospongium' of light microscopy. These
processes, in common with the rest of the glial cytoplasm, are well
supplied with microtubules [Mt']. They are thought to have a trophic
function in supplying the neurone cell body with nutrient molecules
including the precursors of fats and glycogen. To the nerve cell
membrane pushed in by these processes are applied cisternae
[arrows], partially or completely devoid of attached ribosomes, which
may be concerned with the uptake of materials transferred from the
glia.

($\times$ 38,000.)

(*Philips EM 200.*)

88

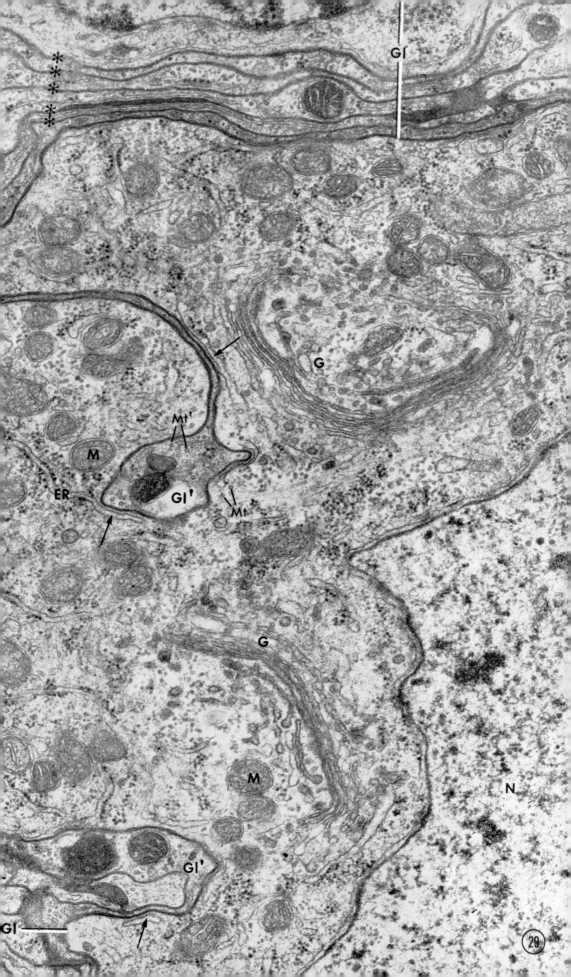

GI

* * * * *

GI

M

ER

Mt'

GI'

Mt

G

G

M

GI'

GI

N

29

Plate 30 ▷

An electron micrograph that shows, at low magnification, the
relationship between the neurone cell bodies, the glial processes that
surround them, and the complex central neuropile, in the hypocerebral
ganglion of the stick insect *Carausius morosus*. At lower centre and
left are included portions of two neurone cell bodies with large
nuclei [N] and cytoplasm containing prominent dictyosomes or Golgi
bodies [G], shown at higher magnification in Plate 29. The neurone
cell bodies here, and throughout the insect central nervous system,
are enveloped by tightly fitting sheets of glial cytoplasm [Gl] arranged
in parallel stacks (cf. Plate 29). In the absence of synapses with the
nerve cell bodies, all synapses within the central ganglia appear to be
relegated to the neuropile. In this field, the profiles of axons and their
branches, ranging in diameter from about 0·1–2 micra, are grouped
together in a compact mass. Slender glial ramifications enter the
neuropile with the axons, and the lipid droplets [L] lie within these
non-nervous processes. The axons within the neuropile contain
neurotubules [Nt] or, in some instances, synaptic vesicles [SV],
while those containing opaque droplets [ND] represent the processes
of neurosecretory cells.

(× 12,000.)

(*Philips EM 200.*)

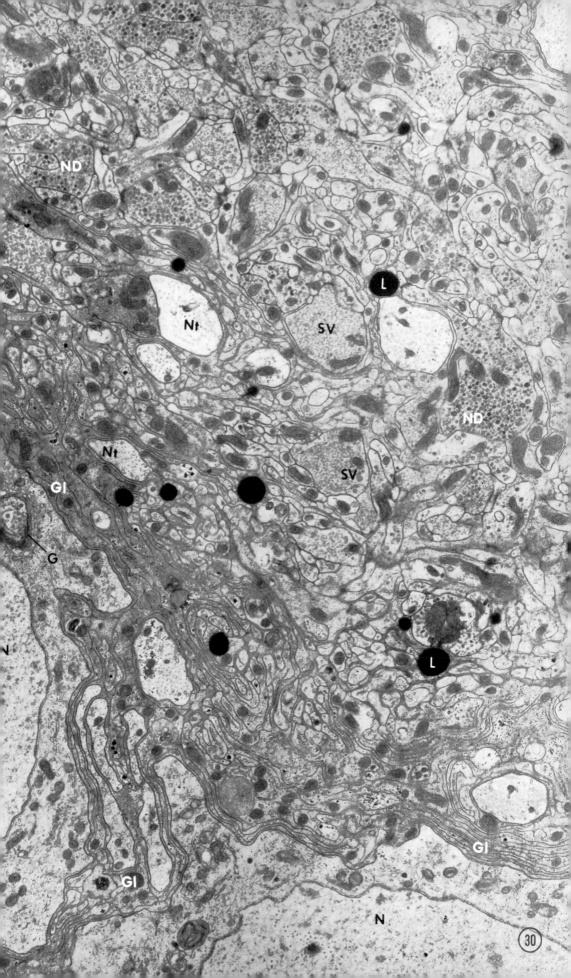

As in the vertebrate body, hormones perform many crucial roles in the control of development and physiological function in insects. According to the definition which will be adopted here, a hormone may be considered as a substance, liberated from a nerve or endocrine gland cell and transferred by diffusion or by means of a circulatory system to a 'target' organ, tissue or cell, situated at some distance from its point of release, upon which it exerts a specific effect. The insect corpus cardiacum has been for some time recognised as an organ from which are released neurohormones playing a particularly wide spectrum of roles, having been implicated in the regulation of the moulting cycle, growth of the ovaries, oviposition movements, the rate of heart beat, the activity of certain regions of the central nervous system and epidermal colour change control (Refs. in Scharrer, 1963).

Except in the higher Diptera, where the paired corpora cardiaca are incorporated with the corpora allata into the 'ring gland' encircling the heart, these organs lie behind the brain with which they are linked by small nerve fibres. In almost all insects, the corpora cardiaca are closely associated with similarly paired glandular organs, the corpora allata, which are innervated by axons that have passed through the cardiaca *en route* from the brain, and which perform important endocrine functions (p. 107).

The electron microscope has provided us with much useful information about the cellular organisation of the corpus cardiacum, its relationship with the brain and the way in which secretory products may be released from it prior to their distribution through the body in the circulating haemolymph. Studies with the light microscope on sectioned material and also on living preparations clearly indicated that this organ functions as a storage depot for neurosecretory substances, synthesised within neurone cell bodies lying within the brain, notably in the protocerebrum, and passed backwards along the axons of the corpus cardiacum nerves. An important additional feature was recognised by Scharrer (1963) in an electron microscopic study; that, in addition to receiving axons from the brain, the corpus cardiacum is also equipped with its own intrinsic secretory cells which in many respects resemble neurosecretory neurones, and which are accompanied by cells apparently corresponding to the glial elements of the central nervous system.

A word should be said at this point about the concept of a neurosecretory nerve cell. In many nervous systems lie cells which have the form of 'typical' neurones, but which differ from these in possessing stainable material, synthesised within the cell body and passed out along the axon. In many instances, it has been shown that these cells are engaged in producing hormones. The electron microscope has suggested that this stainable material is contained within droplets or vesicles, ranging in size from 1000–3000 Å and which often, though not always, bind osmium strongly and hence are opaque to the electron beam. These droplets are thought to include hormones, perhaps combined with 'carrier' proteins. In some cases, at least, these cells are able to sustain action potentials, and, as suggested by Bargmann (1966), are perhaps best regarded as 'normal' neurones that in addition to their conductive ability also possess glandular properties. Such neurosecretory cells are widespread throughout the Phyla, and from one group to the next vary greatly in their number and distribution. The extensive literature on these cells has been brought together by Gabe (1966) in a recent book, and Bargmann (1966) has reviewed our present understanding of the nature and identification of neurosecretory materials. An account of the distribution of neurosecretory pathways in insects and other invertebrates has been given by Bern and Hagadorn (1965).

Unlike the corpus allatum, which seems to be curiously variable in its fine structure (p. 107), the cellular construction of corpora cardiaca seems to be more standardised. Electron microscopic studies on these organs have been made by Willey and Chapman (1960) on the cockroaches *Leucophaea* and *Periplaneta*, Scharrer (1963) on *Leucophaea*, Meyer and Pflugfelder (1958) and Smith and Smith (1966) on the stick insect *Carausius*, Normann (1965) and Johnson (1966) on the blowfly *Calliphora*, and Bowers and Johnson (1966) on the aphid *Myzus*. The micrographs that have been selected here to illustrate some of the structural features of the corpus cardiacum have been prepared from the stick insect.

At first sight, the organisation of the corpus cardiacum appears to be very complex, especially when a large area is surveyed at low magnification (Plate 31). At this level, the fabric of the organ is resolved as a mass of loosely fitting cells and cell processes containing, most obviously, large numbers of droplets—the majority electron-opaque and a minority transparent. Interpretation of these structures becomes a good deal easier when it is remembered that the organ contains not only intrinsic secretory cells, but also axons whose cell bodies lie within the brain, some of which appear to release their contents within the cardiacum, while others merely pass through the cardiacum to terminate in the adjoining corpus allatum and also, as shown by Johnson and Bowers (1963), in association with the gut, salivary glands, prothoracic glands, heart and abdominal muscles, and so on. First, let us consider the contribution made by the brain. Peripheral axons typically contain scattered mitochondria and neurotubules, but axons passing to the corpus cardiacum possess, in addition, 'neurosecretory granules' formed within the cell body of the neurone and fixed for electron microscopic examination as they travel along the axon towards its terminal. In the stick insect, these may be divided into two general groups (Plate 32) on the basis of their osmium-binding capacity: in some axons, the granules or droplets are heavily 'stained' while others possess droplets with an electron-transparent content and in which the membrane limiting each is revealed. While both groups are present within a single corpus cardiacum nerve, each individual axon contains one type or the other without mixing or intergradation, a feature suggesting that while different nerve cell bodies produce different secreted materials, each axon transports unchanged the material it receives, or, at least, without change that is reflected in its ability to bind osmium.

These neurosecretory droplets, of extrinsic origin, account for many of the profiles within the cardiacum itself and this feature aids our understanding of the structure of the organ, which, as Scharrer showed, also contains large cells which have several of the characteristics of secretory neurones. These intrinsic cells are represented in Plate 33, and they differ from typical neurones in that the axon-like process is short and wide and does not appear to extend beyond the confines of the organ. The organisation of the cytoplasm of the perikaryon of these cells is shown at higher magnification

94

in Plate 34, which reveals the presence of the membranes associated with the synthetic role of the cell. Cisternae of the ribosome-bearing endoplasmic reticulum and unattached ribosomes are plentiful, and as in typical insect nerve cells (Plate 30) these are spread irregularly through the cytoplasm and not deployed in the compact 'Nissl bodies' of vertebrate neurones. Agranular cisternae are present in groups forming the dictyosomes or Golgi bodies. Within the perikaryon lie abundant droplets of secretion which bind osmium strongly and thus resemble many of the neurosecretory products reaching the cardiacum from the brain, and in each of these instances the droplets first make their appearance in small vesicles associated with the Golgi bodies (Plate 34). Whether the latter represent the sole site of synthesis of the secretory material, or whether, for example, protein is passed on from the ribosome-bearing cisternae and incorporated into the developing droplet is not known. The intrinsic droplets become aggregated in large numbers in the stubby axon-like processes of the cells (Plate 33), but fortunately for our analysis of the construction of the corpus cardiacum, these processes also contain ribosomes and occasional cisternae of the rough-surfaced endoplasmic reticulum and are thus distinguishable from axons of extrinsic cells which do not contain these structures. A similar mode of synthesis of neurosecretory droplets has been described, for example, in the earthworm (Scharrer and Brown, 1961) and in vertebrates (Sloper and Bateson, 1965; Bargmann, 1966).

The axons of the corpus cardiacum nerves are enveloped, as is usual in peripheral nerves, by glial cells. Axons that merely pass through the cardiacum presumably retain these glial sheaths all the way to their terminations in the corpus allatum or elsewhere in the body. It is a general rule in nervous systems that the glial covering of a nerve cell is interrupted at points where it receives synaptic endings of other neurones, or where pharmacologically active substances are released from it, and this rule seems to be followed within the cardiacum. In the stick insect, many of the axons received from the brain end within the cardiacum, rather than passing through towards other organs, and these axons, containing the electron-opaque and transparent neurosecretory droplets, show areas where the glial investment is broken and the axon plasma membrane is thereby exposed directly to the extracellular space. Likewise, the surface of the intrinsic cardiacum cells is largely covered by processes of glial (or 'interstitial') cells (Plate 34) which are, again, locally incomplete over the axon-like extensions.

The corpus cardiacum has for some time been thought of as a neurohaemal organ, that is, a storage depot from which neurosecretory material is liberated into the circulatory system. As mentioned above, the electron microscope has shown that provision seems to be made for the release both of products manufactured within the organ and of those conveyed thence from the brain. Some uncertainty at present remains concerning the manner in which this release takes place. In the stick insect and the blowfly, there is evidence that both extrinsic and intrinsic secretory droplets may be liberated across the axon membrane, where the glia is interrupted, by a mechanism akin to that employed in the release of zymogen granules from the exocrine pancreatic cell, that is, by fusion of the limiting membrane surrounding the droplet with the plasma membrane of the axon (Smith and Smith, 1966; Normann, 1965). This mechanism is also believed to be employed in the release of transmitter molecules from the synaptic vesicles of axons terminating on skeletal muscle fibres (p. 60) and elsewhere. Furthermore, this appears to be at least one of the means by which endocrine secretion is liberated from the cells of the adenohypophysis (Weiss, 1965). On the other hand, Johnson (1966) has suggested, from his work on the blowfly, that the neurosecretory

95

droplets may first fragment into smaller vesicles prior to release, and that these may discharge across the axon membrane. In either instance, the material liberated must traverse an extracellular basement membrane or basal lamina before reaching the haemolymph. Further studies will doubtless tell us more about the way in which secretions leave the cells of the cardiacum, and the means by which this release is triggered and controlled.

While the electron microscope has been of great assistance in tracing the structure and general mode of function of the corpus cardiacum, our methods cannot at present do justice to the diversity of physiological effects controlled by the substances passed into the circulatory system from this organ. Except for the brain hormone, released from the cardiacum and triggering the liberation of moulting hormone from the pro-thoracic glands, we do not know which effects are controlled by extrinsic and which by intrinsic products. Furthermore, it should be stressed that while crude grouping of secretory droplets, on the basis of their opacity or transparency after treatment with osmium, provides an aid in sorting out the origins of the contents of the cardiacum, it is probable that similarity in the 'staining' properties of droplets in various axons and in different intrinsic cell, masks crucial biochemical and physiological differences that we are at present unable to recognise.

Attention has often been drawn to the parallels that exist between the corpus allatum–corpus cardiacum complex of the insect and the hypothalamo–hypophyseal system of the vertebrate. As Wigglesworth (1954) points out, in each case an endocrine gland of non-nervous origin (respectively the corpus allatum and the adenohypophysis) is closely associated with a nervous derivative (the corpus cardiacum and the neuro-hypophysis), from which neurohormones are liberated into the circulatory system. Furthermore, the neurosecretory cells within the protocerebrum of the insect brain which send their axons to the corpus cardiacum have their morphological parallel in the hormone-secreting neurones whose cell bodies lie in the supraoptic and paraven-tricular nuclei of the hypothalamus and send their axons along the infundibular stalk, to end in the infundibular process of the neurohypophysis. While this structural analogy between parts of the endocrine systems of insects and vertebrates is an interesting one, it should not be pressed too far; for, unlike the corpus cardiacum, the neurohypophysis possesses no intrinsic secretory cell bodies and, of course, the hormones associated with the two complexes are entirely different in their effects.

In short, despite the attention that has been paid to the corpus cardiacum, several questions concerning its function remain unanswered. Future work will no doubt clarify the question of which extrinsic and intrinsic hormones are released within it, and which are merely conveyed through it along axons of neurosecretory cells and in this way distributed to various target organs throughout the body.

Although the corpus cardiacum and the nerves that pass through it constitute the best-known neurohaemal system in insects, it is now realised that release of neuro-secretory material takes place, in addition, from other parts of the nervous system. For example, Maddrell proposed that a diuretic hormone is released from the fused meso-thoracic ganglion mass of the blood-sucking bug *Rhodnius*, but he has recently shown (Maddrell, 1966) that in fact this hormone is channelled out of the ganglion along axons which end in swellings lying immediately beneath the extracellular sheath of the abdominal nerves, and he has obtained electron micrographs suggesting that neuro-secretory droplets are thence discharged into the haemolymph. Furthermore, discrete segmentally arranged neurohaemal organs have been found in the medial nervous system of several insects—a branching system of axons arising from the central ganglia and including the motor nerve supply of the spiracular muscles. These organs take the form of local swellings, superficially resembling small ganglia. The electron microscope has shown, however, (Brady and Maddrell, 1967) that they contain a closely packed mass of bulbous axon endings from which neurosecretory material may be liberated into the circulatory system, together with ordinary axons passing through *en route* for the spiracles. Unlike a ganglion or the corpus cardiacum, these organs possess no intrinsic nerve cell bodies. The part played by the hormone or hormones released from these special regions of the nervous system is not yet known.

REFERENCES

BARGMANN, W. 1966. Neurosecretion. *Int. Rev. Cytol.*, **19**, 183–201.
BERN, H. A., and HAGADORN, I. R. 1965. Neurosecretion. In *Structure and Function in the Nervous Systems of Invertebrates* by T. H. Bullock and G. A. Horridge, Vol. 1, pp. 353–429. W. H. Freeman, San Francisco and London.
*BOWERS, B., and JOHNSON, B. 1966. An electron microscope study of the corpora cardiaca and secretory neurones in the aphid, *Myzus persicae* (Sulz.). *Gen. compar. Endocr.*, **6**, 213–230.
*BRADY, J., and MADDRELL, S. H. P. 1967. Neurohaemal organs in the medial nervous system of insects. *Z. Zellforsch. mikrosk. Anat.*, **76**, 389–404.
GABE, M. 1966. *Neurosecretion* (R. Crawford, trans.). Pergamon Press, Oxford.
*JOHNSON, B. 1966. Ultrastructure of probable sites of release of neurosecretory materials in an insect, *Calliphora stygia* Fabr. (Diptera). *Gen. compar. Endocr.*, **6**, 99–108.
*JOHNSON, B., and BOWERS, B. 1963. Transport of neurohormones from the corpora cardiaca in insects. *Science*, **141**, 264–266.
*MADDRELL, S. H. P. 1966. The site of release of the diuretic hormone in *Rhodnius*—a new neurohaemal system in insects. *J. exp. Biol.*, **45**, 499–508.
*MEYER, G. F., and PFLUGFELDER, O. 1958. Elektronenmikroskopische Untersuchungen an den Corpora Cardiaca von *Carausius morosus* Br. *Z. Zellforsch. mikrosk. Anat.*, **48**, 556–564.
*NORMANN, T. C. 1965. The neurosecretory system of the adult *Calliphora erythrocephala*. I. The fine structure of the corpus cardiacum with some observations on adjacent organs. *Z. Zellforsch. mikrosk. Anat.*, **67**, 461–501.
*SCHARRER, B. 1963. Neurosecretion. XIII. The ultrastructure of the corpus cardiacum of the insect *Leucophaea maderae*. *Z. Zellforsch. mikrosk. Anat.*, **60**, 761–796.
SCHARRER, E., and BROWN, S. 1961. Neurosecretion. XII. The formation of neurosecretory granules in the earthworm, *Lumbricus terrestris* L. *Z. Zellforsch. mikrosk. Anat.*, **54**, 530–540.
SLOPER, J. C., and BATESON, R. G. 1965. Ultrastructure of neurosecretory cells in the supraoptic nucleus of the dog and rat. *J. Endocr.*, **31**, 139–150.
*SMITH, U., and SMITH, D. S. 1966. Observations on the secretory processes in the corpus cardiacum of the stick insect, *Carausius morosus*. *J. Cell Sci.* **1**, 59–66.
WEISS, M. 1965. The release of pituitary secretion in the platyfish, *Xiphophorus maculatus* (Guenther). *Z. Zellforsch. mikrosk. Anat.*, **68**, 783–794.
WIGGLESWORTH, V. B. 1954. *The Physiology of Insect Metamorphosis*. Cambridge University Press.
*WILLEY, R. B., and CHAPMAN, G. B. 1960. The ultrastructure of certain components of the corpus cardiacum in orthopteroid insects. *J. Ultrastruct. Res.*, **4**, 1–14.

Plates 31–34 ▷

H

Plate 31 ▷

The corpus cardiacum is a loosely-knit organ, in which the cell surfaces are separated by wide extracellular spaces [ES] illustrated here in material prepared from the stick insect. In addition to axons received from the brain, the cardiacum contains large intrinsic neurone-like secretory cells, the nuclei and perikarya of which are seen at N and Pk. Each perikaryon includes a large number of opaque secretory droplets [ND_3], the formation of which is illustrated at higher magnification in Plate 34. These droplets are passed in large numbers into axon-like processes of the intrinsic cells (Plate 33) whence they are probably released into the extracellular channels ramifying through the organ. They resemble, in density, many of the extrinsic droplets reaching the cardiacum through axons from the brain (Plate 32). A few of the latter are included in this micrograph [ND_1] within axons containing neurotubules, while the aggregates of droplets [ND_3] in the left half of the field are set in dense cytoplasm containing ribosomes, and are probably of intrinsic origin. The vesicles with transparent contents within the axons at ND_2 represent neurosecretion passed back from the brain, and seen in transit to the cardiacum in Plate 32. The large opaque inclusions [*] are perhaps formed by confluence of smaller secretory droplets, or alternatively may represent lipid spheres.

(× 9000.)

(Philips EM 200. Micrograph prepared in collaboration with Dr U. Smith.)

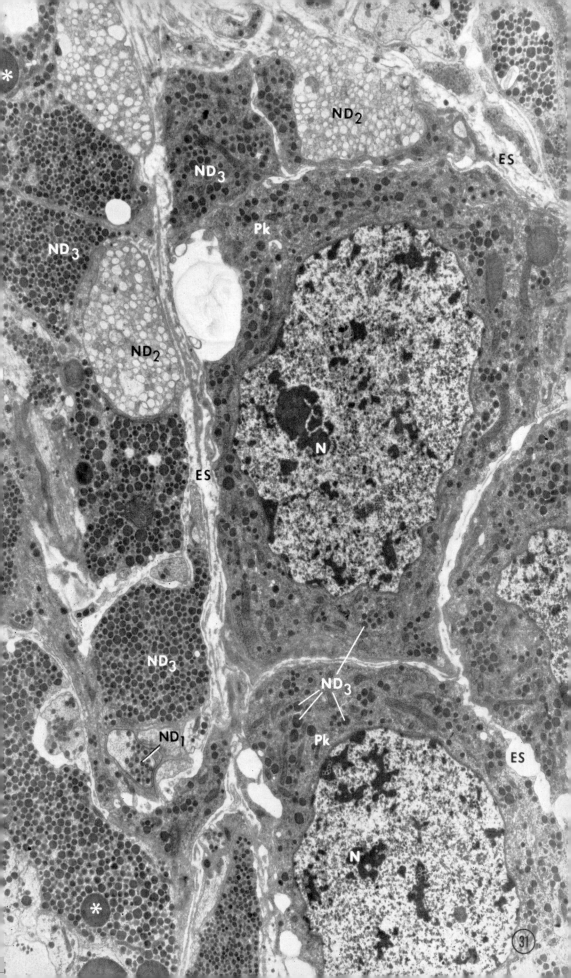

Plate 32 ▷

Some of the cellular structures and types of neurosecretory droplet occurring within the corpus cardiacum of the stick insect are illustrated in Plates 31 and 33. The droplets found within the organ are in part intrinsic and in part extrinsic in origin, and the task of distinguishing one from the other becomes somewhat simplified when, as in the micrograph shown here, we observe the contents of axons *en route* to the cardiacum from their cell bodies in the protocerebrum of the brain. In this insect, these nerves (nervi corporis cardiaci) contain two main categories of neurosecretory droplet or vesicle, one electron-opaque [ND_1] and the other with transparent contents [ND_2]. The axoplasm also contains small mitochondria, and prominent neurotubules [Nt.] As in the case of other peripheral nerves, the axons are ensheathed by glial processes [Gl], and a portion of a glial nucleus is seen at the bottom left [N.] Some of these axons are thought to end, within the corpus cardiacum, in bulbous processes from which the neurosecretory material is released into the wide extracellular channels permeating the organ (Plate 33), thence passing into the haemolymph through the surface sheath or basement membrane. Some axons from the brain do not end within the cardiacum, but pass on through it to the corpus allatum and other tissues of the body. In addition to these axons of extrinsic origin, the corpus cardiacum contains its own neurone-like cells, within which the intrinsic neurosecretory materials are synthesised (Plate 34).

($\times$ 40,000.)

(*Philips EM 200. Micrograph prepared in collaboration with Dr U. Smith.*)

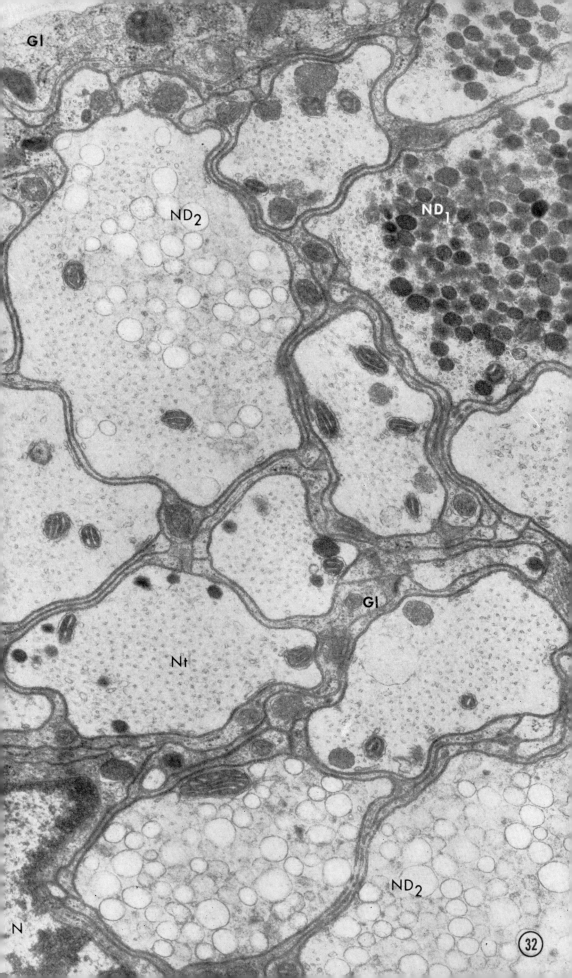

Plate 33 ▷

The corpus cardiacum is ensheathed by a layered basement membrane [arrow] containing collagen, and strands of similar material lie in the extracellular spaces between the cell surfaces within the organ [*], where they probably have a connective function. This field includes portions of two perikarya of intrinsic secretory cells [Pk] from which extend axon-like processes [Ax']. These contain numerous secretory droplets, which are passed down to be stored in bulbous swellings at the end of each process (Plate 31). A profile of one of these swellings, packed with neurosecretion [ND$_3$], is included on the right. In addition occur aggregates of transparent droplets [ND$_2$] believed to be among the extrinsic products (Plate 32) reaching the cardiacum from the brain. It is probable that both extrinsic and intrinsic neurohormones are released within the cardiacum, from which they may pass into the surrounding haemolymph after traversing the basement membrane.

($\times$ 13,000.)

(*Philips EM 200. Micrograph prepared in collaboration with Dr U. Smith.*)

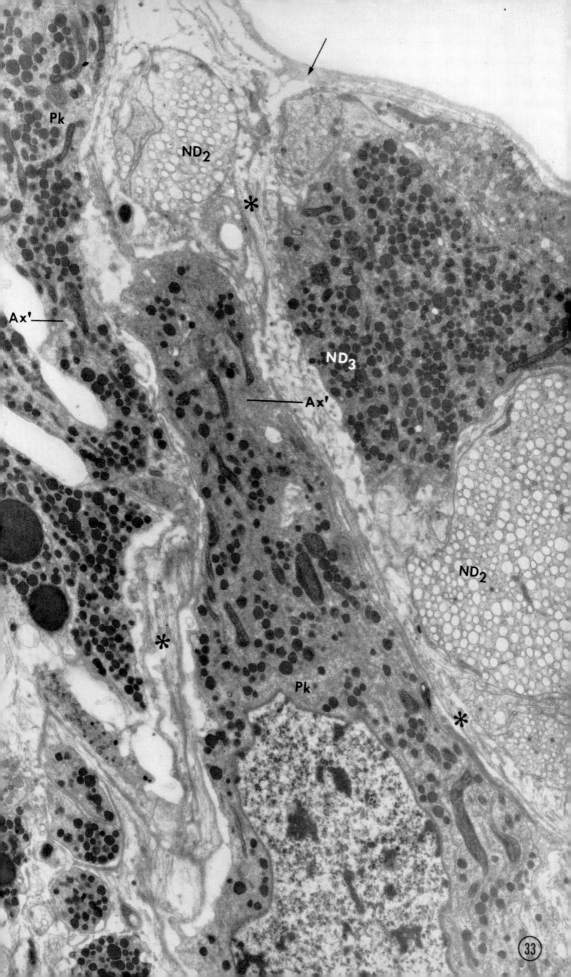

Plate 34 ▷

The intrinsic secretory cells of the corpus cardiacum resemble typical neurosecretory nerve cells except that the axon-like process arising from each cell body is short and bulbous, and unlike a true axon contains ribosomes, both free and attached to occasional cisternae of the endoplasmic reticulum. The field shown here, from the stick insect, includes a portion of the large nucleus of an intrinsic cell [N]. The surrounding cytoplasm is clearly engaged in the synthesis of opaque droplets [ND] seen at low magnification in Plate 33. Ribosome-bearing cisternae of the endoplasmic reticulum [ER] together with many free ribosomes are spread plentifully through the perikaryon. Agranular cisternae are stacked together in Golgi bodies [G], where secretory material is packaged : within these membranes are resolved small dense deposits [*]—the precursors of the larger neurosecretory droplets. In mature droplets, the opaque contents generally obscures the limiting membrane, but this may sometimes be distinguished after the forming droplet has separated from the Golgi region [arrow]. It is probable that protein material, synthesised in association with the ribosomes on the reticulum cisternae, is passed for packaging and export from the cell to the Golgi cisternae—a common sequence of events in secretory tissues, and one that is shared by typical neurosecretory neurones in vertebrates and invertebrates. Mitochondria with longitudinally oriented cristae [M] are present in the micrograph shown here, while the structure seen at M′ containing concentrically arranged pairs of membranes is frequently met with in these cells, and perhaps represents a mitochondrion of unusual form. The surface of the cell body and process of these cardiacum cells is partially covered by thin sheets of glia, seen here at the upper left of the field (Gl].

(× 60,000.)

(Philips EM 200. Micrograph prepared in collaboration with Dr U. Smith.)

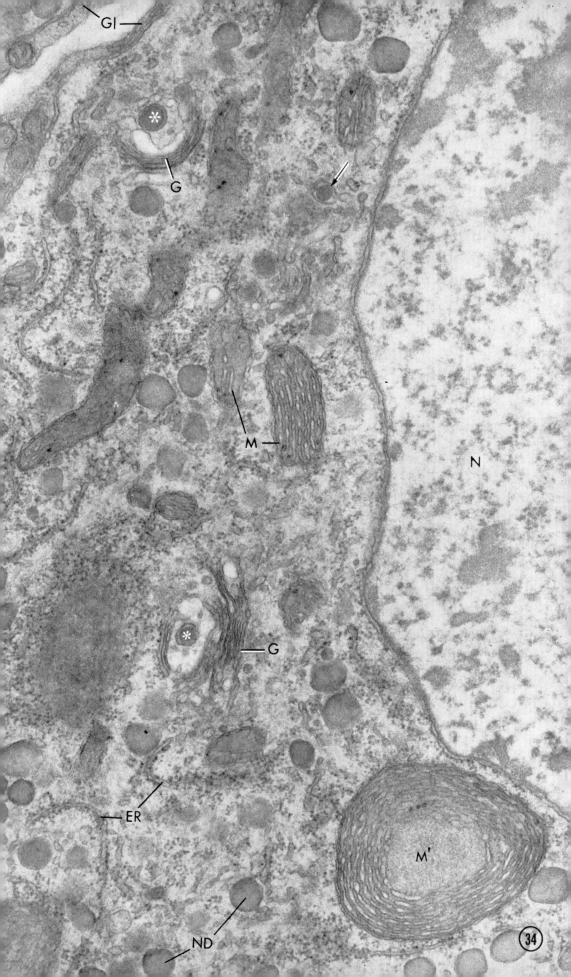

The corpora allata are small, usually paired, glandular organs, which lie either behind the corpora cardiaca or more or less fused with them. These organs are non-nervous, and have for some time been recognised as possessing very important endocrine functions. Each corpus allatum is innervated by axons of neurosecretory cells whose cell bodies lie in the brain, and which first traverse the corpus cardiacum, and the analogy that has been drawn between the allatum–cardiacum complex and the vertebrate hypothalamo–hypophyseal system has already been mentioned (p. 96).

During most of the insect's larval life, the corpora allata produce the juvenile hormone (neotenin) which prevents precocious maturation, and it is the eventual absence of this hormone that allows development to proceed to adulthood. After the last moult to the adult stage has occurred, the corpora allata may again become active and influence a variety of functions which in various insects include the general level of metabolism, reproductive behaviour, oocyte yolk deposition, spermatophore secretion, and, in locusts, changes in phase and colour (Refs. in Wigglesworth, 1965).

Reflecting the importance of the corpus allatum in the development and function of the insect body, the fine structure of this organ has been studied in several species. Schultze (1960) and Waku and Gilbert (1964) described some features of the allata of the moths *Celerio* and *Hyalophora*, while other insects that have been considered include the cockroach *Leucophaea* (Scharrer, 1964), the fruitfly *Drosophila* (King and others, 1966), the beetle *Hypera* (Tombes and Smith, 1968), and the desert locust *Schistocerca* (Odhiambo, 1966a, 1966b). Two striking features have emerged from this work: first, the presence of neurosecretory droplets within the axons entering the corpus allatum, and, second, the surprisingly variable structure of the allatum cells, from one species to the next, which provides conflicting indications of the nature of their secretion. As an example of corpus allatum organisation, a section from *Hypera* is shown in Plate 35: the neurosecretory axons infiltrating the organ and spreading over its surface are thought to release neurohumors from their endings among the gland cells, and thus control the synthesis and/or liberation of allatum hormone.

The chemical nature of the juvenile hormone of the larva, and of the hormone secreted by the corpus allatum in the adult, is not yet known, nor, indeed, has it been clearly established whether one or more hormones are synthesised by the gland throughout life. The moulting hormone, ecdysone, secreted by the prothoracic glands, is now known to be a steroid (Refs. in Scharrer, 1965), and it would be of great interest to know whether or not the corpus allatum produces chemically related molecules. As Scharrer (1965) suggests, the membranes of the allatum cells, viewed against a wide variety of secretory cells, might provide us with a circumstantial clue about the secretion they produce. Steroid-secreting cells of the mammalian testis (p. 183) possess a remarkably rich system of smooth-membraned tubules of the endoplasmic reticulum, and in the two most detailed studies of allatum cells (King and others, 1966; Odhiambo, 1966a), smooth-surfaced cisternae and vesicles were found to dominate the intracellular scene. In particular, Odhiambo showed that active allatum cells of the locust become crowded with arrays of smooth-membraned cisternae and vesicles, and that vesicles, perhaps containing secreted material, enlarge as they approach the surface of the cell. In these cases, ribosome-studded cisternae, usually associated with cells that are secreting protein for export, are very inconspicuous, and the cellular architecture is at least consistent with the manufacture of a steroid or similar molecule. On the other hand, Scharrer (1964) found that active cells of the cockroach corpus allatum possess some smooth-surfaced cisternae, but also conspicuous whorls of ribosome-studded (rough-surfaced) cisternae. In the stick insect *Carausius*, smooth membranes are restricted to the Golgi bodies, and rough-surfaced cisternae virtually fill the cell (Smith, unpublished observations).

Prothoracic glands, secreting ecdysone, are well supplied with smooth-surfaced cisternae (Scharrer, 1964b, 1965), but the variable amounts of rough and smooth cisternae in the corpora allata of various insects calls for further work, perhaps including assay of fractions obtained by centrifugation of homogenised allatum tissue. Further work with these cells, which are so important to the insect, might well add to our knowledge of the nature and mode of secretion of insect hormones.

REFERENCES

*KING, R. C., AGGARWAL, K., and BODENSTEIN, D. 1966. The comparative submicroscopic cytology of the corpus allatum–corpus cardiacum complex of wild type and *fes* adult female *Drosophila melanogaster*. *J. exp. Zool.*, **161**, 151–176.

*ODHIAMBO, T. R. 1966a. The fine structure of the corpus allatum of the sexually mature male of the desert locust. *J. Insect Physiol.*, **12**, 819–828.

*ODHIAMBO, T. R. 1966b. Ultrastructure of the development of the corpus allatum in the adult male of the desert locust. *J. Insect Physiol.*, **12**, 995–1002.

*SCHARRER, B. 1964a. Histophysiological studies on the corpus allatum of *Leucophaea maderae*. IV. Ultrastructure during normal activity cycle. *Z. Zellforsch. mikrosk. Anat.*, **62**, 125–148.

*SCHARRER, B. 1964b. Ultrastructural study of the prothoracic glands of *Leucophaea maderae*. *Am. Zoologist*, **4**, 328.

SCHARRER, B. 1965. Recent progress in the study of neuroendocrine mechanisms in insects. *Archs Anat. microsc.*, **54**, 331–342.

*SCHULTZE, R. L. 1960. Electron microscopic observations of the corpora allata and associated nerves in the moth *Celerio lineata*. *J. Ultrastruct. Res.*, **3**, 320–327.

SMITH, U. Unpublished observations on the fine structure of the corpora allata of the stick insect *Carausius morosus*.

*TOMBES, A. S., and SMITH, D. S. 1968. Ultrastructural studies on the corpora cardiaca-allata complex of active and diapausing alfalfa weevil adults, *Hypera postica*. *Proc. Symp. Insect Endocr.*, Brno, 1967, in press.

*WAKU, Y., and GILBERT, L. I. 1964. The corpora allata of the silkmoth, *Hyalophora cecropia*: an ultrastructural study. *J. Morph.*, **115**, 69–96.

WIGGLESWORTH, V. B. 1965. The Principles of Insect Physiology, 6th edn, Ch. 3. Methuen, London.

Plate 35 ▷

Plate 35 ▷

The corpus allatum plays a central role in the regulation of
development before the adult stage is reached, by producing the
juvenile hormone. The interplay between this and the moulting
hormone from the prothoracic glands, upon the cells of the body,
regulates the progressive advance towards metamorphosis. In the
adult, the corpus allatum may resume an endocrine function in
controlling egg production, as in the alfalfa weevil. In adult females
of this insect (*Hypera postica*), each of the pair of corpora allata
consists of a spherical group of closely packed cells, seen in this
micrograph at low magnification. The nucleus [N] of each cell is
surrounded by cytoplasm containing evenly scattered mitochondria,
Golgi bodies, and rough-surfaced endoplasmic reticulum cisternae.
In *Hypera*, axons containing opaque neurosecretory droplets [Ax]
pass backwards from the brain, traverse the corpora cardiaca and, as
shown here, penetrate between the cells of the corpora allata, where
they may control hormone secretion or release. Tracheoles [Tr] also
meander between the allatum cells.

($\times$ 8000.)

(*Philips EM 200. Micrograph produced in collaboration with
Dr A. Tombes.*)

110

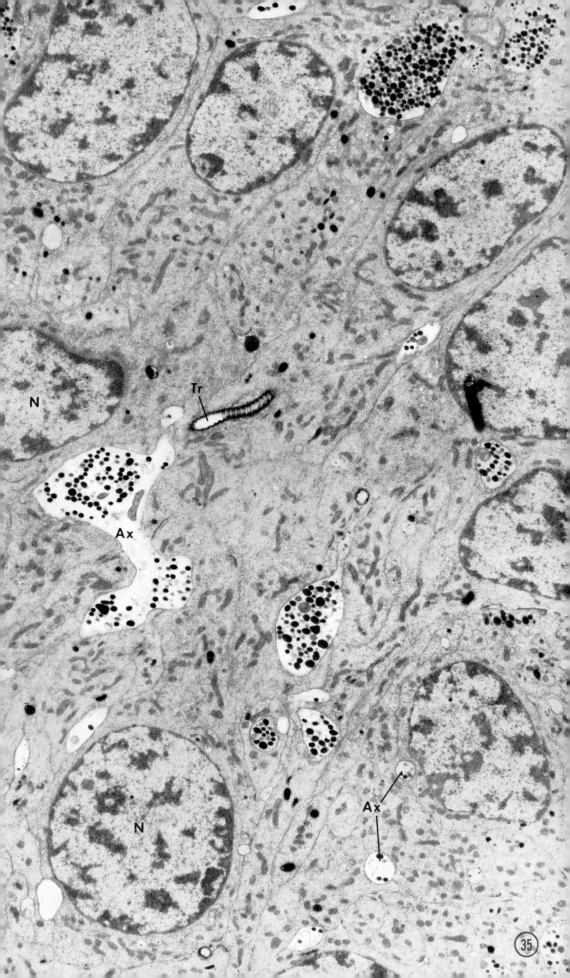

The Compound Eye

The chief sensory systems of the vertebrate body—vision, touch, proprioception, hearing and the chemical senses of taste and smell—all find their functional analogues in insects, though, as might be expected, the great difference in bodily organisation between these two groups of animals are paralleled in the form of their respective sense organs. In particular, the organs receiving stimuli from the external environment around the insect must carry out their function in association with the surface cuticle, which is therefore often specially modified to meet efficiently the physical requirements of the senses they serve.

Much is known of the form and distribution of insect sense organs at the level of the light microscope. Although our knowledge of their fine structure is still very incomplete, the electron microscopic studies at present available have given us new insight into the specialised features of sensory endings. The compound eye, the chief visual organ of adult insects, has been chosen for illustration here, but a brief description and bibliography of work on other parts of the sensory system has been included at the end of the section.

The faceting of the compound eye was impressively figured by Hooke in the *Micrographia* and from the time of Johannes Muller's 'mosaic' theory, ideas on the functioning of this organ in insects and other arthropods have centred on the part played by the single facet and underlying group of sense cells in the perception of a complex visual field. This morphological unit is termed the ommatidium. Each ommatidium consists of a dipotric system made up of the transparent lenticular surface cuticle (the corneal lens) and an underlying 'crystalline cone' secreted in quadrants by the four Semper's cells: this system is thought to collect light from its visual field and convey it to the cylindrical group of retinular cells or primary sensory neurones of the ommatidium. Proximally, each of these neurones gives rise to a short axon process which passes through an extracellular sheath *en route* for the periopticon or first optic ganglion in which occurs the first rank of an extremely complex series of central nervous synapses. In addition, the eye contains non-nervous pigment cells around the crystalline cone and also around each column of retinulae.

It is important to note that the following description and accompanying electron micrographs relate to the compound eye of the cockroach and, briefly, to that of the blowfly, and that considerable variation occurs in different insects, notably in the number and positioning of the cells of the retinula, their spatial relationship with the cone and the disposition of the pigment cells. The possible functional importance of some of these variations is briefly discussed later.

The cone of the cockroach ommatidium, when viewed in the electron microscope, does not in fact show any suggestion of 'crystalline' structure, or of the lamination that was believed by Exner (1891) to confer on the cone the properties of a lens cylinder of

I

graded refractive index. Instead, the cone is secreted and fitted together by four cells whose intercellular membranes form a cruciform pattern when the cone is seen in transverse section (Plate 36). The cytoplasm of these cells is virtually replaced by the material they have secreted—a closely packed mass of granules, each 100–200 Å in diameter. The nuclei of these 'Semper's cells' persist anteriorly to the segments of the cone.

Behind the cone extend the retinular cells, surrounding an axial structure called the rhabdom. In light microscopic studies, the rhabdom was resolved as a refractile rod, believed to be secreted by the sensory cells and acting as a wave guide ensuring that light entering it from the dioptric system will be conducted without loss along the cylinder of sensory receptors. While the rhabdom may well act in this way, the electron microscope has shown it to be not a secreted product, but rather built up from a multitude of short microvillar processes stemming from the inner surface of some or all of the retinular cells and oriented, with precision, perpendicular to their long axis. The evolution of photoreceptors throughout the animal Phyla has followed two morphologically distinct paths: 'rhabdomeric' sensory cells occur not only in insects and other arthropods, but also in rotifers, platyhelminths, annelids and molluscs; while in coelenterates, echinoderms and chordates the fine structure of the photoreceptor cells reveals that they are derived from highly modified cilia (Miller, 1960; Eakin, 1965).

Exner recognised two morphologically distinct types of ommatidia in insect compound eyes: 'apposition' ommatidia in which the rhabdom extends to the base of the cone, and 'superposition' ommatidia in which the rhabdom is formed only at the base of each retinula, and is separated from the cone by a long 'translucent filament', perhaps a distal process of the sensory cells. The eye of the cockroach, and indeed of most insects except some crepuscular and nocturnal species, is of the apposition type and, as may be seen in Plates 36 and 39A, the group of microvilli (or rhabdomere) of each of the four retinular cells comprising the distal portion of this ommatidium lap very tightly around the surface of the cone, and the hexagonal arrangement of the microvilli is seen when the rhabdomere is sectioned transversely (Plate 39B). In the proximal part of the ommatidium, the number of sensory cells is increased to eight. The appearance of these compact cylinders is illustrated at low magnification in Plate 37, and in greater detail in Plate 38. In this insect, the rhabdomeres are clustered together in the axis of the ommatidium, and are surrounded by many pigment granules. Details of the cytoplasmic organisation of the sensory neurones also include scattered mitochondria, endoplasmic reticulum cisternae, and conspicuous vacuoles, together with many oriented microtubules probably corresponding to the 'neurotubules' prominent in the axoplasm elsewhere in the nervous system (Plates 25 and 32). From the appearance of the rhabdom in longitudinal section (Plate 40), its rod-like disposition when examined in the light microscope may readily be understood. These micrographs also illustrate the independence of the ommatidia, which are each surrounded by extracellular spaces, in which lie tracheolar cell processes and the cell bodies and cytoplasmic tendrils of the ensheathing pigment cells.

The way in which the rhabdomeres are disposed varies a good deal. Their juxtaposition to form a compact rhabdom illustrated here in the cockroach has also been adopted, for example, by the locust (Horridge and Barnard, 1965) and grasshopper (Fernández-Morán, 1958), the honey bee *Apis* (Goldsmith, 1962), the moth *Erebus* and a hesperiid butterfly (Fernández-Morán, 1958), and the silk moth (Eguchi *et al.*, 1962). Alternatively, the rhabdomeres may sometimes be isolated from each other and

114

the retinular cells arranged round a central wide extracellular space. This situation has been described in electron micrographs of the water bug *Notonecta* (Ludtke, 1957), the fruit fly *Drosophila* (Waddington and Perry, 1960), the flies *Sarcophaga* and *Lucilia* (Trujillo-Cenóz, 1965a and b), and is illustrated here (Plate 41) in an ommatidium of the blowfly *Calliphora*. As was first described in the allied genus *Musca* by Fernández-Morán (1958), six similar retinular cells are present, accompanied by a much narrower seventh cell, each bearing a rhabdomere of microvilli linked to the cell surface by very short slender stalks. The cavity between the sense cells contains granular material, aggregated into a crescent over each rhabdomere profile. Throughout the retina of these insects, the orientation of the rhabdomere microvilli is repeated constantly from one ommatidium to the next, and within each of these groups of sensory cells, the microvilli of opposite rhabdomeres parallel each other.

In the insect eye, as in other photoreceptors, light energy incident on the sensory neurones or on some specialised part of them is transduced into an electrical signal— the common currency of nervous integration—which is conveyed to the central nervous system. The nature of the transducing mechanism here, and in sensory cells adapted to be triggered into activity by other stimuli, such as mechanical displacement or molecules perceived by taste and smell, remains the greatest general problem in sensory physiology. It is well known that, in vertebrate and many invertebrate eyes, an essential step in the activation of photoreceptors is the absorption of light energy by molecules of visual pigments (of which the most widespread is rhodopsin, a conjugated retinene or vitamin A_1 aldehyde-protein), but an understanding of the photochemistry involved has not yet disclosed the secret of sensory activation. Goldsmith (1964) has reviewed the chemical evidence in insects and this, though very incomplete, suggests that the compound eye contains similar visual pigments. As Goldsmith (1964) points out, the supposition that the rhabdom of the insect ommatidium bears the visual pigment and acts as the site of photoreception is attractive, but as yet unproven. There is a striking morphological similarity between the parallel microvilli of the rhabdomeres, for example, and the stacked membranes of the outer segment of the rods of the vertebrate retina, known to contain rhodopsin. Furthermore, the rhabdom appears to be well placed to receive and contain light passed back from the dioptric system. An additional interesting piece of evidence pointing in the same direction is that in the developing pupa of the silkworm *Bombyx*, the first detectable retinal action potentials as a response to light stimulation, involving depolarisation of the retinular cell membranes, coincides with the first appearance of rhabdomere microvilli along the cell membranes, and that as the microvilli differentiate further, so the retinal response increases in amplitude.

The electron microscope has told us a good deal about the construction of the omma-tidia of the compound eye, but the most important questions concerning the detailed mode of function of the groups of sensory cells await a final answer. According to Exner's mosaic theory of vision in these eyes, each ommatidium is stimulated by light entering it from its own discrete visual field. Rays entering the eye obliquely were believed to be absorbed by the pigment cells surrounding the retinular cells, except in the case of superposition eyes in which distal migration of pigment occurring in con-ditions of low light intensity supposedly permitted convergence of light entering the dioptric systems of several ommatidia upon the rhabdom of a single group of sense cells. As has been pointed out by Goldsmith (1964) in an extensive review on insect vision, recent work has suggested that the mechanism of perception in the compound eye may be a good deal more complex than was earlier supposed. The visual fields of adjoining ommatidia in fact overlap extensively, and yet this overlap may still permit angular resolution as small as, or even smaller than, the interommatidial angle. Furthermore, the postulated formation of superposition images at the level of the layer of sense cells, as a device for increasing the sensitivity of the eye at the cost of reduced resolution, has been called into question, as also has the existence of lens cylinder optics in the corneal lens and crystalline cone.

In the vertebrate retina, the photoreceptor structures are highly modified portions of single cells; the distal segments of the rod and cone cells. In the insect eye, the morphological unit is a group of cells each contributing to the common rhabdom or presumed receptor structure. It has been generally assumed that the ommatidium of the compound eye acts as the functional unit of perception, but the possibility that each retinular cell may be capable of responding individually to light cannot yet be discounted. This and other questions, including the perception of polarised light, colour vision, and the central nervous integration of signals initiated in the sensory cells of the compound eye, are discussed by Goldsmith.

Problems enough remain at the level of the primary sense cells of the compound eye. These are, however, greatly compounded when we seek to follow the way in which these cells are related to the ranks of underlying neurones within the optic lobes of the brain, which, as Cajal and Sánchez showed in their delicate silver-impregnated preparations (1915), contain synaptic areas of great complexity. At the base of the retina, the retinular cells of each ommatidium stay together as a group, but lose the rhabdomere microvilli before passing out of the eye through a connective tissue sheath containing a mat of collagen fibrils (Plate 42). Some interesting features of the first synaptic field have, however, been displayed by Trujillo-Cenóz (1965) in his work on the fine structure of dipteran eyes. In *Sarcophaga* and *Lucilia*, an additional retinular cell is added to the group of seven forming most of the ommatidium (cf. Plate 41) and as in the cockroach clusters of eight axons leave the base of the eye. Reassortment soon occurs, and the first neuropile contains cylindrical 'optic cartridges' each consisting of two large central fibres surrounded by six retinular axons. The former are axons of second-order neurones which, as Trujillo-Cenóz has shown, receive the converging information from their crown of photoreceptor terminals. To add to the complexity of the picture, each of the six photoreceptor axons of the cartridge is contacted by two fibres presynaptic with respect to them and perhaps representing the terminal branches of centrifugal fibres whose cell bodies lie in the deeper regions of the brain. In any analysis of the anatomy of the nervous system, the light microscope is essential for an understanding of the distribution and interrelationships of the constituent neurones, while the value of the electron microscope lies in its ability to show us how these are fitted together to forge synaptic links. While we have travelled only a short distance along the maze of nerve cells directly or indirectly associated with insect vision, both the light and the electron microscope have shown us something of the complexity of cellular patterns upon which this sense is based.

OTHER SENSORY RECEPTORS

The adaptation of peripheral sensory mechanisms to the cuticle-bearing surface of the insect body is well illustrated by the chemoreceptors present on the antennae, palps, mouth-parts and tarsi. These sense organs vary considerably in their morphology, but all share a common requirement: whether they are excited by airborne molecules or substances in solution (serving respectively the senses of smell and taste), provision must be made for the access of these molecules to the sensory cells, through the impermeable cuticle. Electron microscopic studies on a variety of these organs, and particularly on the antennal olfactory sensilla, have indicated that this requirement is met by a common device. Each sensillum generally involves a hair- or peg-like extension of the cuticle, into which pass the distal processes or dendrites of a group of bipolar sensory neurones or fine filamentous branches derived from them. The sensillum may possess an apical pore beneath which lie the ends of these processes, or frequently the cuticle over the sensillum is pierced by many minute pores with diameters in the range of 100–1000 Å, closely associated with the distal processes or their delicate branches. In each instance, that is to say, a direct channel is provided through which molecules may pass unhindered from the exterior to the surface of the receptor cells. A selection of the numerous papers on the fine structure of these interesting members of the insect sensory system is listed below.

The insect body contains a variety of sensory receptors triggered by mechanical stress. The simplest of these are the tactile sensilla, which comprise a projecting articulated hair or spine to the base of which is attached the distal process of a bipolar sensory neurone. Thurm (1965) has described the fine structure of sensilla of this type in the honey bee, and has suggested that firing of the sense cell is initiated by compression or squeezing of the tip of the distal process or 'scolopoid body' occurring when the hair is moved in its socket. Finer hairs of this type may be sensitive to air currents, earthborne vibrations and also to low frequency sound waves. In some insects, however, elaborate auditory organs are present in which groups of receptors, termed chordotonal organs, are associated with a delicate cuticular tympanum. Gray (1960) has described the electron microscopic structure of these cells from the abdominal auditory organ of the locust, and has shown that their distal process includes a cilium-like structure—a feature also shared by chemoreceptors and the sensory neurones of tactile hairs. Again, the nature of the transduction process in these organs is not known, but they are thought to detect displacement of the tympanum to which they are attached and to rely on amplitude modulation rather than frequency discrimination in the reception of a sound pattern.

REFERENCES

Compound Eye

CAJAL, S. R., and SÁNCHEZ, D. 1915. Contribución al conocimiento de los centros nerviosos de los insectos. *Trab. Lab. Invest. biol. Univ. Madr.*, **13**, 1–164.

EAKIN, R. M. 1965. Evolution of photoreceptors. *Cold Spring Harb. Symp. quant. Biol.*, **30**, 363–370.

*EGUCHI, E., NAKA, K.-I., and KUWABARA, M. 1962. The development of the rhabdom and the appearance of the electrical response in the insect eye. *J. gen. Physiol.*, **46**, 143–157.

EXNER, S. 1891. *Die Physiologie der facettierten Augen von Krebsen und Insecten.* Franz Deuticke, Vienna.

*FERNÁNDEZ-MORÁN, H. 1958. Fine structure of the light receptors in the compound eyes of insects. *Expl Cell Res.*, **5**, suppl., 586–644.

*GOLDSMITH, T. H. 1962. Fine structure of the retinulae in the compound eye of the honey-bee. *J. Cell Biol.*, **14**, 489–494.

*GOLDSMITH, T. H. 1964. The visual system of insects. In *The Physiology of Insecta* (M. Rockstein, ed.), Vol. 1, pp. 397–462. Academic Press, New York and London.

*HORRIDGE, G. A., and BARNARD, P. B. T. 1965. Movement of palisade in locust retinula cells when illuminated. *Q. Jl microsc. Sci.*, **106**, 131–135.

LÜDTKE, H. 1957. Beziehungen des Feinbaues im Rückenschwimmeraüge zu seiner Fähigkeit, polarisiertes Licht zu analysieren. *Z. vergl. Physiol.*, **40**, 329–344.

MILLER, W. H. 1960. Visual photoreceptor structures. In *The Cell* (J. Brachet and A. E. Mirsky, eds.), Vol. 4, pp. 325–364. Academic Press, New York and London.

*SHOUP, J. R. 1966. The development of pigment granules in the eyes of wild type and mutant *Drosophila melanogaster*. *J. Cell Biol.*, **29**, 223–249.

*TRUJILLO-CENÓZ, O. 1965a. Some aspects of the structural organization of the arthropod eye. *Cold Spring Harb. Symp. quant. Biol.*, **30**, 371–382.

*TRUJILLO-CENÓZ, O. 1965b. Some aspects of the structural organization of the intermediate retina of dipterans. *J. Ultrastruct. Res.*, **13**, 1–33.

*WADDINGTON, C. H., and PERRY, M. M. 1960. The ultra-structure of the developing eye of *Drosophila*. *Proc. R. Soc. B*, **153**, 155–178.

Chemoreceptors

*ADAMS, J. R., HOLBERT, P. E., and FORGASH, A. J. 1965. Electron microscopy of the contact chemoreceptors of the stable fly, *Stomoxys calcitrans* (Diptera: Muscidae). *Ann. ent. Soc. Am.*, **58**, 909–917.

*DETHIER, V. G., LARSEN, J. R., and ADAMS, J. R. 1963. The fine structure of the olfactory receptors of the blowfly. In *Olfaction and Taste, Proceedings of the First International Symposium*, Wenner-Gren Institute, Stockholm (Y. Zotterman, ed.). Pergamon Press, Oxford.

HODGSON, E. S. 1964. Chemoreception. In *The Physiology of Insecta* (M. Rockstein, ed.), Vol. 1, pp. 363–396. Academic Press, New York and London.

*SLIFER, E. H., and SEKHON, S. S. 1961. Fine structure of the sense organs on the antennal flagellum of the honey bee, *Apis mellifera* Linnaeus. *J. Morph.*, **109**, 351–381.

*SLIFER, E. H., and SEKHON, S. S. 1963. Sense organs on the antennal flagellum of the small milkweed bug, *Lygaeus kalmii* Stal (Hemiptera, Lygaeidae). *J. Morph.*, **112**, 165–193.

*SLIFER, E. H., and SEKHON, S. S. 1964. Fine structure of the sense organs on the antennal flagellum of a flesh fly, *Sarcophaga argyrostoma* R.-D. (Diptera, Sarcophagidae). *J. Morph.*, **114**, 185–208.

*SLIFER, E. H., SEKHON, S. S., and LEES, A. D. 1964. The sense organs on the antennal flagellum of aphids (Homoptera), with special reference to the plate organs. *Q. Jl microsc. Sci.*, **105**, 21–29.

Mechanoreceptors

*GRAY, E. G. 1960. The fine structure of the insect ear. *Phil. Trans. R. Soc. B*, **243**, 75–94.

*THURM, U. 1965. An insect mechanoreceptor, Part I: Fine structure and adequate stimulus. *Cold Spring Harb. Symp. quant. Biol.*, **30**, 75–82.

Plates 36–42 ▷

Plate 36 ▷

A low-power electron micrograph of the compound eye of the
cockroach *Periplaneta americana*, passing through the ommatidia
transversely to their long axis. The plane of section lies close to the
base of the so-called crystalline cones [CC], each of which is built
up from four closely fitting segments, containing granular secreted
material (seen at higher magnification in Plate 39*A*). The distal ends
of the rhabdomeres [R] or microvilli springing from the retinular
sensory cells [Re] lap closely around the cones, and are flanked by
numerous pigment granules [P]. In the extracellular space between
the ommatidia lie pigment cells or 'iris cells' [PC] forming a sheath
around the sensory units; a relationship seen in longitudinal section
in Plate 40. At this level of the eye, the ommatidia comprise four
retinular cells, while proximally these increase in number to eight
(Plates 37 and 42).

(× 7000.)

(*Philips EM 200.*)

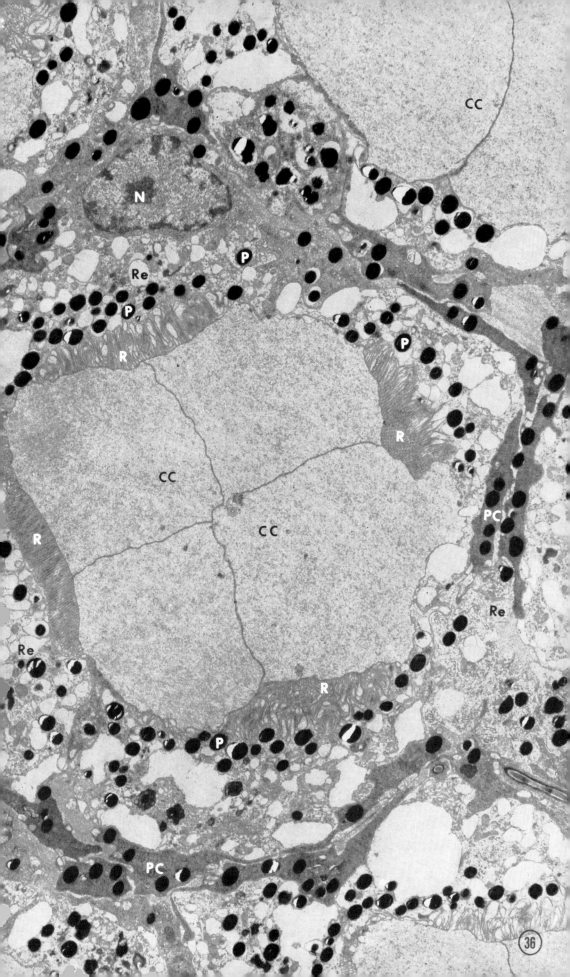

Plate 37 ▷

A section through the cockroach compound eye, similar to that
shown in Plate 36, but passing through the ommatidia beneath the
crystalline cones. At this level, each ommatidium consists of up to
eight close-knit primary sense cells [Re], the inner surfaces of which
meet to form a compact column of microvilli constituting the rhabdom
[R] believed to be the site of the photochemical reaction that triggers
the activity of the sensory cells. The microvilli are flanked by pigment
granules and cytoplasmic vacuoles [V] (cf. Plate 38). Retinular
nuclei are seen at N. The cylindrical groups of retinular cells are set
in an extracellular space [ES] in which lie slender processes of
pigment cells [PC] and tracheoles [Tr].

(× 5000.)

(*Philips EM 200.*)

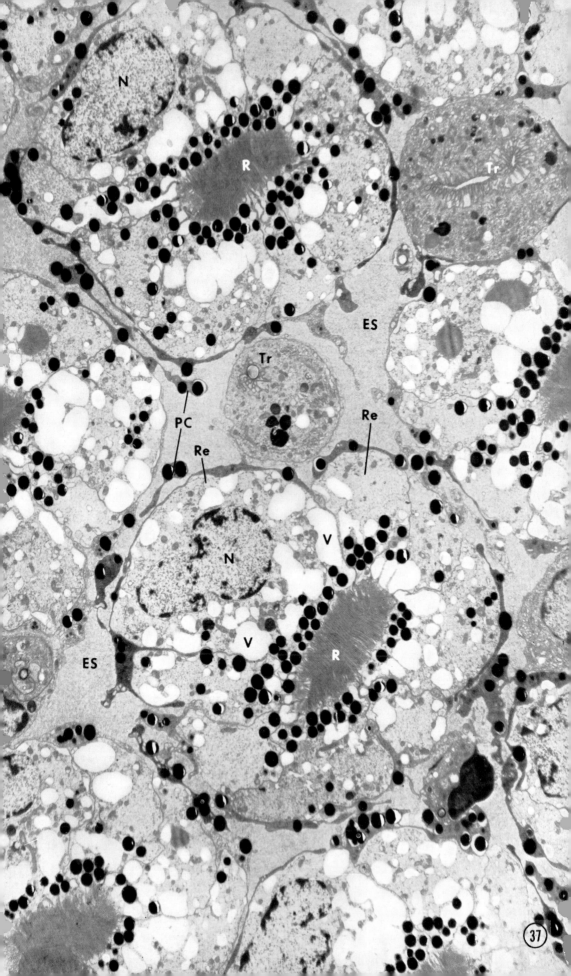

Plate 38 ▷

In the ommatidium of the compound eye of the cockroach, which is of the apposition type, the cylindrical group of retinular cells extends distally to impinge upon the crystalline cone, lying beneath the corneal lens. In the proximal portion of the eye of this insect, eight cells contribute to each ommatidium, and in the section illustrated here, portions of three of these are included [Re_1, Re_2, Re_3]. The nuclei of these sensory neurones [N] are often deeply constricted. The inner surface of each cell is regularly sculptured to produce ranks of microvilli, the closely apposed arrays of which form the rhabdom [R] running down the centre of the receptor complex. Close to the origin of these microvilli, the retinular cells are joined together by short desmosomes [D], and large vacuoles [V] and pigment granules [P] lie within the cytoplasm, particularly alongside the rhabdomeres. Elsewhere in the cytoplasm are scattered small mitochondria [M] and large numbers of tubular structures [Nt] which probably represent the neurotubules of these specialised sensory nerve cells. Each ommatidium is surrounded by extracellular space [ES] in which lie arborescent pigment cells containing granules [P′] similar in appearance to those within the retinular units.

($\times$ 20,000.)

(Philips EM 200.)

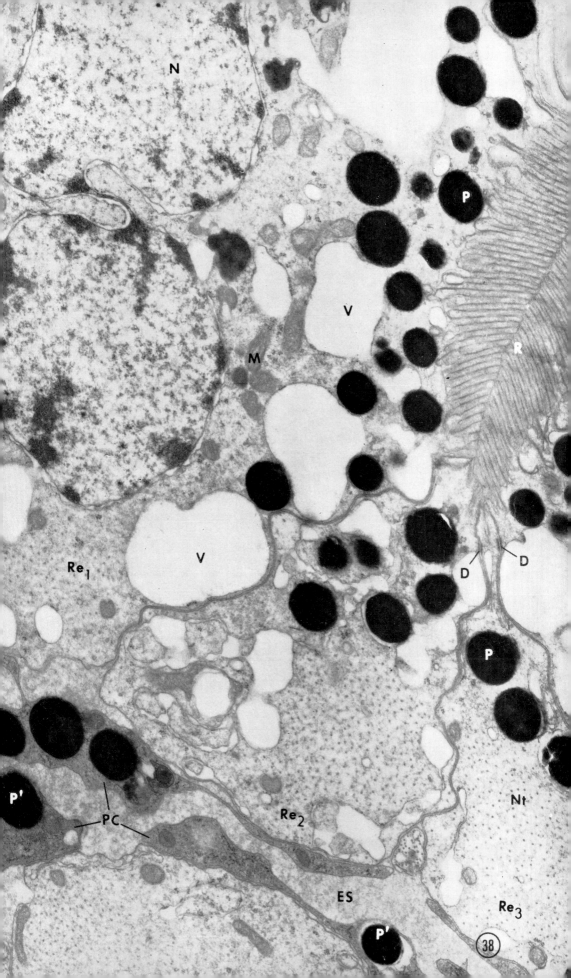

Plate 39 ▷

A. In an apposition eye such as that of the cockroach, the rhabdomeres of the retinular cells are very closely applied to the base of the crystalline cone. Light passed through the cone to the rhabdom is believed to activate a photochemical reaction with molecules of visual pigment associated with the membranes of the rhabdom microvilli, and in this way trigger firing of the cells. In this micrograph, the granular matrix of a segment of the cone [CC] is resolved, together with the aligned microvilli of a rhabdomere [R], the tips of which are separated from the limiting cell membrane of the cone (or Semper's) cells by a gap of only about 150 Å.

B. The regularity of the packing of rhabdomere microvilli is well illustrated when these are seen in transverse section. Each microvillus is polygonal in section, about 750 Å in width, and these prolongations of the cell membrane are compressed into an hexagonal array. Each contains one or more fine filaments, the function of which is not at present known.

(*A* : × 30,000. *B* : × 105,000.)

(*Philips EM 200.*)

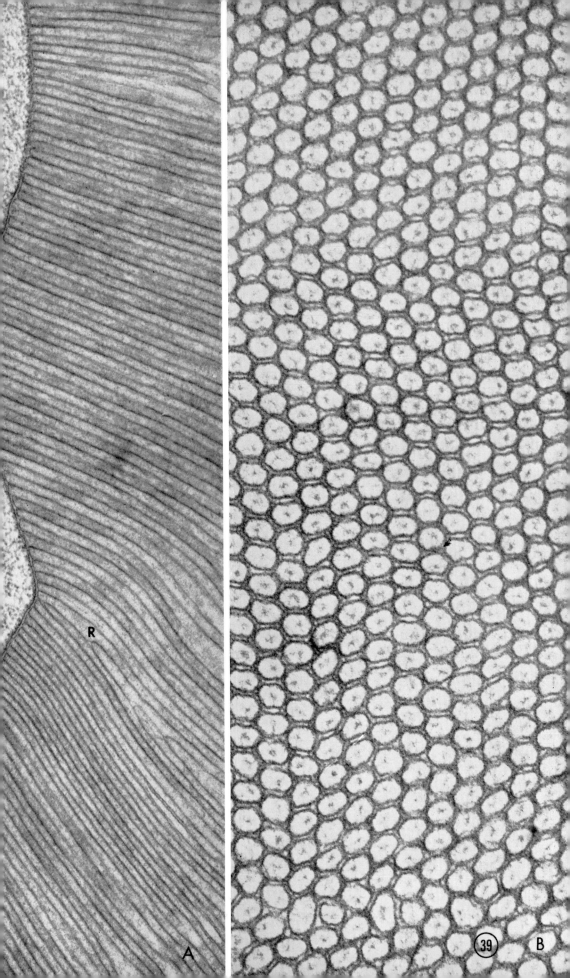

R

39   B

Plate 40 ▷

A longitudinal section through the retinula layer of the eye of the cockroach, perpendicular to that illustrated in Plate 37. Portions of three ommatidia are included in the field, and the tightly packed microvilli of the central rhabdoms [R], described in earlier light microscopic studies as refractile rods, are resolved, surrounded by the retinular cells [Re] from which they are produced. Pigment granules [P] are prominent in the cytoplasm of these cells, and a retinular nucleus is seen at the lower left [N]. These groups of primary sensory neurones are separated by extracellular spaces [ES] containing elongated pigment cells [PC] and their nuclei [N'].

(×9000.)

(*Philips EM 200.*)

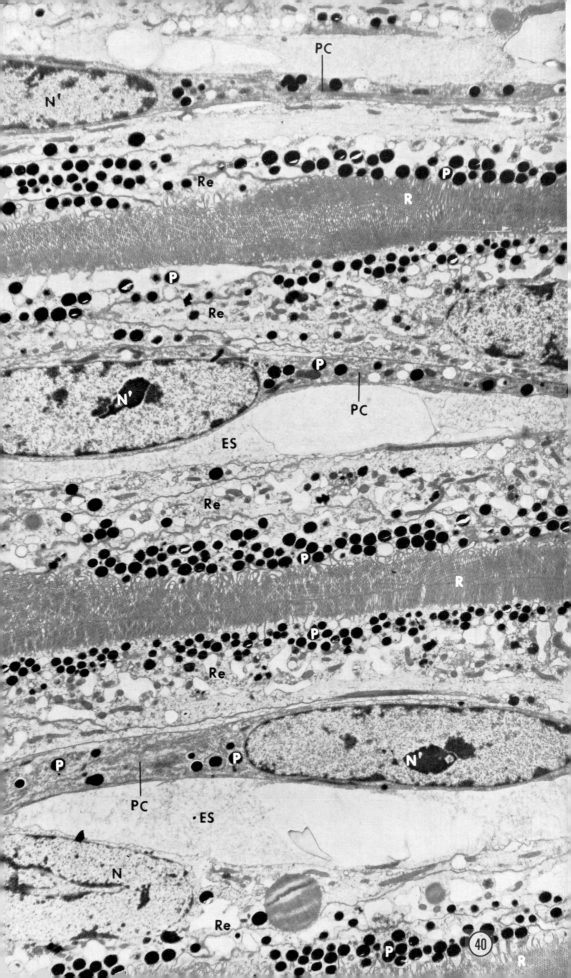

Plate 41 ▷

In most insects, including the cockroach (Plates 37–40), the rhabdomeres of each retinular cell meet to form a compact rhabdom. In the blowfly *Calliphora erythrocephala* and other Diptera the ommatidium is open in construction, with the rhabdomeres widely separated from each other. Each ommatidium in the blowfly, illustrated here in transverse section, comprises seven retinular cells [Re], six of similar size and a seventh smaller cell [Re']. The rhabdomeres [R] are built up, as usual, from ranks of closely packed tubular processes or microvilli borne on the inner surface of each sense cell, protruding into a wide intraommatidial space [*]. The microvilli display precise orientation: those of opposite retinular cells are arranged paralleling each other. The space between these cells contains a finely granular material, which appears to be aggregated close to the surface of each rhabdomere. The sense cells of the ommatidium are linked by short desmosomes [D]; except around their nucleus [N] they are slender and their cytoplasmic contents include mitochondria [M] and numerous pigment granules.

(× 15,000.)

(Philips EM 200.)

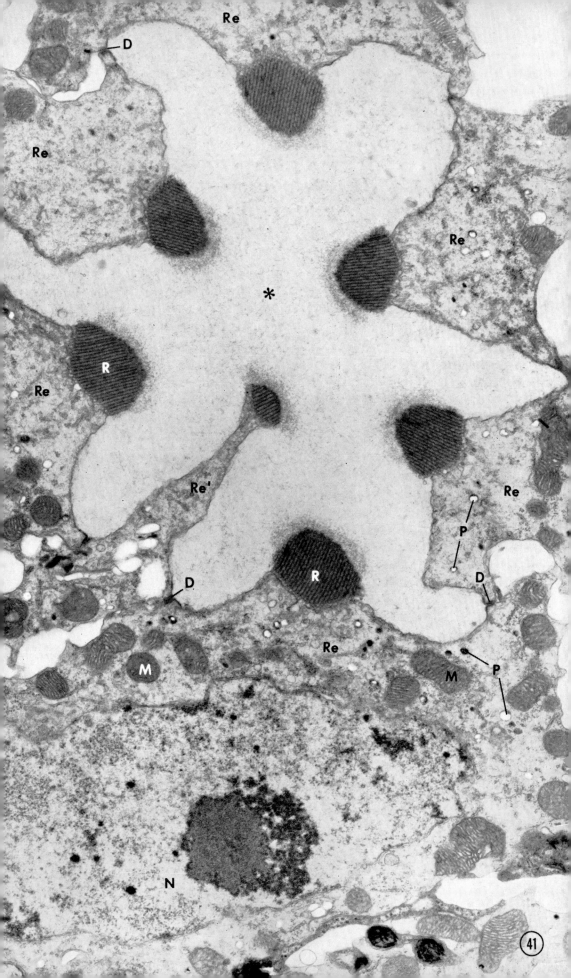

Plate 42 ▷

At the base of the retina, the retinular cells lose the rhabdomere
microvilli, and take on the form of more typical axons just before they
pass out of the eye. In this micrograph from the eye of the blowfly,
a group of eight such axons is seen in transverse section [arrow],
surrounded by a tenuous glial sheet, as it passes through the mat
of collagen fibrils [Co] limiting the proximal surface of the compound
eye. Upon leaving the eye, the primary sensory axons enter the
periopticon or first optic ganglion: the optic lobe of the brain
contains three ganglia, each associated with a neuropile within which
occur very complex series of synapses, integrating the information
initially supplied by the retinular cells.

(× 8000.)

(*Philips EM 200.*)

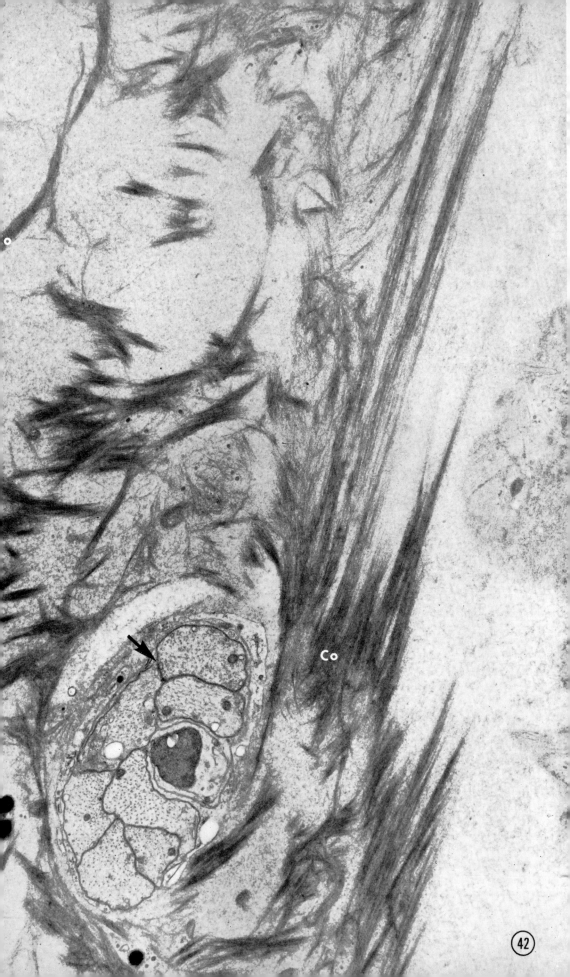

Co

42

The Tracheal System

Respiration in all animals involves the entry of oxygen into the body, its distribution to the sites of oxidative metabolism, and the elimination of carbon dioxide. Generally, these requirements are met by diffusion of respiratory gases across the surface of the body, by the provision of a blood system containing respiratory pigments, or by a combination of the two. In the great majority of insects, however, no respiratory pigment is present, diffusion of oxygen through the surface integument is quite insufficient to satisfy the needs of the animal, and air is brought directly to the tissues by the tracheal system—a complex set of tubules that ultimately open to the exterior of the body through spiracular apertures.

The main tracheal trunks arising from the spiracles are wide, and they branch repeatedly to form progressively smaller tubes which ultimately give rise to very slender tracheoles, less than one micron in diameter, which are generally intimately associated with the tissues of the body. The tracheal system is an inward extension of the body surface, and the respiratory tubes are lined with cuticle, surrounded by an epithelium continuous with the surface epidermis. This cellular sheath may be of considerable thickness around the larger trunks, but often becomes extremely thin in the finest tracheolar branches. Electron micrographs have proved helpful in clarifying the relationship between the cuticular tube and the cells that secrete and maintain it. Transverse sections of trunks and larger branches (Plate 43) show that the tube is often ringed by profiles of two or more epithelial cells, whereas smaller branches may be built up of a single column of cells. In the latter instance (Plate 44), the membrane surrounding the cuticular intima is confluent with the plasma membrane covering the outer surface of the tracheal cell via a 'mestracheon' in a way that seems to be morphologically analogous to the situation in peripheral nerve fibres (Plate 23) where the glial cell membrane encompasses an axon via the invaginated mesaxon fold. In these portions of the tracheal system, the cuticular intima is evidently an extracellular secretory product released across the plasma membrane. Tracheoles generally arise within tracheoblasts or 'tracheal end cells' from which fan out the terminal tendrils of the respiratory system. The tracheolar cuticle is ensheathed by a close-fitting membrane, as in tracheae, but this does not appear to be linked with the surface plasma membrane by a mestracheon (Plate 45). It is not entirely clear whether the tracheolar intima is secreted across a cylindrical invagination of the tracheoblast plasma membrane extending to the blindly ending tip of a tracheoblast process, or whether (Shafiq, 1963) it is laid down within a cylindrical cavity that is initially intracellular. While the cuticular lining of the tracheae is replaced at each moult, that of the tracheoles persists from one instar to the next.

The intercellular membranes of the epithelial cells surrounding larger tracheae, and the paired membranes of the mestracheon folds are linked by extensive septate desmosomes (Plate 43). The cytoplasm of these cells is generally not conspicuously specialised, in terms of its complement of intracellular membranes. In the epithelium enveloping the tracheae, scattered cisternae of the rough-surfaced endoplasmic reticulum are present, presumably taking part in the cyclic synthesis of protein incorporated into the cuticular tubes of successive instars. As in other very elongated cells, including spermatids (Plate 102), the glial sheath of peripheral nerves (Plate 25) and the epidermal prolongations into bristles projecting from the surface cuticle (Plate 5), microtubules are often found, running parallel with the long axis of the tracheal cells (Plate 43). Occasionally, substantial deposits of glycogen are found within the tracheal epithelium (Plate 44). The unusually elaborate tracheal end cells adjoining the photocytes in the luminescent organs of fireflies are equipped with great numbers of large mitochondria (Plate 46), although these organelles are generally sparsely distributed in tracheal cells.

The most striking structural feature of many tracheae, observed in the light microscope, is that the cuticular lining is thrown into a helical fold, often reinforced by a thread-like taenidium. In the seventeenth century, Malpighi found that it is possible to unwind the taenidium by pulling apart the halves of a broken length of trachea, and Harker (1960) used this thread for ligaturing fine nerves. Early electron micrographs of unsectioned tracheoles (Richards and Anderson, 1942a and 1942b; Richards and Korda, 1950; Souza Santos et al., 1954) showed that helical or sometimes annular taenidial folds, beyond the limit of resolution in the light microscope, extend right to the tips of these terminal respiratory processes. Furthermore, a study of thin sections of tracheae and tracheoles has made possible a detailed comparison between the fine structure of their cuticle and that of the outer integument (Locke, 1957, 1958, 1964, 1966; Edwards et al., 1958).

The lining of tracheae and tracheoles alike appears, in section, as a continuous opaque layer, about 200 Å or less in thickness (Plate 45). Locke (1966) has concluded that this delicate lining of the cuticular tube represents the lipoprotein cuticulin layer that forms the outer part of the epicuticle (p. 3) elsewhere in the body. It occurs, for example, over the surface cuticular plates or sclerites, over diaphanous intersegmental membranes, over cuticular hairs and bristles, along the cuticular invaginations lining the fore- and hind-gut (Plates 71 and 87) and secretory ducts leading to the body surface (Plate 117). Locke has shown in high resolution electron micrographs that the cuticulin layer contains three dense laminae, the outermost of which perhaps corresponds to a lipid monolayer, and has tentatively suggested that the orderliness of molecular structure within this extracellular layer may prove to be comparable with that of the thinner plasma membrane.

The cuticulin defines the contours of the taenidial folds throughout the tracheal and tracheolar system, and Locke has proposed that this folding results from the operation of simple physical forces during the secretion of cuticulin by the epidermal cells, rather than from a cellular sculpturing feat. Cuticulin is secreted inside the lining due to be moulted in tracheae, or into a tubular lumen extending along a tracheoblast cell process in the case of developing tracheoles. In each instance, it is thought that patches of cuticulin grow in area until they coalesce into a cylinder which then, as more cuticulin is added, buckles to produce the characteristic helical or annular folds (Plate 47). On this model, the diameter of the initial tube is an important parameter in determining the frequency of buckling (Locke, 1958), and the close spacing of the folds in small tracheoles and their wider spacing in larger tracheae, observed in thin sections, was shown to accord with the 'expansion and buckling' hypothesis. The cell membrane across which the cuticulin is released does not follow the taenidial folds, and into these folds where the cuticulin is separated from the surface of the epidermal cell, in tracheae and perhaps some larger tracheoles, is secreted the substance of the taenidial thread. This contains chitin and protein, as in the surface endocuticle (perhaps sometimes partially tanned as in 'exocuticle') (p. 2), and the chitin is apparently oriented in fibrils running longitudinally along the thread (i.e. tangentially with respect to the tracheal tube), providing a strengthening mechanism that resists radial compression and collapse. Contrary to earlier interpretations of histological preparations, a continuous sheet of endocuticle beneath the taenidial folds is not of general occurrence, and is present only in the stoutest tracheal trunks of some species. In a study of the fine structure of tracheae and tracheoles associated with the silk moth prothoracic gland, Beaulaton (1964) found that the larger trunks possess, in addition to the taenidial thread, other cuticular structures including a continuous layer of endocuticle. In most tracheoles, even the taenidial thread is absent (Plate 45), and the lining consists solely of the folded cuticulin cylinder. For more detailed accounts of the structure, growth and development of the tracheal system, the reader is referred to the recent reviews on the integument (Locke, 1964) and aerial gas transport (Miller, 1964) in insects.

While some oxygen may pass across the intima and cellular sheath of the tracheae and thence to the tissues via the general haemolymph, by far the greater part of oxygen transfer is thought to take place from the thin-walled tracheoles which are distributed throughout the body in a way that minimises the diffusion distance between them and the respiring cells. The tracheal supply to different tissues is not uniformly profuse, but appears to be commensurate with their varying rates of oxidative metabolism. Moreover, electron micrographs have shown that while tracheoles are generally closely associated with the cells they serve, this juxtaposition is in some tissues more intimate than in others. Frequently, the tracheoblasts and their slender extensions form a meshwork outside the basal surface of epithelia, providing a type of connective tissue within which the basement membranes of the tracheoblasts may coalesce with those of muscle and nerve fibres to produce an irregular fenestrated sheet, sometimes termed the 'peritoneal membrane'. Tracheoles are abundant in this position around the ovarioles and testes, the mid-gut, salivary glands (Plates 48, 72, etc.) and elsewhere. These are merely cited as examples of tracheolar distribution, and of course every tissue in the body receives its share of the respiratory supply, illustrated in many papers on the fine structure of insect cells.

The relationship between tracheoles and the cells they supply may be so close, as in the fat body, luminescent organs and flight muscles, that 'intracellular' tracheolar endings have often been described in light microscopic studies. The electron microscope has shown, however, that while tracheoles may be tightly inserted between adjacent cells or may indent them as a finger is pushed into a balloon, the intima is always surrounded by a tracheoblast cellular sheath, albeit very attenuated, and that the plasma membrane limiting this sheath is separated by a narrow extracellular gap from that of the tracheated cell. In the richly tracheated luminescent organs of lampyrid fireflies, for example, regularly spaced tracheoles pass between the columnar photocytes and throughout their course (Plate 46) are flanked by concentrations of photocyte mitochondria placed to receive oxygen across the minimum diffusion distance (Beams and Anderson, 1955; Kluss, 1958; Smith, 1963). Other instances of very intimate tracheation are illustrated in micrographs of the corpus allatum (Plate 35) and anal papilla

(Plate 98). Muscle fibres throughout the body are invested with tracheoles: the tracheoblasts incorporated into the 'peritoneal membrane' of the gut and other organs presumably serve the visceral muscles, when present, as well as the underlying epithelial cells (Plate 48). Tracheoles approach the surface of the muscular heart (Plate 56) and lie closely alongside intersegmental (Plate 21) and other skeletal fibres. The tracheal supply to flight muscles, which during activity consume oxygen at an enormously high rate, is especially elaborate and often includes thin-walled tracheal air sacs, ventilated by thoracic or abdominal movements (Refs. in Miller, 1964). This ventilation aids the exchange of respiratory gases between the tracheae and the atmosphere, but as usual oxygen reaches the muscle fibres by diffusion through the smaller tracheae and, ultimately, the tracheoles. In dragonflies, tracheoles pass through the narrow extracellular spaces between the flight muscle fibres, and from the tracheoles oxygen must reach the large mitochondria which alternate with the lamellar fibrils (Plate 16) by diffusing along the radius of the fibre, a distance of about ten micra. In most other flight muscles, whether synchronous or asynchronous in their response to motor nerve impulses (p. 36), the muscle cell membrane is indented by invaginated tracheoles which pass between the fibrils and bring gaseous oxygen to within a few micra of even the most deeply situated mitochondria in fibres that sometimes reach a diameter of several hundred micra (Hodge, 1955; Edwards et al., 1958; Vogell et al., 1959; Smith, 1961, 1967; and others). This respiratory device is illustrated here in flight muscle of a wasp (Plate 18), and also in the sound-producing tymbal muscle of a cicada (Plate 14).

A number of aquatic insects have evolved a special respiratory device, a physical gill or 'plastron'—a 'gas film of constant volume and an extensive water-air interface . . . held in position by a system of hydrofuge structures' (Hinton, 1966a). Several of the remarkable cuticular modifications maintaining the plastron gas layer in Diptera have been examined by Hinton with the aid of the scanning electron microscope (Hinton, 1964, 1966a, 1966b, 1966c, 1967a). Analogous specialisations have also been detected in certain insect egg-shells (Plate 113B) (Hinton, 1962, 1967b).

Electron micrographs have revealed new details of the formation and fine structure of the regions of the tracheal system, and of their relationship with sites of respiratory activity in various types of cell. This information, however, does not reflect the intricacy of the physiological and physical bases of insect respiratory control. The regulation of gas exchange by spiracular movements and ventilatory mechanisms, the physical basis of oxygen and carbon dioxide transport in the gas phase and in solution, and the factors that may determine the distribution of tracheoles in different organs and tissues (reviewed by Miller, 1964, 1966) are all involved in the function of tracheal tubes in the insect body.

REFERENCES

*BEAMS, H. W., and ANDERSON, E. 1955. Light and electron microscope studies on the light organ of the firefly, Photinus pyralis. Biol. Bull., 109, 375–393.

BEAULATON, J. 1964. Les ultrastructures des trachées et de leurs ramifications dans la glande prothoracique du ver à soie tussor (Antheraea pernyi Guér. Lépidoptère, Attacidae). J. Micr., 3, 91–104.

*EDWARDS, G. A., RUSKA, H., and DE HARVEN, E. 1958. The fine structure of insect tracheoblasts, tracheae and tracheoles. Archs Biol., 69, 351–369,

HARKER, J. E. 1960. Endocrine and nervous factors in insect circadian rhythms. Cold Spring Harb. Symp. quant. Biol., 25, 279–287.

*HINTON, H. E. 1962. The fine structure and biology of the egg-shell of the wheat bulb fly, *Leptohylemyia coarctata. Q. Jl microsc. Sci.*, **103**, 243–251.

*HINTON, H. E. 1964. The respiratory efficiency of the spiracular gill of *Simulium. J. Insect Physiol.*, **10**, 73–80.

*HINTON, H. E. 1966a. Plastron respiration in marine insects. *Nature, Lond.*, **209**, 220–221.

*HINTON, H. E. 1966b. Structure of the plastron in *Lipsothrix*, and the polyphyletic origin of plastron respiration in Tipulidae. *Proc. R. ent. Soc. Lond.* A, **42**, 35–38.

*HINTON, H. E. 1966c. The spiracular gill of the fly, *Antocha bifida*, as seen with the scanning electron microscope. *Proc. R. ent. Soc. Lond.* A, **42**, 107–115.

*HINTON, H. E. 1967a. Plastron respiration in the marine fly *Canace. J. mar. biol. Ass. U.K.*, **47**, 319–327.

*HINTON, H. E. 1967b. The respiratory system of the egg-shell of the common housefly. *J. Insect Physiol.*, **13**, 647–651.

*HODGE, A. J. 1955. Studies on the structure of muscle. III. Phase contrast and electron microscopy of dipteran flight muscle. *J. biophys. biochem. Cytol.*, **1**, 361–380.

*KLUSS, B. C. 1958. Light and electron microscope observations on the photogenic organ of the firefly, *Photuris pennsylvanica*, with special reference to the innervation. *J. Morph.*, **103**, 159–185.

*LOCKE, M. J. 1957. The structure of insect tracheae. *Q. Jl microsc. Sci.*, **98**, 487–492.

*LOCKE, M. J. 1958. The formation of tracheae and tracheoles in *Rhodnius prolixus. Q. Jl microsc. Sci.*, **99**, 29–46.

*LOCKE, M. J. 1964. The structure and formation of the integument in insects. In *The Physiology of Insecta* (M. Rockstein, ed.), Vol. 3, pp. 379–470. Academic Press, New York and London.

*LOCKE, M. J. 1966. The structure and formation of the cuticulin layer in the epicuticle of an insect, *Calpodes ethlius* (Lepidoptera, Hesperiidae). *J. Morph.*, **118**, 461–494.

MILLER, P. L. 1964. Respiration—aerial gas transport. In *The Physiology of Insecta* (M. Rockstein, ed.), Vol. 3, pp. 557–615. Academic Press, New York and London.

MILLER, P. L. 1966. The regulation of breathing in insects. In *Advances in Insect Physiology* (J. W. L. Beament, J. E. Treherne and V. B. Wigglesworth, eds.), Vol. 3, pp. 279–354. Academic Press, New York and London.

*RICHARDS, A. G., and ANDERSON, T. F. 1942a. Electron micrographs of insect tracheae. *Jl N.Y. ent. Soc.*, **50**, 147–167.

*RICHARDS, A. G., and ANDERSON, T. F. 1942b. Further electron microscope studies on arthropod tracheae. *Jl N.Y. ent. Soc.*, **50**, 245–247.

*RICHARDS, A. G., and KORDA, F. H. 1950. Studies on arthropod cuticle. IV. An electron microscope survey of the intima of arthropod tracheae. *Ann. ent. Soc. Am.*, **43**, 49–71.

*SANTOS, H. L. S., EDWARDS, G. A., SANTOS, P. S., and SAWAYA, P. 1954. Electron microscopy of insect tracheal structures. *Anais Acad. bras. Cienc.*, **26**, 309–315.

*SHAFIQ, S. A. 1963. Electron microscopy of the development of tracheoles in *Drosophila melanogaster. Q. Jl microsc. Sci.*, **104**, 135–140.

*SMITH, D. S. 1961. The structure of insect fibrillar flight muscle. A study made with special reference to the membrane systems of the fiber. *J. biophys. biochem. Cytol.*, **10**, suppl., 123–158.

*SMITH, D. S. 1963. The organization and innervation of the luminescent organ in a firefly, *Photuris pennsylvanica* (Coleoptera). *J. Cell Biol.*, **16**, 323–359.

*SMITH, D. S. 1967. Structural features associated with gas and metabolite transfer in the insect. (A brief comparison with the vertebrate body.) In *Physical Bases of Circulatory Transport: Regulation and Exchange* (E. B. Reeve and A. C. Guyton, eds.), pp. 277–298. W. B. Saunders, Philadelphia and London.

*VOGELL, W., BISHAI, F. R., BÜCHER, T., KLINGENBERG, M., PETTE, D., and ZEBE, E. 1959. Über strukturelle und enzymatische Muster in Muskeln von *Locusta migratoria. Biochem. Z.*, **332**, 81–117.

Plates 43–48 ▷

Plate 43 ▷

This micrograph illustrates a cluster of tracheal tubes, supplying oxygen to the salivary gland of the milkweed bug *Oncopeltus fasciatus*. Transverse sections of five tracheoles [Tr] and a trachea [TR] are included. The tracheolar lining is smooth, but that of the trachea bears small tubercles [short arrows] and an oblique view of the helically running taenidial fold [long arrow]. At least two epithelial cells encompass this trachea, and the intercellular membranes of these are linked by simple [D] and septate desmosomes [SD], while each of the tracheolar tubes lies in its own sheath drawn out from a tracheoblast or tracheal end cell. The cytoplasm contains short cisternae of the ribosome-studded endoplasmic reticulum [ER], small mitochondria [M] and numerous microtubules oriented parallel with the cuticular tubes [Mt], and the cells are contained within a prominent basement membrane [BM]. On the right lies the edge of a large tracheal trunk [TR'] seen in longitudinal section; a taenidial fold is included, containing a strengthening 'thread' [*] consisting of chitin and protein, while adjoining it the intertaenidial cuticle is, as in the smaller trachea in the centre of the field, produced into tubercles.

($\times$ 55,000.)

(*Philips EM 200. Micrograph produced in collaboration with Miss J. Ross.*)

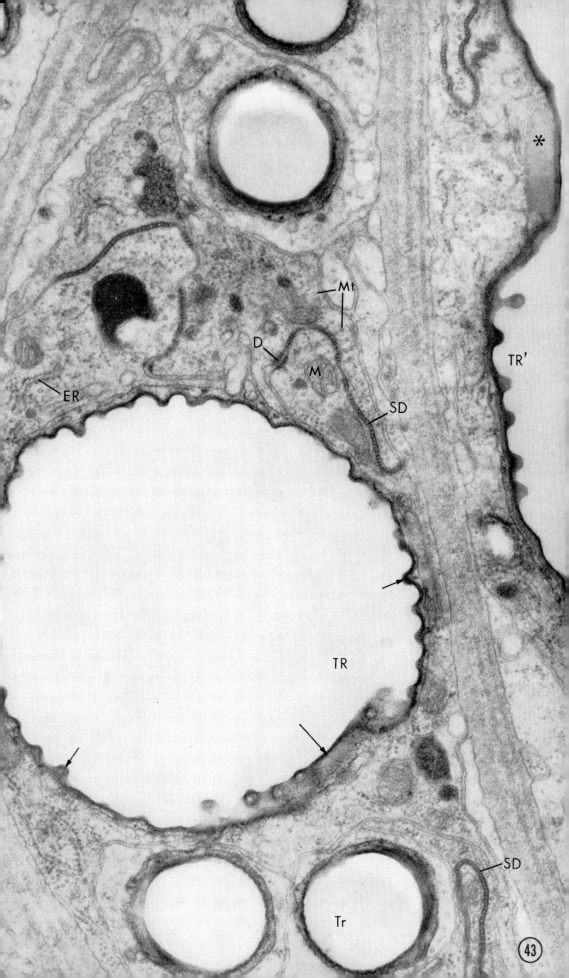

43

Plate 44 ▷

The relative richness or paucity of the tracheal supply to insect tissues and organs appears to be related to their varying rates of oxidative metabolism. The flashing of adult lampyrid fireflies requires oxygen both as a direct participant in the photochemical reaction and for the production of ATP by oxidative phosphorylation, taking place in the mitochondria. Consequently, the light organs receive a profuse and elaborate tracheal supply. The photocytes are supplied by regularly disposed tracheoles, linked with large complex tracheal end cells (Plate 46) which in turn stem from groups of tracheal twigs entering the 'lantern' from the body cavity. Part of one such group of tracheae is included in this micrograph, in transverse section. The cuticular intima or lining of the tracheae, enclosing the gas-filled lumen [TR] is encompassed by cells of the tracheal epithelium, continuous with the surface epidermis. Profiles of the nuclei of these cells are seen at N. The tracheal intima, though contained within the epithelial cells, is an extracellular product (as is the cuticle of the body surface), and is secreted within a cylindrical invagination of the tracheal cell surface plasma membrane, continuous with the cell surface via a folded 'mestracheon' [Mtr], morphologically comparable with the glial 'mesaxon' of a peripheral nerve (Plate 23). The plasma membrane invaginations of the mestracheons separate to enclose the tracheal tubes as a pleated membranous cylinder, closely associated with large mitochondria [M]—a feature that becomes spectacular in the tracheal end cells (Plate 46). The epithelial cells of these light organ tracheae also contain prominent deposits of glycogen, identified in electron micrographs as clusters of electron-opaque granules [Gy]. The tracheal twigs supplying the firefly light organ lie in cylindrical gaps between the photocytes, and in life the extracellular spaces between them [ES] are filled with haemolymph.

(× 15,000.)

(*Philips EM 200.*)

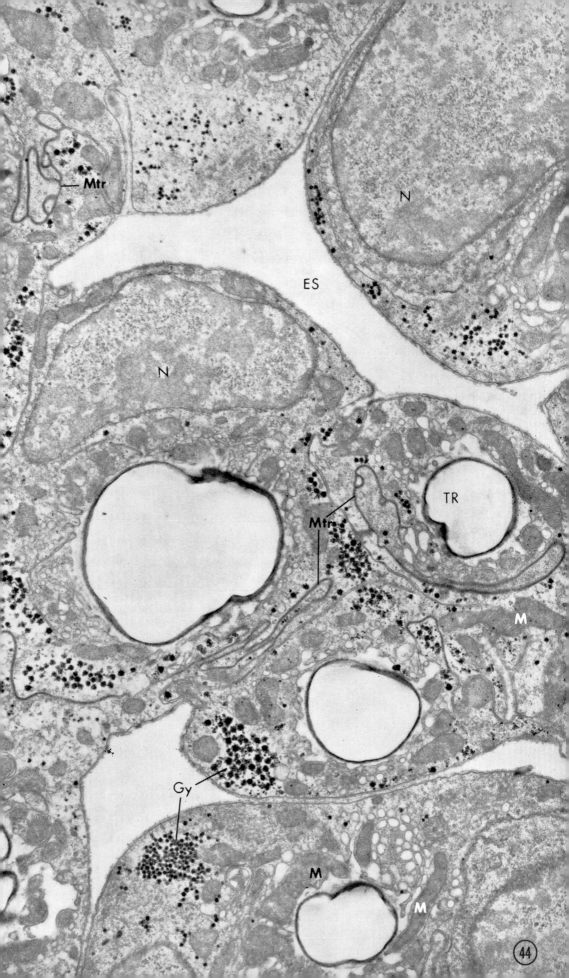

Plate 45 ▷

In most insect tissues, the tracheoles pass close by the surface of the
cells they supply with oxygen, and are only invaginated into cells
which have the most demanding respiratory requirements (e.g. flight
and tymbal muscles; Plates 14 and 18). The mid-gut and other tissues
lying in the body cavity receive a rich meshwork of fine tracheolar
processes, which are spread over the basal surface of the epithelia
where they are sometimes accompanied by visceral muscle fibres.
On the left of this field (from a section of the mid-gut of the larval
flour moth *Ephestia kühniella*), is seen the basal region of an
epithelial cell, containing many extracellular canals formed by
irregular invaginations of the plasma membrane [*]. Immediately
outside the cell lies the basement membrane [BM] including
close-packed fibrils. The tracheoles reaching the surface of the gut
and other tissues of the body are very slender, but the cuticular lining
is always contained within a sheath of tracheoblast cytoplasm, seen
in this section at Cy. The tracheole in the centre of this field [Tr]
weaves in and out of the plane of section, and the membrane across
which the cuticular intima is secreted is indicated by an arrow. The
tracheole on the right of the field [Tr] is cut in longitudinal section,
and clearly illustrates the regularity of helical folding of the cuticulin
lining providing the strengthening taenidium. The basement membrane
of the tracheoblast extensions [BM'] may link up with that of visceral
muscle fibres (Plate 48) and of the tracheated epithelial cells to
provide a connective sheath or 'peritoneal membrane'.

($\times$35,000.)

(*Philips EM 200.*)

144

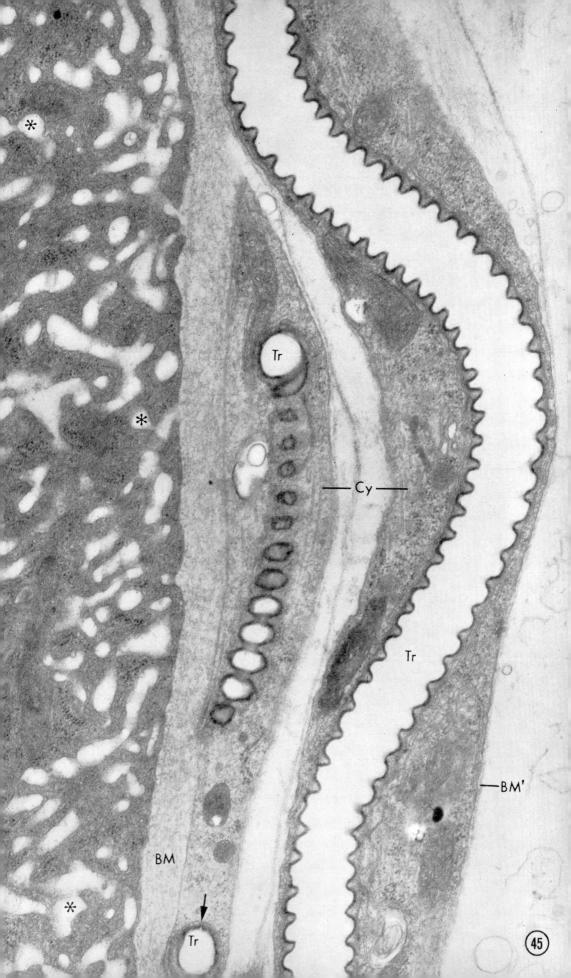

45

Plate 46 ▷

Although the best-known motor nerve endings in the insect body are those associated with muscle fibres, endings showing rather similar axoplasmic organisation have been identified in electron micrographs of luminescent organs, such as that of the firefly *Photuris pennsylvanica*, shown here. This organ is built up of large photocytes [1] containing many mitochondria [M] and conspicuous granules apparently involved in the synthesis of some component of the light-producing reaction, closely associated with specialised tracheal and tracheolar cells [2, 3] which are likewise abundantly supplied with mitochondria [M]. In this species, nerve terminals are tightly inserted between these last two cells [*], and their axoplasm contains both synaptic vesicles and opaque neurosecretory droplets.

(× 18,000.)

(Philips EM 200. From Smith (1963). Reproduced by courtesy of the Journal of Cell Biology.)

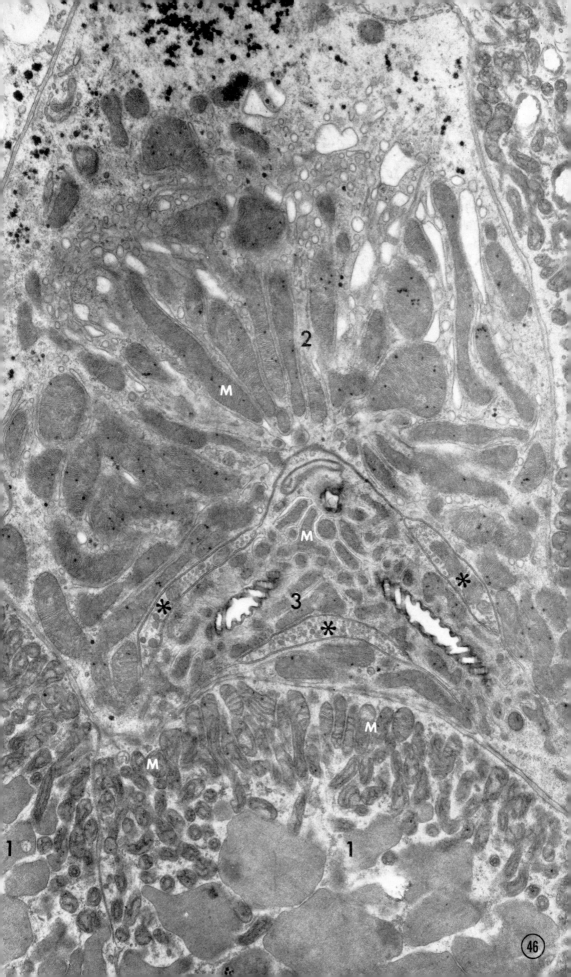

Plate 47 ▷

A micrograph that includes part of two intact tracheoles, prepared by the technique of negative staining. This technique has proved of great value in studying the macromolecular construction of viruses and protein crystals, and the structure of such subcellular entities as ribosomes, mitochondria and myofilaments. In this case, a suspension of homogenised blowfly flight muscle was mixed with a neutral one per cent solution of potassium phosphotungstate and placed on a supporting film on a specimen grid: most of the drop was withdrawn from the grid by touching it with filter paper, and the remaining fluid was allowed to dry.

The neutral heavy metal salt is not bound to or adsorbed upon the structures present in the original suspension, to produce positive contrast. Instead, it dries on and around the structures, revealing their form and sculpturing in negative contrast. In this micrograph the electron-opaque stain has outlined the collapsed tracheolar tubes, together with their helical taenidial folds which in this case appear to be double.

($\times$ 72,000.)

(*Philips EM 200. Specimen prepared by the author. From Miller (1966). Reproduced by courtesy of Dr P. L. Miller and Academic Press.*)

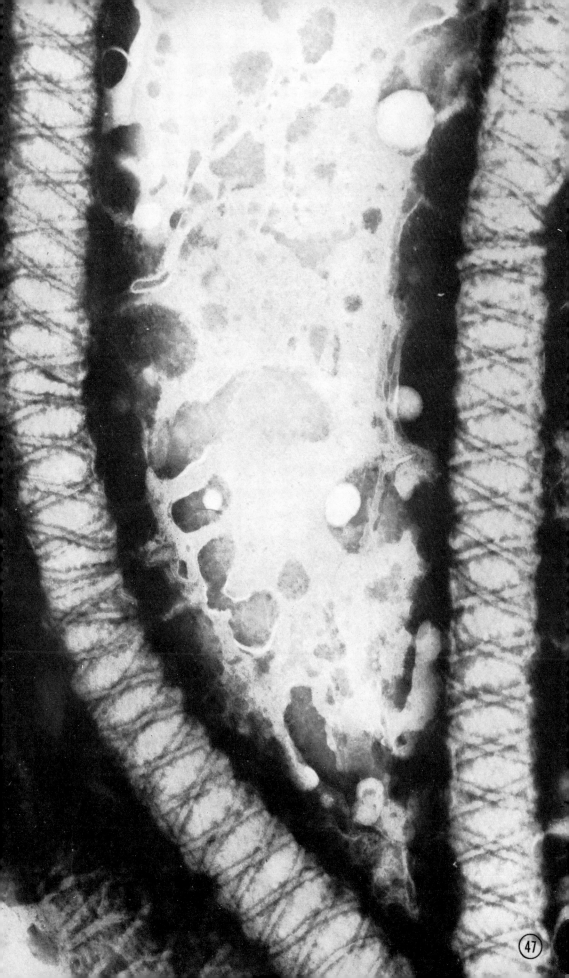

Plate 48 ▷

A micrograph illustrating the arrangement of tracheal cells and visceral muscle fibres around a salivary gland of the milkweed bug *Oncopeltus fasciatus*. The edge of the gland epithelium [Ep] and the adjoining basement membrane [BM] are included at lower left. Many small tracheoles [Tr], and two profiles of a trachea [TR] enmesh the epithelium: in all of these, the cuticular intima is helically folded to form the taenidium, but this feature is most clearly seen here in the lining of the trachea [Tn]. Between these processes of the respiratory system lie small muscle fibres [MF], in which the contractile material is not split up into separate fibrils. The muscles and tracheoles are knit together by sheets of extracellular material [*], probably representing their respective basement membranes, while the outermost of these sheets [BM'] separates the entire tracheal and muscular sheath from the haemolymph.

(× 9000.)

(Philips EM 200. Micrograph produced in collaboration with Miss Jean Ross.)

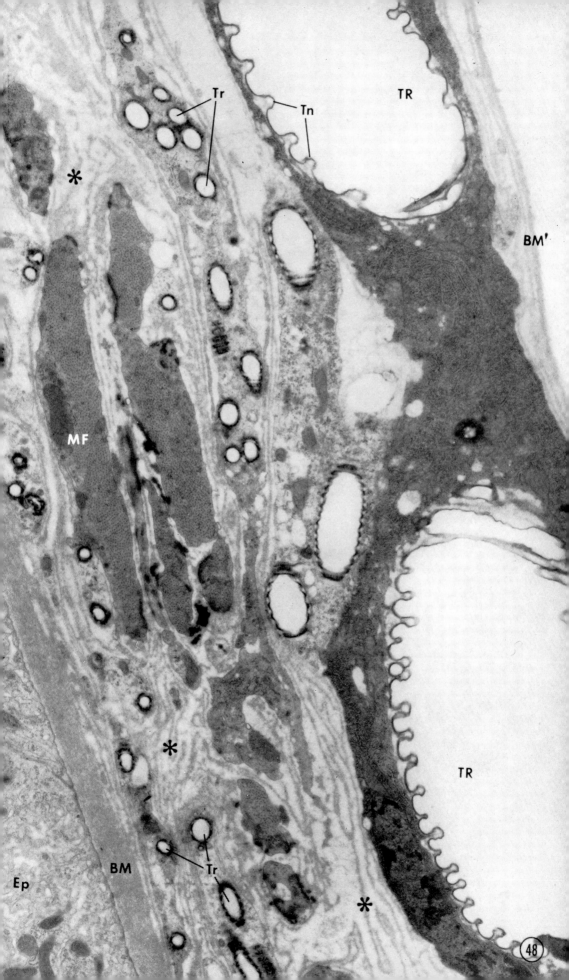

The Dorsal Vessel and Haemocytes

In the vertebrate body, the capillary circulatory system plays a vital role in the respiratory exchange between the blood and the tissues, and also in the absorptive and excretory functions of the intestinal and renal systems. In the insect, the dorsal vessel, responsible for the circulation of the haemolymph, plays little direct part in respiration since molecular oxygen is brought very close to the respiring cells throughout the body by the tracheae and their ultimate tracheolar branches. However, the haemolymph acts as a medium for the distribution of hormones and the exchange of metabolites between the tissues bathed by or contained within it. In addition, the haemolymph contains a variety of blood cells or haemocytes that include among their functions the cleansing of the circulated fluid from micro-organisms, parasites and solid particles including tissue fragments.

The circulation of the haemolymph is accomplished primarily by a dorsal muscular tube comprising a posterior 'heart' and an anterior 'aorta'. The haemolymph is aspirated into the heart through segmental valved pores or ostia during dilation, then passed forwards and out of the open aorta during contraction. The dorsal vessel is usually separated from the general body cavity by a connective tissue diaphragm or pericardial septum, and is often suspended from the dorsal surface of the body by connective filaments. Histological preparations together with electron micrographs (Edwards and Challice, 1960) showed that the muscle fibres making up the dorsal vessel possess striated fibrils, and that these fibrils may either be arranged in a circular fashion around the contractile tube, or may also include longitudinally arranged components. In the cockroach *Periplaneta americana*, the great majority of fibrils are circular and hence, when the heart is examined in transverse section as in Plate 56, are seen in longitudinal profile with the sarcomeres demarcated by Z bands. On the other hand, longitudinal sections of the wall of the heart (Plate 49) pass transversely through the irregular fibrils, which almost fill the muscle cell except in the nuclear region, which often includes a bulge of sarcoplasm. As in the vertebrate, these cardiac fibres must work unremittingly throughout life, and are likewise well supplied with mitochondria providing the contractile material with energy-rich molecules of ATP.

While the mechanics of haemolymph movement by the dorsal vessel—in via the ostia and out through the aorta—are simple, the contraction and relaxation of the muscular tube appears to be governed by a complex control system. The isolated heart, or even small segments of it, is able to maintain rhythmic beating, and in the intact animal this myogenic rhythm is modified in rate and amplitude by direct nervous control, and also by a factor released from the nearby pericardial cells (p. 172) when these are triggered by a hormone that is present within the corpora cardiaca (Refs. in Wigglesworth, 1965).

The electron microscope has proved very valuable in revealing some of the structural features that appear to be connected with the complex control of heart beat. Edwards and Challice (1960) described neurosecretory droplets in many of the axons that pass out of the corpora cardiaca and run alongside the heart in the lateral cardiac nerves, and in a more recent series of papers (Johnson and Bowers, 1963; Johnson, 1966; Bowers and Johnson, 1966), further important details have been added. It is now known, for example, that axons containing neurosecretory material (much or all of which probably originates in neurone cell bodies in the brain) leave the corpora cardiaca *en route* for a variety of target organs—not only to the heart, but also to the corpora allata, salivary and prothoracic glands, visceral muscles and elsewhere. Direct neuromuscular synapses with the cardiac fibres are present, but there is also evidence suggesting that the cardiac nerves act, in addition, as neurohaemal organs, liberating neurosecretory material in the vicinity of the heart and pericardial cells, and it is probably this material, acting as a local hormone, that controls the release of a heart-accelerating indolalkylamine from the pericardial cells. A transverse section of the lateral nerve accompanying the cockroach heart is illustrated in Plate 24.

Electron micrographs of the pericardial septum underlying the heart of the cockroach are shown in Plate 50A and B. This sheet often bears the alary muscles whose contraction aids the dilation of the heart and hence the entry of haemolymph through the ostial openings. In *Periplaneta* this septum is fenestrated, and the haemolymph passes through the fenestrae into the pericardial sinus before passing into the heart. This sheet, and also the ventral diaphragm that is sometimes present overlying the central nerve cord, has been described in light microscopic studies as 'fibrous', but at the level of the electron microscope is found to consist of a delicate sheet of extremely flattened cells sandwiched between relatively thick extracellular layers of finely fibrillar material, apparently secreted by the septal cells.

The insect haemolymph contains no erythrocytes or other cells playing a role in respiration, but it possesses a variety of blood cells that float in the circulating fluid or adhere to the tissues of the body cavity. These haemocytes are very variable in their histological appearance, and our knowledge of their fine structure and function is at present too scanty to support a general scheme of classification comparable with that achieved in the case of vertebrate leucocytes. Crossley (1964, 1965) recognised several haemocyte types in the blowfly *Calliphora*, on the basis of their histochemical properties and morphology, and described the fine structure of phagocytic cells that are abundant in the haemolymph shortly before pupation. The surface of these cells is produced into many slender processes or pseudopodia, which are active in the engulfing of droplets of haemolymph and fragments of histolysing larval muscles and other tissues that are destined not to survive into the adult stage. The cytoplasm of the phagocytes contains vacuoles perhaps including degraded protein, similar in appearance to those seen in proximal convoluted tubule cells of the kidney, together with dense structures that probably represent lysosomes containing hydrolytic enzymes used in the breakdown of materials taken into the cell. In addition to their phagocytic function at moulting and before metamorphosis, blood cells may remove foreign particles, including bacteria, from the haemolymph. An example of a haemocyte from an adult stick insect, the morphology of which points to a phagocytic role, is shown in Plate 51, while the spherical cell from the blood of an *Ephestia* larva (Plate 52) bears no pseudopodia, but is actively taking in droplets of the surrounding haemolymph by pinocytosis.

A further well-documented function of haemocytes is that they may provide an insect with immunity to metazoan parasites, by forming a cyst or capsule around the invading body. The eggs and larvae of hymenopterous parasites, laid in their normal lepidopterous hosts, resist encapsulation and develop normally, but in unusual hosts may be encysted and killed. These delicate and often highly specific interactions have been reviewed by Salt (1963). Blood cell aggregation may also be studied experimentally, after foreign bodies such as fragments of polymerised Araldite (or parasite eggs) are inserted into the body of the insect, and electron micrographs of the cellular cysts that result are illustrated in Plates 53 to 55. In larvae of the flour moth *Ephestia*, haemocytes cluster around the implant, become extremely flattened and are piled upon one another to form a very compact isolating tissue (Plate 53; Grimstone and others, 1967). In the stick insect *Carausius morosus*, the blood cells that collect around an experimentally introduced egg of the parasitic wasp *Nemeritis* are less closely packed (Plate 54), but develop local areas of contact that hold together the cellular spongework (Reik, unpublished observations). In common with vertebrate leucocytes, insect haemocytes are sometimes unusually rich in their complement of cytoplasmic structures. Haemocytes of the stick insect for example (Plate 55) may contain lysosomes, cytolysomes, microtubules, and lipid droplets, in addition to mitochondria, well defined Golgi bodies built up of parallel series of smooth-membraned cisternae and vesicles, together with ribosome-studded cisternae of the endoplasmic reticulum and unattached ribosomes. These haemocytes also display very prominently a feature that has been described in a wide variety of cell types—the continuity between the endoplasmic reticulum membranes and the outer membrane of the nuclear envelope. To conclude this list, these cells are engaged in the absorption of materials (perhaps specific proteins) from the haemolymph, by means of coated vesicles pinched off from the plasma membrane (see pp. 171, 338).

Haemocytes have been implicated in a variety of other functions, including blood clotting, the movement of nutrients about the body and the manufacture of haemolymph proteins (Refs. in Wigglesworth, 1965). Wider studies with the electron microscope on the range of fine structure displayed by these cells would not only provide a surer basis for their morphological classification than have histological preparations, but would also throw more light upon the diverse roles that they may play in the insect body.

REFERENCES

*BOWERS, B., and JOHNSON, B. 1966. An electron microscope study of the corpora cardiaca and secretory neurones in the aphid, *Myzus persicae* (Sulz.). *Gen. compar. Endocr.*, **6**, 213–230.
*CROSSLEY, A. C. S. 1964. An experimental analysis of the origins and physiology of haemocytes in the blue blow-fly *Calliphora erythrocephala*, (Meig), *J. exp. Zool.*, **157**, 375–398.
*CROSSLEY, A. C. S. 1965. Transformations in the abdominal muscles of the blue blow-fly, *Calliphora erythrocephala* (Meig), during metamorphosis. *J. Embryol. exp. Morph.*, **14**, 89–110.
*EDWARDS, G. A., and CHALLICE, C. E. 1960. The ultrastructure of the heart of the cockroach, *Blattella germanica*. *Ann. ent. Soc. Am.*, **53**, 369–383.
*GRIMSTONE, A. V., ROTHERAM, S., and SALT, G. 1967. An electron microscope study of capsule formation by insect blood cells. *J. Cell Sci.*, **2**, 281–292.
*JOHNSON, B. 1966. Fine structure of the lateral cardiac nerves of the cockroach *Periplaneta americana* (L.). *J. Insect Physiol.*, **12**, 645–653.
*JOHNSON, B., and BOWERS, B. 1963. Transport of neurohormones from the corpora cardiaca in insects. *Science*, **141**, 264–266.
*REIK, L. Unpublished observations on the fine structure of haemocyte capsules.
SALT, G. 1963. The defence reactions of insects to metazoan parasites. *Parasitology*, **53**, 527–642.
WIGGLESWORTH, V. B. 1965. *The Principles of Insect Physiology*, 6th edn, Ch. 10. Methuen, London.

Plates 49–55 ▷

Plate 49 ▷

The insect dorsal vessel, responsible for the circulation of the haemolymph, is a muscular tube. Haemolymph enters the posterior part of the vessel (the 'heart') through valved apertures or ostia during dilation of the tube, and during contraction is passed forwards and out of the anterior part of the vessel (the 'aorta'). The wall of the vessel consists of a single layer of muscle cells in which the fibrils are striated (Plate 56) and run either irregularly or, as illustrated here in a transverse section of the heart of the cockroach *Periplaneta americana*, are arranged in a circular fashion. Generally, cardiac muscle fibres are virtually filled with the contractile material [F] and numerous mitochondria [M], but sometimes the cell nuclei are contained within a large bulge protruding into the lumen of the vessel. This field includes two nuclei [N] set in regions of granular cytoplasm [Cy] containing a few mitochondria but hardly a trace of myofibrils. The cardiac fibres are fitted together along prominent intercellular junctions [CJ] that often involve septate desmosomes. The outer surface of the heart, facing the body cavity, lies at the lower right of the field, and the granular material [He] at upper left has been precipitated from the haemolymph contained within the heart lumen.

(× 12,000.)

(*Philips EM 200.*)

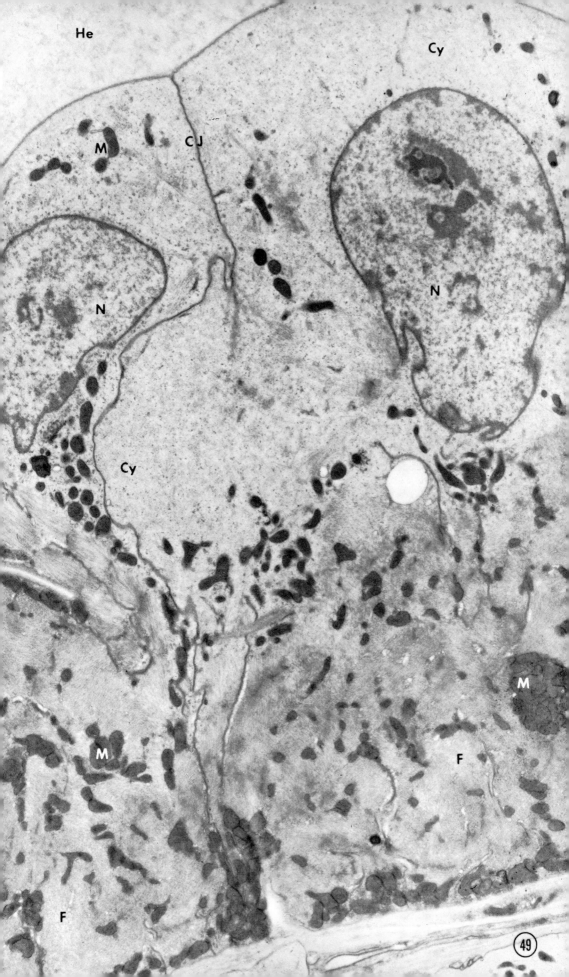

Plate 50 ▷

The insect heart is generally attached to the lateral body wall by the pericardial septum or dorsal diaphragm that lies beneath it, and in addition is often suspended from the dorsal body wall by connective filaments. The pericardial septum frequently bears alary muscles which aid the dilation of the heart and the entry of haemolymph through the ostia. In the cockroach *Periplaneta americana* the septum is fenestrated, and haemolymph passes through it from the general body cavity into the pericardial sinus surrounding the heart, before being aspirated into the vessel. The fine structure of this cellular septum is illustrated in the pair of micrographs shown here. As may be seen at low magnification (left), the sheet of septum cells is often little more than a micron in thickness; the nuclei [N] are extremely flattened and the cytoplasm surrounding them is sparse. The intercellular membranes [IM] between them are merely closely apposed, and do not seem to possess desmosome attachments. At higher magnification (right) the cytoplasm is found to contain clusters of Golgi vesicles [G] lying near the poles of the nuclei, and prominent cisternae of the rough-surfaced endoplasmic reticulum [ER]. The latter are often swollen with finely granular material [*] that is perhaps passed to the Golgi vesicles and thence released from the cell to contribute to the thick basement membrane-like sheath [BM] present on the upper and lower faces of the septum. Other cytoplasmic inclusions in these cells are occasional mitochondria [M] and lipid droplets [L].

(A : × 18,000. B : × 28,000.)

(*Philips EM 200.*)

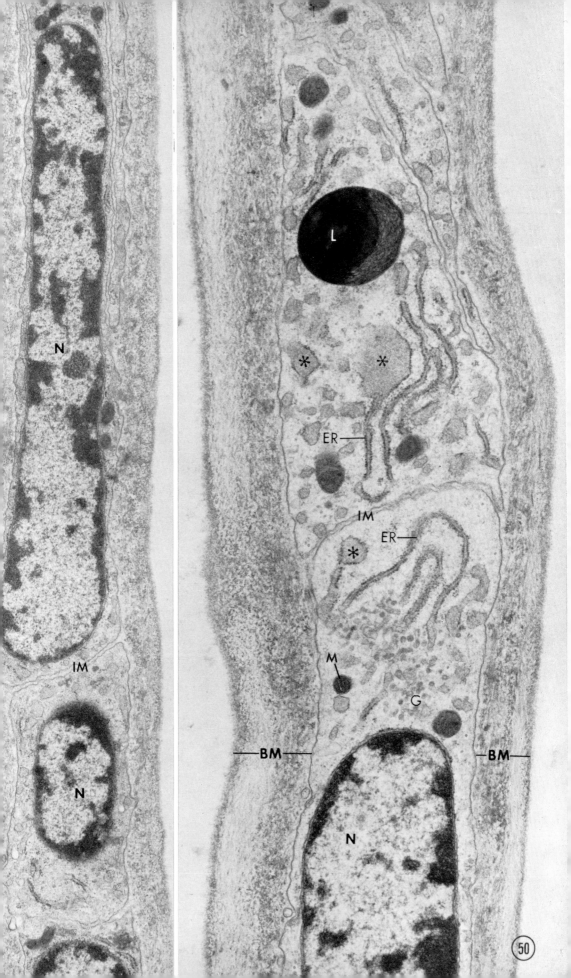

50

Plate 51 ▷

Insect haemocytes vary considerably in their histological appearance,
and play several functional roles. Some of these cells are phagocytic,
removing from the haemolymph bacteria or other foreign bodies,
engulfing fragments of histolysing cells that are present during
moulting and before metamorphosis. This electron micrograph is
included as an example of a blood cell from the stick insect
Carausius morosus that appears to be adapted for such a role. The
cell surface is very irregular and bears small pseudopodia [arrows],
seemingly engaged in engulfing droplets of the surrounding
haemolymph. The opaque bodies which are abundant in the
cytoplasm [*] may be lysosomes, containing hydrolytic enzymes
concerned in the breakdown of ingested material. The nucleus [N] is
elongated and sinuous. Examples of other haemocytes are shown in
Plates 52–55.

($\times$ 23,000.)

(*Philips EM 200.*)

160

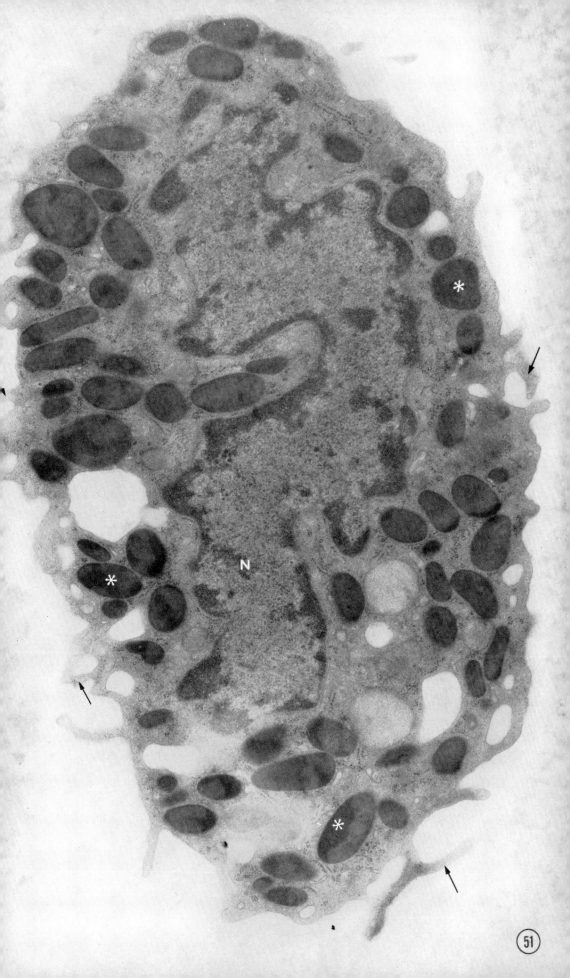

Plate 52 ▷

A micrograph of a spherical haemocyte from a larva of the flour moth *Ephestia kühniella*. This cell appears to be ingesting droplets of the surrounding haemolymph, but accomplishes this by the formation of pinocytic vesicles [arrow] rather than by means of pseudopodial processes (cf. Plate 51). Small vesicles [*] scattered through the cytoplasm have probably been pinched off from the cell surface in this way, and often contain granular material similar to the precipitated plasma of the haemolymph [He] surrounding the cell. Most sections of these cells contain Golgi bodies comprising smooth-surfaced cisternae and vesicles, such as that seen here at G. In addition, the cytoplasm includes small dense lysosomes, mitochondria [M], ribosome-studded cisternae of the endoplasmic reticulum [ER] and large numbers of unattached ribosomes. N represents a profile of the centrally placed nucleus. Haemocytes that have encapsulated a foreign body, in this insect, present a very different appearance from the cell shown here (cf. Plate 53).

($\times$ 35,000.)

(*Philips EM 200. Micrograph reproduced by courtesy of Drs A. V. Grimstone, S. Rotheram and G. Salt.*)

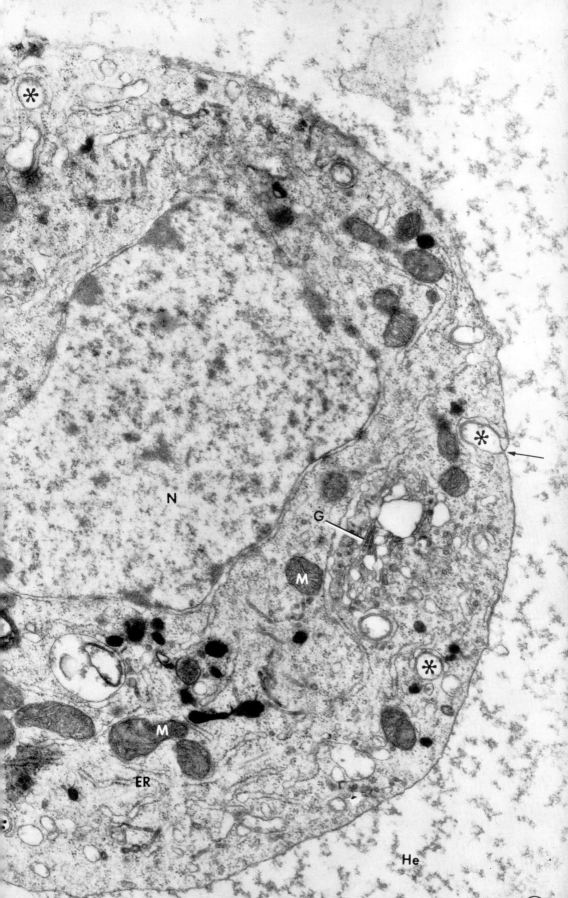

Plate 53 ▷

An electron micrograph illustrating the compact haemocyte tissue
that encapsulates a foreign body within the body cavity of *Ephestia*.
In this instance, the foreign body was a small piece of Araldite, injected
into the animal. The innermost cells of the capsule 72 hours after
implantation of the fragment are generally necrotic, and contain
numerous very large cytolysomes, while the middle region of the
capsule, included here, comprises large numbers of closely apposed
and extremely flattened blood cells. These are thickest in the vicinity
of the nucleus [N] but taper peripherally to thin sheets [arrows], only
a fraction of a micron thick. The formation of capsules or clumps of
haemocytes provides the insect with a defence against metazoan
parasites, and is further illustrated in Plates 54 and 55.

(×21,000.)

(*Philips EM 200. From Grimstone, Rotheram and Salt (1967).
Micrograph reproduced by courtesy of the authors and the* Journal of
Cell Science.)

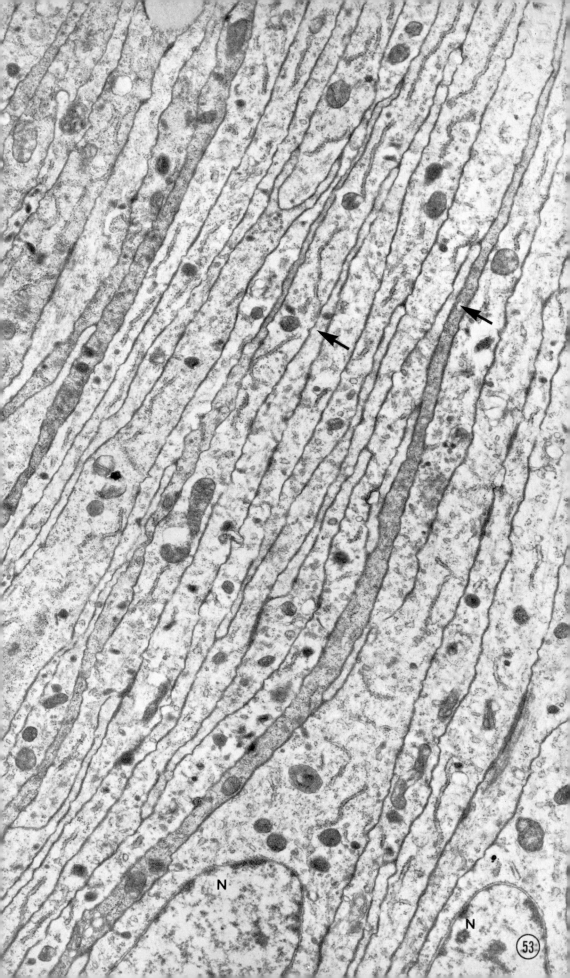

N

N

53

Plate 54 ▷

An electron micrograph showing several haemocytes from a clump
forming around an egg of the parasitic wasp *Nemeritis* that has been
experimentally implanted into a stick insect. Unlike the cells of the
capsule that isolates a foreign body in the flour moth (Plate 53),
these haemocytes are loosely packed and stuck together only at local
areas of close contact [arrows]. The opaque granules often present in
these cells [*] are perhaps lysosomes, containing hydrolytic enzymes
(cf. Plate 51). Lobed nuclei are seen at N. The extracellular spaces
between the spongework of cells contain material precipitated from
the haemolymph plasma [He].

($\times$ 15,000.)

(Philips EM 200. Micrograph reproduced by courtesy of Mr L. Reik Jr.)

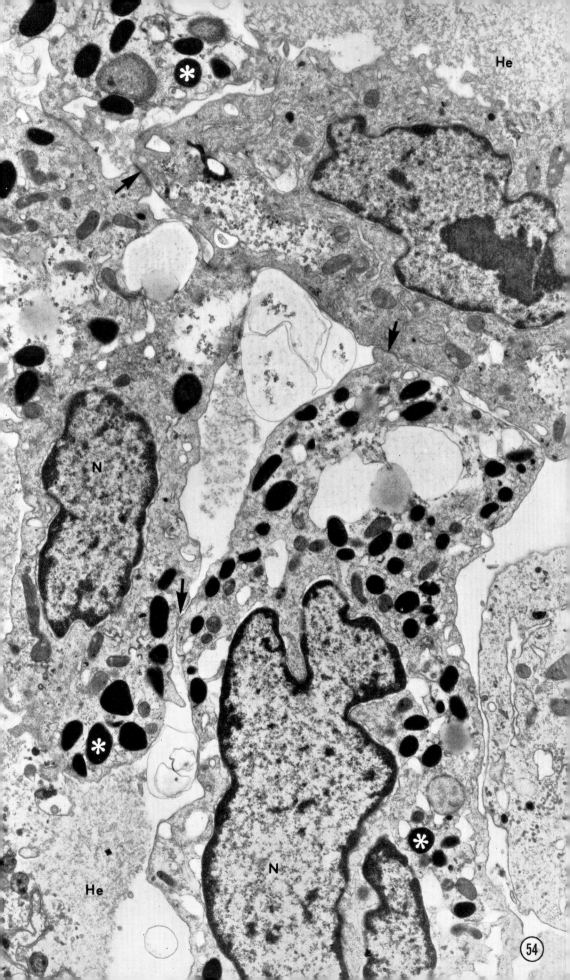

Plate 55 ▷

A micrograph of a *Carausius* haemocyte from the same material as in Plate 54, at higher magnification. These cells possess an unusually rich variety of cytoplasmic structures, and are a close natural approximation to the 'generalised cells' occurring in textbooks. The structures resolved here include mitochondria [M], compact Golgi bodies [G], cytolysomes containing membranous remnants [Cl], small opaque lysosomes, microtubules and lipid droplets [L]. Ribosomes are abundant, both unattached within the cytoplasm and studding the surface of cisternae of the endoplasmic reticulum [ER], the membranes of which are in several places [*] seen to be continuous with the outer membrane of the nuclear envelope.

($\times$ 30,000.)

(Philips EM 200. Micrograph reproduced by courtesy of Mr L. Reik Jr.)

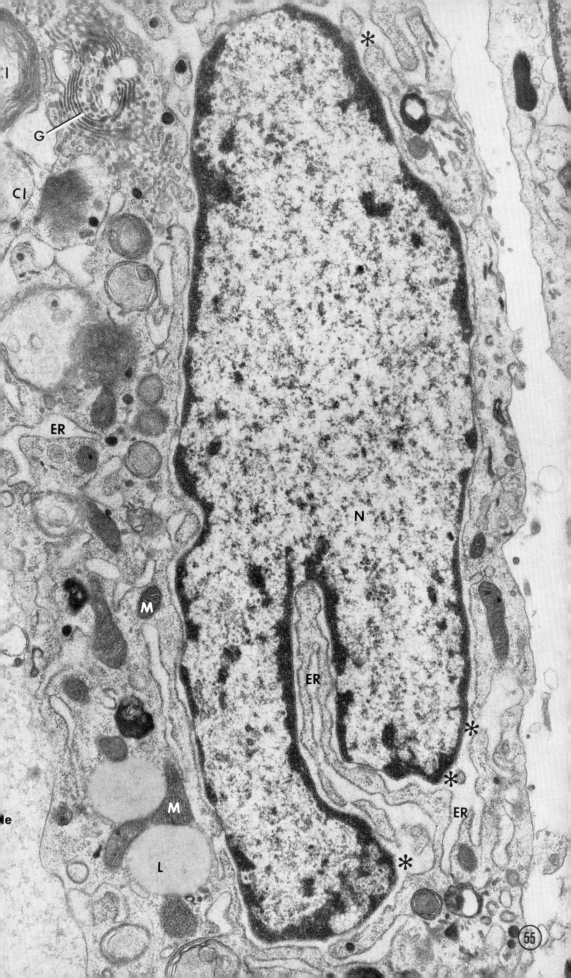

The pericardial cells of insects are present around the outer surface of the tubular heart and often extend onto the underlying pericardial septum and alary muscles. At the level of the light microscope, these cells were found to contain many vacuoles and granules, and unlike the haemocytes, which are likewise of mesodermal origin, they are sessile and never enter the haemolymph circulation. It has been shown experimentally that the pericardial cells are able to absorb certain substances—notably proteins and acid dyes—from the haemolymph (Hollande, 1921), and it is now thought that while the haemocytes rid the haemolymph of foreign bodies and tissue fragments, the pericardial cells perform a function comparable with that of the vertebrate reticulo–endothelial system.

We owe much of our present knowledge of the fine structure of pericardial cells to a preliminary account by Kessel (1961) and a more recent and detailed study by Bowers (1964), respectively on material from a grasshopper, *Melanoplus differentialis*, and from an aphid, *Myzus persicae*. In particular, Bowers approached the organisation of these cells from the point of view of their ability to absorb substances from the blood which bathes them, and showed that they make use of a structural device shared by a variety of cells in insects and vertebrates that are able to carry out the selective absorption of protein. Some of the features of these cells in the cockroach are illustrated in Plates 56 to 59.

In this insect, the pericardial cells are plentifully grouped around the muscular tube of the heart (Plate 56), and at low magnification, where most cellular fine details are barely resolved, their most obvious feature is the presence of many large vacuoles or droplets, some with opaque contents and others containing material of low or intermediate density (Plate 57). These bodies, even when they are very abundant, do not extend to the cell surface; they are always excluded from a narrow cortical zone, a few micra in width, which Bowers showed to be very complicated in its organisation, and which provides structural clues to the function of the cell. Cell surfaces across which materials are transported are often folded in various ways (Plates 74, 90, 94 and 98, for example) which achieve an increase in membrane surface area that enhances the efficiency of their transporting function. This is true of the pericardial cell, but the pattern of folding that has been adopted is quite unusual. Much of the cell surface is thrown into pleats or folds, often shallow but sometimes penetrating for a distance of a few micra into the cortex, and the lips of these folds are held together by desmosomes that resemble stitches, when seen in transverse section. Conventional desmosomes link the surfaces of two adjoining cells rather than, as in this case, the edges of indentations of a single cell. These features are illustrated in Plates 58 and 59.

Closer examination of the pericardial cell cortex indicates that material is taken into the cell from the outside by pinching off of small vesicles, that first arise as pits in the

171

surface membrane. In the cockroach, as in the aphid, these vesicles seem to be formed only at special sites which are marked by clumps of dense material outside the cell membrane, and by the presence of minute fibrils attached to the cytoplasmic side of the membrane (Plate 59A). The great interest of this point of fine detail lies in the fact that comparative studies have shown that the formation of similar 'coated vesicles' bearing a minutely sculptured layer of alveoli occurs in several cells that are engaged in the absorption of proteins (Refs. in Bowers, 1964). In insects, specialised micropino-cytic structures of this type have been found at the surface of the oocyte during protein yolk formation (Plate 112B), in blood cells (Plate 55), and in vertebrate cells including neurones, erythroblasts and the epithelium of kidney tubules (Refs. in Bowers, 1964).

The subsequent fate of the coated vesicles and the material they contain, which perhaps includes foreign or denatured protein, has not yet clearly emerged from electron microscopic observations. The cortical zone of the cell possesses large numbers of tubular structures, up to about a micron in length and bearing a bulbous swelling on one end (Plate 59), and Bowers suggests that these bulbs may enlarge and fuse to produce the vacuoles with light contents that are prominent in electron micrographs. It is certainly tempting to suppose that this link between the tubules and the large vacuoles represents a means of pooling material within the cell, since there are striking similarities between the structures mentioned above and components of kidney tubule cells as they take up and digest haemoglobin (Miller, 1960). From his studies on the kidney, Miller concluded that this protein is taken into the cell and passed to vacuoles via tubular structures, and that the contents of these vacuoles condenses to form opaque granules where hydrolysis of the haemoglobin occurs. However, as Bowers points out, while the tubules and the various vacuoles and granules of pericardial cells may indeed be related to protein accumulation and metabolism, important gaps in the story have still be to filled—in particular, no connection between the tubules and the cell membrane or the coated vesicles has been observed. In a paper based on electron micrographs of *Drosophila* pericardial cells, Mills and King (1965) have also concluded that these are responsible for the uptake and degradation of unwanted molecules, present in the haemolymph.

Electron micrographs show that pericardial cells vary greatly in the number and size of their vacuoles and granular inclusions, and as reported by Hollande from his light microscopic studies, they may well undergo cyclic changes in contents. Mills and King have suggested that these changes may trace a pattern of ingestion of material from the haemolymph, and its subsequent digestion within the cell, and the elimination of products that result. Further information on the fine structural basis of these changes would be most valuable; it would be interesting, for example, to know details of the fine structure of *Rhodnius* pericardial cells which were found by Wigglesworth (1965) to parallel the Kupffer cells of the liver and other members of the vertebrate reticulo–endothelial system in the way in which they break down molecules of haemoglobin.

Finally, another and entirely different function has been traced to the pericardial cells: they were found by Davey (Refs. in Wigglesworth, 1965) to secrete a substance (probably an indolalkylamine) that causes acceleration in the rate of heart beat, when triggered by a hormone present in corpus cardiacum extracts. Johnson and Bowers (1963) were able to show that this hormone does not seem to be liberated from the corpus cardiacum directly, but rather is conducted to the vicinity of the heart along axons of the cardiac nerves. More recently (Bowers and Johnson, 1966; Johnson, 1966), electron micrographs have been obtained which suggest that neurosecretory material is indeed released from these axons close to the surface of the pericardial cells (p. 153). The cellular details of the synthesis and secretion of the indolalkylamine by the pericardial cells, which is an important part of the complex control of insect heart beat, awaits further study.

REFERENCES

*BOWERS, B. 1964. Coated vesicles in the pericardial cells of the aphid (*Myzus persicae* Sulz). *Protoplasma*, **59**, 351–367.
*BOWERS, B., and JOHNSON, B. 1966. An electron microscope study of the corpora cardiaca and secretory neurones in the aphid, *Myzus persicae* (Sulz.). *Gen. compar. Endocr.*, **6**, 213–230.
HOLLANDE, A. 1921. La cellule pericardiale des insectes. *Archs Anat. microsc.*, **18**, 85–307.
*JOHNSON, B. 1966. Fine structure of the lateral cardiac nerves of the cockroach *Periplaneta americana* (L.). *J. Insect Physiol.*, **12**, 645–653.
*JOHNSON, B., and BOWERS, B. 1963. Transport of neurohormones from the corpora cardiaca in insects. *Science*, **141**, 244–246.
*KESSEL, R. G. 1961. Electron microscope observations on the submicroscopic component of the subesophageal body and pericardial cells of the grasshopper, *Melanoplus differentialis differentialis* (Thomas). *Expl Cell Res.*, **22**, 108–119.
MILLER, F. 1960. Hemoglobin absorption by the cells of the proximal convoluted tubule in mouse kidney. *J. biophys. biochem. Cytol.*, **8**, 689–718.
*MILLS, R. P., and KING, R. C. 1965. The pericardial cells of *Drosophila melanogaster*. *Q. Jl microsc. Sci.*, **106**, 261–268.
WIGGLESWORTH, V. B. 1965. *The Principles of Insect Physiology*, 6th edn, Ch. 10. Methuen, London.

Plates 56–59 ▷

Plate 56 ▷

A low-power electron micrograph illustrating the arrangement of cells
in and around the heart, in the abdomen of the cockroach
Periplaneta americana. This section passes transversely through the
tubular heart, and hence the circularly disposed striated myofibrils of
the cardiac muscle fibres [MF] are seen in longitudinal profile. Part of
the nucleus [N] of one of these cells, and the edge of the heart lumen,
are included in the field at bottom right. The granular material within
the heart [*] and outside it [He] represents protein or other substances
precipitated from the haemolymph during fixation. Tracheoles [Tr]
and a small nerve fibre [NF] approach the outer surface of the
vessel. Clustered around the heart and attached to the pericardial
septum are 'nephrocytes' or pericardial cells [arrows], which are
thought to carry out the selective uptake of unwanted proteins from
the haemolymph, and also appear to release a heart-stimulating
substance when triggered by a hormone from the corpus cardiacum.
Details of the fine structure of these large and complex cells are
illustrated in Plates 57 to 59.

(× 6000.)

(*Philips EM 200.*)

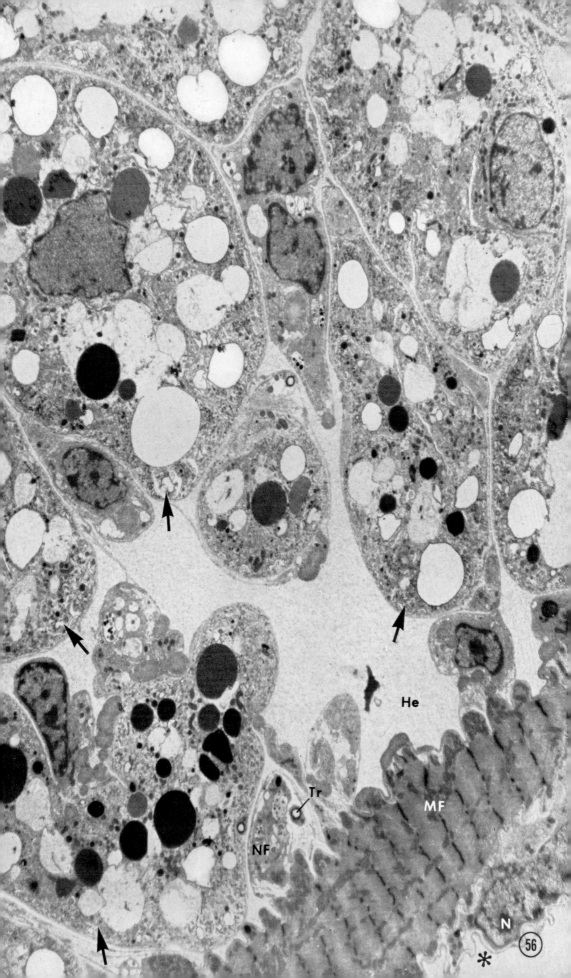

He

Tr

NF

MF

N

*

56

Plate 57 ▷

The most conspicuous structures within the pericardial cells are large
opaque granules [*], and vesicles [Ve] containing varying amounts
of granular material. Each cell possesses a well-defined cortical region
[arrows] which presents a complex structural picture when examined
at higher magnification (Plates 58 and 59), and which appears to be
adapted for the uptake of proteins from the surrounding haemolymph.
The edge of a nucleus is included at N.

($\times$ 11,000.)

(*Philips EM 200.*)

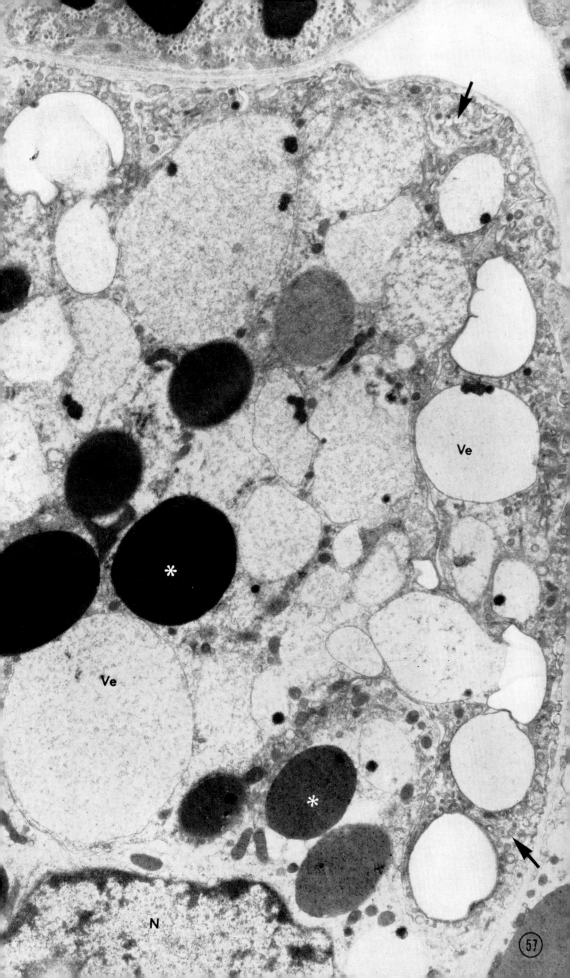

Plate 58 ▷

A micrograph illustrating some aspects of the fine structure of a cockroach pericardial cell. The cell is ensheathed by a basement membrane [BM] containing granular material and very fine fibrils. The cell surface is thrown into a series of folds and finger-like processes 'stitched together' (Plate 59) by septate desmosomes, and the cell membrane is also extended along channels [black asterisks] that penetrate more deeply into the cell. From these folds and channels, specialised 'coated vesicles' are pinched off into the cytoplasm [arrows]. These vesicles are thought to carry out the selective absorption of proteins from the haemolymph, and their appearance is further illustrated in Plates 59A and 112B. In addition, the cortical cytoplasm contains small tubular elements [Tu] of unknown function, which are often found to be confluent with cytoplasmic vesicles (Plate 59B). Interspersed among the larger vesicles and granules illustrated in the last plate are small opaque granules [white asterisks], together with cisternae of the endoplasmic reticulum [ER] and a few mitochondria [M].

($\times$ 30,000.)

(*Philips EM 200.*)

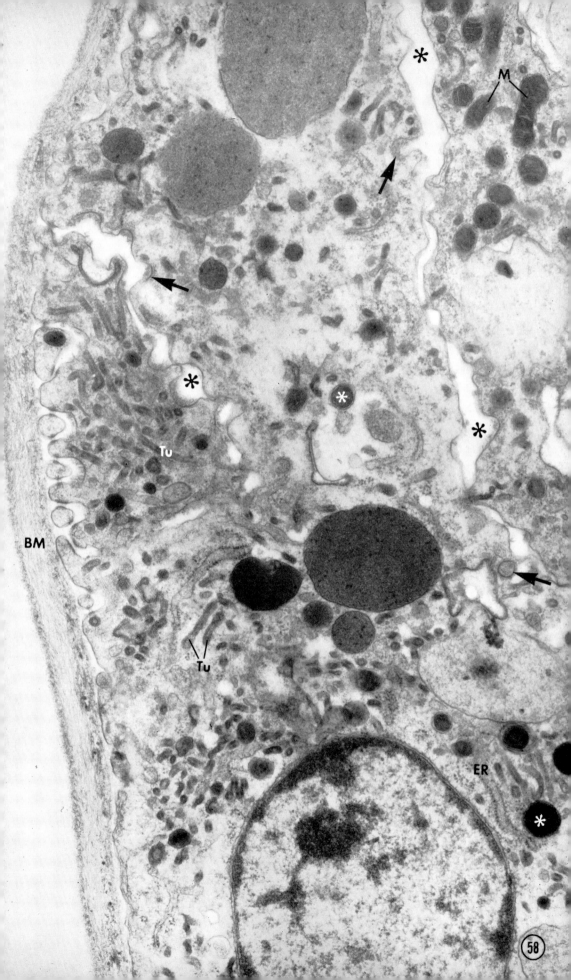

Plate 59 ▷

A. A higher magnification field illustrating¡ n more detail the origin of coated vesicles from pinched off pits that form along the plasma membrane of the pericardial cell. At 1 a pit is seen apparently during its formation, while that at 2 has almost separated from the surface. A vesicle that has already been pinched off into the cytoplasm is included at 3. These differ from pinocytic vesicles in possessing, on the cytoplasmic side of their membrane, a sculptured coat of minute alveoli, and moreover they form in places where dense extracellular material (perhaps selectively adsorbed proteins) becomes aggregated close by the cell surface. This micrograph also demonstrates the stitch-like desmosomes [arrows] that link together the lips of the surface membrane folds and processes.

B. A field similar to the last, but illustrating the fusion between cortical tubules [Tu] and vesicles [Ve] in the pericardial cell. It is possible that these tubular structures may be concerned in some way with the accumulation of materials taken up by the cell, but unlike the coated vesicles do not seem to stem from the plasma membrane. An axon [Ax] of the cardiac nerve, flanked by the extracellular sheath or neural lamella [*], is included on the left.

($A: \times 90,000. B: \times 55,000.$)

(*Philips EM 200.*)

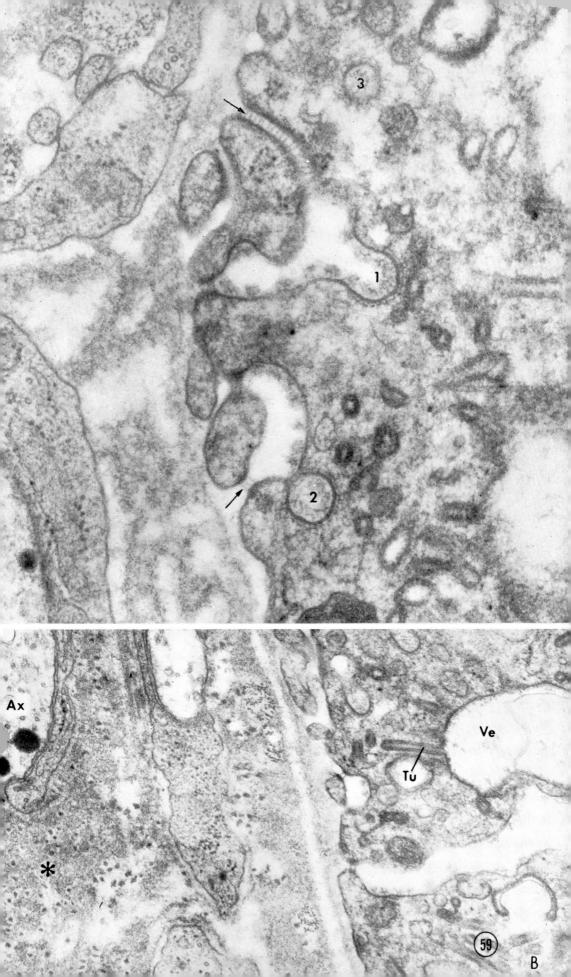

Scattered throughout the insect body cavity are very large cells, termed 'oenocytes' in recognition of the yellowish colour that they often display in fresh preparations. These cells are of ectodermal origin, but while they often accompany the epidermal cells beneath the cuticle of the body surface, they are also found elsewhere, for example between the epidermis and underlying muscle fibres, around the spiracles and, more deeply situated, interspersed with the mesodermal cells of the fat body.

While it has been generally supposed that oenocytes play a part in intermediary metabolism, their precise role, in their various locations, is still by no means clear. The fine structure of these cells has hitherto received little attention, but, as mentioned below, preliminary studies made with the electron microscope have shown that they possess a cytoplasmic organisation that is strikingly different from that of other insect cells, and that provides a clue to their function.

In the larvae and adults of the stick insect *Carausius*, the epidermal cells are charged with great numbers of pigment granules. Accompanying them, and inserted between the inner surface of the cuticle and the epidermal basement membrane, lie spherical or flattened oenocytes, often 100 micra or so in diameter. A portion of one of these large cells is shown in Plate 60, and even at the low magnification of this micrograph the unusually uniform construction of the cytoplasm may be seen. Small groups of ribosome-bearing cisternae of the endoplasmic reticulum are present, especially around the surface of the nucleus, and long slender mitochondria are evenly dispersed through the cell. The bulk of the cytoplasm is filled with an irregular meshwork of interlacing tubules of the agranular or smooth-surfaced reticulum, more readily observed at higher magnification in Plate 61. Such extreme hypertrophy of this membrane system is, so far as is at present known, unique amongst insect cells, but finds an interesting counterpart in the vertebrate body.

In vertebrate tissues, the presence of an extensive agranular reticulum has been associated with a variety of different functions. In the interstitial cells of the testis, these membranes are believed to be concerned with the biosynthesis of the steroid testosterone, responsible for the development of the male secondary sexual characters (Christensen, 1965), and are also present in the ovarian corpus luteum within which the steroid progesterone is synthesised. Elsewhere, agranular cisternae may be linked with other roles: they appear to be involved in ion transport in the 'chloride cells' of fish gills, in the synthesis of triglycerides in the absorptive cells of the intestine and in the breakdown of drugs within the liver (Fawcett, 1966). Insects possess no sex hormones corresponding precisely to those of vertebrates, but an interesting comparison between functionally comparable vertebrate and insect cells is provided by the prothoracic glands of the latter, which synthesise the moulting hormone ecdysone, probably a steroid, and which contain considerable amounts of agranular reticulum.

183

So far as is known, on the other hand, oenocytes are not involved in steroid production or metabolism, and the significance of their cytoplasmic fine structure may be sought elsewhere.

There is evidence from light microscopic studies that the oenocytes may synthesise lipid or lipoprotein material of the cuticulin of the epicuticle, laid down before moulting (p. 4), and that they may also be involved in the production of wax deposited on the surface of the cuticle, perhaps by supplying the epidermal cells with wax precursors. Furthermore, it has been suggested that in adult female insects the oenocytes undertake a further role in supplying the ovaries with cuticulin-like material used in the formation of the egg shells (Refs. in Wigglesworth, 1965). While electron micrographs of oenocytes so far produced show little evidence of well developed rough-surfaced cisternae, which would be expected in cells manufacturing protein for export, their abundant smooth-surfaced reticulum is at least consistent with their proposed role in the synthesis of lipids, although the details of this function are not at present known.

A further aspect of oenocyte organisation is illustrated in Plate 61. In a butterfly larva (*Calpodes*), prior to pupation, the oenocytes contain degenerating cellular material, isolated from the general cytoplasm in very large cytolysomes (Locke, unpublished observations). Locke has found that to these bodies are added proteins, taken up into the oenocyte from the haemolymph; a mechanism that finds a parallel in cells of the fat body at the same stage of development (p. 191). The significance of this complicated sequence of events has not been established, although it is possible that the cytolysomes in oenocytes and fat body cells represent a storage device, and that the proteinaceous and other material they contain may later be reused. These cellular events certainly reflect the metabolic and cellular flux that accompanies metamorphosis.

REFERENCES

CHRISTENSEN, A. K. 1965. The fine structure of testicular interstitial cells in guinea pigs. *J. Cell Biol.*, **26**, 911–935.

FAWCETT, D. W. 1966. *The Cell. An Atlas of Fine Structure*. W. B. Saunders, Philadelphia and London.

*LOCKE, M. 1968. The ultrastructure of the oenocytes in the molt/intermolt cycle of an insect (*Calpodes ethlius* Stoll). *Tissue & Cell*, **1**, in 103–164.

*SMITH, U., and SMITH, D. S. Unpublished observations on the fine structure of oenocytes in larvae and adults of the stick insect, *Carausius morosus*.

WIGGLESWORTH, V. B. 1965. *The Principles of Insect Physiology*, 6th edn, Ch. 10. Methuen, London.

Plates 60–61 ▷

Plate 60 ▷

An electron micrograph of a portion of an oenocyte associated with the epidermis in an adult egg-laying female of the stick insect *Carausius morosus*. Part of the nucleus is included at the left [N]; the nucleoplasm includes nucleolar material [white asterisk] and aggregates of chromatin [black asterisks]. The cytoplasm of these large cells is of uniform construction, unlike, for example, epithelial cells, which are typically divided into distinct zones. Throughout the cytoplasm is present a tangled meshwork of tubules, representing the smooth-surfaced endoplasmic reticulum [SER]. Parallel arrays of short cisternae of the rough-surfaced reticulum, studded with ribosomes, are uncommon and virtually restricted to the neighbourhood of the nucleus [ER]. Slender mitochondria [M] are dispersed plentifully through the cytoplasm.

($\times$ 12,000.)

(*Philips EM 200. Micrograph produced in collaboration with Dr U. Smith.*)

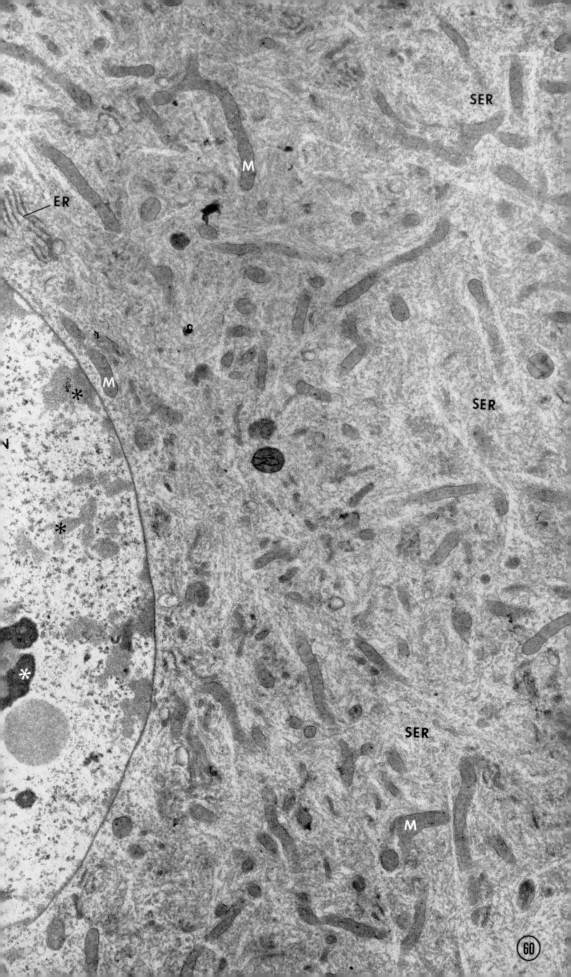

SER

M

ER

M

*

N

*

*

SER

SER

M

60

Plate 61 ▷

A micrograph illustrating the cytoplasmic organisation of an oenocyte from the last larval instar of the butterfly *Calpodes ethlius*. As in the last plate, the cell contains sinuous and branching tubules [SER] representing the smooth-surfaced endoplasmic reticulum, small mitochondria [M], together with scattered unattached ribosomes [Rb]. In this species, before pupation, the oenocytes exhibit very large cytolysomes—complex bodies within which cytoplasmic structures are isolated from the rest of the cell and undergo degeneration. Much of this field is occupied by one of these bodies, which is made up of many spheres of cytoplasm, each contained within a membranous coat, set in a dense granular matrix [*]. In some cases, these spheres include still recognisable structures— endoplasmic reticulum cisternae [SER'] and aggregates of ribosomes [Rb']. Fat body cells at the same stage of development follow the same pattern (Plate 64), and it is possible that in each case the materials segregated within the cytolysomes are later reused by the animal.

($\times$ 61,000.)

(RCA EMU 4. Micrograph reproduced by courtesy of Dr M. J. Locke.)

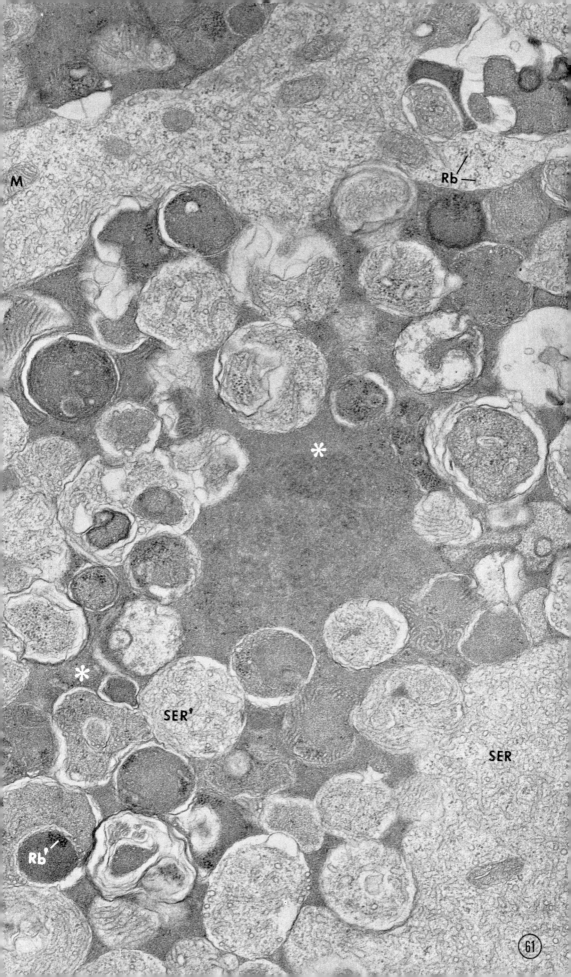

61

The Fat Body

The cells of the insect fat body are generally diffusely distributed within the body cavity, and their arrangement varies considerably. They may be disposed in sheets, lobules or ribbons, typically most abundant in the abdomen but sometimes extending into the thorax and head. This tissue is often represented by a sheet beneath the epidermis, and may be present as a sheath around the gut and ventral nerve cord. The term 'fat body' does scant justice to this versatile tissue, for not only does it provide a storage depot for reserve protein and carbohydrate in addition to fat, but is also a major centre of intermediary metabolism, performing a role in some respects comparable with that of the vertebrate liver. The available information on the many biochemical processes occurring in fat body cells has recently been reviewed by Kilby (1963).

The amount and nature of food reserves within the fat body varies with the nutritional state, with the moulting cycle and also with the developmental stage of the insect. Several light microscopic studies have traced the changes occurring in the fat body contents through growth and metamorphosis, and during feeding and starvation, and the electron microscopic studies of Gaudecker (1963) on *Drosophila* larvae, of Ishizaki (1965) on silkmoth larvae, and of Locke and Collins (1965) on the fat body of larvae of a butterfly, *Calpodes ethlius*, have shown that gross changes in the cell contents are accompanied by complex events at the fine structural level. Throughout most of the larval life of *Calpodes*, lipid droplets are the most conspicuous food reserve in the fat body cells (Plate 62), though clusters of glycogen granules may also occur. At this time, the presence of a very extensive rough-surfaced endoplasmic reticulum provides the cellular machinery for protein synthesis, but through the fourth larval instar no protein is retained for storage. As is generally the case in holometabolous insects, the fat body cells of this insect show intense storage activity as the time of pupation approaches, in readiness for the heavy demands on food reserves that are made during the period of tissue reorganisation and replacement that occurs as the adult body is formed. During the fifth (final) larval instar, granules of stored protein make their appearance (Plate 63), and Locke and Collins have traced the intricate steps in their formation and have found that these granules are of two types, distinct both in their appearance and origin (Plate 64). The first type appears about thirty hours before pupation, when the chitin and protein of the larval endocuticle is being resorbed: these form by coalescence of small vesicles derived from the Golgi bodies in which protein manufactured in the reticulum cisternae is packaged, augmented by vesicles of protein picked up by the fat body cell from the surrounding haemolymph. Formation of the second type of granule starts about ten hours before the larva moults to the pupal stage. These arise when mitochondria or small packets of cytoplasm containing rough-surfaced cisternae are 'isolated' within membranes derived from the Golgi bodies; the structures within these cytolysomes becomes progressively less well-defined as lysis continues, until eventually

191

the cytolysomes contain only a granular matrix of protein and, sometimes, closely packed clumps of ribosomes. These protein reserves, together with stores of lipid and glycogen, are presumably later mobilised from the fat body and used elsewhere.

Structures described as lysosomes and cytolysomes occur in many cells, and are very variable in their fine structure but are thought to have a common feature in possessing hydrolytic enzymes. A convenient system of nomenclature is of great importance in organising our observations, whether on animal species or subcellular structures, and De Duve and Wattiaux (1966) have recently proposed a lysosome taxonomy that takes into account the variable appearance and origin of these structures. According to this classification, the protein granules and cytolysomes described above may respectively be termed 'heterophagosomes' and 'autophagosomes'—since the latter are derived from structures occurring within the cell, while the former include material from two sources. The functional analogy between the fat body and the liver has been mentioned before, and the similarity between the two is reflected not only at the biochemical level, but also in their structure. For example, autophagosomes containing identifiable remnants of cellular structures occur in liver cells, although their role in protein storage has not been established in this case. Furthermore, structures similar in appearance to the 'microbodies' which are plentiful in liver cells and which probably represent another type of lysosome, have their counterpart in the fat body.

Many aspects of fat body fine structure await attention. Among these may be mentioned the mechanism of uptake of materials from the haemolymph into these cells, and of the release of nutrients from them. In addition, the synthesis and storage of uric acid and a variety of pigments, occurring in the fat body of some insects (Refs. in Kilby, 1963), are biochemical features that may prove to be associated with interesting processes at the level of cellular fine structure. The metabolic role of the fat body is by no means ended when adulthood is reached, since it may then provide reserves for such varied functions as egg production, hibernation and flight, but electron microscopic studies on this tissue in adult insects are not at present available.

Interspersed among the typical fat body cells of some insects are unusual cells which contain large numbers of supposedly symbiotic micro-organisms, and the fine structure and possible function of these 'mycetocytes' are considered in the next section.

REFERENCES

DE DUVE, C., and WATTIAUX, R. 1966. Functions of lysosomes. *A. Rev. Physiol.*, **28**, 435–492.
*GAUDECKER, B. 1963. Über den Formwechsel einiger Zellorganelle bei der Bildung der Reservestoffe im Fettkörper von *Drosophila*-Larven. *Z. Zellforsch. mikrosk. Anat.*, **61**, 56–95.
*ISHIZAKI, H. 1965. Electron microscopic study of changes in the subcellular organization during metamorphosis of the fat-body cell of *Philosamia cynthia ricini* (Lepidoptera). *J. Insect Physiol.*, **11**, 845–855.
KILBY, B. A. 1963. The biochemistry of the insect fat body. In *Advances in Insect Physiology* (J. W. L. Beament, J. E. Treherne and V. B. Wigglesworth, eds.), Vol. 1, pp. 112–174. Academic Press, London and New York.
*LOCKE, M., and COLLINS, J. V. 1965. The structure and formation of protein granules in the fat body of an insect. *J. Cell Biol.*, **26**, 857–884.

Plates 62–64 ▷

o

Plate 62 ▷

A survey electron micrograph of part of a fat-body cell from a young
larva of the butterfly *Calpodes ethlius*, containing stored nutrients.
Large lipid droplets [L] and many clusters of glycogen granules [Gy]
are present. The cisternae of the rough-surfaced endoplasmic
reticulum [ER] are distended, presumably by protein synthesised in
association with the ribosomes they bear. Mitochondria [M] are
distributed throughout the cytoplasm, and a profile of the spherical
nucleus is included at N. The edge of the cell is dissected into
irregular processes [*] and is ensheathed by a delicate basement
membrane [BM].

($\times$ 16,000.)

*(RCA EMU 4. Micrograph reproduced by courtesy of
Dr M. J. Locke.)*

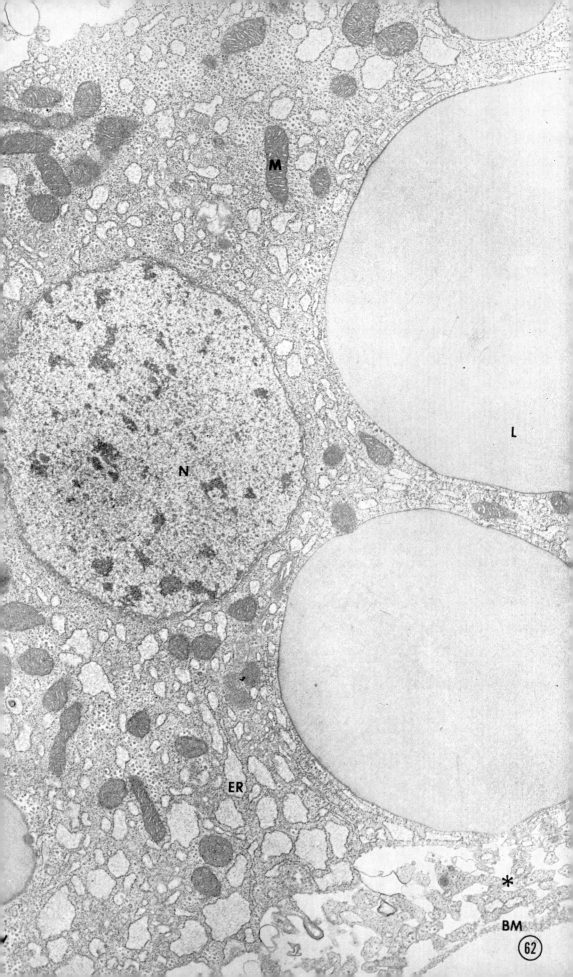

Plate 63 ▷

Insect fat-body cells do not merely serve as storage depots for food reserves, but also play an important part in intermediary metabolism and the synthesis of nutrients. The cell profile shown here, from the fat body of a young larva of a butterfly, *Calpodes ethlius*, displays a very extensive system of vesicles and cisternae of the rough-surfaced endoplasmic reticulum [ER]—necessary cellular equipment for the synthesis of protein for export. A small Golgi body comprising smooth-surfaced membranes is included at lower right [G], and the edge of a large protein granule [Pr] appears at upper right.

($\times$ 36,000.)

(RCA EMU 4. Micrograph reproduced by courtesy of Dr M. J. Locke.)

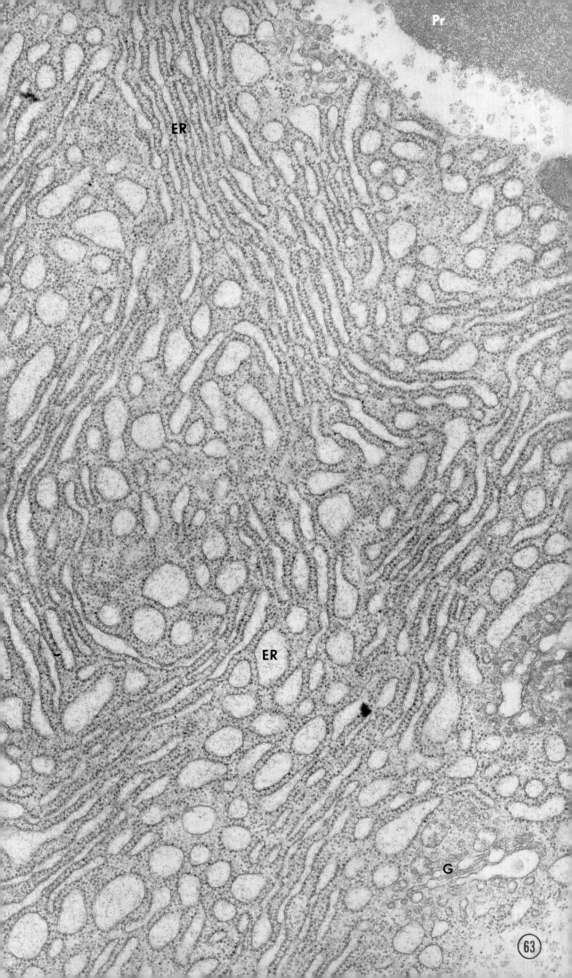

Plate 64 ▷

As the time of pupation approaches, the fat-body cells in the larva of
the butterfly *Calpodes ethlius* become engaged in the massive storage
of protein. The fine structural changes that occur in these cells during
the last larval instar have revealed that protein granules are formed in
two quite distinct ways. At lower left lies a protein granule [Pr],
apparently produced by the aggregation and confluence of large
numbers of small smooth-surfaced vesicles, some of which still
remain intact [arrows] within it. These vesicles are believed to contain
protein synthesised in the rough-surfaced endoplasmic reticulum,
passed to the Golgi cisternae from which the vesicles are pinched off.
A second mode of protein granule formation involves the isolation and
degradation of packets of cellular material in cytolysomes, one of
which is included here [Cl]. This example contains a granular matrix,
membrane fragments [*] and a still recognisable mitochondrion [M'],
and these bodies frequently contain, in addition, reticulum cisternae,
ribosomes and other cellular material. Ultimately, the cytolysome
contents may become uniformly granular, or may retain closely packed
groups of ribosomes in the protein matrix, and it is possible that the
materials stored in this way are later mobilised and reused by the
body.

(× 65,000.)

*(RCA EMU 4. From Locke and Collins (1965). Reproduced by
courtesy of the authors and the* Journal of Cell Biology.)

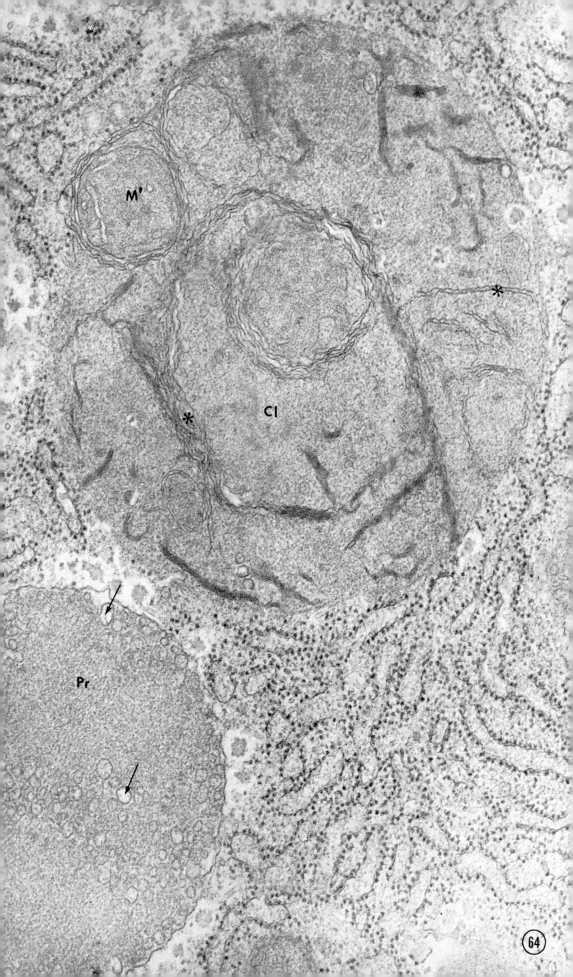

Mycetocytes

The non-pathogenic occurrence of micro-organisms in the body of insects is considerably more fully documented than are the possible physiological relationships involved in these associations. An intestinal bacterial flora carries out the digestion of cellulose in some mammals, and while bacteria with similar properties are presumably taken in and digested by many wood-feeding insects, a special 'fermentation chamber' has been developed in the hind-gut of certain beetle larvae, in which cellulose digestion may continue to the benefit of the insect. The spectacular flagellate fauna of the termite hind-gut (or perhaps the bacteria that these protozoa contain) contributes to the metabolic pool of the host by carrying out cellulose digestion under anaerobic conditions, and the astonishingly complex fine structure of these organisms has been investigated by Gibbons and Grimstone (1960), Grimstone and Gibbons (1966), and others.

A more intimate association between micro-organisms and insect cells is often found, however, where the former (usually yeasts or bacteria) are passed from one generation to the next, often by means of elaborate devices (Wigglesworth, 1965). These organisms may be contained within the gut lumen, or they may be aggregated into special cells termed mycetocytes, situated in the mid-gut, Malpighian tubules or, in the body cavity, within the gonads and the fat body. As Wigglesworth (1965) points out, it is not possible to generalise about the role of these 'symbionts', and while in some cases they may merely be tolerated by the insect, in other instances they may be useful or even necessary for normal growth and reproduction.

In *Periplaneta* and other cockroaches, bacteroids (bacterium-like organisms) are present between the ovarian follicle cells and the surface of the developing oocytes (Plates 111 and 112), and in due course enter the ooplasm (p. 339). In larvae and adults, mycetocytes are scattered throughout the fat body, and examples of electron micrographs of these cells are shown in Plates 65 and 66. The mycetocyte cytoplasm is more or less reduced in extent, but may include large lipid droplets and clusters of glycogen deposits. Rod-like bacteroid cells, possessing a cell membrane and a cell wall, are abundant, each lying within a membrane-lined cavity. These are somewhat variable in size, but are generally about 2·5 μ in length and 1 μ in diameter. In addition to these cells, large vacuoles are often present within the mycetocyte, containing a variety of less readily identified objects, which perhaps include other types or stages of micro-organism, and/or degenerating bacteroid cells. Milburn (1966) has carried out a detailed study of the fine structure of bacteroids occurring in the ovaries and mycetocytes of several genera of cockroaches. She found that in *Periplaneta* and *Leucophaea* mycetocytes large rod-like bacteroids, together with a few smaller dense rods are found in both larvae and adults, but that in other cockroaches the symbionts undergo a striking 'metamorphosis' during the period of oocyte development and at other times when the demands on lipid and glycogen stores in the fat body are very high. In the course of these changes, the bacteroids enlarge, lose their cell walls and become filled with concentric layers of strands. Milburn suggests that this transformation may be under the control of a hormone from the corpus cardiacum. The fine structure of micro-organisms in mycetocytes of the fat body and mid-gut of the beetle *Sitophilus* has been described by Grinyer and Musgrave (1966).

Intracellular bacteria isolated from cockroach fat body (Keller, 1950) were found to resemble, in their morphology and physiology, bacteria of legume roots (*Rhizobium leguminosarum*), and since they were able to use uric acid as a nitrogen source, were named *Rhizobium uricophilum*. Kilby (1963) has pointed out that this ability to utilise uric acid as a metabolite may play a part in making available to the insect the nitrogen contained within this excretory molecule, but that these micro-organisms may play a more important part in supplying factors needed for normal reproductive capacity. However, another bacterium, *Corynebacterium periplanetae*, has been reportedly cultured from cockroaches (Refs. in Wigglesworth, 1965), and the identity of the organisms present in the fat-body cells could perhaps best be established by correlated microbiological and electron microscopic study.

Clearly, the range of fine structure, disposition and transmission of symbionts in insects afford problems that deserve further attention from electron microscopists, who have the advantage, in the selection of material, of a wide and varied literature.

REFERENCES

GIBBONS, I. R., and GRIMSTONE, A. V. 1960. On flagellar structure in certain flagellates. *J. biophys. biochem. Cytol.*, **7**, 697–716.

GRIMSTONE, A. V., and GIBBONS, I. R. 1966. The fine structure of the centriolar apparatus and associated structures in the complex flagellates *Trichonympha* and *Pseudotrichonympha*. *Phil. Trans. R. Soc. B*, **250**, 215–242.

*GRINYER, I., and MUSGRAVE, A. J. 1966. Ultrastructure and peripheral membranes of the mycetomal micro-organisms of *Sitophilus granarius* (L.) (Coleoptera). *J. Cell Sci.*, **1**, 181–186.

KELLER, H. 1950. Die Kultur der intrazellularen Symbionten von *Periplaneta orientalis*. *Z. Naturforsch.*, **5**b, 269–273.

KILBY, B. A. 1963. The biochemistry of the insect fat body. In *Advances in Insect Physiology* (J. W. L. Beament, J. E. Treherne and V. B. Wigglesworth, eds.), Vol. 1, pp. 112–174. Academic Press, London and New York.

*MILBURN, N. S. 1966. Fine structure of the pleomorphic bacteroids in the mycetocytes and ovaries of several genera of cockroaches. *J. Insect Physiol.*, **12**, 1245–1254.

WIGGLESWORTH, V. B. 1965. *The Principles of Insect Physiology*, 6th edn, Ch. 11. Methuen, London.

Plates 65–66 ▷

Plate 65 ▷

Mycetocytes, or cells containing micro-organisms, are found in various parts of the body in a number of insects. These intracellular micro-organisms, generally bacteria or yeasts, may in some instances at least act as symbionts that supply the insect with useful molecules. In the cockroach *Periplaneta americana* mycetocytes are scattered throughout the fat body, and part of one of these cells is included in this micrograph. The cytoplasm contains small mitochondria [M] and many clusters of glycogen granules [Gy], together with bacteroid cells [Ba] lying within membrane-lined vacuoles [black asterisks]. In addition, a variety of smaller structures [arrows and white asterisks] are aggregated inside larger vacuoles, and perhaps represent other members of the symbiotic microflora of the fat body, or symbiont cells that are undergoing degeneration.

(×15,000.)

(*Philips EM 200.*)

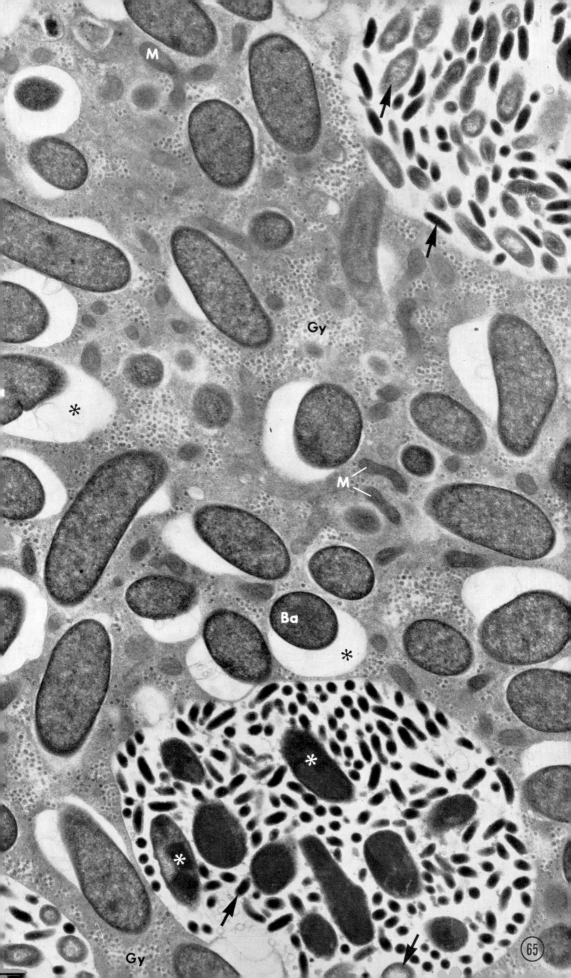

Plate 66 ▷

Another section of a cockroach fat-body mycetocyte, including the
nucleus [N], stores of glycogen granules [Gy] and large lipid droplets
[L]. The greater part of this field is occupied by large vacuoles
containing a variety of inclusions [arrows and asterisks] which may
represent living and/or degenerating micro-organisms, which cannot
at present be identified further.

(×10,000).

(*Philips EM 200.*)

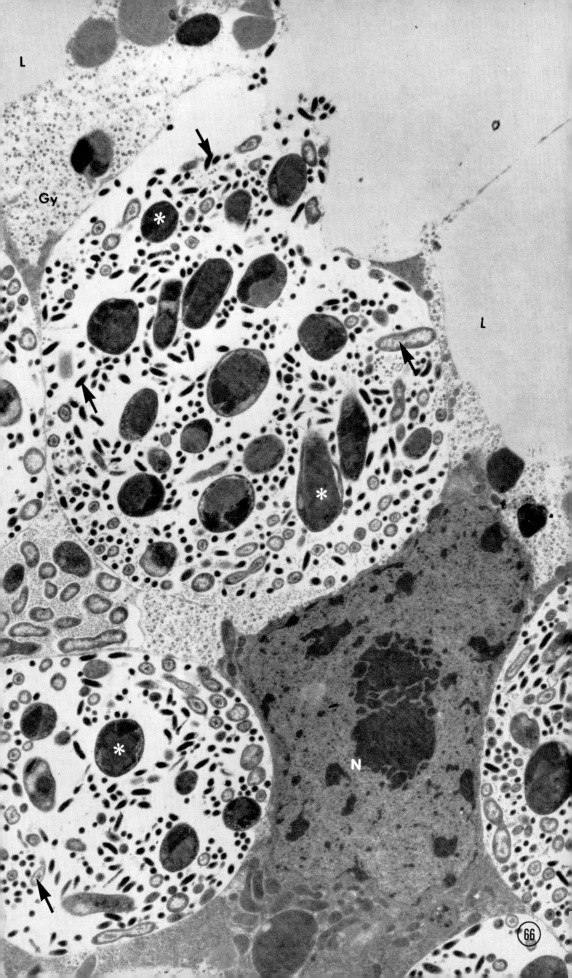

Salivary Glands and Silk Glands

In most insects, the bulk of digestion is carried out by enzymes secreted by the cells of the mid-gut, but in some species the salivary glands, opening into the mouth-parts, play a greater or lesser part in the breakdown of food material. The salivary glands are of ectodermal origin, and are members of a long list of dermal or integumentary glands whose ducts are lined with cuticle and open onto the surface of the body or into one of its invaginations (p. 351). The saliva is usually produced by the labial glands associated with the mouth-parts, but when these are devoted to other functions (for example the production of silk), glands of the maxillary or mandibular segments may assume the role of saliva secretion. The saliva may serve to moisten the food; it may lubricate and clean the mouth-parts, especially in species that feed on blood or plant juices by means of a 'hypodermic' stylet, and sometimes contains enzymes, most commonly amylase and invertase (Wigglesworth, 1965). In bees, the salivary secretions play an important part in the behaviour and maintenance of the colony; the mandibular glands produce pheromones, and the pharyngeal glands secrete the 'royal jelly' in young workers, which affords a special diet that results in the development of queens (p. 351), and later change to the production of a more conventional saliva containing carbohydrases.

Light microscopic studies showed that these glands vary a good deal in their size and arrangement, from simple elongated tubes to more complex systems of branches or lobes. The electron microscope has revealed that, as in the spermatheca (Plates 116 and 117) and other integumentary glands, the secretory cells are lined with porous material, and that the secretory products are transported to the exterior along cuticular ducts that are surrounded by non-glandular epithelial cells. Two types of secretory cell have been described by Kessel and Beams (1963) in salivary glands of the cockroach, while in a series of fine-structural studies on the complex glands of an aphid *Myzus*, which not only secrete the saliva but also manufacture a sheath which surrounds the stylets as they penetrate the plant tissues during feeding, no less than four structurally distinct gland cells have been recognised (Moericke and Wohlfarth-Botterman, 1960a, 1960b, 1963; Wohlfarth-Botterman and Moericke, 1960).

The salivary glands of Diptera have proved of great value in cytogenetic studies, since their nuclei contain giant polytene chromosomes which display, by the formation of localised 'puffs', patterns of activity that involve various chromosomal loci. These transient puffs occur sometimes at a particular stage of development, though often in patterns independent of this, and may control changes in cytoplasmic events. The bands of these polytene chromosomes are visible in electron micrographs as areas of compacted chromatin, and the chromosomal puffs, the nucleoli and other nuclear structures are also identifiable (Phillips, 1965). Phillips and Swift (1965) have studied the fine structural changes that occur in the cytoplasm of salivary glands of a fungus gnat *Sciara*, at different stages in larval life, and have suggested that the changing pattern of secretory activity that they found may be used as the basis of further enquiries into the relationship between chromosomal and cytoplasmic activity. Each of the paired glands of *Sciara* is an elongated tube, longer, indeed, than the larva itself, passing secreted material into a narrow duct and thence via a common duct into the fore-gut. Phillips and Swift found that three different types of secretion are manufactured in the anterior gland cells, and released into the gland lumen; in each case products synthesised within the rough-surfaced endoplasmic reticulum cisternae appeared to be passed in small vesicles to the abundant Golgi bodies, prior to release across the apical cell membrane. One type of secretion, an electron-transparent granule, occurs throughout most of larval life, disappearing only when feeding ceases before pupation; a small opaque granule type appears in late larvae, while another opaque granule of characteristic ellipsoidal shape may be found sporadically at all times. Phillips and Swift suggested, from these results, that the first secretion may contain digestive enzymes, while the other granules may contribute mucoprotein to the pupal cocoon and to the slime covering the larva, and they point out that the Golgi bodies appear to handle different materials, at different periods of larval life, as the endoplasmic reticulum varies its pattern of synthesis. Following a different line of approach, Berendes and Holt (1965) have compared nuclear and cytoplasmic changes in *Drosophila* mucopolysaccharide-secreting salivary gland cells during normal larval development, and in larval glands that have been implanted into the body of adults.

Other electron microscopic accounts of the salivary glands of flies include those of Jacob and Jurand (1963, 1965) on a sciarid and a chironomid, and more recently Macgregor and Mackie (1967) have described the formation and release of secretory products in the glands of the blackfly *Simulium*.

Salivary glands of insects not only provide very promising material for further studies on nucleo-cytoplasmic relations, but have also proved suitable for an entirely different purpose—for investigating the physiological importance of specialised cell-to-cell junctions, resolved in electron micrographs. Farquhar and Palade (1963) found that the adjoining lateral or intercellular membranes of various vertebrate epithelia may include narrow zones where membrane fusion occurs (*zonulae occludentes* or tight junctions), forming an effective seal that prevents passage of materials along the intracellular path between the cells. In addition to these junctions, a variety of desmosomes (*maculae* and *zonulae adhaerentes*) are present, whose function is probably to maintain the attachment of one cell to the next. In insects, similar tight junctions are also found in some epithelia (Plates 79B and 89), and extensive septate desmosomes, characterised in transverse section by regular bridges of dense material placed between the cell membranes (Plates 43, 89, etc.), have been described in many tissues of insects and other invertebrates, and investigated in detail by Locke (1965). Loewenstein and Kanno (1964) have pointed out that it has been generally assumed that the plasma membrane coating a cell presents a uniform barrier to ion flow over its entire surface—an assumption based on the behaviour of such special cells as erythrocytes, which are not connected one to another, and striated muscle and nerve cells, in which connections only occur at points of synapse. Electron micrographs of salivary glands showed that the secretory cells are linked by prominent septate desmosomes (Kessel and Beams, 1963; Wiener and others, 1964), and Loewenstein considered the question of whether these links are simply mechanical, for adhesion, or whether they play an additional role in the epithelium.

In brief, Loewenstein and Kanno were able to show, by the use of intracellular micro-electrode techniques, that while there is a very high resistance to the movement of ions across the epithelium of *Drosophila* salivary glands, along the intercellular spaces, the resistance to lateral ion flow between one cell and the next is little more than that in extruded cytoplasm. This conclusion was supported by the fact that the dye fluorescein, injected into a cell, readily diffused into its neighbours through the junctional membranes, but did not leak out into the extracellular spaces surrounding the epithelium. While there is no direct evidence concerning the structures that permit cell-to-cell movements of ions and molecules but prevent movements between the gland lumen and the space surrounding the gland, the septate desmosomes seem a possible candidate. Sometimes, as in the mid-gut and rectal papillae (Plates 79 and 89), both these and tight junctions occur together, and their respective roles provide an interesting and open problem.

The sealing off of the direct intercellular pathway across epithelia is of general occurrence, and it is this feature separating the apical and basal milieux that enables the cells to carry out efficiently such directional functions as the release of various secretions and the intracellular transport of water, ions and molecules.

Some details of the fine structure of *Calliphora* salivary glands are shown in Plates 67 and 68. The synthesis and release of secretion has not been followed in this insect, and these fields are included to illustrate the arrangement of intercellular membranes in the cuboidal epithelium. Alongside the basal half of the cell, each pair of adjacent lateral membranes are separated by an obvious gap, but then there abruptly intervenes a region, about 3–4 micra in length, where the membrane surfaces are joined by a series of septate desmosomes. Close to the apical border lies a narrow desmosomal collar or *zonula adhaerens*, which presumably contributes to the mechanical integrity of the epithelium.

SILK GLANDS

Silk is one of a wide variety of materials synthesised by integumentary glands of insects, and the most familiar example of this function is, of course, the spinning of silk by the labial (modified salivary glands) glands of lepidopterous larvae. Silk consists of two protein components, the strong elastic 'fibroin' and the gelatinous 'sericin'. Within the gland, the silk protein is water soluble, but upon being forced through the narrow orifice of the spinneret is formed into an insoluble fibre, in which the denatured protein molecules are unfolded and arranged longitudinally in a crystalline manner (Refs. in Wigglesworth, 1965). As might be expected, the fine structure of silk-secreting cells reflects their function in massive protein synthesis and export. Voigt (1965a, 1965b) and Akai (1963, 1964) have described the appearance of labial gland cells of the commercial silk-moth *Bombyx mori*: their cytoplasm contains an extremely profuse rough-surfaced endoplasmic reticulum, together with many Golgi bodies, and here, and in the glands secreting the silk used by caddis fly larvae in case building (Beams and Sekhon, 1966), these membranes appear to play a role similar to that described in other protein secreting cells. Proteins synthesised in association with the ribosomes attached to the reticulum cisternae appear to be transported to and concentrated within the Golgi bodies, from which secretion vesicles move through the cytoplasm to release their contents into the gland lumen.

The micrographs that have been selected to illustrate this aspect of insect cell function have been prepared from the larva of a fungus gnat, *Platyura fultoni*. The main claim to fame of this insect is that its larva is luminescent, and it snares its prey in a silken web studded with viscous droplets. Each of the paired silk glands consists of a long epithelial tube of secretory cells, connected to the mouth-parts by a narrow cuticle-lined duct. Virtually the whole of the cytoplasm of the secretory cells is filled with a tangled skein of ribosome-studded tubular elements of the endoplasmic reticulum (Plates 69 and 70). Scattered throughout the cell are many clusters of smooth-surfaced vesicles and short flattened cisternae, representing the Golgi bodies, containing small opaque droplets of material, presumably of protein that has been received from the surrounding reticulum and concentrated. Electron micrographs suggest that these droplets become pooled by progressive fusion of the smaller vesicles, and that the large sacs, containing many droplets that are formed in this way move to the apical surface of the cell, where the secretion is discharged into the lumen of the gland. The nucleus of this type of cell in *Platyura* is very large, often about 20 micra in diameter, and as in the homologous salivary glands of *Drosophila*, *Sciara*, and other related flies, contains many nucleoli and giant polytene chromosomes, identifiable in electron micrographs (Plate 69). The nuclear envelope, which in many cells is smoothly extended around the nuclear contents, is in this case deeply pleated.

With the versatility that is one of the characteristic features of insects, parts of the body other than the labial salivary glands are sometimes adapted for silk synthesis. Many examples are described by Lespéron (1937), and include tarsal glands, accessory genital glands and specialised regions of the Malpighian tubules, offering interesting material for further studies on the relationship between fine structure and function in insect cells.

REFERENCES

*AKAI, H. 1963. Electron microscopical observations on the fibroin formation in the silk gland of the silkworm, *Bombyx mori* L. *Bull. seric. Exp. Stn Japan*, **18**, 271–282.

*AKAI, H. 1964. Micromorphological changes of the glandular cell in the posterior division of the silk gland during the 5th larval instar of the silkworm, *Bombyx mori*. *Bull. seric. Exp. Stn Japan*, **18**, 475–511.

*BEAMS, H. W., and SEKHON, S. S. 1966. Morphological studies on secretion in the silk glands of the caddis fly larvae, *Platyphylax designatus* Walker. *Z. Zellforsch. mikrosk. Anat.*, **72**, 408–414.

*BERENDES, H. D., and HOLT, T. K. H. 1965. Differentiation of transplanted larval salivary glands of *Drosophila hydei* in adults of the same species. *J. exp. Zool.*, **160**, 299–318.

FARQUHAR, M. G., and PALADE, G. E. 1963. Junctional complexes in various epithelia. *J. Cell Biol.*, **17**, 375–412.

*JACOB, J., and JURAND, A. 1963. Electron microscope studies on salivary gland cells of *Bradysia mycorum* Frey (Sciaridae)—III. The structure of cytoplasm. *J. Insect Physiol.*, **9**, 849–857.

*JACOB, J., and JURAND, A. 1965. Electron microscope studies on salivary gland cells. V. The cytoplasm of *Smittia parthenogenetica* (Chironomidae). *J. Insect Physiol.*, **11**, 1337–1343.

*KESSEL, R. G., and BEAMS, H. W. 1963. Electron microscope observations on the salivary gland of the cockroach, *Periplaneta americana*. *Z. Zellforsch. mikrosk. Anat.*, **59**, 857–877.

LESPÉRON, L. 1937. Recherches cytologiques et expérimentales sur la secrétion de la soie. *Archs Zool. exp. gén.*, **79**, 1–156.

*LOCKE, M. 1965. The structure of septate desmosomes. *J. Cell Biol.*, **25**, 166–169.

LOEWENSTEIN, W. R., and KANNO, Y. 1964. Studies on an epithelial (gland) cell junction. I. Modifications of surface membrane permeability. *J. Cell Biol.*, **22**, 565–586.

*MACGREGOR, H. C., and MACKIE, J. B. 1967. Fine structure of the cytoplasm in salivary glands of *Simulium*. *J. Cell Sci.*, **2**, 137–144.

*MOERICKE, V., and WOHLFARTH-BOTTERMAN, K. E. 1960a. Zur funktionellen Morphologie der Speicheldrüsen von Homopteren. I. Mitteilung. Die Hauptzellen der Hauptdrüse von *Myzus persicae* (Sulz.), Aphididae. *Z. Zellforsch. mikrosk. Anat.*, **51**, 157–184.

*MOERICKE, V., and WOHLFARTH-BOTTERMAN, K. E. 1960b. Zur funktionellen Morphologie der Speicheldrüsen von Homopteren. IV. Mitteilung. Die Ausführgänge der Speicheldrüsen von *Myzus persicae* (Sulz.), Aphididae. *Z. Zellforsch. mikrosk. Anat.*, **53**, 25–49.

*MOERICKE, V., and WOLFARTH-BOTTERMAN, K. E. 1963. Zur funktionellen Morphologie der Speicheldrüsen von Homopteren. II. Mitteilung. Die Deck- und die Zentrallzellen der Speicheldrüse von *Myzus persicae* (Sulz.), Aphididae. *Z. Zellforsch. mikrosk. Anat.*, **59**, 165–183.

*PHILLIPS, D. M. 1965. An ordered filamentous component in *Sciara* (Diptera) salivary gland cell nuclei. *J. Cell Biol.*, **26**, 677–683.

*PHILLIPS, D. M., and SWIFT, H. 1965. Cytoplasmic fine structure of *Sciara* salivary glands. I. Secretion. *J. Cell Biol.*, **27**, 395–409.

*VOIGT, W.-H. 1965a. Zur funktionellen Morphologie der Fibroin- und Sericin-Sekretion der Seidendrüse von *Bombyx mori* L. I. Mitteilung. Der proximale Abschnitt der Seidendrüse. *Z. Zellforsch. mikrosk. Anat.*, **66**, 548–570.

*VOIGT, W.-H. 1965b. Zur funktionellen Morphologie der Fibroin- und Sericin-Sekretion der Seidendrüse von *Bombyx mori* L. II. Mitteilung. Der mediale Abschnitt der Seidendrüse. *Z. Zellforsch. mikrosk. Anat.*, **66**, 571–582.

*WIENER, J., SPIRO, D., and LOEWENSTEIN, W. R. 1964. Studies on an epithelial (gland) cell junction. II. Surface structure. *J. Cell Biol.*, **22**, 587–598.

WIGGLESWORTH, V. B. 1965. *The Principles of Insect Physiology*, 6th edn, Ch. 13. Methuen, London.

*WOHLFARTH-BOTTERMAN, K. E., and MOERICKE, V. 1960. Zur funktionellen Morphologie der Speicheldrüsen von Homopteren. III. Mitteilung. Die Nebendrüse von *Myzus persicae* (Sulz.) Aphididae. *Z. Zellforsch. mikrosk. Anat.*, **52**, 346–361.

Plates 67–70 ▷

Plate 67 ▷

An electron micrograph of part of two cells in the secretory salivary gland epithelium of an adult blowfly, *Calliphora erythrocephala*. The cuboidal cells rest on a delicate basement membrane [BM], which is closely associated with tracheoles. The spherical or ovoid nucleus [N] is often placed in the apical half of the cell. The details of synthesis and release of salivary secretions have not been followed in this insect, and at the stage shown here the cells are not filled with the conspicuous secretion droplets that have been described in the salivary glands of other species. The chief feature of interest in this field lies in the arrangement of the intercellular membranes; over much of their extent, the adjoining lateral membranes are loosely apposed across a wide gap, but in the apical region of the cell [CJ] a close intercellular junction is present, which includes a series of septate desmosomes. This junction is shown at higher magnification in the next plate; it has been suggested that this specialised region of the epithelium facilitates passage of materials from one cell to the next, but closes the intercellular channel between the apical and basal sides of the epithelium.

(× 14,000.)

(*Philips EM 200.*)

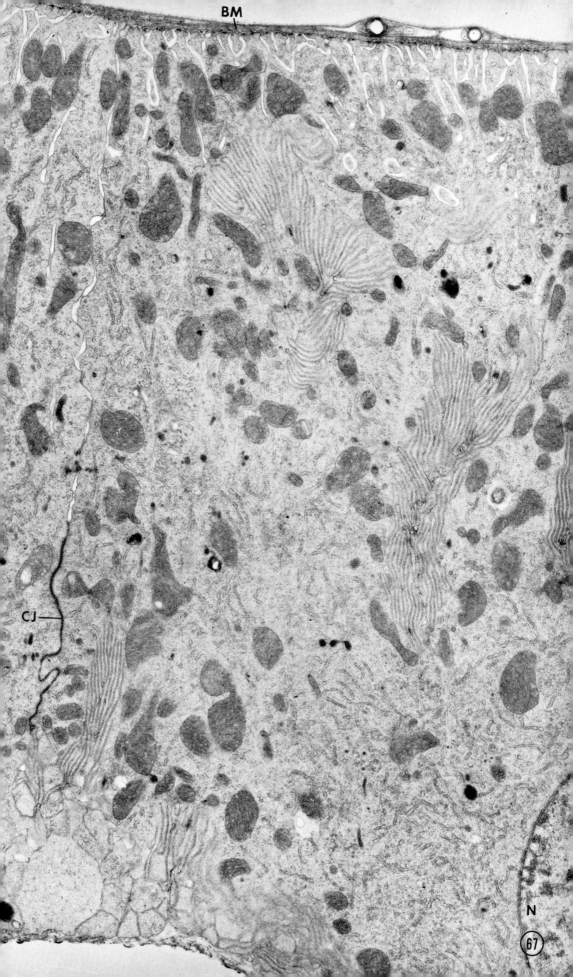

BM

CJ

N

67

Plate 68 ▷

A region of intercellular junction between two salivary gland cells
from *Calliphora*, similar to that shown in Plate 67, but at higher
magnification. Close to the apical surface of the cells, the lateral
membranes are linked by a series of septate desmosomes [SD], and
a desmosome region of the zonula adhaerens type [D] ringing the
cell and presumably playing a part in maintaining the integrity of the
epithelium. These septate desmosomes perhaps provide the observed
high resistence to intercellular movement of ions and molecules
between the inside and outside of the gland, and may at the same
time facilitate lateral transfer of these from one cell to the next along
the epithelium. Microtubules [Mt] are present in the cytoplasm, and
this field also illustrates the folding of the apical cell membrane to
form closely packed leaflets [*].

(× 70,000.)

(*Philips EM 200.*)

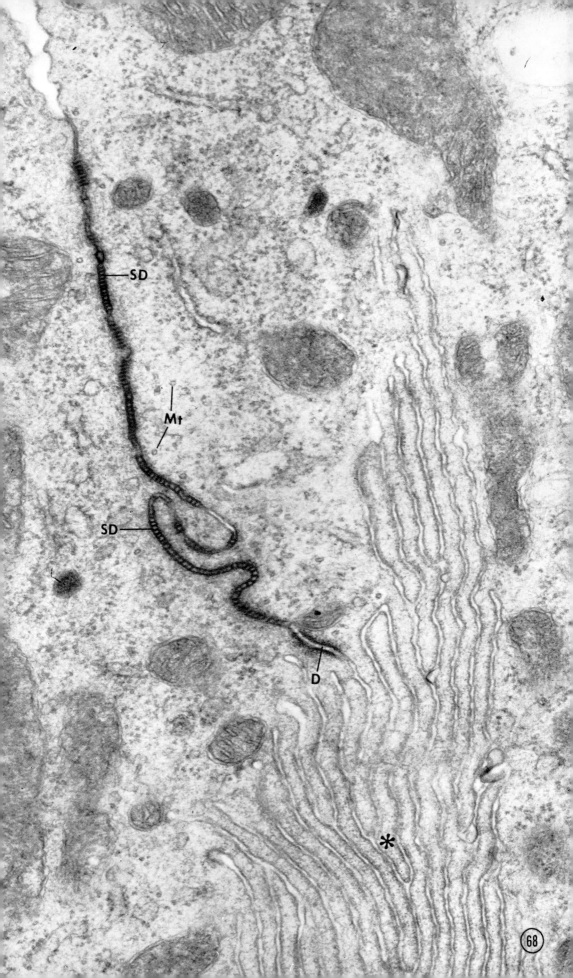

SD

Mt

SD

D

*

68

Plate 69 ▷

A micrograph including part of the nucleus and the surrounding
cytoplasm in a silk-secreting labial gland cell from a larva of the fungus
gnat (mycetophilid) *Platyura*. As in the salivary glands of *Drosophila*
and allied Diptera, the nuclei of these cells contain giant polytene
chromosomes, the chromatin bands of which are resolved here [white
asterisks], together with nucleolar profiles [thick arrows]. The
nuclear envelope is folded into deep ridges and troughs [arrows],
and mitochondria [M] lie in the adjacent cytoplasm. The cytoplasm
of these cells is virtually filled with intertwining tubules of the rough-
surfaced endoplasmic reticulum [ER], within which are collected the
silk proteins, synthesised in association with the ribosomes studding
the tubules, and these proteins are believed to be passed to and
concentrated within the membranes of the Golgi bodies, prior to their
release from the cell.

($\times$ 18,000.)

(*Philips EM 200.*)

218

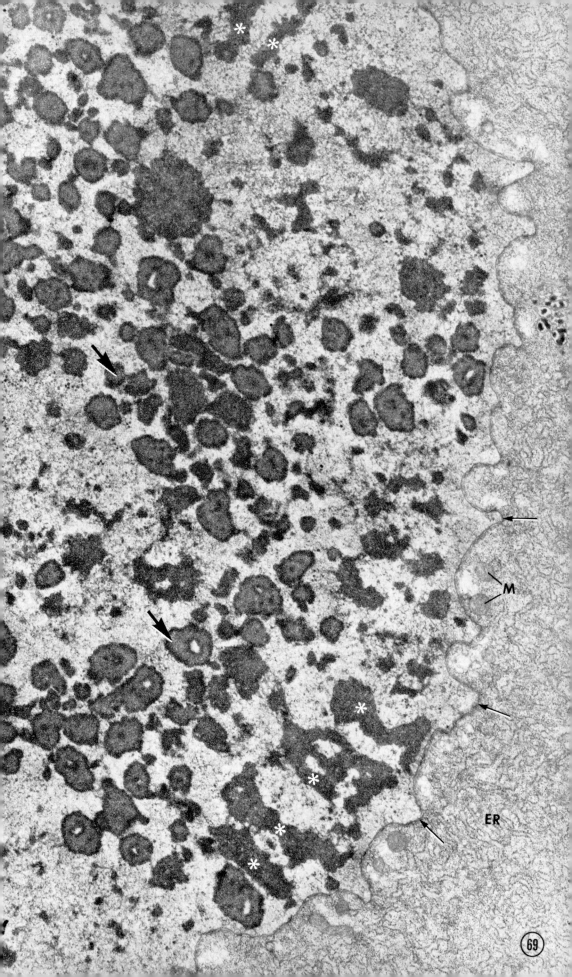

ER

M

Plate 70 ▷

A field showing the cytoplasmic features of the basal portion of a silk
gland in the larva of a fungus gnat, *Platyura fultoni*. The thin basement
membrane [BM] is shown at upper left, and small mitochondria [M]
are fairly abundant in the underlying basal edge of the cell—perhaps
playing a part in the entry of silk protein precursors from the
surrounding haemolymph. The great bulk of the cytoplasm of these
specialised cells is occupied by rough-surfaced tubular elements of
the endoplasmic reticulum [ER], engaged in the synthesis of the
proteins of the silk. Golgi bodies [G] contain small cisternae and
vesicles, clustered together and lacking attached ribosomes: within
these are sequestered small opaque droplets, thought to arise by
concentration of secreted material passed to them from the rough-
surfaced endoplasmic reticulum. Larger secretion vesicles [VS] arise
by coalesence of the smaller Golgi vesicles, and these migrate to the
apical cell surface and discharge their contents into the gland lumen.
A small portion of the large nucleus [N] is included at lower right,
surrounded by numerous mitochondria [M], and further details of
nuclear structure are shown in the next plate.

($\times$ 28,000.)

(*Philips EM 200.*)

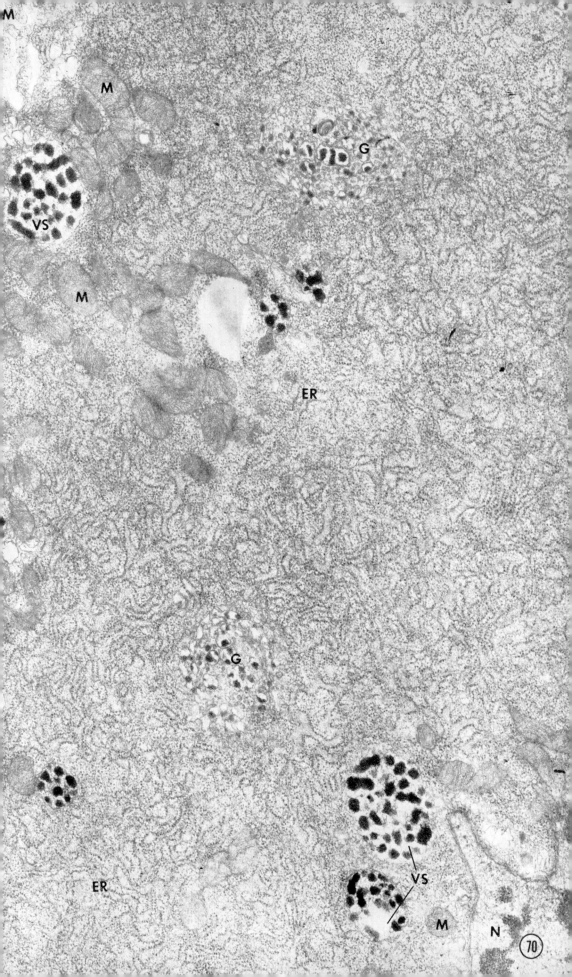

The Fore-gut, Mid-gut and Peritrophic Membrane

The intestinal tract of the insect comprises three structurally and embryologically distinct regions, arranged in sequence to form an epithelial tube, continuous from mouth to anus. The first and last of these regions, the fore-gut and the hind-gut, are ectodermal in origin and in common with other ectodermal invaginations within the body (including, for example, the tracheae and lower genital ducts) are lined with cuticle continuous with that of the body surface. The intervening mid-gut is endodermal, and possesses no cuticular intima.

Over the range of insects, the fore-gut shows a good deal of variation in its morphology, but three main regions are generally recognised: the buccal cavity, the pharynx and the oesophagus. All of these regions are equipped with visceral muscle fibres, and this muscular investment is particularly robust around the pharynx, which is responsible for the ingestion and backward passage of food towards the mid-gut. The oesophagus is sometimes represented by a narrow tube, but often includes a crop provided by a simple dilatation or by a lateral oesophageal diverticulum. The passage of food from the fore-gut to the mid-gut is controlled by a muscular sphincter at the posterior end of the former, and this region is sometimes distinguishable as the proventriculus, which may be equipped with cuticular spines or teeth which filter or crush food particles leaving the fore-gut. The divisions and morphological diversity of the fore-gut are achieved within the simple framework of the muscular sheath, and a generally thin epithelial layer of cells together with the cuticle they secrete. As an example of the fine structure exhibited by this part of the intestinal tract, a micrograph of the blowfly crop is shown in Plate 71.

The crop may serve merely as a storage depot for ingested food, prior to its passage into the mid-gut. In some species, however, a limited amount of digestion may occur in the crop when its contents receive salivary or mid-gut secretions. Little or no absorption of nutrients into the haemolymph takes place across the crop wall, and the crop (for example of the cockroach and blowfly) resists evaporative water loss for long periods, when removed from the body. This impermeability is a general feature of the fore-gut and, by contrast, much of the uptake of the products of digestion takes place along the mid-gut (p. 226), while the hind-gut is often an important site of water and ion reabsorption (p. 264).

The diaphanous wall of the crop (Plate 71) is invested with a network of slender muscle fibres, the contraction of which regulates the extrusion of the fluid contents of the reservoir. As in other small visceral fibres (Plates 12 and 108), the contractile material virtually fills the cell and the sarcoplasmic reticulum (p. 36) is very poorly developed. The epithelial cells rest on a narrow basement membrane, which lies closely against the extracellular sheath or sarcolemma of the muscles. This epithelial layer is extremely thin; indeed, it is in places thinner than the cuticular lining that it secretes.

In the field shown here, the latter is about 1 micron in thickness and displays the 'bottle-brush' appearance often seen in electron micrographs of the endocuticle at the surface of the animal (Plate 3). The probable arrangement of chitin and protein within the cuticle resulting in this pattern is mentioned further on p. 2. Adjoining the lumen of the crop lies a narrow layer of dense epicuticle, and it is this part of the lining that is thought to render the crop wall so impermeable. The lining of the rectum of the same insect, it is interesting to note, must lack a waterproofing device allowing it to play an important part in osmoregulation. The basis of this physical difference between gut cuticles that are quite similar in appearance and thickness may lie in the presence or absence of an epicuticular lipid layer comparable with that preventing water loss over the general body surface.

THE MID-GUT

The design of the vertebrate gut employs extensive division of labour in which different cells are responsible for the secretion of digestive enzymes, the production of mucus, and the absorption of digested nutrient materials. Furthermore, the breakdown of food carried out by enzymes released from gland cells of the stomach and intestine is augmented by the enzymes of the pancreatic juice, and by the bile secreted by the liver which facilitates the breakdown and absorption of fat. The cells comprising the insect mid-gut tube are clearly differentiated, both structurally and functionally, from the epithelia of the rest of the digestive tract, but in some cases, at least, the same cells are able both to secrete digestive enzymes into the gut lumen and to absorb the products of digestion. In addition, these cells may act as storage depots for food reserves, and may be involved in the synthesis of specific proteins (p. 338) including those incorporated into the yolk of developing oocytes.

An extensive literature exists on the organisation of the mid-gut in a wide variety of insects. While light microscopic studies have established the histological features of this part of the digestive tract, details of the processes of secretion and absorption are by no means clear. The mid-gut consists primarily of columnar cells, which bear a 'striated border' along their apical surface bordering the lumen. This epithelium rests on a basement membrane and is invested with circular and longitudinal visceral muscle fibres. Along the basal portion of the epithelium are inserted small undifferentiated cells, arranged singly or in groups, which are responsible for the maintenance of the mid-gut through the replacement of cells lost by degeneration. Among the mid-gut epithelial cells of some insects, notably in the larvae of Lepidoptera, are interspersed cells in which the apical surface is invaginated to form a large flask-shaped cavity: the function of these 'goblet cells' has for long been in doubt, although they are clearly unrelated to the mucus-secreting goblet cells of vertebrates to which they bear a superficial resemblance.

Aspects of the fine structure of mid-gut cells have been described in several electron microscopic studies, including those of Beams and Anderson (1957) on *Malacosoma* and *Melanoplus*, Waterhouse and Wright (1960) on *Calliphora*, Bertram and Bird (1961) and Roth and Porter (1964) on *Aëdes*, Khan and Ford (1962) on *Dysdercus* and, most recently, in the work of Anderson and Harvey (1966) on *Cecropia*. The micrographs reproduced here have been prepared from the mid-gut of the cockroach *Periplaneta* (Plate 72), the flour moth *Ephestia* (Plates 74 to 79), and the blowfly *Calliphora* Plate 73).

224

Plate 72 illustrates the appearance of the basal border of the cockroach mid-gut, together with the various cellular and extracellular components that surround it. The circular and longitudinal muscle fibres disposed around the gut may be as little as a micron in thickness. These visceral muscles, as is always the case in the insect body, are striated, but they are functionally comparable with the smooth fibres of the vertebrate gut in their ability to perform slow peristaltic contractions which move the food along the intestinal tract. These cells are set in a thick extracellular matrix which contains collagen fibrils, and this connective tissue binding presumably acts as a mechanical link through which the muscles may exert their effect on the underlying cellular tube. Many nerve axons, generally containing opaque neurosecretory droplets, course through the sheath surrounding the mid-gut. These evidently include motor units of the stomatogastric (visceral) nervous system, which terminate on the gut muscles. There is some evidence (Refs. in Wigglesworth, 1965) that the secretion of digestive enzymes in the mid-gut may be under hormonal control, and while such a hormone might be released elsewhere, to reach the gut cells via the circulating haemolymph, it seems possible, alternatively, that this release could take place in the vicinity of the gut surface from some of the neurosecretory axons within the connective tissue sheath. Details of the musculature and tracheolar supply of mid-gut cells of the blowfly are illustrated in Plate 73.

The mid-gut cells rest on a basement membrane, about 0·5 micron in thickness. As in other species (Roth and Porter, 1964; Anderson and Harvey, 1966, etc.) the basal region of the columnar cells of the cockroach mid-gut is deeply dissected by irregular infoldings of the cell membrane, and many mitochondria lie in the resulting narrow cytoplasmic sheets. In *Cecropia*, the extracellular spaces formed by these infoldings may extend two-thirds of the way to the apical border, beyond the level of the nucleus. These invaginations enormously enhance the area of basal plasma membrane possessed by each cell, across which materials may pass from the cytoplasm to the haemolymph and vice versa.

In *Periplaneta*, the undifferentiated replacement cells are collected together in groups or 'nests' (nidi). As is illustrated in Plate 72, they are crescentic in form and contain an elongated nucleus set within a very restricted cytoplasm. As in other undifferentiated cells (for example the myoblasts of muscle, and spermatogonia), the cytoplasm is organised very simply and contains few membranes but large numbers of unattached ribosomes. As they differentiate to replace degenerating mid-gut cells, they elongate and acquire, along one line of development, the apical microvilli of columnar epithelial cells, or alternatively the complex cavity of goblet cells. How the developmental fate of the individual cell is determined, and indeed how differentiation is triggered, are interesting and unsolved morphogenetic problems.

The 'striated border' resolved in the light microscope along the apical margin of the absorptive cells of the vertebrate intestine and most epithelial cells of the insect mid-gut is represented, in the electron microscope, by great numbers of cylindrical processes or microvilli, projecting into the gut lumen. In *Ephestia* these are about 0·1 micron in diameter and reach a length of about 4 micra (Plate 74). Transverse sections through this microvillar 'brush border' (Plate 78A) show that the projections are arranged in a regular hexagonal array. The similarity between these gut microvilli in insects and vertebrates extends to the fine details of their structure: in each group of animals, the cytoplasm of the microvilli contains many very slender fibrils which extend for a short distance into the main body of the cell (Plate 74A), and in each case the plasma

Q

membrane covering the microvilli bears a fine coat (the 'glycocalyx'), probably of mucopolysaccharide material. Pinocytic vesicles, pinched off into the cytoplasm from small pits arising between the microvilli, are sometimes observed (Plate 74A).

Little is known, as yet, of the ways in which nutrient molecules are taken up from the lumen of the insect gut into the adjoining cells. Some materials are undoubtedly absorbed by pinocytosis; in *Ephestia* larvae fed on meal mixed with ferritin (a ferric hydroxide-protein complex), particles of this electron opaque marker enter the cells in this way (Smith *et al.*). However, it seems probable that much, perhaps most nutrients are taken up directly through the apical plasma membrane in the form of small molecules, not detectable in thin sections examined in the electron microscope. In the intestine of mammals fed on lipid, for example, droplets of fat appear within smooth-surfaced cisternae in the apical region of the absorptive cells, and these are thought to be built up from monoglycerides and fatty acids passing through the plasma membrane (Fawcett, 1966). The apical brush border greatly increases the membrane facing the lumen, by a factor of about 18 in *Ephestia*, and hence improves the efficiency of food absorption.

The cytoplasm of columnar mid-gut cells is richly supplied with cisternae of the rough-surfaced endoplasmic reticulum, and agranular cisternae collected into Golgi bodies are of frequent occurrence, especially in the vicinity of the nucleus (Plate 75). While it is probable that these membranes play a part in the synthesis and release of digestive enzymes, the details of this function, in terms of fine structure, are not well understood and indeed may vary from one insect species to another. It is tempting to suppose that the dense droplets present within the Golgi cisternae in *Ephestia* gut cells may represent secreted material comparable with the zymogen granules of pancreatic cells, but at present this is mere conjecture, since the release of this material into the lumen has not been observed. Moreover, these insect cells appear to lack the intra-cisternal granules enclosed by rough membranes that mark the early stages of zymogen secretion. Bertram and Bird (1961) have described in adult female mosquitos a remarkable cycle of changes in the arrangement of the endoplasmic reticulum that is connected with the nutritional state of the insect. In unfed individuals, the rough-surfaced cisternae are disposed in tight whorls within the mid-gut cytoplasm, which unfurl to distribute the cisternae throughout the cell some hours after the insect has taken a blood meal, and re-form after the blood has been digested. However, this behaviour may be related either to the digestion of protein, the absorption of the products of digestion, or perhaps to the synthesis of specific proteins within the gut cells, passed on to the developing oocytes (p. 338).

The suggestion has frequently been made that secretion of digestive enzymes in the mid-gut is holocrine or merocrine, involving the splitting off or extrusion of globules of cytoplasm from the columnar cells. Khan and Ford (1962) have shown that, in *Dysdercus* at least, this interpretation is erroneous. In this insect, loss of the brush border, vacuolation of the cytoplasm, shedding of globules of cytoplasm and, ultimately, loss of the nucleus are degenerative changes that afflict the mid-gut cells progressively, during starvation, and this breakdown is rapidly checked when the insect is fed.

Histological studies revealed the presence of specialised 'goblet cells', distributed amongst the columnar epithelium of the mid-gut in some insect groups, including mayflies and larvae of butterflies and moths. The characteristic feature of these cells was recognised to be the invagination of the apical border to form a deep cavity which confines the nucleus to the basal region. The function of these goblet cells has been quite obscure, and in the past they have sometimes been regarded as inactive or senescent forms of typical epithelial cells. However, Anderson and Harvey (1966) have found, with the electron microscope, that these are not merely indented epithelial cells, but possess a detailed fine structure that differs markedly from that of neighbouring columnar cells and which is thought to reflect a role not in secretion and absorption, but in ion transport between the haemolymph and the gut lumen.

Some of the structural features of these cells, in the mid-gut of *Ephestia*, are illustrated in Plates 76, 77 and 78B. The light microscope showed that a 'striated border' accompanies the apical invagination lining the cavity of the cell, and as elsewhere along the mid-gut this striation arises from the presence of microvilli, projecting from the cell surface. Unlike those of the columnar cells, the microvilli of the goblet cavity are irregular in thickness and arrangement and, moreover, particularly towards the basal region of the cavity possess tightly inserted mitochondria. The cavity of the goblet cell is not intracellular but, as illustrated by Anderson and Harvey, communicates with the gut lumen through a narrow tortuous channel between microvilli plugging the neck.

Plant-feeding insects, including lepidopterous larvae, have to overcome a special physiological problem posed by their diet. The electrical potential difference maintained across the surface membrane of most animal cells (notably nerve axons and muscle fibres) results from a high internal and low external concentration of potassium ions. In plant materials, however, the concentration of potassium ions is very high, while that of sodium ions is very low, and phytophagous animals must prevent the potassium level in the body fluids from equilibrating with that of their food. In plant-feeding vertebrates, excess of this cation entering the body through the gut wall is removed by the kidneys, while in many insects a similar service is rendered by the Malpighian tubules (p. 286), the cells of which actively transport potassium from the haemolymph into the tubule lumen. Harvey and his colleagues have shown that in larvae of the silkmoth *Cecropia*, the mid-gut also shows this regulatory capacity to a remarkable degree (Refs. in Anderson and Harvey, 1966), and from their work on mid-gut fine structure Anderson and Harvey have put forward good reasons for supposing that this transport is carried out by the goblet cells. First, these represent an unusual component of the mid-gut, while columnar cells of the type found in Lepidoptera are of general occurrence in other insect Orders. A more telling point is that the close association between mitochondria and the cell membrane (in this case in the microvilli of the goblet cavity) is found in many cells that carry out transport functions. These include, for example, distal convoluted tubules in the kidney, striated ducts of the parotid gland, the salt gland of marine birds (Refs. in Fawcett, 1962), and in the insect body in Malpighian tubules, anal and rectal papillae, and elsewhere (pp. 264, 286). Indeed, there is a further point of similarity between the goblet cell microvilli and the apical pleats of rectal papilla cells in that in each case the plasma membrane lying beside the mitochondria is studded with small particles (Plates 78B and 90): of the function of these particles we know nothing at present, but it is conceivable that they are part of the machinery for moving ions across the cell membrane. Whether the goblet mitochondria are placed near the membrane of the microvilli in order to provide the energy needed to transport ions out of the cell, or whether they are themselves able to take up and concentrate potassium before it is expelled (a possibility raised by Anderson and Harvey) is by no means clear. Lastly, these investigators have suggested that the fluid within the goblet cavity may contain lower concentrations of potassium than the gut lumen, and may thus be a device for reducing the metabolic work required to extrude potassium from the cell.

An additional feature of interest that has been brought to light by electron microscopy concerns the cell-to-cell links that are found in the mid-gut. In *Cecropia*, one or more tight junctions are present along the lateral surface of adjoining columnar cells, or between these and the goblet cells. These junctions are similar to those that are believed to seal off the direct intercellular route to water, ions and small water-soluble molecules in vertebrate epithelia (Farquhar and Palade, 1963). In the lepidopteran mid-gut, they may well prevent leakage of potassium ions from the gut lumen back into the haemolymph and thus maintain the regulatory properties of the gut wall. In *Ephestia*, tight junctions are accompanied by septate desmosomes (Plate 79), though whether the latter facilitate the movement of ions between adjacent cells, as has been proposed in insect salivary glands (p. 211), is unknown.

The electron microscope has provided us with new information about the construction of insect mid-gut cells, and has provided answers to some previously unresolved morphological questions. However, it is clear that so far only a preliminary step has been taken towards relating digestive function to cellular fine structure. Even in the columnar cells of the type illustrated here, which make up the greater part of the mid-gut epithelium in the majority of insects, the mode of enzyme secretion, the uptake of digested materials and the way in which these are passed through the basal cell surface into the circulatory system, all require further investigation. Furthermore, as yet little is known of the range of interspecific variation in the types of cell present in the mid-gut: in many flies, for example, this is subdivided into histologically distinct regions in which enzyme secretion and absorption of nutrients and of water from the lumen are said to occur separately. Waterhouse and Wright (1960) have described two cell types within a short segment of the blowfly mid-gut (the 'mosaic epithelium') each differing in fine structure from the columnar cells described above. To quote another example of cell specialisation, the long slender diverticula stemming from the mid-gut of the stick insect contain epithelial cells that are like no other cells so far recognised in insects, but bear some structural resemblance to the acid-secreting oxyntic cells of the vertebrate stomach (Plate 80).

THE PERITROPHIC MEMBRANE

Although the mid-gut epithelium does not secrete a compact cuticular lining, the food in this part of the digestive tract in most insects is separated from the apical surface of the gut cells by an extracellular sheath termed the peritrophic membrane. This structure is generally supposed to play a role similar to that of mucus in the vertebrate gut, in protecting the mid-gut cells from mechanical damage caused by abrasive food particles. Peritrophic membranes are not, however, restricted to species that ingest solid food, in which risk of such damage might be expected, but are also present in some fluid-feeding insects including adult Lepidoptera and Diptera.

Histological studies suggested that peritrophic membranes are formed in two main ways. In representatives of several Orders (Orthoptera, Ephemeroptera, Odonata, Lepidoptera, Coleoptera and Hymenoptera) this sheath is reportedly formed along the length of the mid-gut, presumably as a secretory product of the epithelial cells. In these insects, several peritrophic cylinders, delaminated at intervals, may accumulate within the mid-gut lumen. A second mode of formation has been described in larval and adult flies, and in a few other forms. Here, a viscous secretion produced by specialised columnar cells at the anterior limit of the mid-gut is supposedly formed into a tube upon being pressed out through an annular mould provided by the narrow cleft situated between these cells and the surface of a flange of fore-gut tissue protruding into the mid-gut. On an industrial scale, this principle of the annular mould is used in the production of plastic tubing.

Much of our knowledge of cell architecture at the level of the electron microscope has stemmed from the examination of very thin sections of intact tissues. Before the development of microtomes capable of providing sections of the required thinness (0·1 micron or less), electron microscopists were restricted in their choice of biological material to whole mounts of objects thin enough, when dried upon a supporting film, to permit the formation of an image. By this simple technique, for example, the endoplasmic reticulum was first detected in the cytoplasm of fibroblast cells and taenidial thickenings were found to extend along the finest ramifications of the tracheal system (p. 136). In this way also, the fine structure of the delicate peritrophic membranes of several insect species was investigated by Huber (1950), Huber and Haasser (1950), Mercer and Day (1952), and others referred to in a review of the subject of insect digestion by Waterhouse (1957). These studies showed that in most cases the intact membrane comprises a network of fine fibrils, in some species irregularly arranged and in others forming square or hexagonal lattices, together with a thin amorphous film filling the interstices. Chemically, peritrophic membranes have been shown to resemble the inner layers of the cuticle, in possessing both chitin and protein (Refs. in Waterhouse, 1957; Wigglesworth, 1965).

The electron micrographs illustrating the fine structure of this component of the alimentary tract have been prepared from thin sections of the proventriculus and adjoining mid-gut epithelium of adults of the blowfly *Calliphora*, and are shown in Plates 81 to 85. In this insect, as in mosquitos (Wigglesworth, 1930), an annular press is present, provided by a mushroom-shaped invagination of the fore-gut and a ring of tall columnar mid-gut cells, and in each instance material secreted by the latter is extruded as a tube which extends backwards along the gut lumen. However, the 'peritrophic membrane' of the blowfly has proved more complex than was earlier suspected, and the extruded tube is in fact only one of three components of the 'membrane', each distinct in fine structure and origin.

The most anterior cells of the mid-gut epithelium, for some time recognised to be involved in peritrophic membrane formation in some species, are arranged in a double ring separated by a narrow cleft. They are tall and each fans out from a very narrow basal 'tail' to a broader apical surface which, as in most other mid-gut cells (p. 225) bears a brush border of microvilli (Plate 81). The nuclei lie in the expanded apical half of the cell, and throughout the cytoplasm membrane systems are very richly developed. Conspicuous Golgi bodies, consisting of clusters of vesicles up to 0·3 micron in diameter, containing finely granular material, are generously distributed, while ribosome-studded cisternae of the endoplasmic reticulum are abundant in the intervening cytoplasm. Vesicles derived from the Golgi bodies congregate along the apical surface of the cell, and appear to discharge their secretory contents into the extracellular space between the microvilli. The outer ring of columnar cells is similarly constructed, but appears to manufacture a more homogeneous, opaque secretion, perhaps a second constituent of the membrane that forms in the extracellular cleft between the two epithelial rings.

229

The fabric of this membrane first becomes visible midway along the cleft, between the tips of the opposed ranks of microvilli (Plate 81), and becomes progressively thicker until it is finally spun off the inner epithelial ring into the space adjoining the oesophageal invagination (Plates 82 and 83). As this membrane leaves the epithelium that has produced it, it presents a reticular appearance (Plate 82), but soon narrows down to a uniform sheet about 0·1–0·2 micron in thickness, built up of a pair of interrupted laminae linked by transverse struts (Plates 84 and 85). The abundance of rough-surfaced cisternae within the cells secreting this structure suggests that it contains at least part of the protein known to be present in the peritrophic membrane.

As the first component of the peritrophic membrane passes by the surface of the oesophageal invagination (Plate 83), it is joined by a second sheet that peels away from these fore-gut cells: this is about 0·3–0·4 micron in total thickness and includes a very narrow opaque zone, somewhat resembling the cuticulin layer of the epicuticle in appearance. Chitin is present in the peritrophic membrane, but it is not known whether this polysaccharide is contributed by the ectodermal fore-gut cells, by the endodermal mid-gut cells, or by both of these epithelia.

Behind the specialised cells secreting the first membrane, the mid-gut epithelium proper is thinner; the cells contain fewer Golgi bodies and bear a more regular brush border facing the gut lumen. Above the microvilli of this brush border, the third component of the peritrophic membrane of the blowfly gut makes its appearance (Plate 84): this is a very thin sheet, and comprises a dense layer about 200 Å in thickness, to which are attached wisps of fibrous material. These three distinctive extracellular structures extend apparently unaltered through the mid-gut, and continue through the lumen of the hind-gut. They are seen together, in a transverse section of the posterior mid-gut lumen, in Plate 85.

Light microscopic studies revealed two modes of peritrophic membrane formation, and also gave some indication that both delamination from the mid-gut surface and extrusion through an annular press may sometimes contribute to the membrane of a single species. In the adult blowfly, this certainly seems to be the case, and the picture is further complicated by a contribution added by the fore-gut. However, it would be most rash to draw any general conclusions from the situation in one insect, and further fine structural work is needed to establish the extent to which the picture described here obtains elsewhere.

Our knowledge of the structure and formation of the peritrophic membrane outweighs our understanding of its function. In some insects, it may indeed protect the mid-gut cells from damage, but the provision of an elaborate triple membrane ensheathing the food in a fluid-feeding insect such as the blowfly seems to point to an additional and more sophisticated role. In some species, it has been shown to act as a fine filter towards ingested test materials (Refs. in Wigglesworth, 1965), retaining large colloidal gold and dye molecules; it must, however, be permeable to digestive enzymes released from the mid-gut cells and likewise to the breakdown products of their action on the food material.

REFERENCES

*ANDERSON, E., and HARVEY, W. R. 1966. Active transport by *Cecropia* midgut. II. Fine structure of the midgut epithelium. *J. Cell Biol.*, **31**, 107–134.
*BEAMS, H. W., and ANDERSON, E. 1957. Light and electron microscope studies on the striated border of the intestinal epithelial cells of insects. *J. Morphol.*, **100**, 601–619.

*BERTRAM, D. S., and BIRD, R. G. 1961. Studies on mosquito-borne viruses in their vectors. I. The normal fine structure of the mid-gut epithelium of the adult female *Aëdes aegypti* (L) and the functional significance of its modification following a blood meal. *Trans. R. Soc. trop. Med. Hyg.*, **55**, 404–423.

FARQUHAR, M. G., and PALADE, G. E. 1963. Junctional complexes in various epithelia. *J. Cell Biol.*, **17**, 375–412.

FAWCETT, D. W. 1962. Physiologically significant specializations of the cell surface. *Circulation*, **26**, 1105–1132.

FAWCETT, D. W. 1966. *The Cell. An Atlas of Fine Structure*. W. B. Saunders, Philadelphia and London.

*HUBER, W. 1950. Recherches sur la structure submicroscopique de la membrane péritrophique de l'intestin moyen chez quelques insectes. *Archs Anat. Histol. Embryol.*, **33**, 1–19.

*HUBER, W., and HAASSER, C. 1950. Electron-microscope study of the peritrophic membrane in *Dixippus morosus*. *Nature, Lond.*, **165**, 397.

*KHAN, M. R., and FORD, J. B. 1962. Studies on digestive enzyme production and its relationship to the cytology of the mid-gut epithelium in *Dysdercus fasciatus* Sign. (Hemiptera, Pyrrhocoridae). *J. Insect Physiol.*, **8**, 597–608

*MERCER, E. H., and DAY, M. F. 1952. The fine structure of the peritrophic membranes of certain insects. *Biol. Bull.*, **103**, 384–394.

MILLER, D., and CRANE, R. K. 1961. The digestive function of the epithelium of the small intestine: II. Localization of disaccharide hydrolysis in the brush border portion of intestinal epithelial cells. *Biochim. biophys. Acta*, **52**, 293–298,

*ROTH, T. F., and PORTER, K. R. 1964. Yolk protein uptake in the oocyte of the mosquito *Aëdes aegypti*. *J. Cell Biol.*, **20**, 313–332.

*SMITH, D. S., COMPHER, K., JANNERS, M., SCOLA, C., and WITTLE, L. The organization of the mid-gut epithelium in the larva of a moth, *Ephestia kühniella*, with observations on the mode of absorption and fate of ferritin. (In preparation.)

WATERHOUSE, D. F. 1957. Digestion in insects. *A. Rev. Ent.*, **2**, 1–18.

×*WATERHOUSE, D. F., and WRIGHT, M. 1960. The fine structure of the mosaic mid-gut epithelium of blowfly larvae. *J. Insect Physiol.*, **5**, 230–239.

WIGGLESWORTH, V. B. 1930. The formation of the peritrophic membrane in insects with special reference to the larvae of mosquitoes. *Q. Jl microsc. Sci.*, **73**, 593–616.

WIGGLESWORTH, V. B. 1965. *The Principles of Insect Physiology*, 6th edn, Ch. 11. Methuen, London.

Plates 71–85 ▷

Plate 71 ▷

A micrograph illustrating the fine structure of the crop wall in an adult blowfly, *Calliphora erythrocephala*. In this insect, the crop is a lateral diverticulum of the fore-gut, opening into the oesophagus by a narrow tube, and acts as a storage reservoir for ingested food. Reflecting its derivation from the ectodermal stomodeal invagination, the crop, together with the rest of the fore-gut, is lined with cuticle. While in some insects certain portions of the fore-gut cuticle may be thick, or formed into spines or 'teeth', the lining of the crop [Cu] is very thin and is made up of an endocuticle similar to that often found in the surface integument (Plate 3) and a dense epicuticle [*] that probably incorporates a waterproofing lipid layer, conferring on the crop its remarkable impermeability. The epithelium underlying the cuticle of the crop [Ep] is continuous with that of the surface epidermis (or hypodermis). Here the cells are very attenuated, and contain numerous small mitochondria [M], scattered cisternae of the granular and agranular endoplasmic reticulum, and large numbers of unattached ribosomes. The inner surface of the crop bears a lattice-work of slender visceral muscle fibres [MF], each invested with an extracellular covering or sarcolemma, similar in appearance to, and closely associated with, the basement membrane of the epithelium [BM].

In this field, the wall of the crop follows a convoluted course. This appearance has resulted from the collapse of the sac as its contents escaped, during fixation, through the severed tube linking it with the oesophagus. Such collapse occurs naturally when the crop fluid is expelled by muscular contraction, and when the sac is turgid the folds in the wall are smoothed out.

(× 55,000.)

(*Philips EM 200.*)

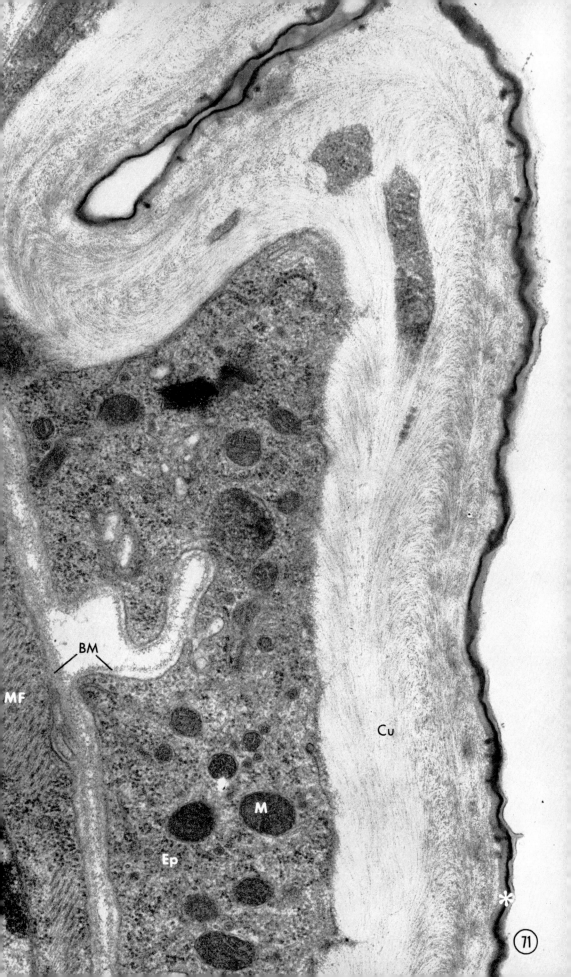

BM

MF

Cu

M

Ep

*

71

Plate 72 ▷

The mid-gut is the principal site of digestion and absorption in the insect digestive tract. It lacks a system of blood capillaries and lymphatic vessels such as that associated with the vertebrate intestine, and absorbed nutrient molecules must traverse a muscular and connective tissue sheath after passing from the epithelial cells *en route* for the haemolymph bathing the gut.

In this longitudinal section of the mid-gut of the cockroach *Periplaneta americana*, the basal region of a columnar epithelial cell is included at the lower left of the field [*]. The basal plasma membrane is profusely infolded, thereby greatly increasing the area of the surface across which ions and molecules may pass into and out of the cell. On the right lies a nidus of 'embryonic' or undifferentiated regenerative cells, containing elongated nuclei [N] and scanty cytoplasm [Cy], the function of which is to differentiate into mature columnar and goblet cells, making good the loss incurred by cell degeneration and death. The cells of the mid-gut are confined within a basement membrane [BM], beyond which extends a deep spongy connective tissue sheath [arrow] containing fibrils of collagen. Within this sheath are embedded tracheoles [Tr] and many small-diameter muscle fibres [MF]. The inner fibres run in a circular fashion around the mid-gut tube and are here seen in transverse section, while the outer fibres run longitudinally; a disposition that is also found, for example, in the smooth muscles of the vertebrate intestine. These visceral muscles are innervated by many small nerve fibres [NF], the axons of which contain opaque neurosecretory droplets.

In life, the haemolymph surrounds and permeates the extracellular sheath of the mid-gut, and through this fluid absorbed nutrients are distributed to the fat body and other tissues.

(×8000.)

(*Philips EM 200.*)

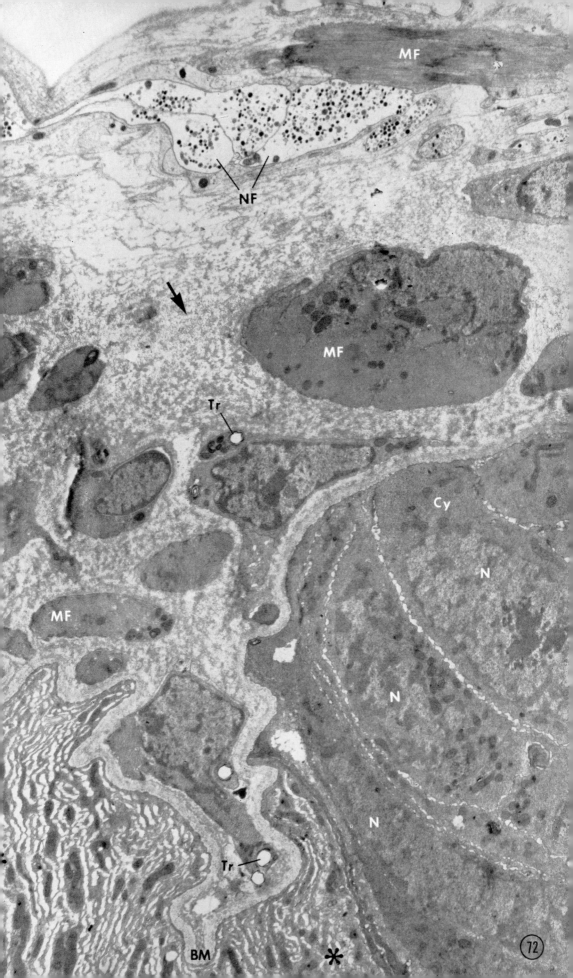

Plate 73 ▷

Micrograph illustrating the disposition of the tracheal and muscular
supply of the posterior mid-gut in an adult blowfly, *Calliphora
erythrocephala*. The basal margins of two cells of the gut epithelium
are included on the right [Ep], bordered by a basement membrane
about 0·2 micron in thickness [BM]. The arrangement of visceral
muscle fibres in longitudinal and circular arrays, seen in this field, is
also adopted in the vertebrate intestinal tract and indeed in many
situations in the body of animals where muscles act on a soft,
deformable tube. In this transverse section of the gut, the fibre closest
to the epithelium [MF_2] is seen in longitudinal profile, and is thus
running in a circular fashion around the gut tube: the narrow band of
contractile material is divided into sarcomeres by Z bands [Z], but
other bands are indistinct. The nucleus of this muscle cell [N]
projects laterally and is surrounded by a thin sheet of sarcoplasm, a
situation that is frequent, though not general, in small-diameter insect
visceral muscles, which sometimes contain centrally placed nuclei.
Outside this cell are included profiles of two muscle fibres [MF_1]
running parallel with the mid-gut, filled with contractile material that
is not dissected into separate fibrils (cf. Plates 12, 108, etc.). These
muscles perform a role analogous to that of unstriated vertebrate
visceral fibres, and perform slow peristaltic contractions that assist in
the backward passage of food material within the gut lumen. This
micrograph also illustrates features of the tracheal supply, which
presumably serves both the mid-gut cells and their muscular
investment. A single tracheole [Tr] is included on the right, adjoining
the mid-gut basement membrane, while at the upper left are seen a
group of tracheoles, each less than one micron in diameter, contained
in a slender process of a tracheoblast or tracheal end cell [Tr]. The
extracellular basement membrane of the latter is confluent with that
of the adjoining muscles [BM′] providing a connective sheath that is
sometimes termed the 'peritoneal membrane'.

(×18,000.)

(*Philips EM 200.*)

236

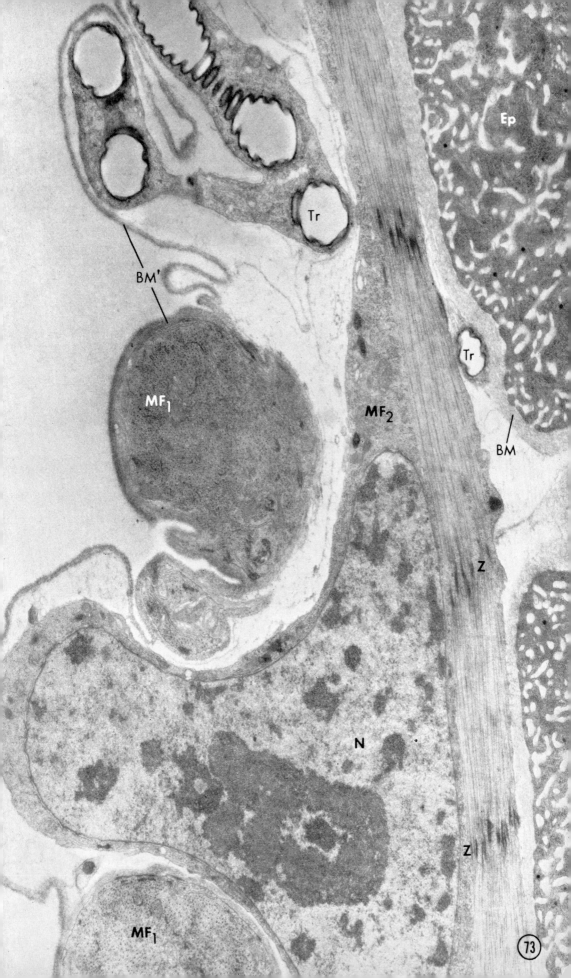

Plate 74 ▷

A pair of micrographs illustrating the fine structure of the apical border of columnar mid-gut epithelial cells in a larva of the flour moth *Ephestia kühniella*.

In field *A*, the apical cell membrane is extended at regular intervals along microvilli, projecting from the cell surface into the gut lumen [Mv]. Unlike cilia and flagella, which they superficially resemble, these projections lack an internal array of tubules, but contain fine fibrils, oriented along their length, which continue for a short distance into the general cytoplasm [*]. Between the microvilli, small pits are formed which are pinched off into the cell as pinocytic vesicles [thick arrows]. In addition to such gross intake of materials from the gut lumen, however, it should be remembered that much absorption probably occurs in the insect mid-gut at the molecular level, through the extensive membrane surface provided by the microvilli.

Field *B* includes longitudinal sections of entire microvilli, which in this insect reach a length of about 4–5 micra, and also illustrates the fine coat or glycocalyx [thin arrows] borne by the membrane covering them.

(*A* : × 65,000. *B* : × 60,000.)

(*Philips EM 200.*)

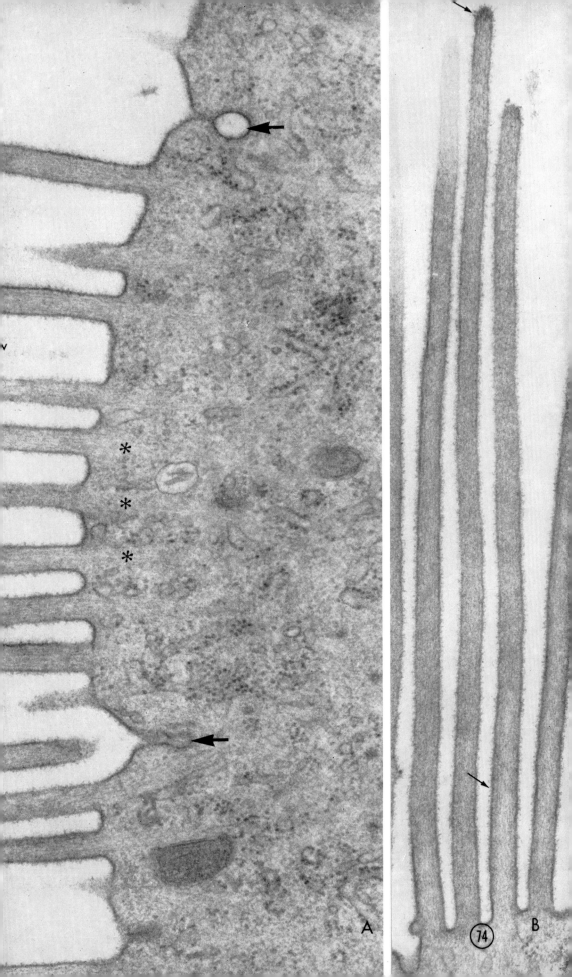

74

Plate 75 ▷

Many insect mid-gut cells are thought to carry out the dual functions of secretion of digestive enzymes and also absorption of digested nutrients from the gut lumen. In addition, nutrient molecules are passed across the basal border of these cells into the haemolymph surrounding the gut.

Little is known of the synthesis of mid-gut enzymes, or of the way in which these are released from the epithelial cells. However, the cytoplasmic organisation of the columnar epithelial cells suggests that they are active in protein synthesis, including, presumably, the synthesis of digestive enzymes. This micrograph represents a field within a mid-gut cell of the larva of the flour moth *Ephestia kühniella*: the cytoplasm abounds in irregularly disposed cisternae of the endoplasmic reticulum, plentifully studded with ribosomes [ER], together with Golgi bodies [G] comprising groups of smooth-surfaced vesicles and cisternae. The Golgi vesicles are often dilated and partially filled with dense droplets [VS], perhaps representing secretory material transferred from the rough-surfaced cisternae or, alternatively, products of digestion absorbed by the cell. Small mitochondria [M] are scattered throughout the cytoplasm, and are plentiful only in the basal region (Plate 72) where they adjoin the infolded cell membrane. This field also included a portion of the cell nucleus [N] limited by the usual pair of enveloping membranes [arrows]. The cytolysome [Cl] at lower right contains granular and membranous cellular debris, and is a common constituent of these mid-gut cells.

(× 35,000.)

(*Philips EM 200.*)

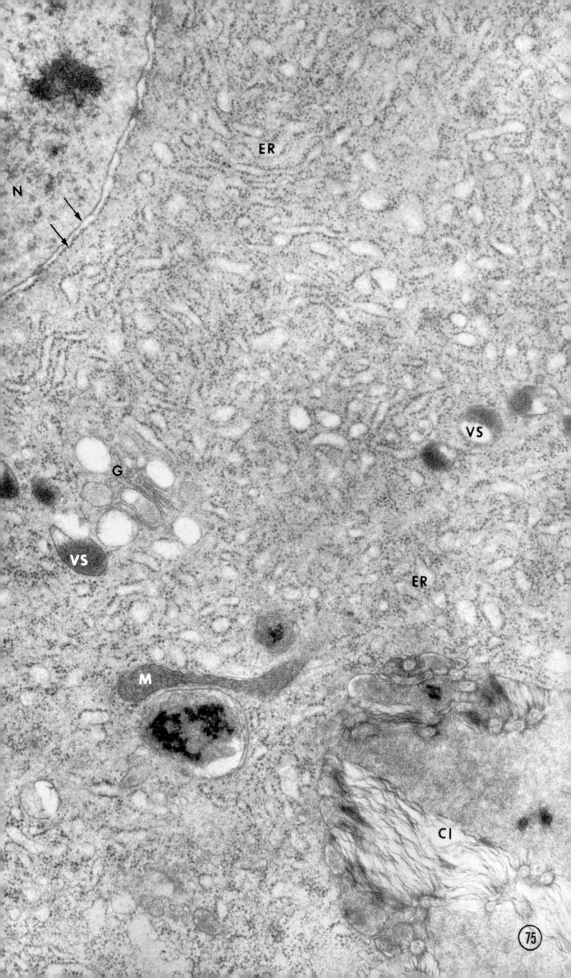

Plate 76 ▷

Interspersed among the columnar epithelial mid-gut cells of some
insects, and especially in the larvae of Lepidoptera, are found 'goblet
cells', which possess a large cavity invaginated from the apical surface.
Profiles of two of these are seen in longitudinal section in this
micrograph of the mid-gut of the larval flour moth *Ephestia
kühniella*. The nucleus of each of these cells [N] lies just above the
deep cavity [*], the surface of which is lined with irregular microvilli
[Mv]. Apically, the goblet cavity communicates with the general
lumen of the gut [Lu] (a portion of which is included in the lower
right corner of the field and contains apical microvilli of the
neighbouring columnar cells) via a narrow channel which lies just out
of the plane of this section. Further structural details of these unusual
cells are illustrated at higher magnification in Plates 77 and 78*B*.

(× 8000.)

(*Philips EM 200.*)

242

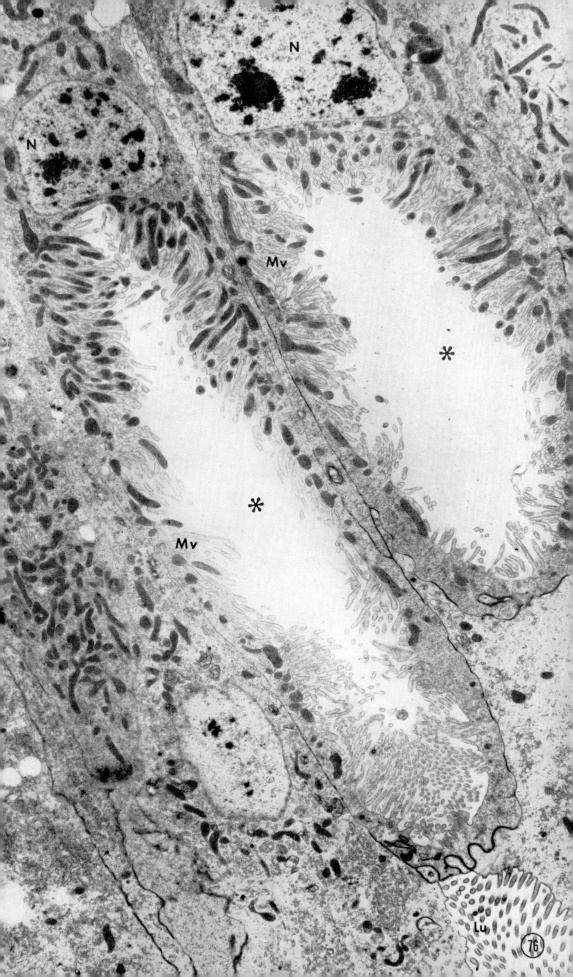

Plate 77 ▷

A portion of the last micrograph, enlarged to show in more detail the structure of the goblet cells of *Ephestia*. The microvilli [Mv] lining the cavity of the goblet cell [*], unlike those borne on the apical surface of the adjoining columnar epithelial cells (Plate 78*A*), are irregularly disposed and in many cases contain elongated mitochondria [M]. These mitochondria are thought to play a part in ion transport, notably in the active extrusion into the goblet cavity of potassium ions that have entered the cytoplasm from the haemolymph.

($\times$ 19,000.)

(*Philips EM 200.*)

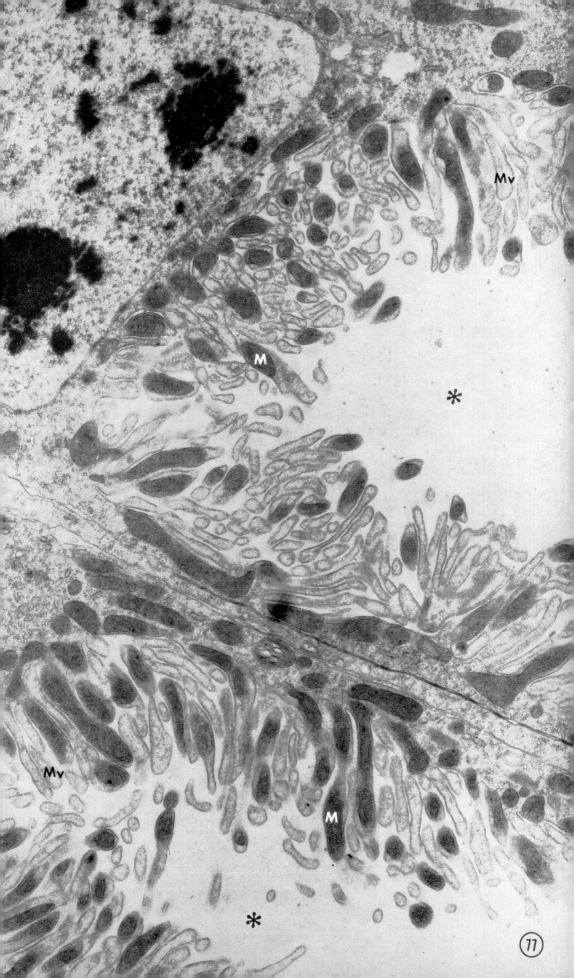

Plate 78 ▷

A. Absorptive cells of the vertebrate intestine are equipped with great numbers of apical microvilli projecting into the gut lumen, and similar structures are borne on most columnar cells of the insect mid-gut. The regular hexagonal arrangement of these cylindrical microvilli is clearly seen in this transverse section through the apical 'brush border' of mid-gut cells in the moth *Ephestia kühniella*. Again as in the vertebrate, the cell membrane limiting these projections is covered with a fine coat of minute fibrils (the 'glycocalyx'), possibly mucopolysaccharide in nature. Within the cytoplasm of each microvillus lie narrow filaments seen here in transverse section as 'dots' [arrows]; in longitudinal sections of the border (Plate 74*A*) these may be traced for a short distance into the apical cytoplasm beyond the bases of the microvilli. It is likely that the greatly enlarged membrane surface area provided by these projections increases the efficiency of uptake of nutrients from the lumen, but it is possible in addition that digestive enzymes are present on the surface of the microvilli.

B. A strikingly different type of microvillus is found in the goblet cells, distributed along the mid-gut epithelium in larval butterflies and moths and a few other insects. As is illustrated in Plates 76 and 77, the goblet cell microvilli line an invaginated extracellular cavity. The section shown here passes transversely through many of these projections; they vary a good deal in size, some profiles are more or less circular but others are flattened. The larger microvilli contain tightly inserted mitochondria [M], another feature distinguishing them from the brush border of the general epithelium. The inner surface of the plasma membrane limiting the goblet cell microvilli is profusely studded with small particles [arrows] similar in appearance to those resolved on the apical surface of osmoregulatory rectal papilla cells (Plate 90).

(*A* : × 50,000. *B* : × 60,000.)

(*Philips EM 200*.)

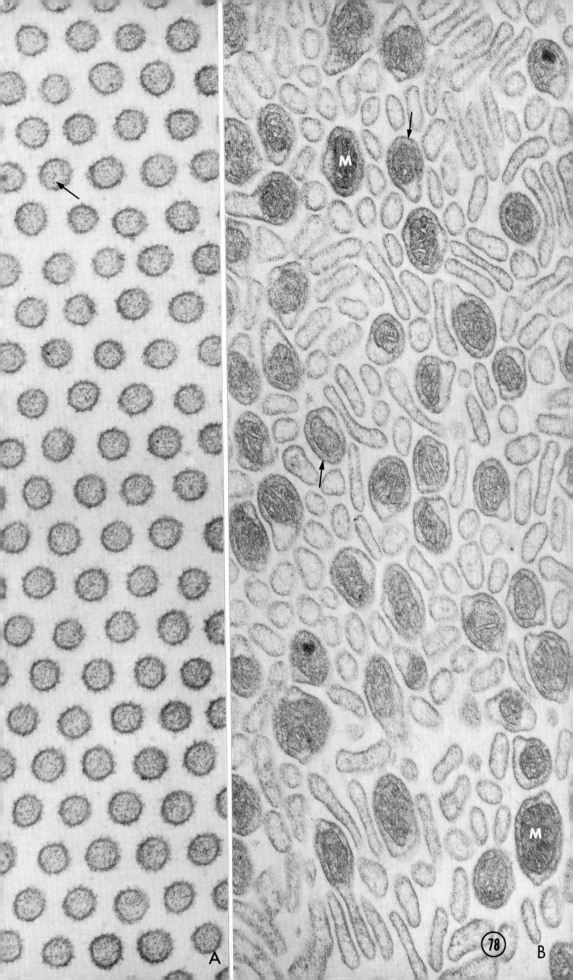

A

B

M

M

M

78

Plate 79 ▷

Three electron micrographs illustrating the fine structure of intercellular junctions in the mid-gut of the flour moth, *Ephestia kühniella*. The area shown in *A* covers a junction between a goblet cell on the left (with microvilli [Mv] lining the invaginated cavity), and an epithelial cell on the right. The apposed lateral cell membranes are linked at intervals by tight junctions [TJ] or *zonulae occludentes*, and septate desmosomes [SD]—shown in more detail elsewhere on this plate. At a tight junction, the unit membranes limiting adjacent cells become partially fused, resulting in obliteration of the intercellular gap, as at TJ in micrograph *B* shown here. Micrograph *C* illustrates the lateral membranes of two epithelial cells, close to the apical surface bordering the gut lumen: in places, the two unit membranes are quite separate [arrows], but elsewhere [SD] are linked together by the regular array of transverse structures characteristic of septate desmosomes, further examples of which are shown in Plates 44, 68, 87, etc.

(*A* : × 78,000. *B* : × 150,000. *C* : × 130,000.)

(*Philips EM 200.*)

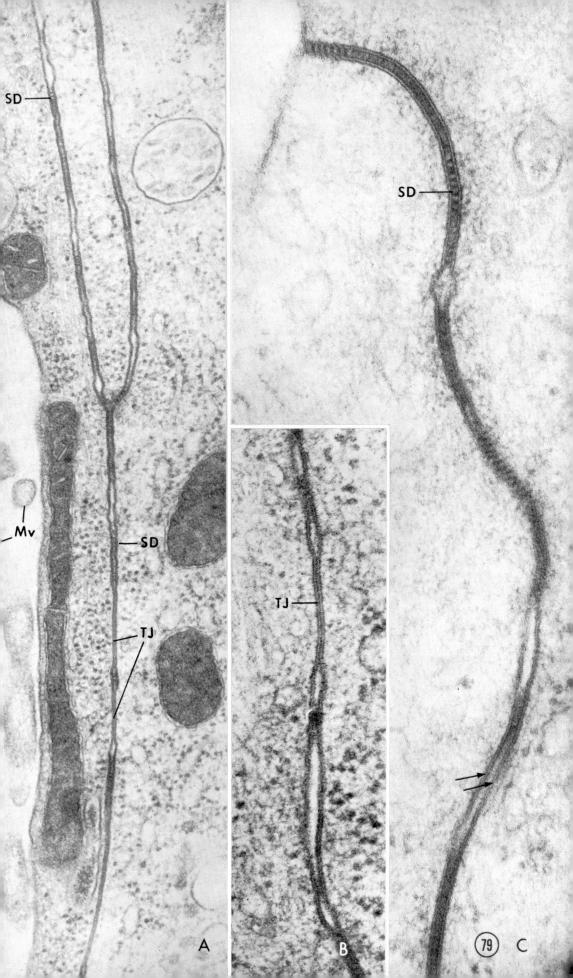

Plate 80 ▷

The mid-gut of the stick insect *Carausius morosus* bears numerous
fine thread-like diverticula, built up of an unusual type of cell, some
features of which are illustrated in this micrograph. The greater part of
the cytoplasm is packed with smooth-membraned tubules [*],
running around and parallel with the elongated nucleus [N]. This
organisation is reminiscent of that of the oxyntic acid-secreting cell of
the vertebrate stomach; a comparison underlined by the fact that the
gut contents over a narrow region close to the opening of these
diverticula is acidic. Similar cells also occur locally in the Malpighian
tubules of this insect.

($\times$ 23,000.)

*(Philips EM 200. Micrograph reproduced by courtesy of
Dr B. L. Gupta.)*

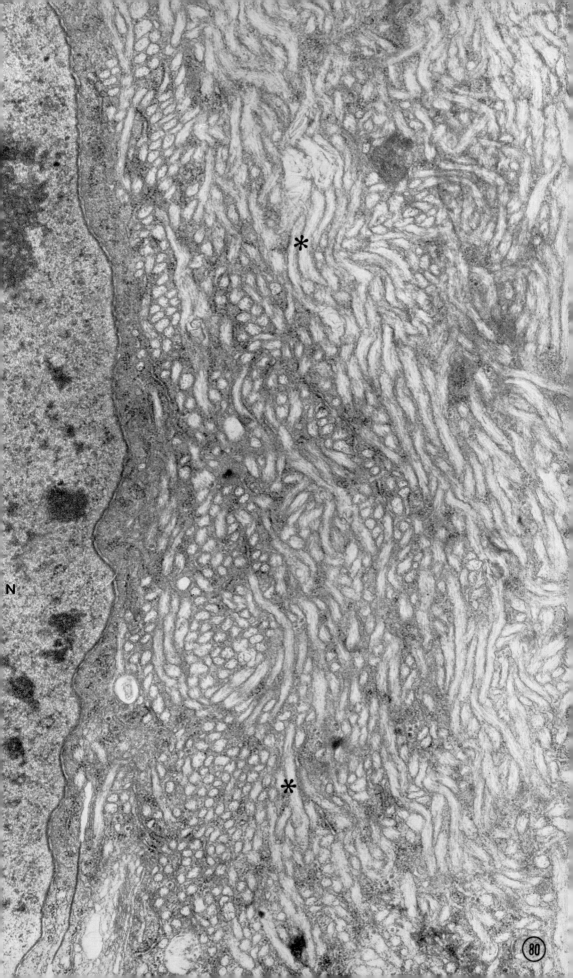

Plate 81 ▷

The peritrophic membrane of the blowfly *Calliphora erythrocephala* is a complex structure, comprising three separate portions, each secreted by a different type of cell. This 'membrane', or extracellular sheath, extends through the mid- and hind-gut, and encloses the food in the former and the faeces in the latter. This micrograph illustrates the fine structure of the most anterior group of cells in the mid-gut epithelium which produce one of the three components of the peritrophic membrane.

These cells are arranged in a double ring [Ep_1, Ep_2] in such a way that the apical microvilli of the two rings [Mv] face each other across a narrow extracellular gap. They are columnar in form, and beyond the central region containing the nucleus [N] they taper sharply into narrow 'tails' [arrows] making up the basal portion of the cell. The cytoplasm contains many Golgi bodies [G] and rough-surfaced cisternae of the endoplasmic reticulum [ER]. The intercellular membranes are linked by prominent cell junctions [CJ] involving septate desmosomes, near the apical border.

Granular secretory material, contained within the Golgi vesicles of the inner ring of cells [Ep_1] is released into the extracellular cleft [*] and is there organised into a structured 'membrane' which progressively thickens and is finally spun off from the surface of the most posterior cells in the ring (Plate 82). It is soon joined by two other extracellular sheets (Plates 83 and 84) which accompany it throughout the remaining course of the digestive tract. The outer ring of cells [Ep_2] flanking the cleft may also contribute secretory material to this portion of the peritrophic membrane.

(×14,000.)

(*Philips EM 200.*)

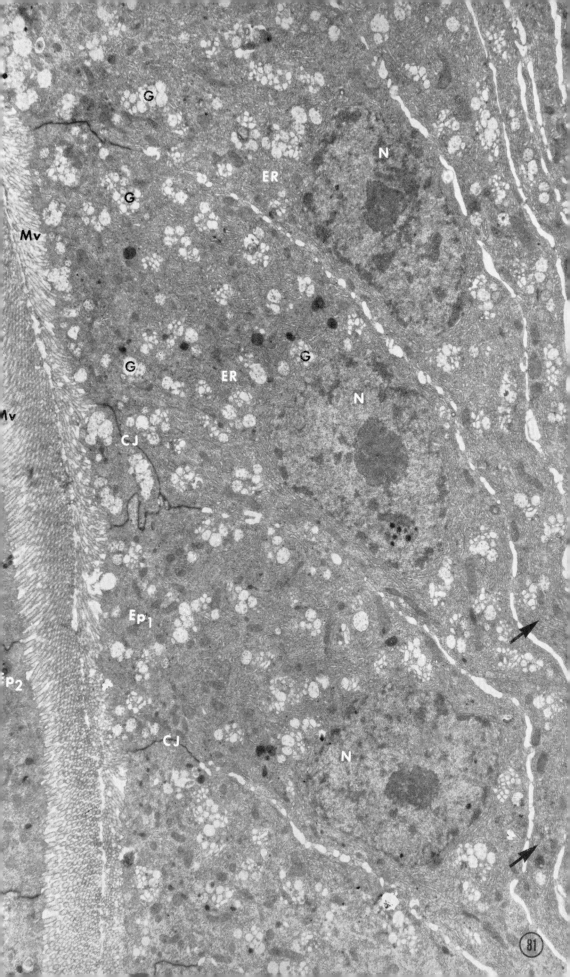

Plate 82 ▷

This micrograph illustrates the 'spinning off' of one component of the peritrophic membrane of the blowfly, from a ring of specialised cells situated at the anterior limit of the mid-gut, and represents a field just posterior to that shown in Plate 81. The granular secretion [long arrows] of the inner ring of epithelial cells [Ep$_1$] appears to be extruded from Golgi vesicles [G] into the extracellular space between the microvilli [Mv] covering the apical surface of the cell. Note the dense apical intercellular junctions [CJ] which include septate desmosomes. Denser secretory material [short arrows] is perhaps released in the same way from the outer ring of cells [Ep$_2$]. Within the narrow cleft between the two opposed ranks of microvilli, the secretory products are formed into a fibrous sheet [*]: this portion of the peritrophic membrane passes backwards [Ptm$_1$] from the cells that secrete it, and as it passes close by the adjoining fore-gut invagination (Plate 83) it is joined by a second membrane of quite different structure.

(×16,000.)

(*Philips EM 200.*)

254

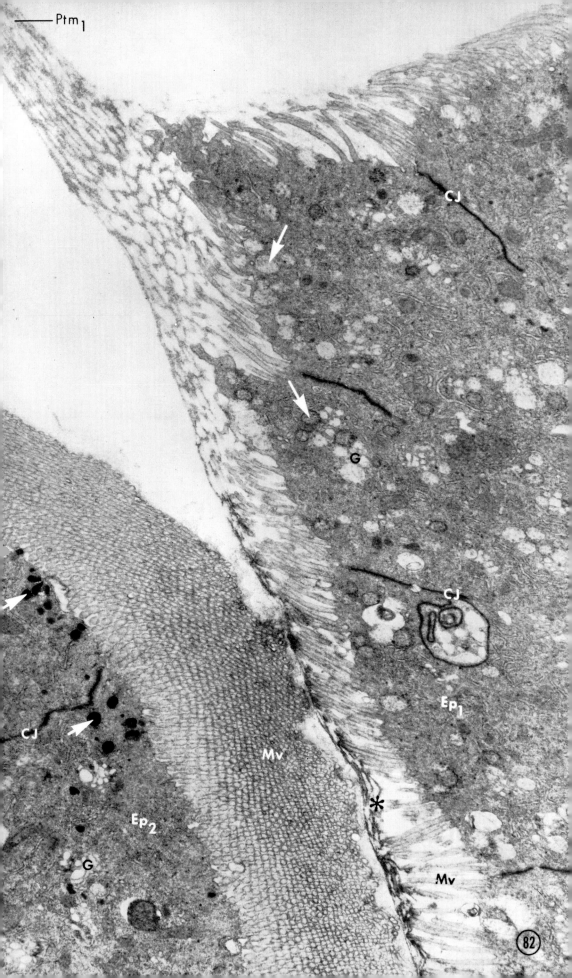

Ptm₁ · CJ · G · CJ · Ep₁ · Mv · * · Mv · CJ · Ep₂ · G · 82

Plate 83 ▷

A low magnification field covering an area immediately behind that
included in Plate 82. The first component of the peritrophic membrane
[Ptm$_1$] passes backwards from the specialised mid-gut cells that
secrete it, and is joined by a second sheet [Ptm$_2$] that peels away
from the surface of the adjoining epithelium of dense fore-gut cells
[white asterisk] invaginated from the oesophagus into the anterior
part of the mid-gut. A region similar to that encircled is shown at
higher magnification in the insert. The peritrophic membrane
surrounding the food within the gut lumen is completed by the
addition of a third component, secreted by the general mid-gut
epithelium, the edge of which lies along the left-hand margin of this
field [arrows].

During the preparation of the section shown here, some distortion
has been introduced, and in life the fore-gut invagination is probably
pressed closely against the anterior rings of mid-gut cells, occluding
the space [black asterisk] that is seen in this micrograph.

($\times$ 58,000. *Insert*: $\times$ 18,000.)

(*Philips EM 200.*)

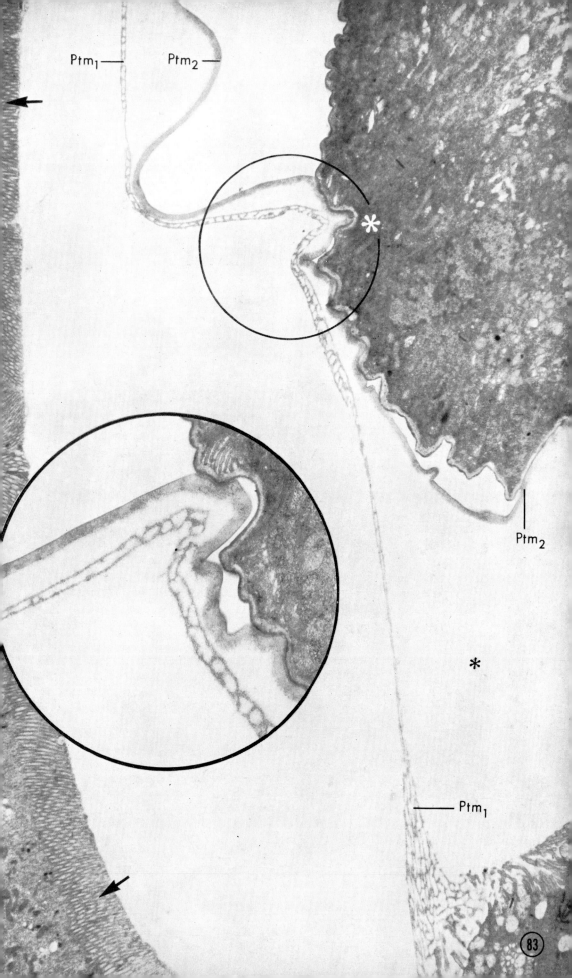

Ptm$_1$ Ptm$_2$

Ptm$_2$

*

Ptm$_1$

83

Plate 84 ▷

Two portions of the peritrophic membrane of the blowfly are contributed by fore- and mid-gut cells lying near the junction of these two segments of the digestive tract (Plate 83). As is illustrated in this micrograph, a third portion is added by the narrower mid-gut tube that follows.

The mid-gut cells lying behind the oesophageal invagination form a cuboidal or columnar epithelium. They bear a more regular apical brush border of microvilli [Mv] than the cells secreting the first component of the peritrophic membrane (Plate 82) and, in addition, contain fewer Golgi bodies [G] and endoplasmic reticulum cisternae [ER]. Mitochondria [M] and part of a nucleus [N] are also included in this field. Lifting away from the surface of the brush border of these cells is a delicate extracellular sheet [Ptm_3] which accompanies the other two components of the composite peritrophic membrane [Ptm_1, Ptm_2] throughout the remainder of the digestive tract (Plate 85).

It should be remembered that each of the three portions of the peritrophic membrane, here seen in transverse section, forms a complete cylinder within the lumen of the gut.

($\times$ 11,000.)

(*Philips EM 200.*)

258

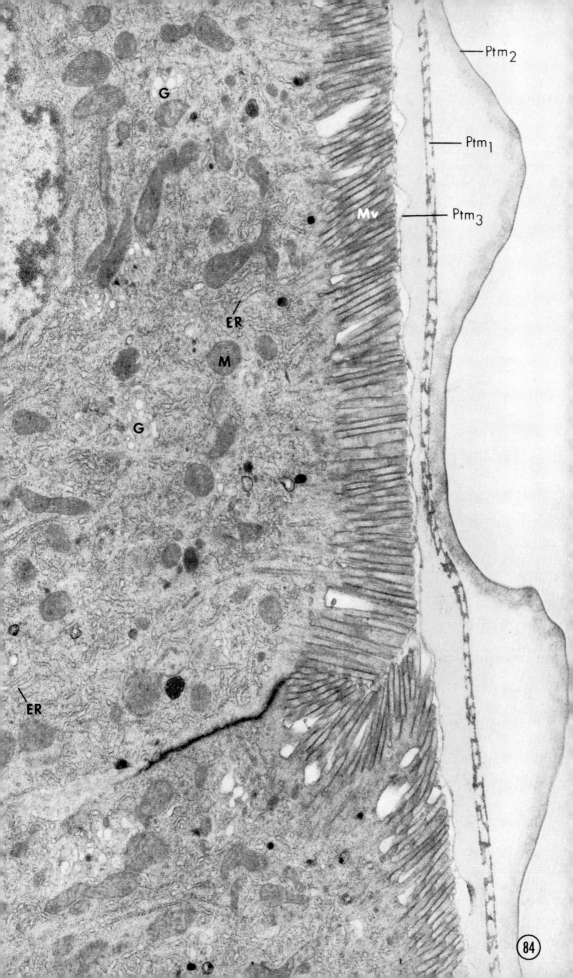

Ptm₂

Ptm₁

Ptm₃

Mv

G

ER

M

G

ER

84

Plate 85 ▷

In this micrograph, the three components of the peritrophic membrane
are seen together, in a transverse section of the posterior mid-gut of
the blowfly, *Calliphora erythrocephala*. In Plate 84 these are present
in a neat parallel array, but here they are thrown into deep folds. The
membrane originating from the anterior mid-gut cells [Ptm_1] appears
to be built up of two incomplete laminae, linked by transverse struts,
and is about 0·1–0·2 micron in overall thickness. The second component
derived from mid-gut cells [Ptm_2] consists of a dense layer, only
ca. 200 Å thick, bearing on one side an indistinct coat of fibrils. The
third portion of the peritrophic membrane [Ptm_2] arises from the
apical surface of fore-gut cells.

($\times$ 26,000.)

(*Philips EM 200.*)

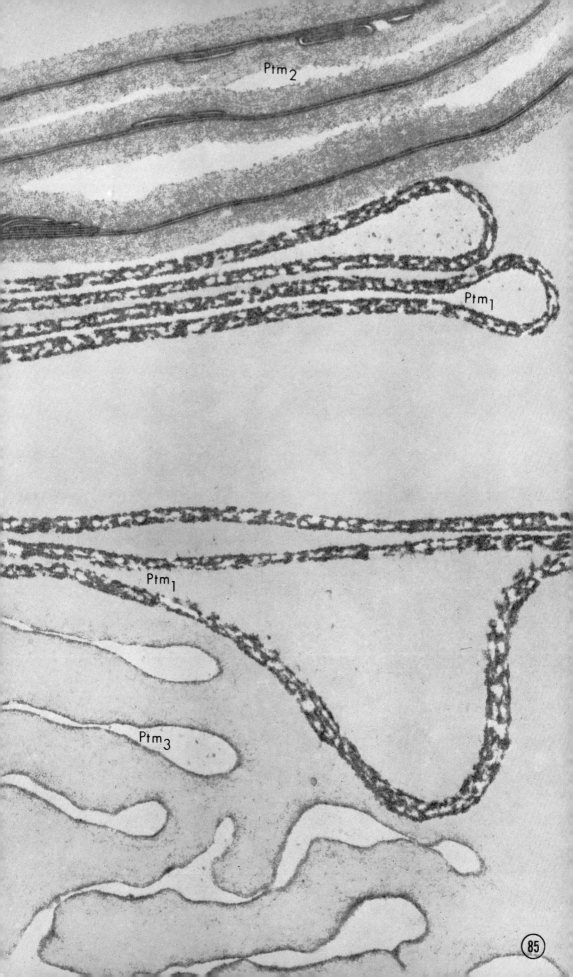

Ptm₂

Ptm₁

Ptm₁

Ptm₃

85

The Hind-gut: Rectum and Rectal Papillae

In many insects, and particularly in those species living under conditions of constant or occasional water shortage, conservation of water passed into the gut by the Malpighian tubules and taken up with the food, may assume vital importance in the maintenance of the normal osmotic milieu of the haemolymph, bathing the tissues of the body. The most probable site of such water reabsorption, and also of the uptake of ions, has for some time been recognised to be the hind-gut, situated between the insertion of the Malpighian tubules into the digestive tract and the anus. The hind-gut consists of a narrow tube lined, like the fore-gut, with a delicate cylinder of cuticle, and is often dilated posteriorly to form a 'rectum' or 'rectal pouch'. While the epithelial cells of the rectum are generally flattened and of rather simple construction (Plates 86 and 87), closely resembling those of the crop associated with the fore-gut (Plate 71), certain of the rectal cells in many species present an entirely different structural picture, being greatly enlarged and often columnar in form. It is thought that this specialised part of the epithelium, constituting the so-called rectal 'glands', 'pads' or 'papillae' are adapted to fulfil the role of water and solute retention.

In the vertebrate body, knowledge of the way in which cells are fitted together in epithelia whose work involves transport of water and ions, obtained with the electron microscope, has greatly assisted our understanding of the mechanisms underlying their function. In particular, it now seems likely that in cells engaged in water transport against a concentration gradient, this solvent may not be actively transported, but rather moved secondarily, by osmotic flow, following the active uptake and concentration of ions in narrow intercellular spaces situated between the epithelial cells (Diamond, 1965; Diamond and Tormey, 1966). That this elegant physiological device may also be shared by insects has recently been suggested by Gupta and Berridge (1966a and 1966b; 1967) as a result of their investigations on the rectal papillae of adult blowflies.

At the level of the electron microscope, the four rectal papillae possessed by this insect are found to be very complex. In essence, however, each of these is conical, with a circular base protruding into the haemolymph, and an apex protruding into the lumen of the rectal pouch. Each cone is built up of very large elongated cells, fitted together loosely in a way that permits a wide and ramifying intercellular space to intrude between them. The hollow cavity or infundibulum of the cone, facing the haemolymph, contains a rich tracheal supply, connective tissue cells secreting collagen and many nerve axons bearing neurosecretory droplets. The bulk of the cytoplasm of the papillary epithelial cells (Plate 88) presents a very unusual appearance, notably through the presence of great numbers of flat membrane-limited sacs, arranged in regular stacks, which lead to irregular channels that meander through the cell. Close examination of many electron micrographs showed that not only do the sacs branch from the channels, but also that the latter in turn link up with the wide intercellular spaces between the lateral cell surfaces. To complete this picture, it must also be mentioned that the spaces between the cells are themselves confluent and form a channel that has limited access to the infundibular space beyond the base of the epithelium, and thence to the circulating haemolymph. Close to the apical and basal regions, adjoining lateral membranes are sealed together by 'junctional complexes' (Plate 89) involving both tight junctions and septate desmosomes, blocking off a direct pathway for movement of materials between the gut lumen and the blood.

As a further structural feature of interest, the piles of sacs occurring throughout the cell generally lie close beside large flattened mitochondria; an association reminiscent of the simpler 'mitochondrial pumps' of the anal papillae of mosquito larvae (Plate 99) in cells that are likewise believed to play a part in water and ion regulation.

The apical border of the papillary cells (Plate 90) is tightly folded into a series of leaflets, ending just beneath the cuticular lining of the rectal lumen. These leaflets bear, on the cytoplasmic side of the cell membrane, small closely-packed particles resembling those present in a similar position in rectal papillae of a termite (Noirot and Noirot-Timothée, 1966) and along the microvilli of 'goblet cells' within the mid-gut (Plate 78B).

On the basis of the appearance of blowfly rectal papillae under a variety of experimental physiological conditions, Gupta and Berridge made some interesting deductions concerning the probable mode of function of these specialised cells, which may be briefly (and necessarily incompletely) summarised as follows. First and foremost, they have suggested that the papillae remove water from the rectum only as a consequence of active transport of ions from the lumen. They have proposed that an ion, perhaps potassium, is pumped actively and to high concentration into the cavities of the multitudinous piles of sacs throughout the cell, and that water then enters these from the cytoplasm and ultimately from the gut lumen across the apical cell surface, along the osmotic gradient. This water, drawn into the intercellular channels, eventually reaches the haemolymph via the circuitous route mentioned above. The active transport of potassium or other ions from the cytoplasm into the sacs, taking place against the concentration gradient, requires the expenditure of energy—hence, presumably, the strategically placed mitochondria which manufacture and make available the necessary supply of ATP. The hydrolytic enzyme (ATP-ase) responsible for the release of this energy has been located cytochemically on the membranes of the sacs (Plate 91): a good example of the use of the electron microscope not merely to display fine cellular detail, but also to provide a picture of one aspect of the biochemical and physiological pattern that lies behind the structural plan (Berridge and Gupta, 1968).

These authors further propose, tentatively, that the particles attached to the membrane of the apical leaflets may be the site of enzyme systems concerned in the uptake of potassium (or other ions) from the gut lumen prior to their transport to the sacs, perhaps by simultaneous secretion of hydrogen ions from the cell, to maintain the electrochemical balance. Similar particles are being discovered on other insect cell membranes, and whatever functions they may later prove to serve, their presence is of general interest in a study of the biology of cells. These structures illustrate the fact that the physiological and biochemical specialisation of cell membranes which have in common a lipoprotein 'skeleton' may on occasions be achieved by the addition of special macromolecular complexes which reveal their presence in the electron microscope.

In marked contrast to the cells of the rectal papillae, the remainder of the rectal epithelium presents none of the peculiarities that have been linked with water and ion transport. Their apical borders bear no folded leaflets, and no extensive intercellular spaces lie between or within the cells, and their sparse mitochondria and cytoplasmic membranes are evenly distributed throughout (Plate 87). The thin wall of the rectum may be thrown into deep folds (Plate 86), permitting the distention that occurs when this part of the hind-gut is filled with fluid, some time after feeding.

The hollow infundibular space within each rectal papilla of the blowfly hindgut is plugged, except for a narrow channel beneath the basal lamella of the specialised epithelial cells described previously, with a conical sheet of 'medullary cells' (Plate 92) enclosing a core, largely filled with tracheae and tracheoles together with a loosely packed mass of collagen-like fibrils. The latter is secreted by the medullary cells, and may be regarded as forming a true connective tissue in the sense of the term familiar to vertebrate anatomists.

The medullary cells are elongated, and are linked together by frequent desmosomes of a type more commonly met with in vertebrate epithelia, characterised by dense cytoplasmic plaques. Their cytoplasm contains free ribosomes, microtubules, mitochondria and, most obviously, many cisternae of the rough-surfaced cisternae of the endoplasmic reticulum, often enormously swollen by secreted material. This material is often resolved as being finely granular throughout, but sometimes within the cisternae appear very slender periodically banded fibrils (Plate 93). This evidence of the synthetic activity of the medullary cells not only points them out as the source of the collagen and perhaps of the mucopolysaccharide material within the core of the papilla, but also, in a wider sphere of interest, gives an intriguing pointer to the intracellular biosynthesis of collagen in this insect connective tissue.

This region of the rectal papilla has a further interesting cytological feature to offer: the presence of many nerve axons, often without a glial covering, close by the medullary cells .As is mentioned elsewhere (p. 59, p. 95) peripheral nerves, in insects and other animals, are generally invested with a sheath of glial origin which is omitted only at the point where the axons terminate, as, for example, at a neuromuscular junction (Plate 22). The axons penetrating the medulla of the rectal papilla contain opaque 'neurosecretory droplets' similar to those passing from the brain to the corpus cardiacum (Plate 32) or extending along the axons innervating visceral muscle fibres (Plate 23). No muscular tissue is present within the rectal papilla, however, and the significance of these apparently terminating axons must be sought elsewhere. Gupta and Berridge (1966a) speculate that they may conceivably release an 'antidiuretic hormone', perhaps acting, as in the collecting ducts of the vertebrate kidney and urinary bladder, by changing the permeability of the apical membranes of the papillary cells, and thus regulating the uptake by these cells of water and solutes.

REFERENCES

*BERRIDGE, M. J., and GUPTA, B. L. 1967. Fine-structural changes in relation to ion and water transport in the rectal papillae of the blowfly, *Calliphora*. *J. Cell Sci.*, **2**, 89–112.
*BERRIDGE, M. J. and GUPTA, B. L. 1968. Fine-structural localization of adenosine triphosphatase in the rectum of *Calliphora*. *J. Cell Sci.* **3**, 17–32.
DIAMOND, J. M. 1965. The mechanism of isotonic water absorption and secretion. *Symp. Soc. exp. Biol.*, **19**, 329–347.
DIAMOND, J. M., and TORMEY, J. McD. 1966. Role of long extracellular channels in fluid transport across epithelia. *Nature, Lond.*, **210**, 817–820.

*Gupta, B. L., and Berridge, M. J. 1966a. Fine structural organization of the rectum in the blowfly, *Calliphora erythrocephala* (Meig.) with special reference to connective tissue, tracheae and neurosecretory innervation in the rectal papillae. *J. Morph.*, **120**, 23–82.

*Gupta, B. L., and Berridge, M. J. 1966b. A coat of repeating subunits on the cytoplasmic surface of the plasma membrane in the rectal papillae of the blowfly, *Calliphora erythrocephala* (Meig.) studied *in situ* by electron microscopy. *J. Cell Biol.*, **29**, 376–382.

*Noirot, C., and Noirot-Timothée, C. 1966. Revêtement de la membrane cytoplasmique et absorption des ions dans les papilles rectales d'un termite (Insecta, Isoptera). *C.r. hebd. Séanc. Acad. Sci., Paris*, **263**, 1099–1102.

Plates 86–93 ▷

Plate 86 ▷

The insect hind-gut, together with the fore-gut, tracheal system and
other ectodermal derivatives, is lined with cuticle, continuous with
that of the body surface. The hind-gut is often a simple tube,
conveying waste materials from the mid-gut and Malpighian tubules
to the anus, but in some species portions of this segment of the
digestive tract play an important part in osmoregulation. In the blowfly
Calliphora erythrocephala, the hind-gut is divided into a narrow
anterior portion, and a dilated posterior 'rectum', and while the
general rectal wall, illustrated in this micrograph, consists of a thin
epithelial layer [Ep] lined with cuticle [Cu], highly specialised
'rectal papillae' are interposed (Plates 88–91) regulating water
absorption from the gut lumen. As is seen in this field, the rectal wall
may be thrown into irregular folds, projecting into the lumen
[Lu]; allowing for considerable distention taking place when the
rectum is filled with fluid. As in the case of other divisions of the
intestinal tract, the rectum is invested with a well-developed sheath
of visceral muscle fibres [MF] assisting in the expulsion of urine and
faecal material.

(×15,000.)

*(Philips EM 200. Reproduced by courtesy of Drs B. L. Gupta and
M. J. Berridge.)*

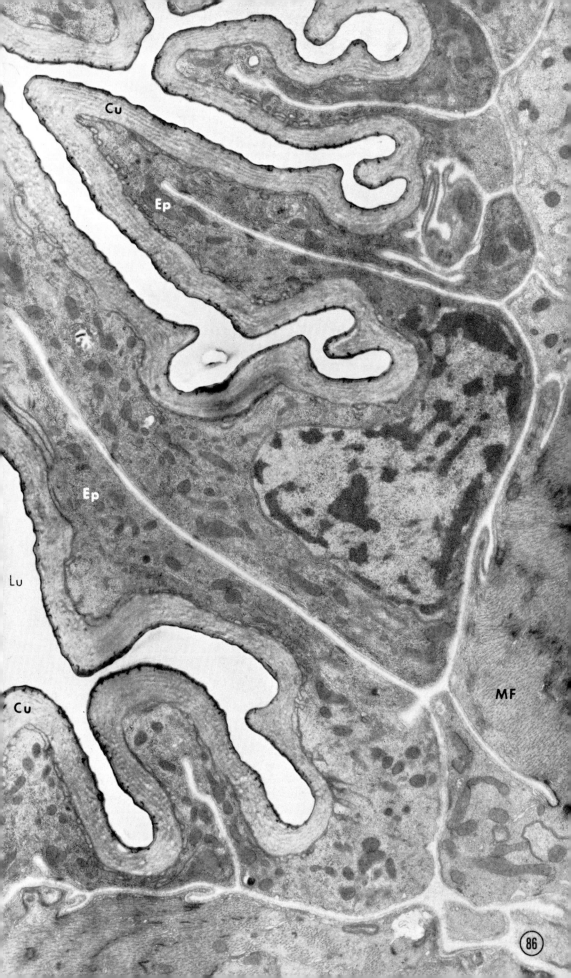

Plate 87 ▷

A field illustrating the structure of the rectal epithelium of the blowfly *Calliphora* at a magnification higher than that of the last plate. It may now be seen that the bulk of the cuticle lining this part of the hind-gut [Cu] is made up of the fibril-containing endocuticle, while the outer epicuticle is represented by a narrow opaque layer. The epithelial cells rest on a basement membrane [BM] and within them the nuclei [N], often irregular in outline, are surrounded by cytoplasm containing occasional mitochondria [M], cisternae of the endoplasmic reticulum and small glycogen deposits [Gy]. Neither the apical nor the basal cell surface is infolded or otherwise shows any evidence of implication in ion or water transport, in striking contrast to the highly specialised columnar cells of the rectal papillae, inserted into the epithelium. Sinuous profiles of the lateral cell membranes link the apical and basal borders; throughout most of their course, the adjoining membranes are merely closely apposed [*], but beneath the apical border become sealed together by extensive septate desmosomes [SD] and a narrow region exhibiting desmosomes [D] of the *macula adhaerens* type.

(× 32,000.)

(*Philips EM 200.*)

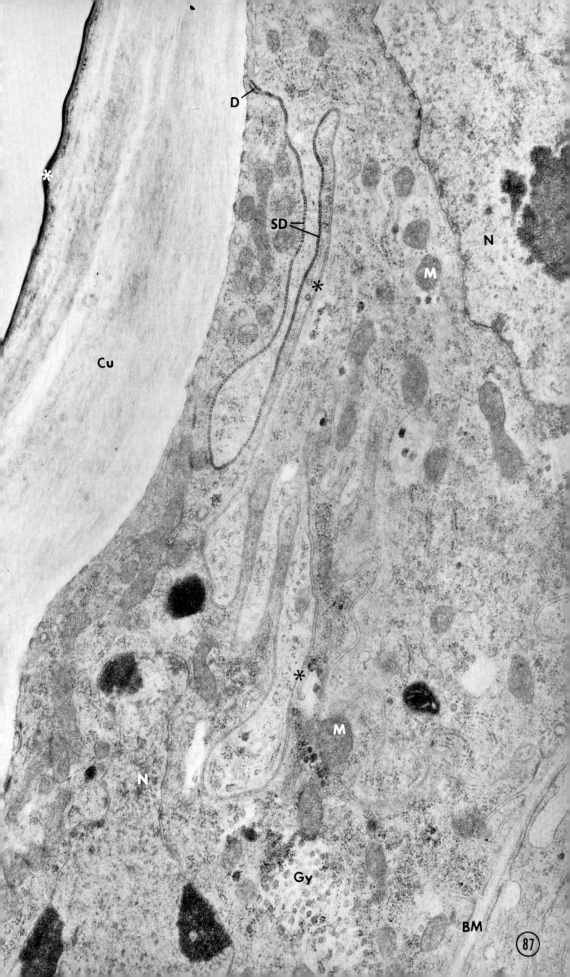

Plate 88 ▷

As is shown in this micrograph, a substantial proportion of the volume
of the blowfly rectal papilla cells is occupied by irregular intercellular
spaces [IS] and regular piles of flattened sacs [*] confluent with
them. The former lead to larger intercellular channels lying between
the lateral cell surfaces; one of these, containing a trachea [TR]
appears in the lower left. As is described more fully in the text
(p. 264) this complex system of interconnected channels is thought
to provide the compartment into which water passes following its
uptake from the hind-gut lumen across the apical border of the cells
of the papilla (Plate 90). The crucial preliminary to this flow is
believed to be the active pumping of ions from the cytoplasm into the
finest intercellular incursions [*], utilising the nearby mitochondria
[M] for the necessary energy, which leads to the subsequent
osmotically controlled escape of water molecules from the cytoplasm.

This survey field includes a portion of the large centrally placed
cell nucleus [N] and extends to the basal surface, which is limited
by a multilayered extracellular sheath [arrow], each member of which
resembles the basement membrane or basal lamella of many other
epithelia.

(× 17,000.)

(*Philips EM 200. Reproduced by courtesy of Drs B. L. Gupta and
M. J. Berridge.*)

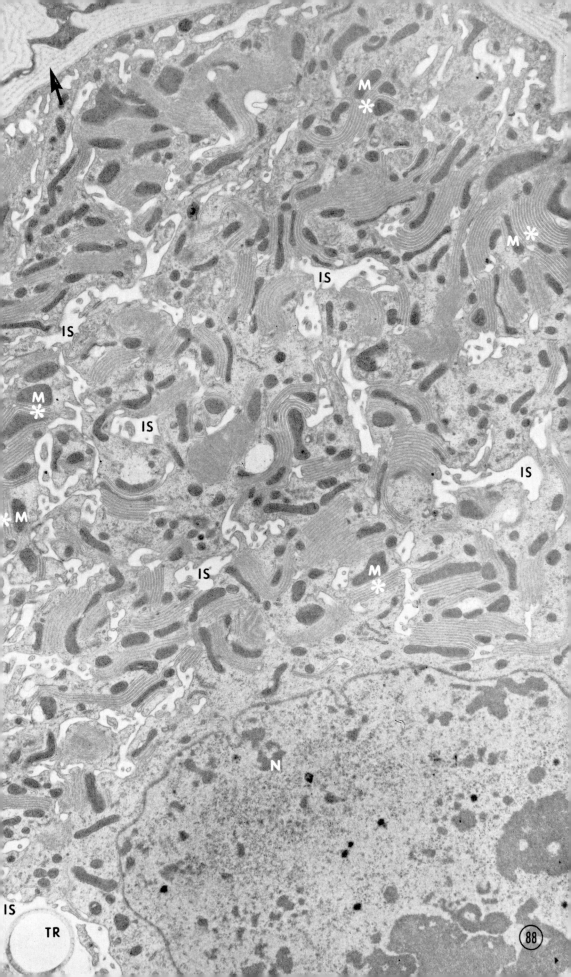

88

Plate 89 ▷

The complex arrays of membranes within the cells of the rectal papilla of the adult blowfly, shown at low magnification in Plate 88, are here seen in greater detail. The close juxtaposition of large mitochondria [M] alongside the regular arrays of flattened sacs, and the narrow lumina of the latter [*] are clearly displayed; likewise, the irregular intercellular spaces [IS] into which these narrow channels lead. Along this tortuous pathway travel water molecules retrieved from the rectal lumen and passed back into the circulating haemolymph.

It is becoming increasingly clear that in vertebrates, insects or, indeed, in any animal group, the functions of epithelia are in large measure permitted or controlled by modifications of the lateral cell boundaries, isolating the different environments maintained within and without the layer of cells. In the present example, the gut lumen is isolated from the haemolymph by intercellular junctional complexes adjoining the apical border and, as shown here, also beneath the basal surface. From under the extracellular sheath at upper left [arrows] adjacent lateral cell membranes are linked together by septate desmosomes [SD] and simple and 'tight' junctions [D and TJ] corresponding to the *zonula* and *macula adhaerens* and *occludens* regions described in vertebrate epithelia.

(× 60,000.)

(*Philips EM 200. From Berridge and Gupta, 1967. Reproduced by courtesy of the authors and the* Journal of Cell Science.)

274

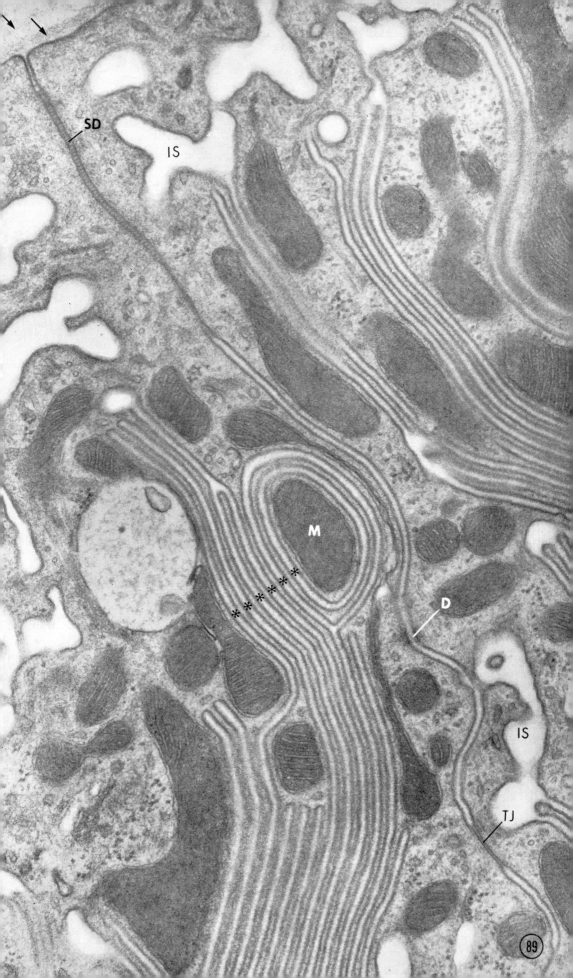

Plate 90 ▷

This micrograph includes a portion of the apical cytoplasm of a papillary cell within the rectum of the blowfly *Calliphora*. These cells, concerned in the uptake of ions and water from the rectal lumen [Lu] are lined with a cuticular sheath [Cu] continuous with that extending throughout the length of the hind-gut. The apical cell membrane is folded into a regular border of leaflets [arrows] which, as may be seen at higher magnification in the insert, bear an array of small particles [arrows] attached to the cytoplasmic side of the unit membrane. Elsewhere, the cytoplasm contains large mitochondria [M], many of which are closely associated with regular stacks of membrane-limited channels [*], believed to play a vital part in the osmoregulatory function of the papilla, and further illustrated in Plates 89 and 90.

Across this apical surface, both water and ions move into the cytoplasm from the gut lumen, after traversing the layer of cuticle. Although the lateral cell borders, over much of their extent, arboresce within the cells to form spaces into which water and ions may pass *en route* for the haemolymph, they are closely linked near the apical and basal borders (Plate 89) by septate desmosomes and tight junctions, which seal off any direct channel across the epithelium.

(× 26,000. *Insert*: × 160,000.)
(*Philips EM 200. From Gupta and Berridge, 1966b. Reproduced by courtesy of the authors and the* Journal of Cell Biology.)

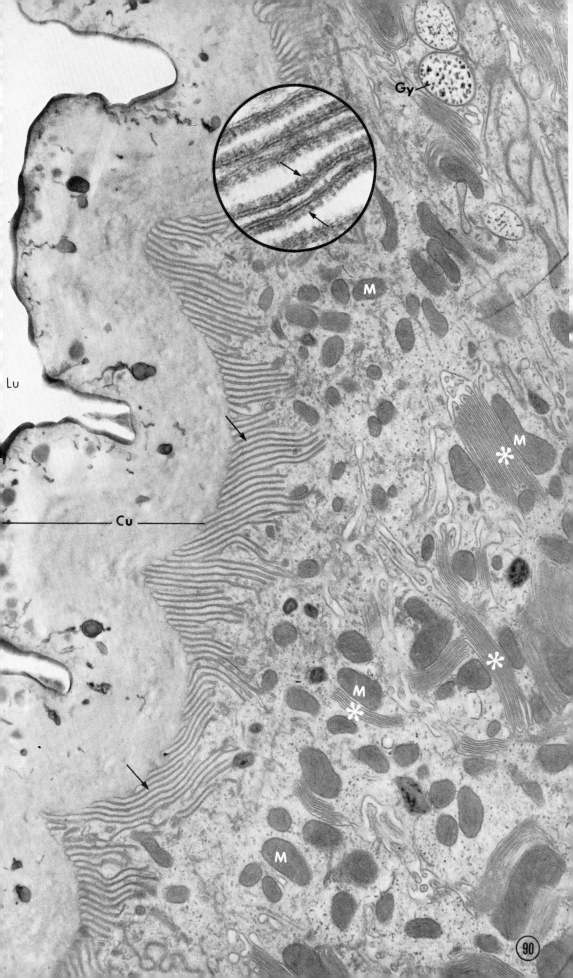

Plate 91 ▷

A low-power field, similar to that shown in Plate 88, but after incubation in a medium devised to reveal the presence and location of phosphatase activity. Small opaque granules of reaction product (in this case lead phosphate) are associated with the membranes bounding the arrays of flattened sacs [*]: more precisely, they lie within the narrow cytoplasmic sheets separating the sacs. No reaction has taken place, for example, in the mitochondria [M] or in other structures within the tissue. The papilla from which this micrograph was prepared was incubated in a solution containing ADP as a substrate and a trace of soluble lead nitrate: where the former was enzymatically split, the inorganic phosphate produced reacted with the lead nitrate to form the highly insoluble and electron opaque lead phosphate, providing a map of the distribution of the enzyme throughout the cell. With ATP as substrate, the reaction product is identically situated and even more intense. The importance of these results is that they corroborate the suggestion that ions are pumped actively from the cytoplasm into the sacs, through the mediation of energy supplied by these strategically placed hydrolytic enzymes. Note the extensive intercellular spaces [IS] inserted into the cell.

Such cytochemical localisation of enzyme distribution brings added meaning to the 'conventional' electron microscopic image, and the development of suitable techniques for this purpose presents a flourishing and intriguing field.

(× 23,000.)

(*Philips EM 200. From Berridge and Gupta, 1968. Reproduced by courtesy of the authors and the* Journal of Cell Science.)

278

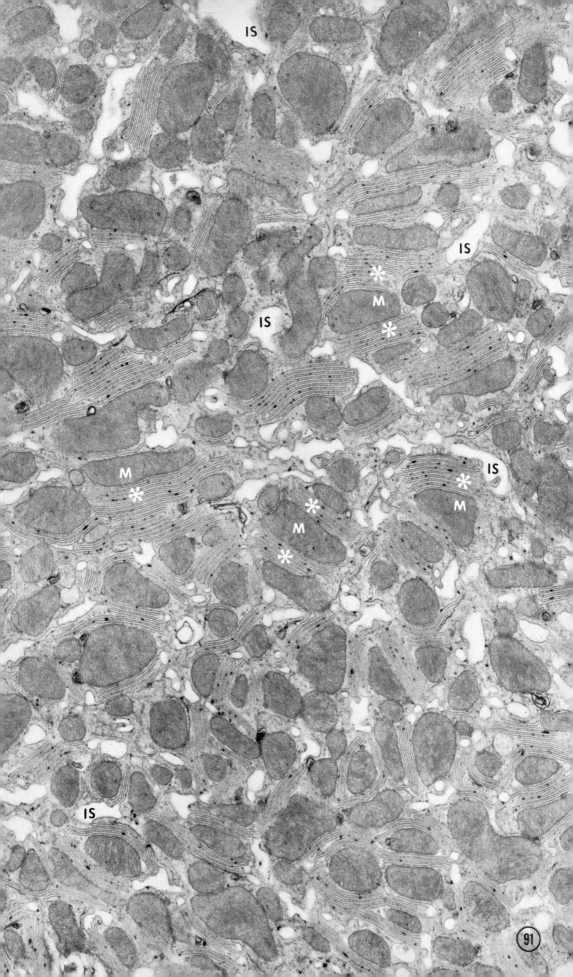

Plate 92 ▷

Within the hollow cavity or 'medulla' of the blowfly rectal papilla lies a sheet of cells encompassing a central core of loosely packed strands of collagen fibrils. These 'medullary cells', shown here, are elongated, and contain ovoid nuclei [N]. They are linked together by frequent desmosomes [D] marked by pairs of dense cytoplasmic plaques. The cellular sheet is lined on both sides by a composite extracellular sheath which may include bundles of collagen fibrils (Co). Within the cytoplasm are present mitochondria [M], many unattached ribosomes and (Plate 93, A and B) dilated cisternae of the rough-surfaced endoplasmic reticulum [*] within which the collagen or a precursor appears to be synthesised. A tracheal trunk passes through the medulla *en route* for the papillary epithelium, and lateral branches also end amongst the connective tissue cells: a profile of a tracheal twig is seen in this micrograph at TR. Axons containing a rather heterogeneous population of opaque neurosecretory droplets [Ax] occur abundantly throughout the medulla, but the identity of their 'target organ' is as yet a matter for speculation.

(× 22,000.)

(*Philips EM 200. Reproduced by courtesy of Drs B. L. Gupta and M. J. Berridge.*)

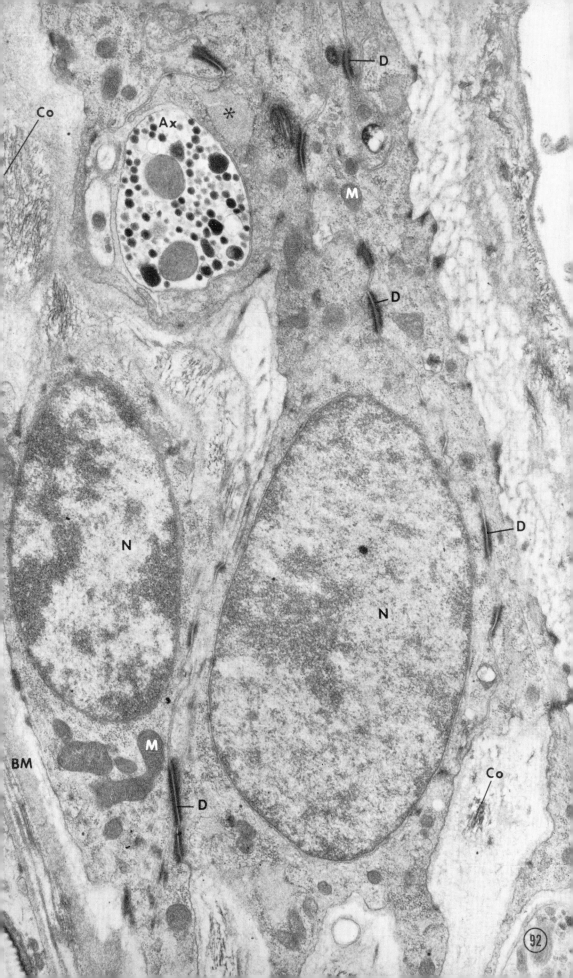

Plate 93 ▷

A pair of micrographs illustrating the mode of formation of collagen-like fibrils in medullary cells of the blowfly rectal papilla.

In *A*, ribosome-studded cisternae of the endoplasmic reticulum [ER] within the medullary cell are greatly swollen with granular secreted material [*]. This micrograph also includes other cellular structures including mitochondria [M], and a desmosome link [D] between the surfaces of adjacent cells (cf. Plate 92).

The field shown in *B* is similar, but in places fine fibrils have appeared, embedded in the granular contents of the cisternae [*]: these fibrils exhibit a collagen-like periodic striation [thin arrows], and on the left [thick arrows] are seen in transverse section. These fibrils appear to be released into the medulla of the papilla by breakdown of the cells in which they are formed.

(*A* : × 30,000. *B* : × 65,000.)

(*Philips EM 200. Micrographs reproduced by courtesy of Dr B. L. Gupta.*)

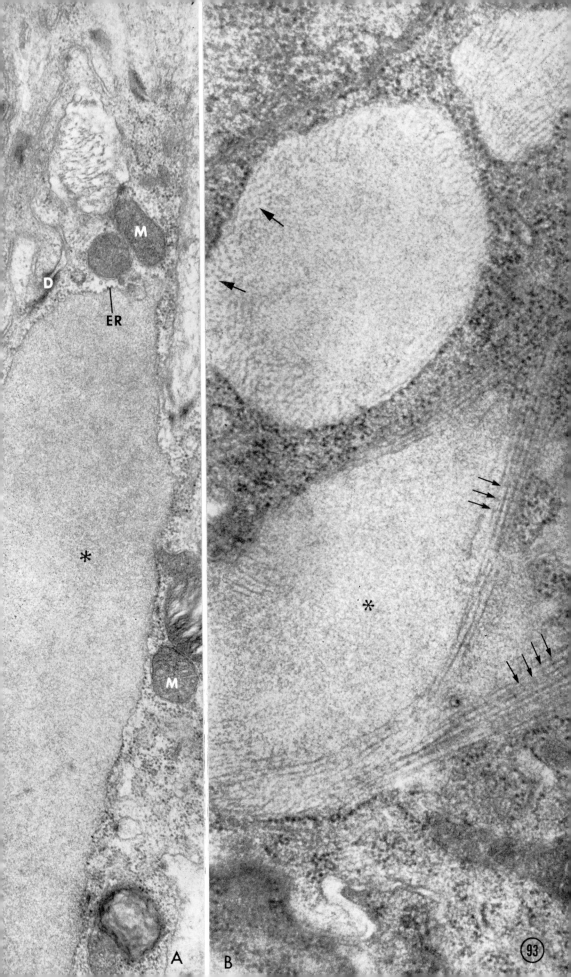

A

B

93

Malpighian Tubules

The first anatomical description of the urinary tubules of the insect was given by Marcello Malpighi in 1668, in his study of the internal organisation of the silkworm, though their function was not established until the early part of the nineteenth century. The Malpighian tubules end blindly, and open into the digestive tract at, or close to, the junction of the mid- and hind-gut; they generally lie freely within the body cavity, where they are bathed in the haemolymph.

In insects and vertebrates alike, the role of the urinary excretory system is to remove waste materials from the circulation, and where the initial formation of urine is accompanied by loss of useful substances, the system also provides for the reabsorption of these before the urine is eliminated from the body. In the glomerular kidney of vertebrates, urine is first formed in the renal corpuscle by ultrafiltration from the blood capillaries, and its composition is subsequently modified as it passes along the kidney tubules by the retention of part of its content of water and solutes. On the other hand, ultrafiltration plays no part in the formation of the initial urine in Malpighian tubules, as is also the case in the tubules of the aglomerular kidney (Bulger, 1965), and instead these rely on the processes of secretion and diffusion for the intake of materials from the blood.

Malpighian tubules vary greatly in number throughout the range of insects; some coccids and larvae of parasitic Hymenoptera, for example, possess only a pair, while as many as 200 may be found in certain Orthoptera. They may be short, especially when present in large numbers, or considerably longer than the entire body. Each tubule contains a lumen usually ringed by two or three epithelial cells; the tubule may be histologically similar along its length, but is often divided into regions where, for example, urine secretion and reabsorption of water and ions may occur separately. Sometimes, the excretory system shows a further division of labour where, as in the blowfly, much or all of the reabsorptive modification of the urine takes place after it has passed from the Malpighian tubule into the rectum (p. 263).

The fine structure of Malpighian tubule cells has received a good deal of attention, and electron microscopic studies include those of Beams *et al.*, 1955; Berkaloff, 1958, 1959, 1960; Smith and Littau, 1960; Tsubo and Brandt, 1962; Wigglesworth and Salpeter, 1962; Mazzi and Baccetti, 1963; Baccetti *et al.*, 1963.

As might be expected, these studies show that one cannot consider the organisation of a 'typical' tubule cell, since differences in detailed structure are met with between one species and the next, linearly along a single tubule and probably between comparable cells examined at different times or under different physiological conditions. However, it is clear that the commonest type of cell in the range of tubules so far investigated with the electron microscope possesses structural features that are frequently associated with the function of water and solute transport. As is illustrated in

Plates 94 and 95, representing sections of tubule cells from the milkweed bug and the blowfly, the basal cell surface is more or less extensively infolded, and the apical surface is produced into a series of microvilli, facing into the lumen. These modifications greatly increase the effective area of the tubule surfaces across which materials may pass between the haemolymph and cytoplasm, and between the cytoplasm and the urinary space—areas that are clearly impressively large when it is realised (Refs. in Wigglesworth, 1965) that the surface area of the tubules themselves may be about 400–500 mm² per mg of body weight. Mitochondria are abundant in these cells; they lie within the sheets of cytoplasm into which the basal part of the cell is dissected, in the main body of the cell, and are often tightly inserted into the apical microvilli.

These fine structural features become especially interesting when the physiology of urine secretion is considered further. Berridge (1967) has pointed out that Malpighian tubules provide unusually favourable material for studying the movement of fluid across an epithelium, since these are basically simple in construction (unlike the renal system of a mammal or frog skin, which have also been used for this purpose), and moreover their secretory output is readily measurable and experimented upon. Berridge has made extensive use of a preparation originally devised by Ramsay, in which urine secreted by a single isolated tubule accumulates within an oil droplet as a growing sphere, the diameter of which may be measured and the volume calculated. With the aid of blowfly tubules arranged in this way, it has been shown that urine secretion is an active process, requiring hydrolysis of ATP as a source of energy, and while the metabolic substrates needed for ATP synthesis are not yet known, Berridge has suggested that the entry of one likely substrate, the disaccharide trehalose, into the tubule cells, may be regulated by a diuretic hormone, perhaps much as insulin controls the access of glucose into mammalian cells. The energy required for urine secretion is believed to be expended in pumping potassium ions into the tubule cells and thence into the lumen, water and anions then following the same course along the osmotic and electrochemical gradients. The concentration of mitochondria along the basal and apical surfaces of the blowfly tubule cells (Plate 95) appears to represent a device for the efficient transport of ions across the cell membrane, and this conclusion is supported by electron micrographs showing that the enzyme ATP-ase is associated both with the basal (Plate 96) and apical surfaces of the cell (Gupta and Berridge, unpublished observations). In the blowfly, part of the water secreted with the initial urine is taken back into the haemolymph, after the urine has passed on to the rectum, as an osmotic consequence of active transport of ions from the gut lumen into the intercellular spaces between the specialised rectal papilla cells (p. 263).

These experiments provide us with interesting information on what may be a widespread mechanism of urine flow into the Malpighian tubules of insects, but so far we have not considered the prime role of these tubules—the elimination of unwanted materials, particularly nitrogenous waste, from the haemolymph. In mammals and aquatic vertebrates, the most important nitrogenous waste product is the highly soluble urea, whereas in most insects, as in birds and reptiles, where water conservation is of prime importance, much nitrogen is excreted in the form of the very insoluble uric acid. Wigglesworth and Ramsay (Refs. in Wigglesworth, 1965) have studied the details of urine formation in the Malpighian tubules of the blood-sucking bug *Rhodnius*, in which spheres of uric acid are present within the tubule lumen proximal to the gut, but in which the distal portion of the lumen contains a clear fluid. Wigglesworth has suggested that soluble acid urates are secreted across the distal tubule cells, where the lumen contents are slightly alkaline, and that uric acid is precipitated in the proximal region of the lumen, which is at an acid pH and from which water and bases (bicarbonates) are reabsorbed into the haemolymph. In this insect, further reabsorption of ions and water probably takes place in the rectum. In the electron microscope, the fine structure of the secretory and absorptive cells is found to be rather similar (Wigglesworth and Salpeter, 1962): mitochondria are associated with basal infoldings in each case, and although the apical microvilli of the secretory cells are unusually tightly packed (the 'honeycomb border' of light microscopy), while those of the absorptive cell 'brush border' are more widely spaced, mitochondria are inserted into the microvilli of each cell type.

A comparison is often drawn between the structure of Malpighian tubule cells and those of the proximal tubule of the mammalian kidney, but it should be remembered that juxtaposition of mitochondria and the cell membrane points to the presence of an active transport mechanism, but does not give an indication of the direction in which this transport occurs. In the proximal tubule, absorbed materials are passed out of the cell through the infolded basal cell membrane, while in Malpighian tubules, mitochondria alongside basal infoldings may provide energy for the transport of materials into secreting cells or out of absorbing cells, and the same is true of mitochondria associated with apical microvilli. In short, one cannot safely interpret the fine structural details of a Malpighian tubule or other transporting system without knowing something of its secretory or absorptive role.

In addition to the exchange of ions and molecules between the haemolymph and urine, controlled by active transport and diffusion, movement of large molecules across the tubule cells may sometimes occur through the formation and migration of pinocytic vesicles (Wessing, 1965).

In the lumen of the proximal part of *Rhodnius* tubules, the refractile uric acid spheres, so prominent in fresh preparations, are dissolved out by processing for electron microscopy, perhaps by the slightly alkaline fixative. However, their erstwhile presence is revealed in electron micrographs, where the brush border has been displaced to accommodate them. The same appearance is found in sections of Malpighian tubules of adult blowflies, and is illustrated in Plate 95. In a series of studies on the Malpighian tubules of the house cricket *Gryllus*, Berkaloff (1958, 1959, 1960) has described the intracellular formation, growth and subsequent release into the lumen of ovoid or spherical granules, that have a striking concentric lamination when seen in thin sections. Similar granules in cells of the proximal segment of *Rhodnius* tubules have also been described by Wigglesworth and Salpeter, and these authors regard them as mineralised deposits, probably containing phosphates or carbonates of calcium and magnesium. Berkaloff, on the other hand, has suggested that the granules in the intact tubule may be partly organic and partly inorganic in composition, perhaps containing uric acid, calcium phosphate and urate together with protein and mucopolysaccharide material. An example of these interesting calculi, within the lumen of a stick insect Malpighian tubule, is shown in Plate 97.

This brief survey by no means covers the range of structural and functional variety of Malpighian tubule cells. Pigment granules are present in many species, and Wessing and Bonse (1966) have described the changes that occur in the tubule cells of 'red' mutant *Drosophila* as 3-hydroxy-kynurenine is converted to ommochrome pigments. One of the four regions of each tubule in leaf hoppers and related Homoptera manufactures and releases a bizarre secretory product, the brochosomes—minute lipid- and

287

protein-containing bodies consisting of hollow polyhedra, upon the pentagonal and hexagonal facets of which are constructed sculptured compartments (Smith and Littau, 1960; Gouranton and Maillet, 1967). Wigglesworth (1965) has listed numerous examples of species whose Malpighian tubules are in part specialised for functions other than urine secretion. Silk for cocoon spinning is usually secreted by the labial glands (p. 211), but this is supplied by Malpighian tubule cells in larvae of the lacewing *Chrysopa*, the ant-lion *Myrmeleo*, the weevil *Phytonomus*, and other insects. Calcium carbonate secreted by the Malpighian tubules in a cercopid *Ptyelus* is formed into a spiral shell, larvae of the wood-boring beetle *Cerambyx* use a similar secretion to plug their burrow, while female stick insects include lime from the tubules in producing the chorion of the eggs. Finally, in this brief and incomplete list, it may be added that one of the most spectacular bioluminescent displays—the blue light of the 'glow-worm caves' of New Zealand—stems from specialised cells in the Malpighian tubules of myriads of larvae of the fly *Bolitophilus*. These varied specialisations offer a wealth of interesting material for future electron microscopic work.

REFERENCES

*BACCETTI, B., MAZZI, V., and MASSIMELLO, G. 1963. Ricerche istochimiche e al microscopio elettronico sui tubi Malpighiani di *Dacus oleae* Gmel. II. L'adulto. *Redia*, **48**, 47–68.
*BEAMS, H. W., TAHMISIAN, T. N., and DEVINE, R. L. 1955. Electron microscope studies on the cells of the Malpighian tubules of the grasshopper (Orthoptera, Acrididae). *J. biophys. biochem. Cytol.*, **1**, 197–202.
*BERKALOFF, A. 1958. Les grains de secrétion des tubes de Malpighi de *Gryllus domesticus* (Orthoptère, Gryllidae). *C.r. hebd. Séanc. Acad. Sci., Paris,* **246**, 2807–2809.
*BERKALOFF, A. 1959. Variations de l'ultrastructure des tubes de Malpighi et leur fonctionnement chez *Gryllus domesticus* (Orthoptère, Gryllidae). *C.r. hebd. Séanc. Acad. Sci., Paris*, **248**, 466–469.
*BERKALOFF, A. 1960. Contribution à l'étude des tubes de Malpighi et de l'excrétion chez les insectes. *Annls Sci. Nat., Zool.*, 12e sér., **2**, 869–947.
 BERRIDGE. M. J. 1967. Ion and water transport across epithelia, In *Insects and Physiology* (J. W. L. Beament and J. E. Treherne, eds.). Oliver and Boyd, Edinburgh.
 BULGER, R. E. 1965. The fine structure of the aglomerular nephron of the toadfish, *Opsanus tau*. *Am. J. Anat.*, **171**, 171–192.
*GOURANTON, J., and MAILLET, P-L. 1967. Origine et structure des brochosomes. *J. Micr.*, **6**, 53–64.
*GUPTA, B. L., and BERRIDGE, M. J. Unpublished observations on the fine structure and ATP-ase activity of Malpighian tubules of adult blowflies, *Calliphora erythrocephala*.
*MAZZI, V., and BACCETTI, B. 1963. Ricerche istochimiche e al microscopio elettronico sui tubi Malpighiani di *Dacus oleae* Gmel. I. La larva. *Z. Zellforsch. mikrosk. Anat.*, **59**, 47–70.
*SMITH, D. S., and LITTAU, V. C. 1960. Cellular specialization in the execretory epithelia of an insect, *Macrosteles fascifrons* Stål (Homoptera). *J. biophys. biochem. Cytol.*, **8**, 103–133.
*TSUBO, I., and BRANDT, P. W. 1962. An electron microscopic study of the Malpighian tubules of the grasshopper, *Dissosteira carolina. J. Ultrastruct. Res.*, **6**, 28–35.
*WESSING, A. 1965. Die Funktion der malpighischen Gefässe. In *Funktionelle und morphologische Organisation der Zelle, Sekretion und Exkretion.* Springer-Verlag, Berlin, Heidelberg and New York.
*WESSING, A., and BONSE, A. 1966. Natur und Bildung des roten Farbstoffes in den Nierentubuli der Mutante 'red' von *Drosophila melanogaster. Z. Naturf.*, **21**, 1219–1223.
 WIGGLESWORTH, V. B. 1965. *The Principles of Insect Physiology*, 6th edn, Ch. 12. Methuen, London.
*WIGGLESWORTH, V. B., and SALPETER, M. M. 1962. Histology of the Malpighian tubules in *Rhodnius prolixus* Stål (Hemiptera). *J. Insect Physiol.*, **8**, 299–307.

Plates 94–97 ▷

U

Plate 94 ▷

An electron micrograph of the epithelial wall of a Malpighian tubule from the milkweed bug *Oncopeltus fasciatus*. These cells perform the function of withdrawing waste materials from the haemolymph and secreting the urine, and also in many cases are responsible for absorbing useful components of the urine before it leaves the tubule and enters the hind-gut. As in many transporting cells (e.g. the epithelium of the proximal renal tubule), the basal cytoplasm is dissected into narrow leaflets and extracellular spaces [*] by extensive infolding of the basal cell membrane—a device that enormously increases the surface area of this face of the cell. The plentiful mitochondria [M] which lie in the cytoplasmic sheets are thought to provide energy for active transport of ions either from haemolymph to cytoplasm in urine-secreting Malpighian tubule cells, or in the reverse direction in cells that are engaged in absorption. The basal surface of the epithelium rests upon a basement membrane [BM], sometimes flanked by small muscle fibres and tracheoles, and beyond this extracellular sheet, in life, lies the haemolymph [He]. The apical surface of the cells bears a brush border of microvilli [Mv]; in this micrograph, mitochondria [M] are abundant in the adjoining cytoplasm, but frequently (Plate 95) tubular mitochondria are squeezed into the microvilli, and again, these appear to play a part in the active transport of materials into or out of the cell. The lateral cell membranes may be quite loosely apposed over much of their extent, but close to the apical border, in this field, a well-defined zone of intercellular junction [CJ] is present, involving septate desmosomes. A similar situation is found in other epithelia, and is a general device for sealing off the direct intercellular route between one side of the epithelium and the other. The organisation of the cytoplasm of Malpighian tubule cells varies greatly, and in the example shown here, ranks of rough-surfaced endoplasmic reticulum cisternae are prominent [ER]. Portions of nuclei are also included [N].

(× 9000.)

(*Philips EM 200.*)

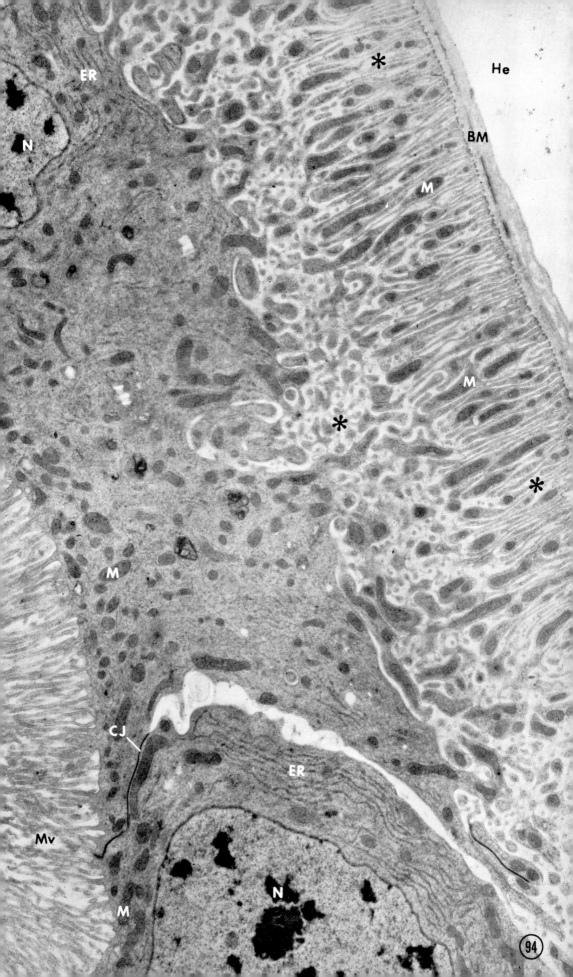

Plate 95 ▷

A micrograph covering part of a cell from a Malpighian tubule of an adult blowfly, *Calliphora erythrocephala*. The space beyond the basal surface of the cell, included at upper left, is in life filled with haemolymph. The cell rests on a basement membrane [BM], adjoining which is a small tracheole [Tr]. The basal plasma membrane is very deeply infolded—more irregularly than in the cell from the milkweed bug shown in the last plate—and the infoldings define extracellular spaces [arrows] that extend almost to the apical surface. Mitochondria [M] are found in large numbers alongside these membrane folds, where they are strategically placed to provide ATP for the active transport of ions across the cell surface. The apical border, as in most Malpighian tubule cells, is produced into microvilli [Mv]. In the blowfly, some of these microvilli contain mitochondria [M′] while others are narrow, and lack these organelles, and it is possible that this variation reflects a permanent functional division between different elements of the brush border, but it is also possible that changes in the mitochondrial supply of the microvilli along the tubule may occur transiently, reflecting changes in the physiological state of the cells. These mitochondria and also those crowded into the apical cytoplasm indicate that active transport of materials takes place between the cell and the tubule lumen (and/or vice versa), as well as across the basal cell surface. The principal nitrogenous excretory product of adult blowflies, and indeed of most insects, is uric acid, which often forms crystalline spheres within the lumen of the Malpighian tubules. These spheres dissolve at some point during preparation of the material for electron microscopy, but evidence of their former presence is found where the brush border has been pushed apart to accommodate them [light asterisk]. A variety of clear vacuoles are seen within the cytoplasm [heavy asterisks], perhaps representing collecting depots for urates or other excretory products. Some insects excrete from the tubule cells spherical multilayered granules (Plate 97), probably containing organic and inorganic material.

(×30,000.)

(*Philips EM 200. Micrograph reproduced by courtesy of Drs B. L. Gupta and M. J. Berridge.*)

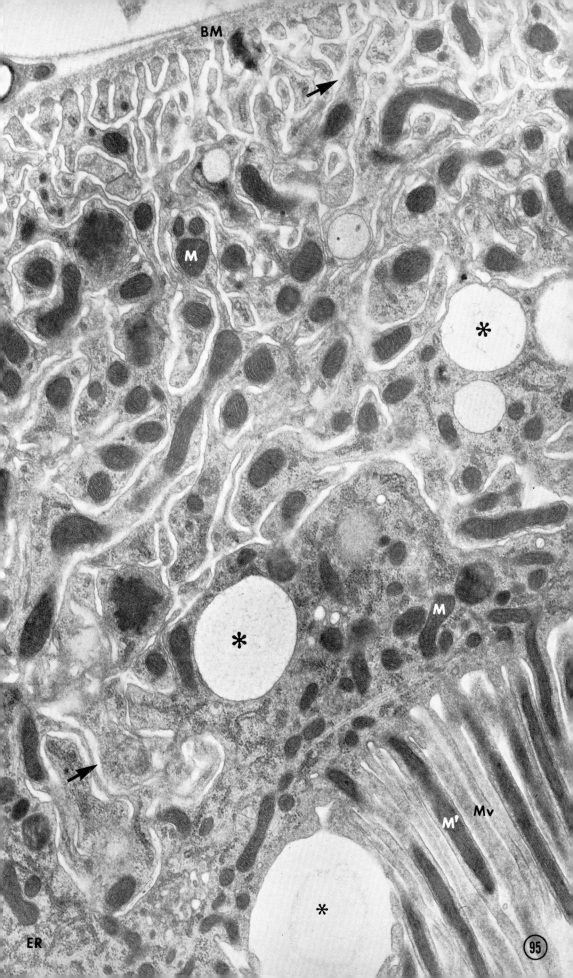

BM

M

*

*

M

M'

Mv

ER

95

Plate 96 ▷

Part of a Malpighian tubule cell of an adult blowfly, similar to that shown in the last plate, but fixed after having been treated in a way designed to reveal the presence of sites of ATP-ase activity. The tubule was incubated in a medium containing magnesium ions, ATP as an enzyme substrate, and a trace of soluble lead nitrate—the medium being buffered at a slightly acid pH (6·8). Where ATP is split, with the formation of inorganic phosphate, the latter reacts with the lead nitrate in solution to produce highly insoluble lead phosphate, which is precipitated as an electron-opaque marker close to the site of enzyme action. Under the conditions used here, granules of reaction product are formed along the infolded basal cell membrane [arrows], indicating the presence of an ATP-base presumably involved in active transport of ions into or out of the cell. This enzyme is active only in the presence of magnesium ions, and if calcium is substituted in the incubation mixture, no reaction product forms. The dusting of dense granules in the basement membrane [BM] is due not to enzyme activity, but to the presence of anion groups which bind lead. If the incubation is carried out at a slightly alkaline pH (7·2), the picture obtained is quite different: the enzyme associated with the basal cell membrane is inactive, but an ATP-ase associated with the apical surface is brought into play, and the microvilli [Mv], which here show no localisation of activity, become studded with granules of lead phosphate. This apical enzyme is likewise thought to play a part in the active transfer of materials across the membrane of the cell. The large vacuoles within the cytoplasm [*] may represent depots where waste substances are accumulated, prior to their release into the lumen of the tubule. Note the numerous mitochondria [M].

(× 34,000.)

(*Philips EM 200. Micrograph reproduced by courtesy of Drs B. L. Gupta and M. J. Berridge.*)

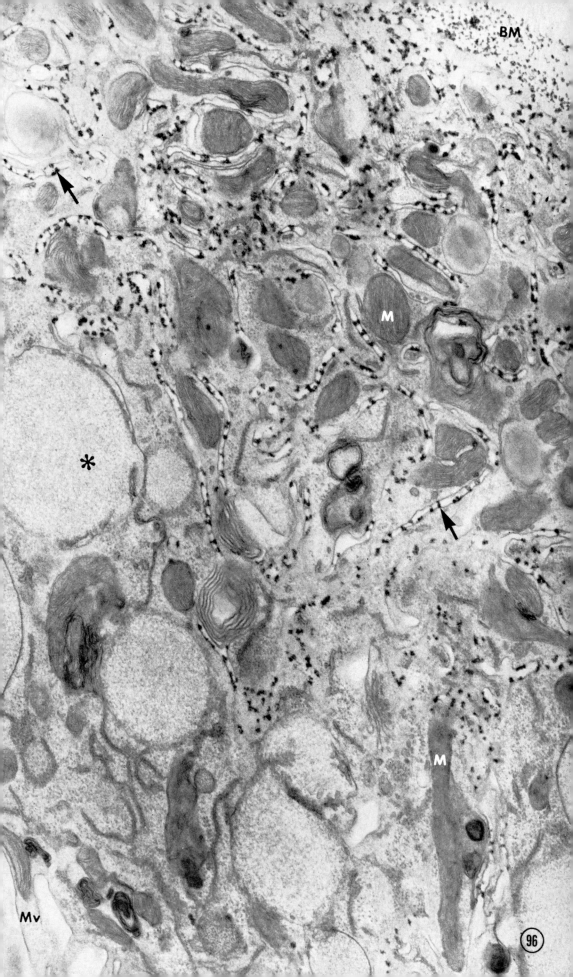

BM

M

*

M

Mv

96

Plate 97 ▷

Some insects, e.g. the house cricket *Gryllus* and the stick insect *Carausius*, liberate into the lumen of the Malpighian tubule spherical granules containing material that, in part at least, survives processing for electron microscopy. As is shown here, in a field within the lumen [Lu] of the stick insect, these granules possess a striking concentrically layered organisation of opaque and clear zones. These excretory bodies are chemically inhomogeneous, and before fixation and subsequent processing perhaps contain inorganic salts, in addition to uric acid, urates and proteinaceous or other organic material. Profiles of microvilli are included [Mv].

($\times$ 60,000.)

(*Philips EM 200. Micrograph reproduced by courtesy of Dr B. L. Gupta.*)

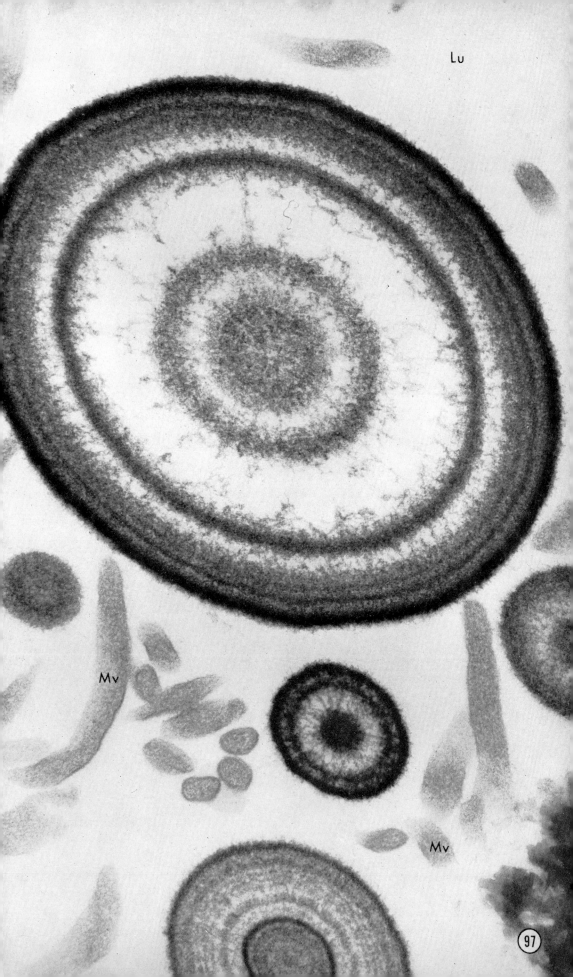

Lu

Mv

Mv

97

Anal Papillae

The maintenance of a favourable salt and water balance within the insect body is a complex and well regulated function. Water and salts are ingested with the food, or in some aquatic species are taken in through specialised regions of the cuticle, and their balance in the haemolymph and tissue fluids may be delicately controlled by a combination of loss through urine production in the Malpighian tubules and reabsorption across the epithelia of the mid-gut or rectum (pp. 227, 285).

Around the anus of mosquito larvae is placed a group of haemolymph-filled papillae consisting of a thin layer of epidermal cells beneath a diaphanous covering of cuticle. These have on occasions been referred to as anal 'gills' in the belief that they serve as respiratory organs, allowing inward diffusion of oxygen from the surrounding water into the body. However, these aquatic larvae breathe atmospheric air by means of a respiratory siphon attached to the water surface, and the physiological importance of the anal papillae has been shown to lie in their ability to absorb ions from the external medium, against the concentration gradient. Furthermore, the size of these projections has been found to vary with the dilution of the medium, becoming largest in water with the lowest salinity (Refs. in Wigglesworth, 1965). The part played by these papillae in maintaining a high haemolymph salt concentration, while the insect is surrounded by a very dilute medium, has been reviewed by Treherne (1965). It has been established, for example, that the papilla epithelium actively transports sodium, chloride, and probably other ions, and that a normal haemolymph concentration of 95–100 mM sodium is maintained in a medium that contains this ion at a concentration of 2 mM.

Copeland (1964) has examined the fine structure of anal papilla epidermal cells in larvae of *Culex quinquefasciatus* that were reared in distilled water to which a few dead larvae were added to provide a total salinity of only nine parts per million. Two of Copeland's electron micrographs are reproduced here (Plates 98 and 99), and these display interesting structural features that may be related to the absorptive role of the papilla cells. The apical cell surface, adjoining the thin cuticular covering, is thrown into a regular series of parallel folds along the inner margin of which lie numerous mitochondria. The basal cell membrane, facing the haemolymph contained within the papilla, is deeply and irregularly infolded into the cell to form a series of meandering canaliculi. Frequently, as illustrated in Plate 99, flattened portions of the canaliculi become tightly sandwiched between pairs of large mitochondria; this striking configuration was termed a 'mitochondrial pump' by Copeland, who suggested that it may be connected with the transporting function of the cell. It is interesting to discover that the general plan of these cells is in some respects markedly similar to that of the absorptive rectal papillae of the blowfly (Plates 88 and 90), which also possess apical leaflets and in which the lateral rather than the basal membrane is infolded to form complex canaliculi, specifically associated with mitochondria.

In rectal papillae (p. 264) it has been proposed that ions are actively taken into the cell by a transport mechanism associated with the apical surface, and thence actively concentrated in the intercellular spaces provided by the infolded lateral membranes, and that water then follows from the gut lumen and through the cytoplasm along an osmotic gradient, eventually passing, with the absorbed ions, into the haemolymph. In anal papillae, the apical pleating achieves a tenfold increase in the surface area of the cell membrane, while the area of the basal membrane is increased considerably by the ramifying infoldings: by this device, the surfaces engaged in the uptake of ions from the water and their secretion into the haemolymph attain a much greater extent than the small size of the papillae would at first sight suggest. Furthermore, the placing of mitochondria close to both the apical and basal membranes suggests that energy provided by ATP is required for the active transport of ions across each of these—that is, from the medium into the cell and from the cell into the haemolymph.

In a subsequent paper, Sohal and Copeland (1966) have examined the effects of different environmental salinity levels upon the structure of the anal papillae in another mosquito, *Aëdes aegypti*. They found that in larvae placed in a medium hypotonic to the blood, the apical surface of the papilla cells is tightly folded, as in *Culex*. In isotonic or progressively hypertonic media, these infoldings were found to decrease in extent, thus reducing the surface area of the cell membrane bordering the cuticular covering of the organ, and this alteration is accompanied by a reduction in the number of mitochondria in the cell. Eventually, in hypertonic solutions, the epithelium undergoes degenerative changes, and its capacity for salt regulation breaks down. Sohal and Copeland suggest that under the experimental conditions used, the intake of inorganic ions through the papillae may be controlled by the device of varying the extent of the membrane across which they enter the cells.

Although the ability to collect salts from fresh water has been most fully studied in mosquito larvae, it is likely that other aquatic insects are able to maintain their haemolymph salt concentration in a similar way. For example, it is possible that dragonfly nymphs take in salts through the thin walled 'gills' present within the rectum, from the water that is periodically taken in and expelled, and it would be of much interest to discover whether the rectal epithelium of these insects includes cells that show the specialisations found in the osmoregulatory anal papillae.

REFERENCES

*COPELAND, E. 1964. A mitochondrial pump in the cells of the anal papillae of mosquito larvae. *J. Cell Biol.*, **23**, 253–263.
*SOHAL, R. S., and COPELAND, E. 1966. Ultrastructural variations in the anal papillae of *Aëdes aegypti* (L.) at different environmental salinities. *J. Insect Physiol.*, **12**, 429–439.
TREHERNE, J. E. 1965. Active transport in insects. In *Aspects of Insect Biochemistry*. Academic Press, London and New York.
WIGGLESWORTH, V. B. 1965. *Principles of Insect Physiology*, 6th edn, Ch. 11. Methuen, London.

Plates 98–99 ▷

Plate 98 ▷

The anal papillae of mosquito larvae are important osmoregulatory organs, and are able to withdraw salts from low concentrations in the water surrounding the insect, and to pass these into the haemolymph. The structural features of the epithelial cells lining the papillae are illustrated in this micrograph and the next. Each papilla is covered with a thin layer of cuticle [Cu] continuous with that of the general body surface, and permeable to ions and probably to water molecules. Beneath this layer, the apical surface of the specialised epidermal cells is tightly folded into a series of parallel leaflets [arrows], similar to those of the rectal papilla cells of the blowfly (Plate 90). The basal cell membrane, facing the haemolymph, rests upon a thin basement membrane [BM], and is deeply infolded into the cell to form a series of irregular channels or canaliculi [*]. These canaliculi are frequently locally compressed between pairs of large mitochondria [M]—a feature more clearly seen, at higher magnification, in the next plate. Other mitochondria [M'] are collected in the cytoplasm near the base of the apical leaflets. A portion of the centrally placed nucleus is included on the left of the field [N]. A tracheole [Tr] indents the basal surface of the anal papilla cell.

(×30,000.)

(Philips EM 200. From Copeland (1964). Micrograph reproduced by courtesy of Dr E. Copeland and the Journal of Cell Biology.)

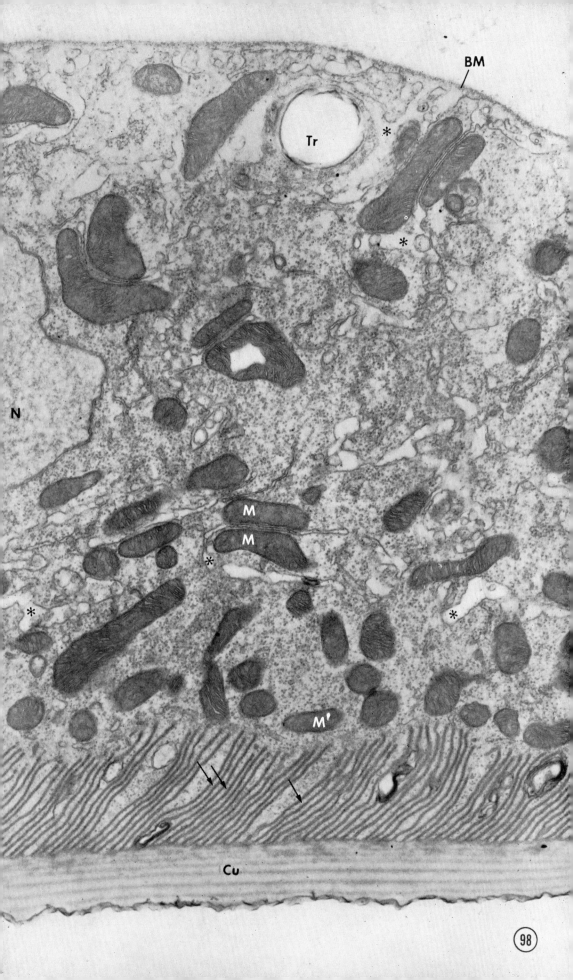

Plate 99 ▷

An electron micrograph of the basal region of an anal papilla cell of a
larval mosquito (*Culex quinquefasciatus*), at higher magnification than
in the last plate. The basement membrane [BM] is included on the
left. In these cells, the basal cell membrane is deeply infolded to form
a complex series of canaliculi or extracellular channels. The mouths
of two of these channels are indicated by arrows, while black asterisks
mark some of the ramifying extracellular spaces. Frequently, the cell
membrane limiting these spaces is tightly inserted [white asterisks]
between pairs or trios of large mitochondria [M]. It is likely that these
mitochondria provide ATP as a source of energy for the active
transport of ions from the cytoplasm into the neighbouring
extracellular spaces, and that these ions are then able to diffuse
through the basement membrane into the circulating haemolymph.
Ions transferred in this way must first be actively absorbed from the
external medium into the cell by way of the permeable cuticle
overlying the papilla, and the tightly pleated apical cell membrane
(Plate 98). The cytoplasm of the anal papilla cells contains sparsely
distributed cisternae of the rough-surfaced endoplasmic reticulum
[ER] together with many granules [Rb], about 150 Å in diameter,
which represent free ribosomes and/or glycogen granules.

($\times$ 64,000.)

(*Philips EM 200. From Copeland (1964). Micrograph reproduced by
courtesy of Dr E. Copeland and the* Journal of Cell Biology.)

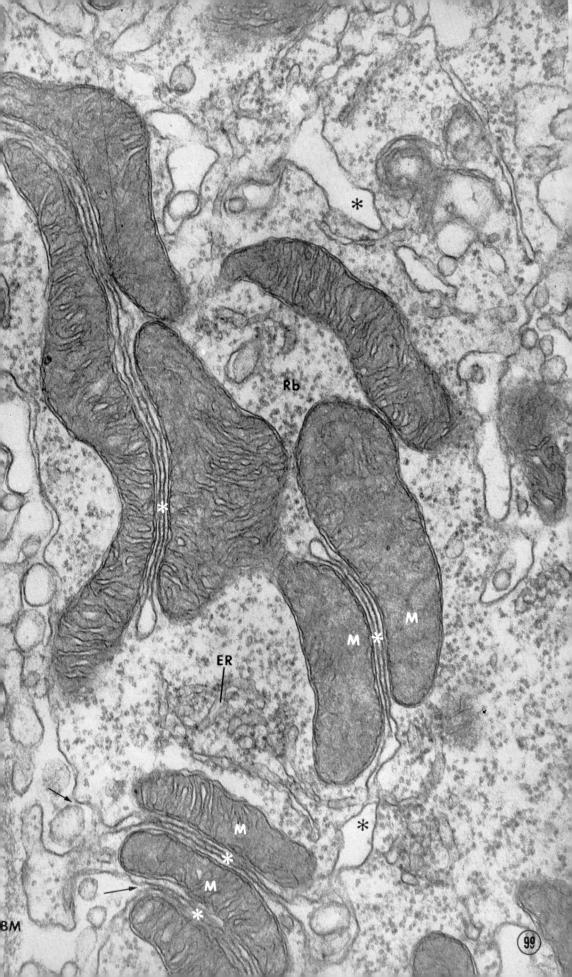

The Testis, Vas Deferens and Accessory Glands

The sequence of events taking place in the formation and maturation of the spermatozoa within the insect testis presents a fascinating problem in cellular differentiation, and one that attracted a good deal of attention in past years, by the methods of classical cytology and the light microscope. More recently, the electron microscope has served to clarify some controversial aspects of male gamete development. However, at the same time, the greatly enhanced resolution and magnification permitted by the electron microscope has revealed that not only are the cellular changes leading to maturation even more complex, within a species, than was earlier suspected, but also that interspecific variation in detail and plan is wide, and at present incompletely documented and understood.

As in the ovary of the insect, the germ cells within the testis are often arranged in a sequence that reflects the temporal changes involved in spermatogenesis. Thus, at the apex of the testis generally lie the undifferentiated primordial germ cells or spermatogonia. These are followed by a zone in which the products of spermatogonial mitotic division, the primary spermatocytes, become grouped into 'cysts', each of which contains the daughter cells derived from a single primordial cell enclosed within a follicle or sheath of somatic cells. Next arise, respectively by the first and second meiotic divisions, the secondary spermatocytes and the spermatids, and soon after the latter division ensues the striking series of morphological changes during which a rounded cell becomes transformed into an elongated flagellate gamete.

It is unnecessary here to attempt to review in any detail the changes involved during sperm elongation; the elegant early work of Bowen and others on this subject is discussed fully by Wilson (1925). Suffice it to say that while the mature insect spermatozoon may be of extreme length (in some instances several millimetres), it is generally 'typical', by vertebrate standards, in possessing from the anterior end backwards an acrosome, nucleus and centriole from which stems a motile flagellum around which are arranged one or two helically disposed mitochondria. A few of the major contributions that have been provided through use of the electron microscope may be mentioned. The formation of the acrosome, which effects penetration of the egg cell at fertilisation, was found to take place within Golgi cisternae (Kay, 1962), confirming the earliest well-documented instance of the secretory role played by this region of the cell. The origin of the flagellum extending from the cell before the onset of elongation (Plate 100) has been examined in detail, and in common with other ciliated and flagellated cells the motile apparatus has been found to arise in association with a centriole (Gall, 1961). A further contribution made by recent studies concerns the identity of the 'Nebenkern' body, the behaviour of which proved so perplexing at the level of the light microscope: this structure, within the spermatocyte, was revealed as a fused mass of mitochondria which later becomes organised into twin organelles,

307

accompanying the elongating cell and coiling around the flagellum. Complex nuclear changes occur as the gamete differentiates and matures, and these have been discussed by Kay and Kay (1966) and others.

In addition to the above, hitherto unsuspected alterations in fine detail have come to light in the course of electron microscopic studies on insect spermatozoa. The fibres of the flagellum, for example, undergo elaborate changes in the maturing spermatid (Cameron, 1965). At the same time, the adjoining mitochondria which at an early stage possess typical cristae, despite their extremely elongated form, become progressively transformed into membrane-limited rods containing paracrystalline material. These lack cristae, but nevertheless retain respiratory enzymes. These remarkable changes within the mitochondria are readily seen in thin sections, and, in addition, lend themselves well to the technique of 'negative staining' with heavy metal salts (Meyer, 1964). This technique has proved valuable in studies on the organisation of such structures as virus particles, protein crystals and muscle filaments, and in this instance displays many details of the substructure of the paracrystalline rods of the sperm tail.

Stages showing some of the above changes, within the testis of the flour moth *Ephestia kühniella*, are illustrated in Plates 100 to 104. In this insect, the flagellum is acquired in the late spermatocyte, when the mitochondria are still small and scattered, prior to their involvement in the Nebenkern complex and subsequent elongation of the cell (Plate 100). In a cyst containing early spermatids (Plate 101A) seen in transverse section at a level behind the nucleus and centriole, the paired mitochondria derived from the Nebenkern are placed on either side of the flagellum, which at this point of development possesses an arrangement of fibres commonly found, for example, in cilia and flagella of Protozoa, and in ciliated epithelia such as lamellibranch gills and the vertebrate trachea. This arrangement comprises nine outer double fibres and an inner pair—the 9+2 configuration that was one of the early revelations of electron microscopy. At a slightly later stage (Plate 101B), while the mitochondria are still of normal appearance, an extra ring of nine 'accessory' fibres has been added, apparently from lateral flanges borne by the original outer doublets (Cameron, 1965). Subsequently, paracrystalline material first makes its appearance within the mitochondria (Plate 102), which become aligned in parallel alongside the flagellum. Furthermore, the accessory fibres have become opaque, and in this respect are soon followed by the inner pair. These flagellar changes have not been followed in more detail in *Ephestia*, but recent work by Phillips (1966) has brought to light further remarkable details of the organisation of maturing flagella of the fly *Sepsis*, which may be mentioned here as an excellent instance of the resolving power of the electron microscope, employed to reveal a further degree of order in a biological structure. In the *Sepsis* spermatid, the 'opacity' seen at low magnification in the fibres described above is due to the presence within each of a central fibre or tubule. Moreover, each flagellar fibre has been resolved into subunits or 'protofibrils' resembling those constituting the cytoplasmic microtubules that are found, after glutaraldehyde fixation, in many types of animal and plant cell. Interestingly enough, the accessory and inner flagellar fibres of the sperm tail and certain microtubules (Ledbetter and Porter, 1963), are each made up of thirteen subunits—a feature that may point to a close similarity between these cellular components. As Phillips suggests, the fact that the doublets of the flagellum may have a slightly different construction may reflect functional divisions between the elements responsible for the movement of the flagellum. Furthermore, Behnke and Forer (1967) have found that in cranefly spermatids and other motile cells the cytoplasmic microtubules and the various tubules of the flagellum may comprise several classes characterised by different physical and/or chemical properties.

At the stage shown in Plate 102, the germ cells within the cyst are enclosed by the follicular epithelium, but later, pseudopodia from these (or perhaps from special nutritive or regulatory 'sustentacular cells') grow into the cyst and meander between the spermatids (Plate 103). Meanwhile, the transformation of the mitochondria has continued, and a dense rod, attached to the surface of each cell by septa, has been developed. The latter structure provides merely one example of the incompleteness of our present understanding of the events of maturation; its appearance in thin sections has been noted by André (1962) and by Yasuzumi and Oura (1965), but neither its mode of origin nor its function is known. In the late spermatid (Plate 104), the flagellum, together with the mitochondria, now no longer paired but fused into a single body, virtually fill the cell at this level. Each cell now bears a mantle of radial 'spokes' made up of fine laminae (André, 1962; Yasuzumi and Oura, 1965)—a structure that is later discarded and which is at present as baffling as it is striking.

The micrographs included here illustrate merely one aspect of the complexity of the developmental events, precisely synchronised within each cyst, occurring within each gamete prior to its emission through the follicular epithelium before being transferred to the female during copulation. They may serve as a reminder that the electron microscope is providing us with structural information that at present goes beyond our knowledge of parallel physiological and biochemical aspects of insect sperm development.

By no means all insect spermatozoa may be considered as 'typical', according to the criteria of Nath (1965), in possessing the linear sequence of components mentioned earlier in this section. Many unusual male gametes, throughout the Animal Kingdom, have for long been recognised and in some instances have been reinvestigated in the electron microscope. For example, in the spermatozoa of the fire-brat *Thermobia* and the silverfish *Lepisma*, the flagellar centriole, instead of migrating to the posterior pole of the nucleus as in most insects, passes up to the anterior end, with the result that the flagellum flanks the nucleus before extending beyond it; moreover, the acrosome is displaced from the apex of the cell and takes up a position behind the nucleus (Bawa, 1964; Werner, 1964). A similar arrangement is arrived at during maturation in the tiger beetle *Cicindela* (Werner, 1965).

Even the familiar 9 + 2 arrangement of flagellar microtubules or fibres is evidently not the only configuration that will permit motility. In the sperm of mosquitos, the pair of central fibres usually present in the axis of the flagellum is replaced by a single structure to form a 9 + 1 configuration (Breland, Gassner, Riess and Biesele, 1966). The sperm of the fungus gnat *Sciara* possess an axial structure involving up to 76 pairs or doublets of microtubules, in the absence of a conventional flagellum (Makielski, 1966). Undoubtedly the most bizarre insect spermatozoa hitherto examined in the electron microscope are those of the coccid *Steatococcus* (Moses and Coleman, 1964): here the spermatid lacks flagellum, mitochondria and nuclear envelope and is reduced to a membrane-limited cylinder containing chromosomal material surrounded by microtubules. Despite this radical simplification (Plate 105) the 32 cells within each cyst contrive to be motile.

On the basis of the fairly wide range of insect types that have been examined, it might seem reasonable to expect that when both structures are present, the mitochondria will be disposed around the straight axial flagellum. However, an exception

309

can usually be counted on to refute even the most conservative generalisation concerning these animals—perhaps not to be wondered at in a group numbering close to a million species. In this case, the flea provides the exception through reversal of the usual situation, in possessing, within each sperm, a flagellum helically coiled around a pair of straight axial mitochondria (Plate 106) (Gupta and Rothschild, unpublished).

Finally, lest it be supposed that insect male gametes all differ markedly, by virtue of extreme length or peculiarity of organisation, from typical vertebrate forms, it may be mentioned that in the cockroach the usual great elongation does not occur and the mature sperm is similar, in proportions and structural complement, to that of a mammal.

After leaving the testes, the spermatozoa pass into the paired vasa deferentia, which are slender tubes sometimes provided with a dilated reservoir or vesicula seminalis in which the mature gametes may be stored. The vasa deferentia unite to form a tube that is continuous with the ectodermal cuticle-lined ejaculatory duct leading to the intromittent organ or penis. The manner in which the spermatozoa pass to the vasa deferentia may be quite complex (Davey, 1965), but in the simplest instances the cysts which contain the gametes in the testis disappear after they enter the vasa deferentia, which thus become filled with free sperm cells. The main features of this part of the male reproductive tract are illustrated in Plates 107 and 108, prepared from the milkweed bug *Oncopeltus*.

The section shown in Plate 107 passes transversely through the duct and includes the cellular wall surrounding the lumen which contains a tightly packed mass of spermatozoa, lying parallel within the elongated duct. The epithelial cells of the vas deferens are cuboidal, and are linked by tortuous intercellular membranes (Plate 108). Their nuclei are often deeply lobed, and the cytoplasm contains a representation of the usual subcellular structures, but is not conspicuously specialised as, for example, for secretion or transport of materials across the epithelium. The basal cell membrane shows no infoldings, the apical membrane bears short irregular microvilli, and mitochondria are evenly distributed throughout the cell. In this part of the genital tract, the spermatozoa are non-motile and unable to move of their own accord; their passage along the vas deferens is presumably effected by contractions of the many small muscle fibres that form a robust sheath around the tube (Plate 108). These fibres are knit together into a mechanical unit by connective strands of extracellular material, which also surround the tracheoles and numerous nerve branches that lie between them.

The details of copulation and sperm transfer in insects vary a great deal (Wigglesworth, 1965), but two broad divisions may be recognised. In many insects, the sperm are transferred to the female within a gelatinous spermatophore which is placed into the vagina during copulation and from which the sperm passes to the spermatheca or receptaculum seminis (p. 349) for storage prior to fertilisation of the oocytes. The spermatophore is probably mucoprotein in nature, and is secreted in liquid form by the mesodermal accessory glands that open into the vasa deferentia, and which becomes shaped and jelly-like within the male intromittent organ. This method is employed by the blood-sucking bug *Rhodnius*, whereas the related milkweed bug *Oncopeltus* carries out the transfer of sperm by a quite different method (Davey, 1965). In *Oncopeltus*, the sperm contained within the seminal fluid are passed through a very long intromittent organ directly into the spermatheca. Nevertheless, accessory glands are

310

present in this insect, and their fine structure (Plates 109 and 110) suggests that they secrete a protein-containing material, though their physiological function is at present unknown. The glandular epithelium consists of cuboidal cells, each with a centrally placed and strikingly lobed nucleus. As in several other insect tissues (e.g. Plates 109 and 110), the lateral cell membranes are closely linked by desmosomes (of the septate and zonula adhaerens types) as the apical surface is approached; elsewhere, the adjoining membranes follow a more independent course. In the material at present available, the arrangement of intracellular membranes is reminiscent of that of exocrine pancreatic cells in a starved mammal—the basal half of the cell is packed with orderly curving arrays of ribosome-studded cisternae of the endoplasmic reticulum, and these are also present, though less well aligned, throughout the rest of the cytoplasm. Compact Golgi bodies containing smooth-surfaced cisternae and vesicles are numerous, particularly in the vicinity of the nucleus. The apical cell membrane is produced into irregular microvilli projecting into the gland lumen which is engorged with a dense homogeneous material, presumably secreted by the epithelium. The release of secretion appears to be complete in the cells illustrated here; no intracisternal granules are present in the endoplasmic reticulum, and the Golgi bodies likewise seem to be devoid of material. Further studies on series of accessory glands from this insect or from *Rhodnius*, selected at intervals before and after copulation, might well reveal interesting cyclic changes in these cells, perhaps paralleling those described in the pancreas and other protein-secreting tissues.

REFERENCES

*ANDRÉ, J. 1962. Contribution à la connaissance du chondriome. Étude de ses modifications ultrastructurales pendant la spermatogenèse. *J. Ultrastruct. Res.*, **3** suppl., 1–185.

*BAWA, S. R. 1964. Electron microscope study of spermiogenesis in a firebrat insect *Thermobia domestica*. *J. Cell Biol.*, **23**, 431–446.

*BEHNKE, O., and FORER, A. 1967. Evidence for four classes of microtubules in individual cells. *J. Cell Sci.*, **2**, 169–192.

*BRELAND, O. P., GASSNER, III, G., RIESS, R. W., and BIESELE, J. J. 1966. Certain aspects of the centriole adjunct, spermiogenesis, and the mature sperm of insects. *Can. J. Genet. Cytol.*, **8**, 759–777.

*CAMERON, M. L. 1965. Some details of ultrastructure in the development of flagellar fibers in the *Tenebrio* sperm. *Can. J. Zool.*, **43**, 1005–1010.

DAVEY, K. G. 1965. *Reproduction in the Insects*. Oliver and Boyd, Edinburgh.

GALL, J. G. 1961. Centriole replication. A study of spermatogenesis in the snail *Viviparus*. *J. biophys. biochem. Cytol.*, **10**, 163–193.

*GUPTA, B. L., and ROTHSCHILD, M. (In preparation.)

*KAYE, J. S. 1962. Acrosome formation in the house cricket. *J. Cell Biol.*, **12**, 411–432.

*KAYE, J. S., and KAYE, McM. R. 1966. The fine structure and chemical composition of nuclei during spermiogenesis in the house cricket. I. Initial stages of differentiation and loss of non-histone protein. *J. Cell Biol.*, **31**, 159–179.

LEDBETTER, M. C., and PORTER, K. R. 1963. A 'microtubule' in plant cell fine structure. *J. Cell Biol.*, **19**, 239–250.

*MAKIELSKI, S. K. 1966. The structure and maturation of the spermatozoa of *Sciara coprophila*. *J. Morph.*, **118**, 11–42.

*MEYER, G. 1964. Die parakristallinen Körper in den Spermienschwänzen von *Drosophila* *Z. Zellforsch. mikrosk. Anat.*, **62**, 762–784.

*MOSES, M. J., and COLEMAN, J. R. 1964. Structural patterns and the functional organization of chromosomes. In *The Role of Chromosomes in Development* (M. Locke, ed.). Academic Press, New York and London.

NATH, V 1965 *Animal Gametes (Male)*. Asia Publishing House, London.

*PHILLIPS, D. M. 1966. Substructure of flagellar tubules. *J. Cell Biol.*, **31**, 635–638.

*WERNER, G. 1964. Untersuchungen über die Spermiogenese beim Silberfischen, *Lepisma saccharina* L. *Z. Zellforsch. mikrosk. Anat.*, **63**, 880–912.

*WERNER, G. 1965. Untersuchungen über die Spermiogenese beim Sandläufer, *Cicindela campestris* L. *Z. Zellforsch. mikrosk. Anat.*, **66**, 255–275.

WIGGLESWORTH, V. B. 1965. *The Principles of Insect Physiology*, 6th edn., Ch. 15. Methuen, London.

WILSON, E. B. 1925. *The Cell in Development and Heredity*. Macmillan, New York.

*YASUZUMI, G., and OURA, C. 1965. Spermatogenesis in animals as revealed by electron microscopy. XV. The fine structure of the middle piece in the developing spermatid of the silkworm, *Bombyx mori* Linné. *Z. Zellforsch. mikrosk. Anat.*, **67**, 502–520.

Plates 100–110 ▷

Plate 100 ▷

The formation of the flagellum in the developing insect sperm cell may occur either in the late spermatocyte or after the second meiotic division, in the early spermatid. In the flour moth *Ephestia kühniella*, illustrated here, this occurs at the former stage, identified by the presence of small mitochondria scattered throughout the cell [M], prior to their aggregation in the 'Nebenkern'. The cell nucleus [N] is now large, and resembles that of many other cells, but subsequently undergoes considerable shrinkage and condensation of its contents. The germ cell cytoplasm at this stage reflects the undifferentiated condition of the spermatocyte: only a few small cisternae of the endoplasmic reticulum are present [ER], while free ribosomes [Rb] are abundant. The flagellum [Fl] arises in association with one of a pair of centrioles [Ce_1, Ce_2] placed perpendicularly to each other. Later reorganisation of the cell places the flagellar centriole, or basal body, behind the nucleus in the elongated cell.

($\times$ 30,000.)

(*Philips EM 200.*)

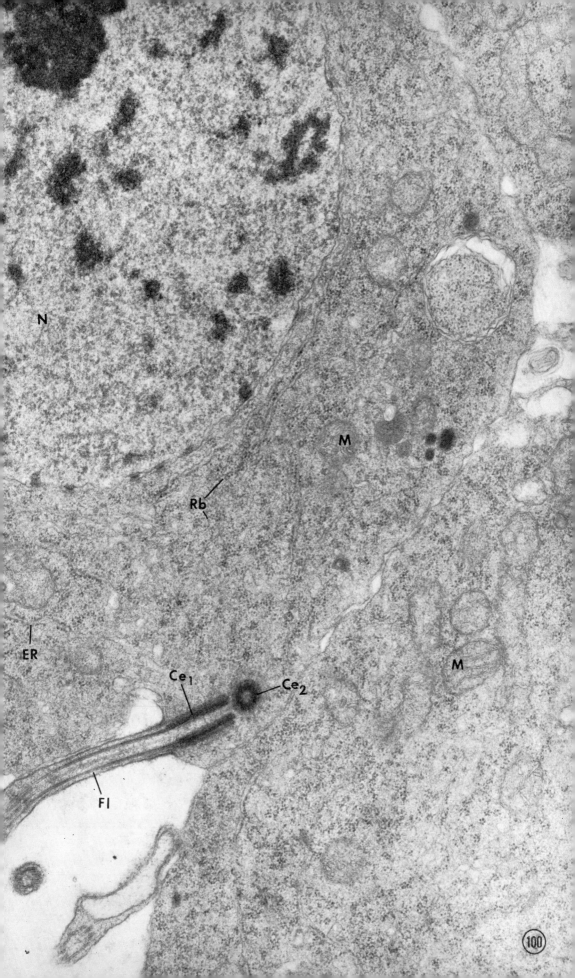

Plate 101 ▷

A pair of electron micrographs of transversely sectioned early spermatids of *Ephestia*, at a level behind the nucleus of the elongating cells. In *A* the paired mitochondria [M] derived from the 'Nebenkern' complex are normal in appearance and contain inner and outer limiting membranes together with small cristae. They lie within a cytoplasmic cylinder containing a few scattered microtubules [Mt]. The flagellum [Fl] includes an outer ring of nine doubled fibres or tubules surrounding an inner pair—the conventional 9 + 2 arrangement found in many cilia and flagella—and the whole structure is surrounded by a cisterna, perhaps referable to the smooth or agranular endoplasmic reticulum [SER]. At a slightly later stage, in *B*, the mitochondria and other cytoplasmic structures are unchanged, but to each of the nine outer doublets of the flagellum has been added an 'accessory' member [arrows]. It should be mentioned here that the changes occurring during sperm maturation are very precisely synchronised throughout every cell in the cyst; a feature seen in these and the following micrographs of thin sections of insect testis.

(*A* : × 55,000. *B* : × 55,000. *Inserts* : × 82,000.)

(*Philips EM 200.*)

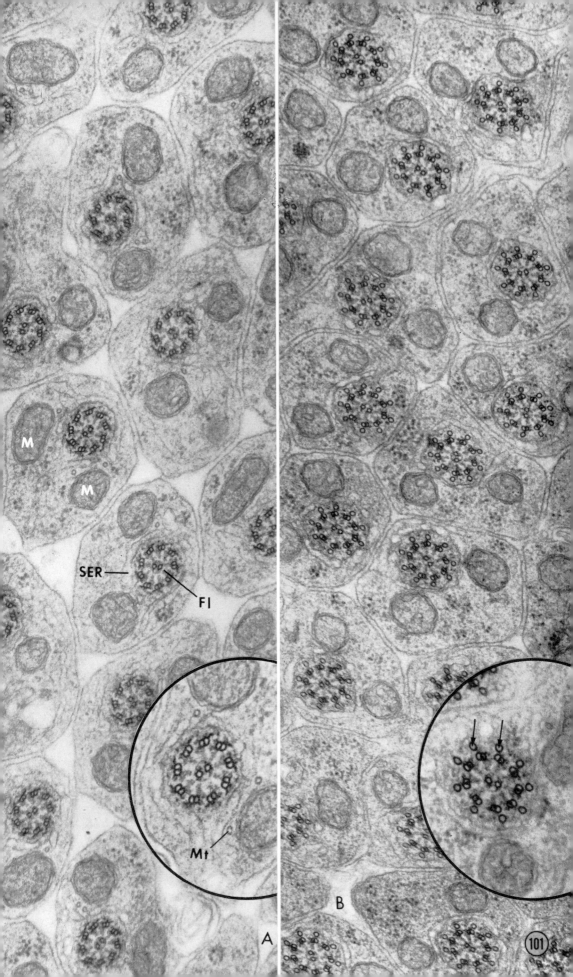

M

M

SER

Fl

Mt

A

B

Plate 102 ▷

At a slightly later stage in spermatid maturation than that shown in the last plate, several changes in organisation have occurred. The flagellum has moved to the periphery of the cell, while the two mitochondria [M] have become aligned in parallel. Within each mitochondrion, the deposition of paracrystalline material in the matrix [*] has commenced. The accessory tubules of the flagellum have become dense [arrows], and the agranular cisterna, which previously enveloped the flagellum, now partially extends around the mitochondria [SER]. Moreover, the microtubules not associated with the flagellum are now aligned [Mt] between and alongside the mitochondria.

($\times$ 45,000. *Insert*: $\times$ 87,000.)

(*Philips EM 200.*)

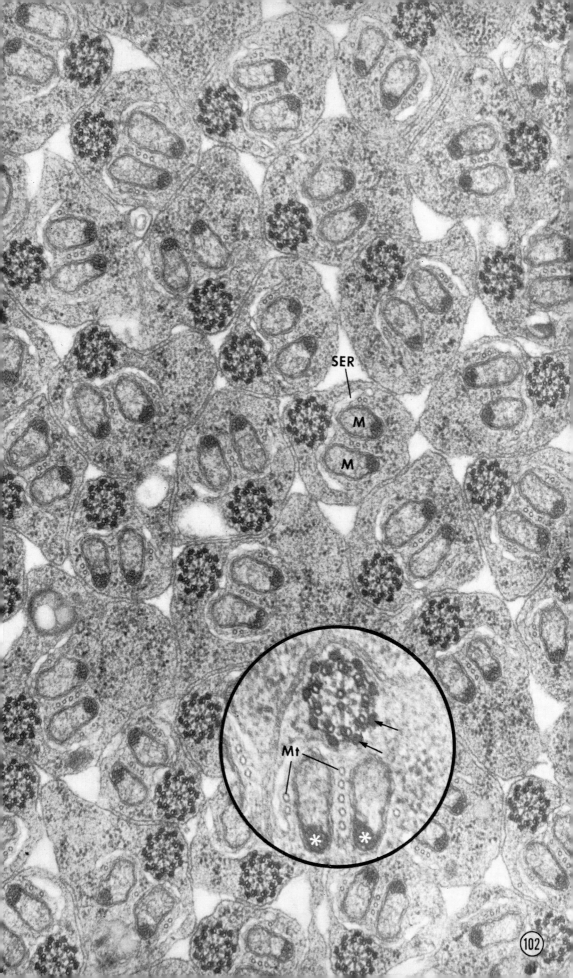

Plate 103 ▷

As spermatid maturation continues beyond the stage illustrated in
Plate 102, substantial changes are encountered. At the stage shown
in this micrograph, the cyst becomes permeated by processes of
follicle (or 'sustentacular') cells [*] which meander between the
spermatids, and perhaps play a part in regulating development in
addition to, or instead of, their generally assumed nutritive role. The
pair of mitochondria within each cell have become very dense and
unequal in size [M], and are flanked by a row of microtubules [Mt].
Smooth-membraned cisternae of the endoplasmic reticulum [SER]
now envelop both the mitochondria and the flagellum. As a further
modification, of unknown significance, each spermatid bears, within
a groove, a dense rod attached to the cell surface by radially arranged
septa [arrows].

($\times$ 25,000. *Insert*: $\times$ 43,000.)

(*Philips EM 200.*)

320

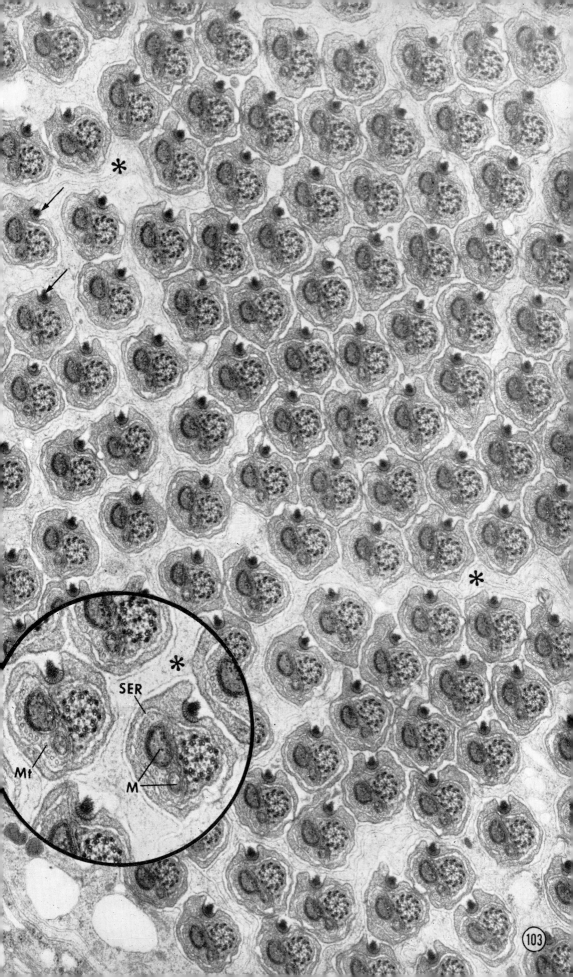

SER

Mt

M

103

Plate 104 ▷

At a still later stage of development within the testis, the cytoplasm of the spermatids of *Ephestia* has become very reduced, and each sperm tail is virtually filled by the flagellum, and the mitochondrial derivatives now fused into a single body [M]. The cell surface, particularly on the side adjoining the mitochondrial rod, bears a mantle of radially arranged 'spokes' of laminated construction [long arrows] in addition to the dense rod [short arrow] depicted in the last plate; this represents another structure of unknown function. Cytoplasmic processes no longer penetrate between the developing cells, although these are still contained within the follicular epithelium, the edge of which is included on the left of the field [Ep]. This micrograph, as well as the four that precede it, illustrate clearly the degree of synchrony achieved within the developing cells of each cyst of the testis.

($\times$ 45,000. *Insert*: $\times$ 70,000.)

(*Philips EM 200.*)

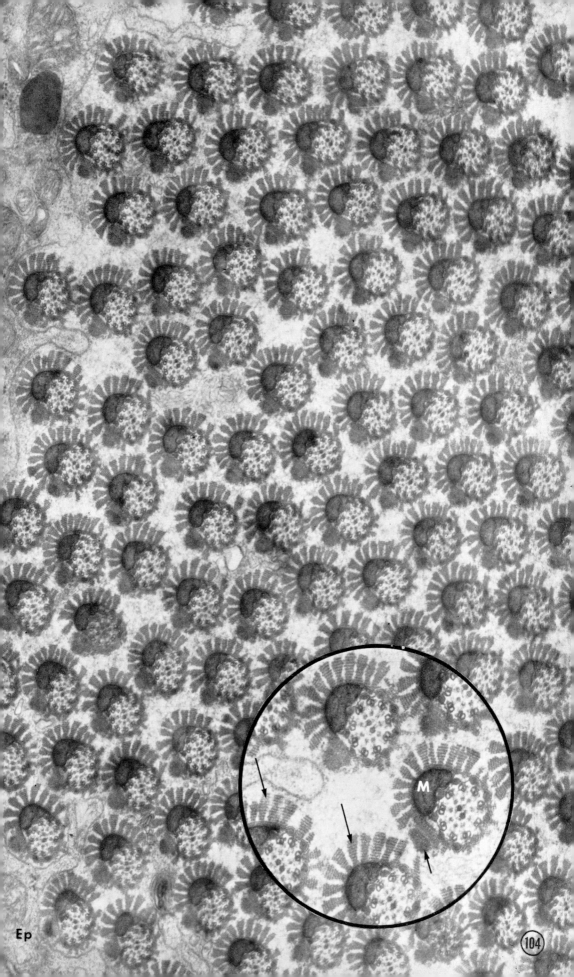

Ep

104

Plate 105 ▷

A pair of micrographs illustrating the structure of the atypical sperm cells of the coccid *Steatococcus tuberculatus*.

A. This field represents a transverse section of two immature sperm cells from a third instar larva. Two complete and one incomplete rings of microtubules [Mt] surround the chromosomal core [*] of each cell: in longitudinal sections this core appears to consist of tightly packed tubules, which yield the stippled texture of the plane of section shown here. Arrows indicate the cell membrane.

The micrograph shown in *B* represents a transversely sectioned sperm bundle from an adult male of this coccid, which contains 32 hexagonally packed spermatozoa. Each sperm is surrounded by a plasma membrane and consists of about three concentric palisades of microtubules [Mt], ensheathing the dense chromosomal core [*]. Except at the periphery of the bundle, each cell is surrounded by six dense triangular bodies, the nature and function of which are unknown.

(A : × 129,000. B : × 70,000.)

(Philips EM 200. Micrographs reproduced by courtesy of Dr M. J. Moses.)

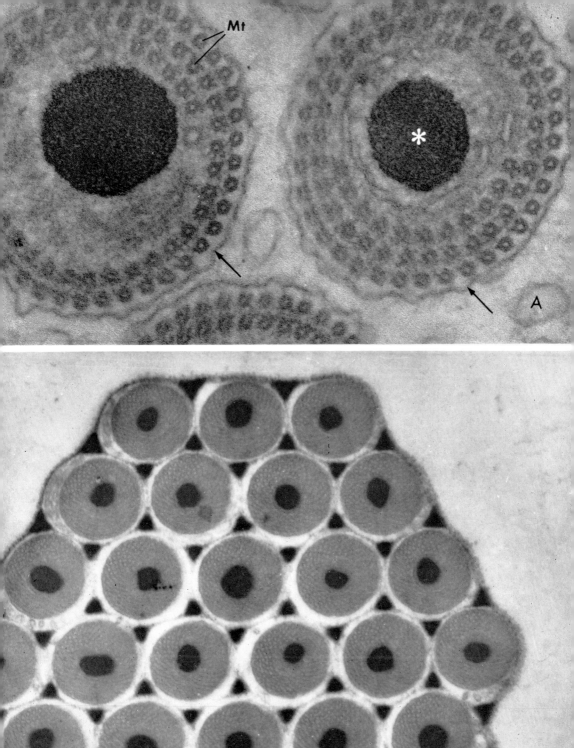

Plate 106 ▷

This longitudinal section through a group of spermatids within the
testis of the flea *Spilopsyllus caniculi* reveals a pattern of organisation
that at present must be regarded as unique amongst male germ
cells of animals. Each sperm tail contains a core of paracrystalline
mitochondrial material [*] around which passes, in a helical fashion,
the motile flagellum [Fl]. In all other flagellate sperm hitherto
examined in the electron microscope, of course, the positions of
these components is reversed, and the mitochondria are deployed
around the axial flagellum.

($\times$ 35,000.)

*(AEI EM 6B. Reproduced by courtesy of Dr B. L. Gupta and
Miriam Rothschild.)*

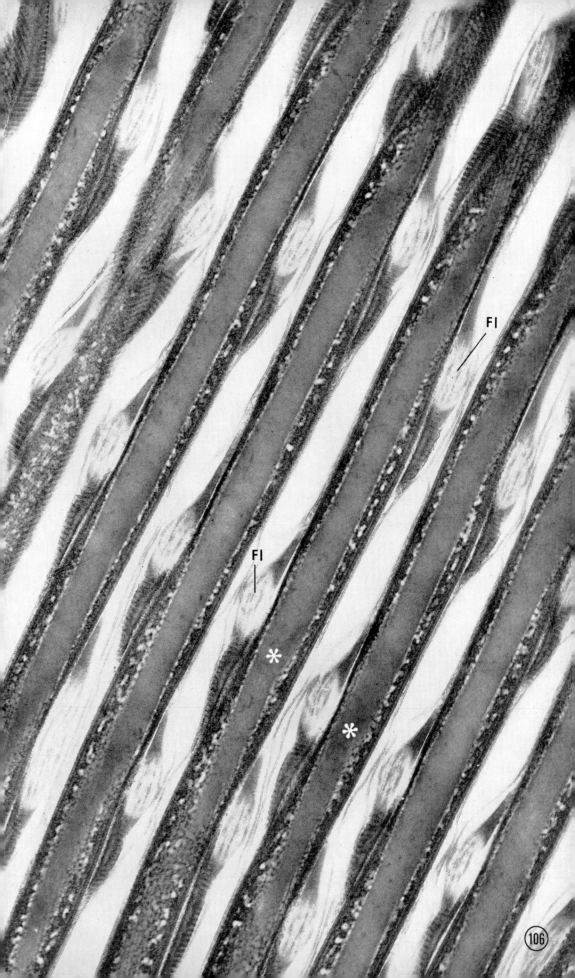

Plate 107 ▷

The paired vasa deferentia are slender tubes that receive
spermatozoa from the testes, and convey them to the ejaculatory duct.
This transverse section through a vas deferens of the milkweed bug
Oncopeltus fasciatus passes through a closely packed group of
sperm [Sp], virtually filling the tubular lumen [Lu]. By now the
gametes are no longer enclosed within cellular cysts, as is the case
within the testis. The epithelium of the vas deferens [Ep] is made up
of cuboidal cells, surrounded by a prominent basement membrane
[BM].

($\times$ 7000.)

(Philips EM 200.)

BM

Sp

Lu

Ep

107

Plate 108 ▷

A micrograph similar to that shown in the last plate, but including the
cellular structures adjoining the vas deferens of the milkweed bug
Oncopeltus. In the lower part of the field, spermatozoa [Sp] lie in the
lumen [Lu] of the vas deferens. The epithelial cells bordering the
lumen are enclosed within a thick layered basement membrane [BM];
the intercellular boundaries follow a very tortuous course, and the
nuclei [N] are irregularly lobed in form. The tube is invested with
many small muscle fibres [MF], the contractions of which force the
non-motile sperm down towards the ejaculatory duct. These visceral
fibres are interspersed with tracheoles [Tr], and numerous nerve fibres
[NF] each containing one or more axons [Ax]. Muscles, nerves and
tracheoles are knit together by connective strands [black asterisks].
Further down the reproductive tract, the secretion produced by the
accessory glands are added to the vasa deferentia; the edge of one of
these glands is seen at upper left [white asterisk].

($\times$ 11,000.)

(*Philips EM 200.*)

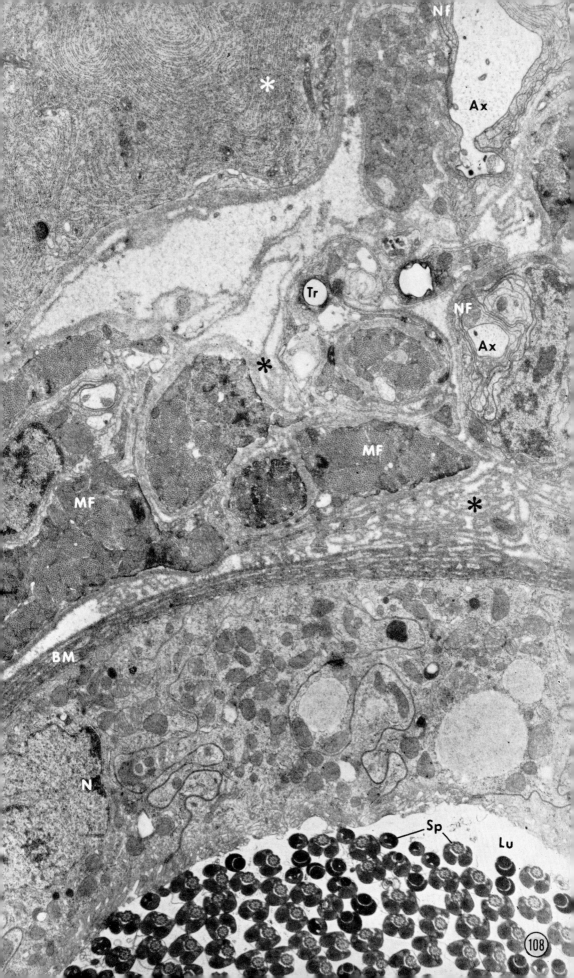

Plate 109 ▷

This field includes a profile of an accessory gland cell of an adult male milkweed bug, *Oncopeltus fasciatus*. In some insects, the accessory glands, opening into the vasa deferentia, secrete a mucoprotein that is formed into a solid plug, the spermatophore, into which the spermatozoa are placed before it is transferred to the female during copulation. In *Oncopeltus*, no spermatophore is produced, and the seminal fluid containing the sperm is transferred directly from the male intromittent organ into the spermatheca of the female. In this case, the role of the accessory gland secretion has not yet been established, but the cells are clearly equipped for protein synthesis. The basal surface of the cell, bordering the haemolymph, rests on a layered basement membrane [BM]. The centrally placed nucleus [N] often presents a bizarre deeply lobed appearance, and the cytoplasm is largely filled with ranks of ribosome-studded cisternae of the endoplasmic reticulum [ER], while Golgi bodies [G] are found near the surface of the nucleus. The apical surface bears microvilli [Mv], and the lumen [Lu] is filled with dense secretion. The lateral cell membranes are loosely apposed, except near the apical border, where they become linked by septate desmosomes [SD] and desmosomes of the zonula adhaerens type [D], running in a ring around each cell.

(× 20,000.)

(*Philips EM 200.*)

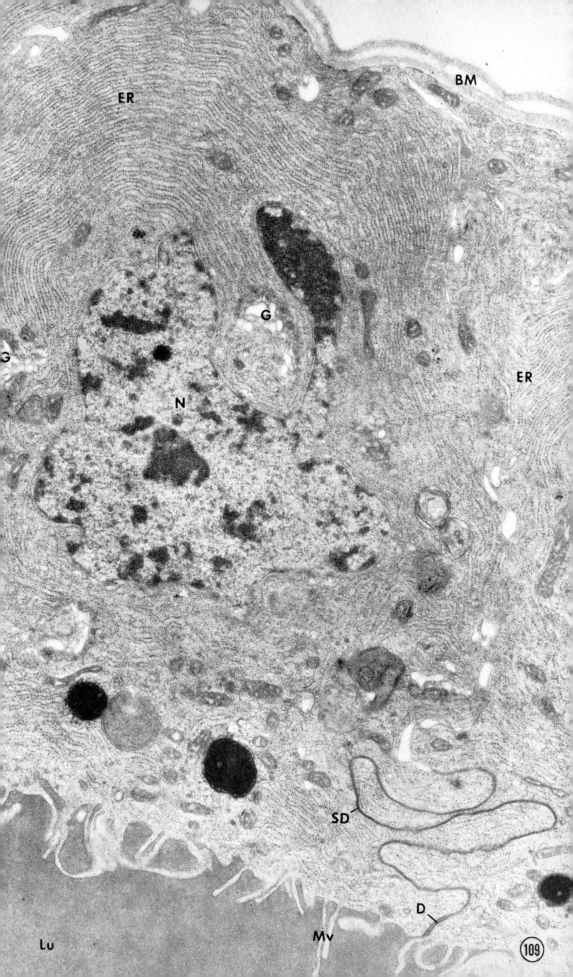

BM

ER

G

G

N

ER

SD

D

Lu

Mv

109

Plate 110 ▷

A micrograph similar to that shown in the last plate, but at higher magnification. Note the usual twin membranes of the nuclear envelope encompassing the lobed nucleus [N]. Curving parallel arrays of rough-surfaced (ribosome-studded) endoplasmic reticulum cisternae [ER] are very prominent in these cells, and indicate that the accessory gland cells are engaged in manufacturing a proteinaceous secretion. Two Golgi bodies [G] adjoin the nucleus, and small mitochondria [M] occur sparsely here, and throughout the cell.

(× 40,000.)

(*Philips EM 200.*)

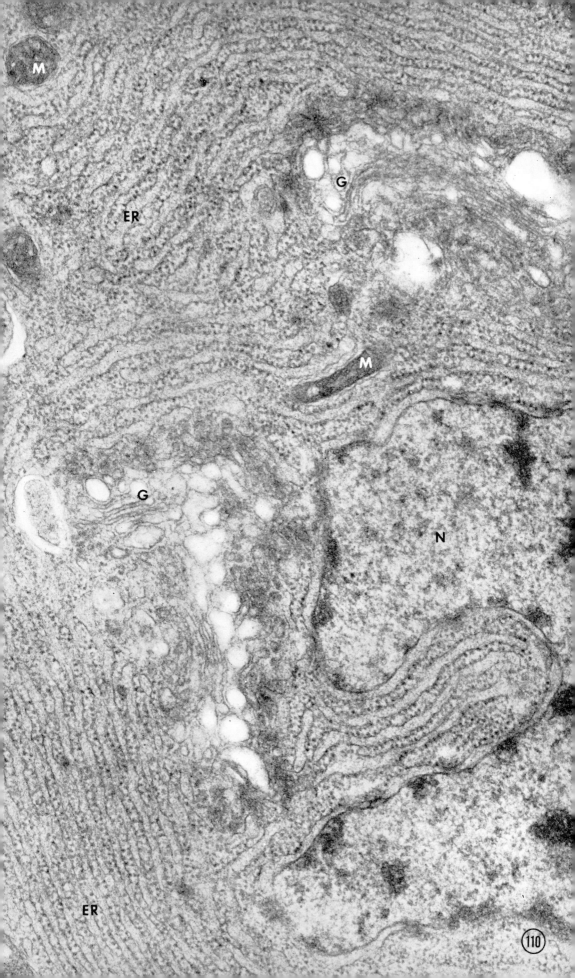

The great majority of insects reproduce sexually, and within the gonads (testes and ovaries) the gametes are differentiated and matured through a sequence of events that involves the cells in complex structural and physiological changes. In the case of sperm development, the electron microscope has clarified many points that remained controversial in earlier studies (p. 307) and this instrument has already played a valuable part in revealing some of the delicately balanced events of oogenesis.

Each of the paired ovaries consists of a variable number of tubular epithelial ovarioles along which are placed the oocytes in a linear sequence that reflects their progressive development. In the narrow anterior part of each ovariole, the germarium, are differentiated the cells that are destined to become the oocytes, and in some insects these are accompanied by other cells which later perform the task of 'nursing' or supplying nutrients to the developing gametes. In other instances, however, special nurse cells are absent, and instead the nutritional responsibility falls upon the epithelium of the oocyte follicles. In the posterior portion of the ovariole, approaching the oviduct, lie increasingly large and advanced oocytes, each contained within a follicular sac. When fully ripe, the oocyte passes to the oviduct after rupture of the follicle; the latter remains behind, but unlike its analogue in the vertebrate ovary (the corpus luteum) is autolysed and plays no part in hormone production. Amongst the changes that occur during maturation, the most striking is the progressive stocking of the ooplasm with stored nutrients, later drawn upon by the developing embryo, and in this connection the findings of electron microscopy have proved of particular interest.

This section is illustrated by micrographs of ovarioles and their contained oocytes in the cockroach *Periplaneta americana*, which are placed in the 'panoistic' group since no nurse cells are included within the follicular sacs. The cuboidal cells of the follicular epithelium (Plate 111) are separated from the general haemolymph, bathing the ovariole, by a robust basement membrane or basal lamina. Their cytoplasm is by no means remarkably specialised, containing only few mitochondria and sparsely distributed cisternae of the endoplasmic reticulum—conspicuously lacking, that is, the abundant complement of cellular membranes to be expected in cells engaged in massive synthesis and export of protein and other materials. Small portions of the oocyte surface, bearing a profusion of microvilli fitting against the wall of the follicle, are included in Plate 112. Between these finger-like projections are inserted many bacterial cells, also seen in Plate 111. At the base of the microvilli are formed large numbers of pits or depressions which pinch off into the oocyte cytoplasm by a mechanism resembling the formation of pinocytic vesicles (e.g. Plate 52), and these structures have provided a clue to the mechanism of protein yolk formation within the ooplasm.

There is evidence in amphibia, birds and mammals that the protein of the yolk is similar to proteins present in the blood serum, and indeed the former is not synthesised within the ovary, but after being produced elsewhere in the body is passed into the circulatory system whence it is sequestered by the developing egg cell. Telfer (1961) has shown, by the use of fluorescein-labelled antibodies against blood proteins, that this method is also shared by saturniid moths: in these experiments, the label was detected in the intercellular spaces between the follicle cells, adjoining the microvillar border of the oocyte, and within yolk droplets of the ooplasm. Telfer suggested that the oocyte surface is capable of the selective uptake of blood proteins by a mechanism perhaps involving combination with a hypothetical 'carrier' on the cell membrane and a mode of ingress 'akin to pinocytosis'.

Roth and Porter (1964) studied the fine structure of maturing follicles of the mosquito *Aëdes*, and obtained evidence of protein uptake that dovetailed well with Telfer's findings. The ovariole of the mosquito is of the polytrophic type, and each follicle contains an oocyte and a group of nurse cells. As in the cockroach, the follicle cells appeared ill-equipped to carry out protein synthesis and secretion, as also did the nurse cells. Roth and Porter described the pits and vesicles forming at the oocyte surface, and moreover found that this activity becomes greatly increased after the mosquito has taken a blood meal, at a time when protein yolk formation within the oocyte is at its height. They detected that this membrane activity differed from conventional pinocytosis in that the pits were always formed from areas of the surface bearing a 'coat' of bristles, about 200 Å in depth, on the cytoplasmic side. Furthermore, these pits contain dense material, thought to represent protein, collected from the extracellular space outside the oocyte and beneath the layer of follicle cells. In the cortex of the oocyte, these coated vesicles coalesce to form large droplets of protein within which paracrystalline structure may be resolved. Some idea of the extraordinary degree of activity achieved by the surface of the oocyte during the peak of protein yolk deposition may be obtained from Roth and Porter's calculation that at this time 300,000 pits may be present around each cell. As was suggested by Telfer, the protein reaches the oocyte from the haemolymph, passing between the follicle cells. The site of synthesis of this egg protein remains a problem. In the mosquito, the mid-gut epithelium seems to be the most probable candidate—these cells contain abundant endoplasmic reticulum cisternae and Golgi bodies, consistent with a role in protein synthesis and secretion. Moreover preliminary autoradiographic studies reported by Roth and Porter suggest that labelled amino acid taken in with the blood meal passes through the mid-gut cells (where it is presumably incorporated into protein), is liberated from the basal surface of the gut cells and later appears in the oocyte protein yolk granules. In this instance, the fat body does not seem to play a part in synthesis. However, the physiological situation found in one species of insect cannot be assumed to hold good in all respects in another, and this is probably true of the processes of vitellogenesis. Anderson (1964) has given a detailed description of protein yolk formation in the cockroach *Periplaneta*, and has shown that this takes place very much as in the mosquito, both as regards the role of coated vesicles and the build-up of yolk granules within the ooplasm. But in this insect, there is histochemical and fine structural evidence (Mills and others, 1966) that both the fat body and the mid-gut are concerned in synthesising the proteins supplied to the oocytes via the blood.

The functions of the follicle cells, and of the nurse cells, when present, present interesting problems. As Telfer points out, the nutritional role of follicle cells during vitellogenesis or yolk deposition appeared to be underlined by the fact that these are present in cephalopods, arthropods and chordates, which possess yolky oocytes, but he mentions that, in insects, there is little evidence of synthetic activity, at least of proteins, in insect follicle cells. However, any generalisation at the present time concerning the function of follicle cells would be hazardous: there is histochemical evidence (Refs. in Wigglesworth, 1965) that these cells play an important role in the synthesis of lipid components of the yolk, and indeed their responsibilities may well vary greatly from one insect to the next. There is also histochemical and autoradiographic evidence that in some species the nurse cells synthesise nucleic acids, and perhaps protein, and convey these to the oocyte via intercytoplasmic connections (Refs. in Wigglesworth, 1965).

The work on mosquito oocytes provides an excellent example of the part that the electron microscope can play in clarifying and bringing into sharper focus aspects of the specialised behaviour of cells, predicted on the basis of their known biochemical and physiological attributes. The coated vesicles, first detected at the oocyte surface, may prove to be of quite general occurrence in cells engaged in the selective uptake of particular protein species. They are also present, for example, in some blood cells (Plate 55), and have been described in detail by Bowers (1965) in pericardial cells (Plate 59A) which are thought to parallel the vertebrate reticulo-endothelial system in removing certain proteins from the circulation. Enticing problems remain concerning the means and pathways by which the insect oocyte is differentiated and stocked with food materials, which should stimulate further study at the level of the electron microscope. These problems obviously include the site of synthesis of yolk proteins in a wider range of insects, the origin of lipid and carbohydrate components of the yolk and the functional relationship between the maturing oocyte and the nurse cells.

The conspicuous bacteroidal flora investing the oocyte of *Periplaneta*, illustrated in the electron micrographs accompanying this section, deserves mention. These microorganisms are believed to reach the oocyte surface from mycetocytes (Plates 65 and 66) lying outside the follicle, and later enter the oocyte insuring 'infection' of the future embryo. In other insects, such transfer may be achieved by more elaborate means. The presence of micro-organisms in insect cells is widespread (p. 201), and while in some instances there is good evidence that these are required for normal growth and development, in other cases their role is more enigmatic. The bacteroids (or bacterium-like cells) associated with cockroach ovaries have been described in electron microscopic studies by Bush and Chapman (1961), Anderson (1964), and Milburn (1966). At the stages in oocyte development illustrated in Plates 111 and 112, the bacteroids lie in the narrow extracellular spaces between a palisade of microvilli that stem from the oocyte surface.

After vitellogenesis is complete, but before the oocyte passes from the ovariole, it is equipped with a protective shell that must allow interchange of respiratory gases between the atmosphere and the developing embryo, after the egg is fertilised and laid. At the same time, this shell must prevent water loss in desiccating conditions, or drowning if the egg should become immersed in water. The inner layer of the shell, the vitelline membrane, appears to be secreted by the oocyte (King and Devine, 1958): beyond this lies the chorion, which is complex in structure and composition and which is secreted by the follicle cells. The architecture of the chorion reflects the fact that the embryo relies solely on gaseous diffusion for its respiratory requirements, and it consists of a thick outer layer and a very thin inner layer, linked by vertical columns and enclosing an air space that has a limited access to the atmosphere. In the egg of the blowfly, this access is provided by a longitudinal band along which the outer layer of the chorion is thin and bears fine perforations, open to the general air space when the egg is dry, and functioning as a respiratory plastron if the egg is submerged, as by rain (Hinton, 1963). The chorion is well adapted to meet a physiological need, and moreover poses the interesting problem of how the ovariole follicle cells secrete so elaborate a structure.

The value of the scanning electron microscope in revealing the fine details of surface pattern in cuticular and other structures has already been mentioned (p. 5). Two striking micrographs obtained with this instrument are reproduced in Plate 113: the first includes a portion of the edge of an egg of the mosquito *Anopheles farauti*, and the second the micropylar area of the egg of a butterfly (*Lysandra bellargus*). Specialisation of the egg-shell associated with a plastron 'physical gill' are further described by Hinton (1962, 1967), and references to analogous respiratory devices are given on p. 138.

REFERENCES

*ANDERSON, E. 1964. Oocyte differentiation and vitellogenesis in the roach *Periplaneta americana*. *J. Cell Biol.*, **20**, 131–155.
*BOWERS, B. 1965. Coated vesicles in the pericardial cells of the aphid (*Myzus persicae* Sulz). *Protoplasma*, **59**, 351–367.
*BUSH, G. L., and CHAPMAN, G. B. 1961. Electron microscopy of symbiotic bacteria in developing oocytes of the American cockroach, *Periplaneta americana*. *J. Bact.*, **81**, 267–276.
*HINTON, H. E. 1962. The fine structure and biology of the egg-shell of the wheat bulb fly, *Leptohylemyia coarctata*. *Q. Jl microsc. Sci.*, **103**, 243-251.
*HINTON, H. E. 1963. The respiratory system of the egg-shell of the blowfly, *Calliphora erythrocephala* Meig., as seen with the electron microscope. *J. Insect Physiol.*, **9**, 121–129.
*HINTON, H. E. 1967. The respiratory system of the egg-shell of the common housefly. *J. Insect Physiol.*, **13**, 647–651.
*KING, R. C., and DEVINE, R. L. 1958. Oogenesis in adult *Drosophila melanogaster*. VII. The submicroscopic morphology of the ovary. *Growth*, **22**, 299–326.
*MILBURN, N. S. 1966. Fine structure of the pleomorphic bacteroids in the mycetocytes and ovaries of several genera of cockroaches. *J. Insect Physiol.*, **12**, 1245–1254.
*MILLS, R. R., GREENSLADE, F. C., and COUCH, E. F. 1966. Studies on vitellogenesis in the American cockroach. *J. Insect Physiol.*, **12**, 767–779.
*ROTH, T. F., and PORTER, K. R. 1964. Yolk protein uptake in the oocyte of the mosquito *Aëdes aegypti* L. *J. Cell Biol.*, **20**, 313–332.
TELFER, W. H. 1961. The route of entry and localization of blood proteins in the oocytes of saturniid moths. *J. biophys. biochem. Cytol.*, **9**, 747–759.
WIGGLESWORTH, V. B. 1965. *The Principles of Insect Physiology*, 6th edn, p. 633. Methuen, London.

Plates 111–113 ▷

Plate 111 ▷

A micrograph showing the cellular structures enveloping the maturing oocyte within the ovarioles of the cockroach *Periplaneta americana*. In this insect, each oocyte is contained within an epithelial layer of follicle cells [Ep], which rest on a thick multilayered sheath or basement membrane [BM]. The apical surface of the follicle cells lies against a dense brush border of microvilli [Mv] stemming from the surface of the oocyte [O]. Between these microvilli, and occasionally invaginated a short distance into the follicle cells, are many bacteroids [Ba], resembling in their general appearance those contained within the mycetocytes of the fat body of the adult (Plates 65 and 66). The follicular cytoplasm shows no evidence of active secretory mechanisms—mitochondria [M] are scattered throughout the cell, and cisternae of the endoplasmic reticulum [ER] are sparsely distributed.

(×13,000.)

(*Philips EM 200.*)

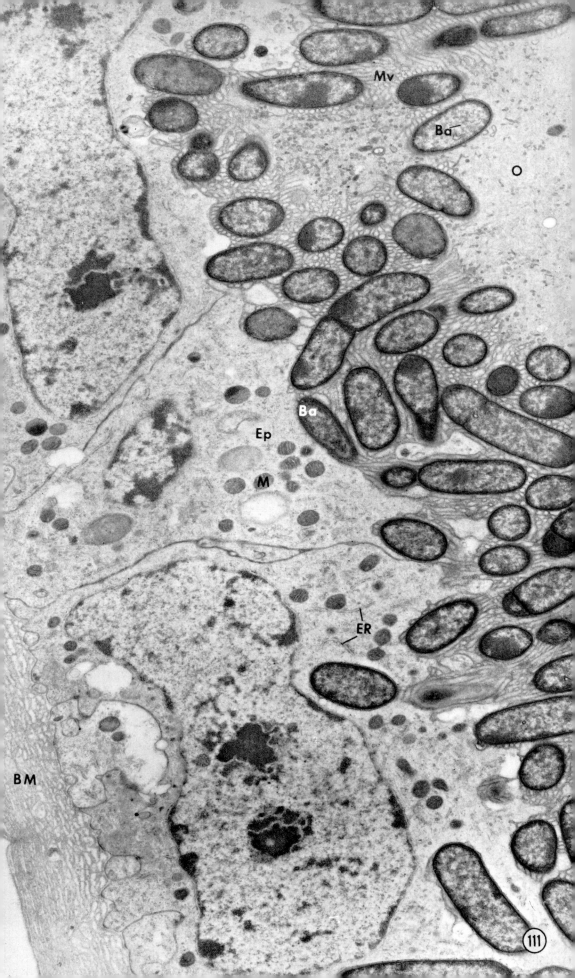

Mv

Ba

O

Ba

Ep

M

ER

BM

111

Plate 112 ▷

A. This field depicts regions of the periphery of two very young oocytes [O_1, O_2] within an ovariole of the cockroach, separated by tongues of the follicular epithelium [Ep] which are linked together by occasional desmosomes [D]. The oocyte on the left contains an homogeneous cytoplasm, rich in free ribosomes, and the plasma membrane has not yet produced the brush border of microvilli, prominent in later development and already acquired by the oocyte of the right [Mv]. These microvilli, when first formed, are regularly arranged around the symbiotic bacteroids [Ba] which in due course enter the oocyte, and presumably stock the mycetocytes of the future embryo, nymph and adult. Neither of these oocytes has commenced the deposition of protein yolk: during this phase of vitellogenesis, protein material is withdrawn from the extracellular space into the oocyte cytoplasm in specialised vesicles by a mechanism resembling micropinocytosis. This process is illustrated in the next micrograph.

B. At a later stage in development, the deposition of protein yolk has commenced. The cytoplasm at the periphery of the oocyte contains numerous small vesicles [Ve] derived by a process of pinching off from small pits or depressions which form along the plasma membrane, between the microvilli [arrows]. At this early stage in vitellogenesis, these vesicles are relatively few in number, but later become very abundant as the passage of material into the cell accelerates. As described more fully in the text, these pits and the vesicles derived from them are characterised by the presence of minute bristles forming a 'coat' on their cytoplasmic side, and are believed to represent localised regions where yolk proteins, synthesised elsewhere and passed to the oocyte between the follicle cells, are picked up by, and taken into, the maturing oocyte.

(*A* : × 27,000. *B* : × 37,000.)

(*Philips EM 200.*)

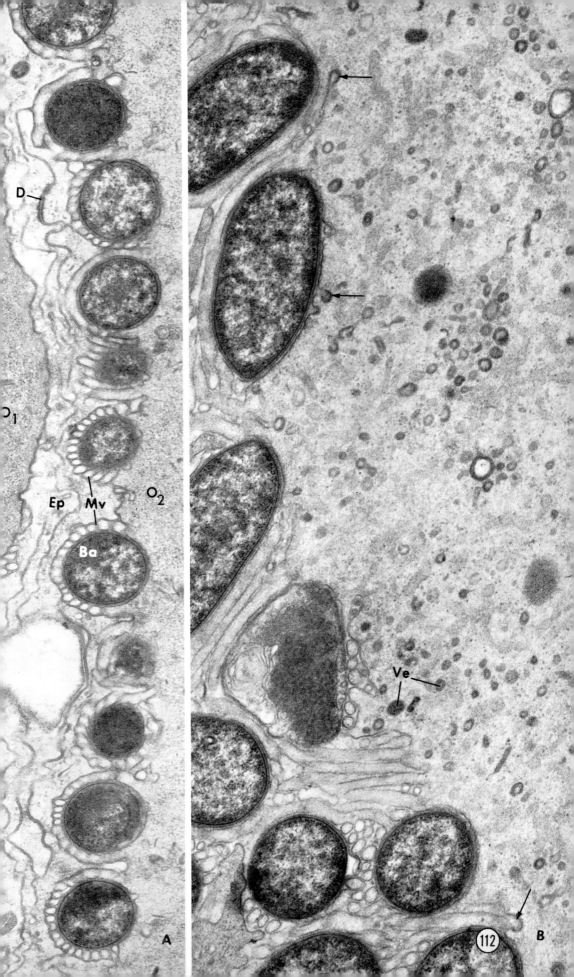

D

O₁

Ep   Mv   O₂

Ba

Ve

A

112   B

Plate 113 ▷

A. A scanning electron micrograph of a portion of the surface of an egg of the mosquito *Anopheles farauti*—an important malarial vector in New Guinea and other regions of the Far East. This micrograph displays the detailed sculpturing of surface deck tubercles [1], lateral frill [2] and float [3] of the egg.

B. A scanning electron micrograph of the micropylar region of an egg of the lycaenid butterfly *Lysandra bellargus*. Access of the spermatozoa to the oocyte surface prior to fertilisation takes place between the polygonal chorion struts [arrows].

(*A* : × 2500. *B* : × 1200.)

(*Stereoscan electron microscope. Micrographs reproduced by courtesy of Dr H. E. Hinton.*)

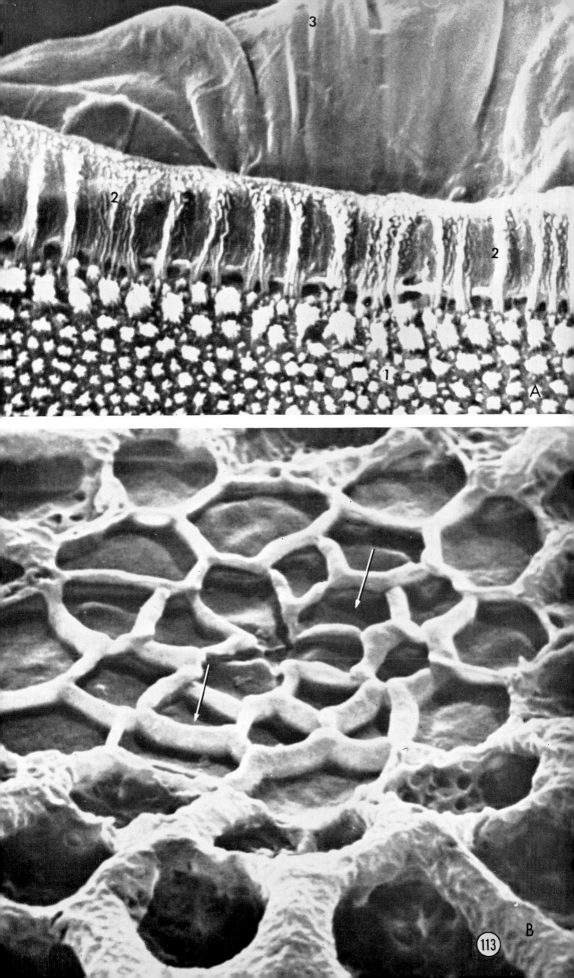

The Spermatheca

During copulation in insects, the spermatozoa, either free or enclosed within a spermatophore secreted by the male accessory glands, are transferred to the female genital tract. In most species, they are initially deposited within the common oviduct or vagina, whence they are passed along a narrow duct to a glandular pouch termed the receptaculum seminis or spermatheca. While spermathecae vary in number and form in different species, each is an ectodermal structure derived by invagination from the surface integument, in common with other glands and ducts of the reproductive system, and hence is lined with cuticle. As is described by Davy (1965) in a recent review of insect reproduction, the spermatozoa may be stored within the lumen of the spermatheca in viable condition for long periods; frequently for a matter of weeks, and in the honey bee and certain ants for up to several years. Fertilisation is achieved when spermatozoa are expelled from the spermatheca following ovulation and meet the egg cell as it enters the common oviduct. There is evidence that the events of oogenesis, ovulation, fertilisation and oviposition are delicately controlled by nervous and humoral mechanisms.

The fact that spermathecae are either partially glandular in their construction, or are associated with tubular 'spermathecal glands', marks out for them a role beyond that of sperm storage alone. The function of these glands and the nature of their secretion is, however, by no means clearly established. The most likely possibility is that they provide an exogenous nutrient source for the spermatozoa: whereas the copious seminal fluid present in mammalian semen provides for the metabolic requirements of the spermatozoa within the female genital ducts, only a small quantity of seminal fluid is added to the gametes by the male accessory glands before copulation, and this is presumably quite insufficient to nurture them during the very lengthy period of storage that may ensue (Davey, 1965).

In the cockroach *Periplaneta americana*, the spermatheca is a bulbous structure, opening into the vagina by a long slender duct. Both the duct and the lumen within the bulb are lined with cuticle forming a tube, surrounded by an epithelium of cells continuous with those of the epidermis at the body surface. Each of the epithelial cells of the bulb is flanked on its basal surface by an elongated glandular or secretory cell. Each pair of cells is structurally adapted to work as a unit in which the products of the gland cell are afforded a channel allowing them to pass through the cuticular intima of the spermatheca into the lumen. At the level of the light microscope, each gland cell appeared to be furnished with an 'intracellular duct' traversing the intima: the electron microscope has not only revealed new details of the way in which the secreted material is formed and released, but has also shown us that the duct is in fact extracellular and made up of two distinct parts, one inserted into the secretory cell and the other encircled by an underlying epithelial cell.

The basal surface of the gland cells occupying the 'cortex' of the spermathecal bulb is covered with a thick fibrous sheath or basement membrane, outside which lie visceral muscle fibres (Plate 114) the contractions of which perhaps compress the bulb and aid the expulsion of spermatozoa, prior to fertilisation. Between these fibres pass many fine nerve branches; some of the axons form neuromuscular junctions in which, as in skeletal fibres, small synaptic vesicles are present (p. 60), while others contain opaque neurosecretory droplets.

The cytoplasm of the glandular cells is richly charged with droplets of secretion, at the stage shown in Plate 114; these display a wide range of electron density, some being quite opaque and others relatively transparent. Although the point is not illustrated in the micrographs included here, the droplets are first formed within smooth-membraned cisternae of the Golgi bodies and probably include protein material transferred from the ribosome-bearing portions of the endoplasmic reticulum. From the apical surface of each of these cells, i.e. from the surface adjoining the epithelial cells surrounding the lumen of the bulb, is invaginated a prominent cavity, lined with slender microvilli. Examination of numerous electron micrographs has shown not only that the secretions of the gland cells are released into this cavity, but also that the secretory activity of the cells follows a cycle. During the first phase of this cycle, the secretory droplets are formed as described above, and the microvilli of the invaginated cavity are pressed closely together, more or less occluding it (Plate 115). As the secretory cycle advances (Plate 116), the size and number of the droplets within the cytoplasm increases, and the microvilli of the invagination move apart as the cavity becomes more voluminous. This distension accommodates the secretion discharged from the cell: large blebs filled with granular or flocculent material protrude into the cavity, and they appear either to pinch off and break down within the cavity or to be released by momentary disruption of the cell membrane covering them.

The cavity within each gland cell is provided with an extracellular duct of unusual structure which is present throughout the entire secretory cycle, affording the channel along which the secretion passes during the first half of its journey to the spermathecal lumen. The wall of this tubular duct is made up of a loose feltwork of fibrils, presenting a porous appearance. Before the secretion is liberated into the cavity, this duct is tightly inserted between the microvilli of the invagination, while later it becomes slung between their tips (Plate 116). The flocculent secretion penetrates the duct wall, and enters the duct lumen, which is about 0·3 micron in diameter. Thus far, the course taken by the secretion is fairly clear, but a more speculative suggestion may be introduced: the transition between the very dense secretion droplets present in the body of the cell and their diffuse condition as they enter the cavity may possibly represent a process of 'liquefaction' facilitating the entry of these materials into the duct.

As has been mentioned above, each gland cell is associated with an underlying cell of the general spermathecal epithelium. The latter provides the second half of the channel along which the secretion passes, via a duct of entirely different construction from that within the gland cell. These cylindrical tubes are seen in the survey micrograph included here (Plate 114), and in greater detail at higher magnification in Plate 117. The wall or intima is compact, and built up of alternating light and dark concentric layers, respectively about 200 Å and 40 Å in width, and inside this laminated zone, adjacent to the duct lumen, the wall becomes electron opaque. Since the epithelial cells are ectodermal, the ducts they secrete are presumably cuticular in nature, in common with the intima of the spermatheca through which they pass to open into the gland lumen. However, although the opaque inner part of the duct apparently corresponds to the cuticulin layer (p. 3; Plates 45 and 71), the laminated part is quite different from the usual fibrillar endocuticle lining the lumen and extending over the surface of the insect's body. The epithelial cells initially secrete the extracellular duct which they surround, and also the general cuticular lining of the lumen. Whether, in addition, they contribute to the formation of the porous duct traversing the gland cell cavity is not known, since no electron miscroscopic studies have been made on the development of the spermatheca. The cytoplasm of the epithelial cells in the adult insect shows no sign of glandular or secretory activity: free ribosomes are plentiful, though cisternae of the endoplasmic reticulum are sparse. Microtubules are present, lying parallel with the duct, and mitochondria are aggregated near the apical cell surface, as shown in Plate 117.

In short, the bulb of the cockroach spermatheca is built up of two distinct layers of cells, one primarily glandular and the other primarily transporting. Where these cell layers meet, their respective ducts are contiguous, thus providing an uninterrupted channel along which passes secretory material supplied to the stored spermatozoa. Further details of the fine structure of the spermatheca, its musculature, and its innervation, are given by Gupta and Smith (1968).

OTHER INTEGUMENTARY GLANDS

The spermatheca provides one example of a very diverse range of insect glands that share a common feature in being derived from the ectoderm. These glands discharge their secretions either directly at the surface of the body, or into cuticle-lined ducts that open onto the surface integument or its invaginations. The 'integumentary glands' include salivary and silk glands, the cement producing dermal glands of the epidermis, various glands associated with the reproductive system in addition to the spermatheca, and glands that secrete an astonishing variety of chemicals which range from noxious substances used for defence to 'pheromones' including sex attractants and chemicals used by social insects for communication or for trail laying.

Several of these glands have been studied in the electron microscope, and while their general morphology varies a good deal from one example to the next, they seem to have adopted a similar device for channeling their secretions to the surface of the cuticle that adjoins them. Each gland cell possesses an invagination lined with porous material, sometimes organised into a cylindrical duct, into which pass the secretory products of the cell. These products are then carried to the exterior either along special cuticular ducts, or along tubular invaginations of the cuticle that lines the gland. The glands listed below are among those where fine structure has been investigated.

The colleterial accessory glands of female cockroaches, which are responsible for secreting the hard tanned protein of the egg capsule or ootheca, and the corresponding glands in mantids and acridiids (Mercer and Brunet, 1959; Baccetti, 1967).

The pharyngeal salivary glands of the worker honey bee, which in the young adult secrete the 'royal jelly', a complex material with proteolytic activity, rich in fatty acids, amino acids, the B-vitamins and other substances, that is fed to the brood at the start of larval life and induces queen development if continued as a diet (Beams and others, 1959).

The mandibular glands of the bumble-bee *Bombus,* which secrete a scented volatile material used as a marker to identify the position of the nest, and perhaps as a sex attractant (Stein, 1962).

The phallic or *conglobate gland* of male cockroaches, of uncertain function (Beams and others, 1962).

The abdominal scent glands of pyrrhocorid stink-bugs, secreting an insect repellant and toxicant (Stein, 1966a, 1966b, 1967).

The terpene-secreting glands of a phasmid, which produce a toxic monoterpene, aniso-morphal, sprayed out as a fine mist from ducts opening behind the head and acting as a means of defence (Happ and others, 1966).

The quinone-secreting glands of a tenebrionid beetle, opening near the anus, which synthesise a noxious irritating fluid containing a mixture of quinones, hydrocarbons and caprylic acid, exuded or squirted from the body as a defence mechanism (Eisner and others, 1964).

REFERENCES

Spermatheca

DAVEY, K. G. 1965. *Reproduction in the Insects.* Oliver and Boyd, Edinburgh.
*GUPTA, B. L., and SMITH, D. S. 1968. Fine structural organization of the spermatheca in the cockroach, *Periplaneta americana. Tissue & Cell,* **1**, in press.

Other integumentary glands

*BACCETTI, B. 1967. L'ultrastruttura delle ghiandole della ooteca in ortotteri acridoidei, blattoidei e mantoidei. *Z. Zellforsch. mikrosk. Anat.,* **77**, 64–79.
*BEAMS, H. W., TAHMISIAN, T. N., ANDERSON, E., and DEVINE, R. L. 1959. An electron micro-scope study on the pharyngeal glands of the honey bee. *J. Ultrastruct. Res.,* **3**, 155–170.
*BEAMS, H. W., ANDERSON, E., and KESSEL, R. 1962. Electron microscope observations on the phallic (conglobate) gland of the cockroach, *Periplaneta americana. Jl R. microsc. Soc.,* **81**, 85–89.
*EISNER, T., MCHENRY, F., and SALPETER, M. M. 1964. Defense mechanisms of arthropods. XV. Morphology of the quinone-producing glands of a tenebrionid beetle (*Eleodes longicollis* Lec). *J. Morph.,* **115**, 355–400.
*HAPP, G. M., STRANDBERG, J. D., and HAPP, C. M. 1966. The terpene-producing glands of a phasmid insect. Cell morphology and histochemistry. *J. Morph.,* **119**, 143–160.
*MERCER, E. H., and BRUNET, P. C. J. 1959. The electron microscopy of the left colleterial gland of the cockroach. *J. biophys. biochem. Cytol.,* **5**, 257–261.
*STEIN, 6, 1962. Über den Feinbau der Mandibeldrüse von Hummelmännchen. *Z. Zellforsch. mikrosk. Anat.,* **57**, 719–736.
*STEIN, G. 1966a. Über den Feinbau der Duftdrüsen von Feuerwanzen (*Pyrrhocoris apterus* L., Geocorisae). I. Mitteilung. Zur funktionellen Morphologie der Drüsenzelle. *Z. Zellforsch. mikrosk. Anat.,* **74**, 271–290.
*STEIN, G. 1966b. Über den Feinbau der Duftdrüsen von Feuerwanzen (*Pyrrhocoris apterus* L., Geocorisae). II. Mitteilung. Das ableitende Kanalsystem und die nichtdrüsigen Anteile. *Z. Zellforsch. mikrosk. Anat.,* **75**, 501–516.
*STEIN, G. 1967. Über den Feinbau der Duftdrüsen von Feuerwanzen (*Pyrrhocoris apterus* L., Geocorisae). Die 2. larvale Abdominaldrüse. *Z. Zellforsch. mikrosk. Anat.,* **79**, 49–63.

Plates 114–117 ▷

Plate 114 ▷

In the cockroach *Periplaneta americana*, the spermatheca, or
receptaculum seminis, consists of a proximal tube opening into the
vagina and a distal glandular bulb within which the spermatozoa are
stored after copulation. The bulb includes an epithelium of specialised
cells lining the cuticular intima, and each of these is closely associated
with a glandular or secretory cell lying in the cortex of the organ.
As is shown in this low-power survey micrograph, the outer surface
of the spermatheca, that is, the basal surface of the gland cells, is
covered with a thick basement membrane [BM] outside which lie
many small visceral muscle fibres [MF]. These fibres are richly
supplied with nerve axons [Ax] which frequently contain droplets
of neurosecretory material (cf. Plate 23). The greater part of the field
illustrated here is occupied by profiles of gland cells, charged with
droplets of secretion [VS] showing varying degrees of electron
opacity. From the apical surface of each cell is invaginated a
prominent cavity [*] lined with microvilli and containing a porous
duct [DS]—features seen in greater detail in Plates 115 and 116.
Each of the underlying epithelial duct cells surrounds a thick-walled
duct (Plate 117) quite different in construction from that of a
secretory cell.

($\times$ 6000.)

*(Philips EM 200. From Gupta and Smith (1968). Micrograph
reproduced by courtesy of Oliver & Boyd.)*

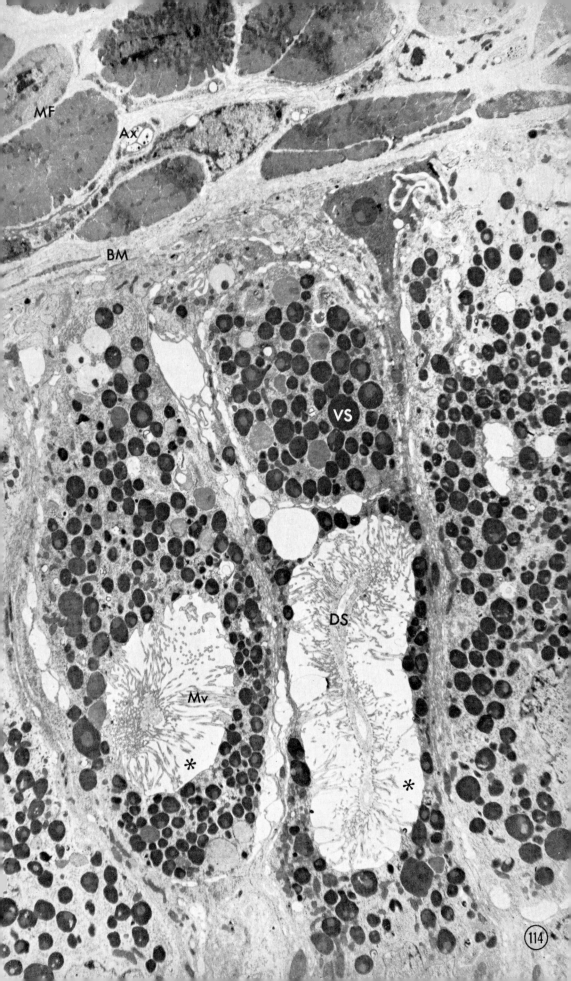

Plate 115 ▷

The glandular cells of the cockroach spermatheca undergo cycles of
activity, during which vesicles containing secreted material build up
within the cytoplasm and are then released from the cell into a cavity
invaginated from the apical surface. Beneath each gland cell lies an
epithelial duct cell, whose function is to convey the secretion to the
general lumen of the spermatheca in which the sperm are stored.
This micrograph includes part of a cell that is in the pre-release phase
of the cycle. The cytoplasm contains droplets of secreted material
enclosed within membrane-limited vesicles [VS], but the microvilli
[Mv] lining the invagination into the cell are grouped in a tight
hexagonal packing, and only become separated when the cavity into
which they extend becomes dilated with released secretion, as in
Plate 116. The invagination contains a duct, *ca*. one micron in
diameter; the lumen of the duct is surrounded by an intima or lining
built up of a meshwork of fibrils [*] each *ca*. 150–200 Å in diameter.
The fine structure of this duct contrasts markedly with that of the
adjoining duct cells, illustrated in Plate 117.

($\times$ 70,000.)

(*Philips EM 200. From Gupta and Smith (1968). Micrograph
reproduced by courtesy of Oliver & Boyd.*)

356

VS

*

Mv

115

Plate 116 ▷

A portion of a gland cell within the cockroach spermatheca at a more advanced stage in the secretory cycle than that shown in the last plate. The invaginated cavity has become greatly distended, and the microvilli [Mv], which at an earlier stage are packed closely together, have become separated and irregularly disposed. Before release, the vesicles of secretion [VS] become less dense; those protruding into the cavity contain finely granular material which is apparently liberated by rupture of the limiting membrane of the vesicle and of the adjoining cell membrane. Similar material [S] may be seen within the cavity, and is thought to pass into the lumen of the duct [DS] through the fibrillar wall [arrow]. The duct follows a sinuous course through the cavity of the gland cell, and often, as here, passes more than once into the plane of section. From this duct, the secretion is channelled into that of the underlying epithelial cell (Plate 117) and thence into the spermathecal lumen.

(× 25,000.)

(*Philips EM 200. From Gupta and Smith (1968). Micrograph reproduced by courtesy of Oliver & Boyd.*)

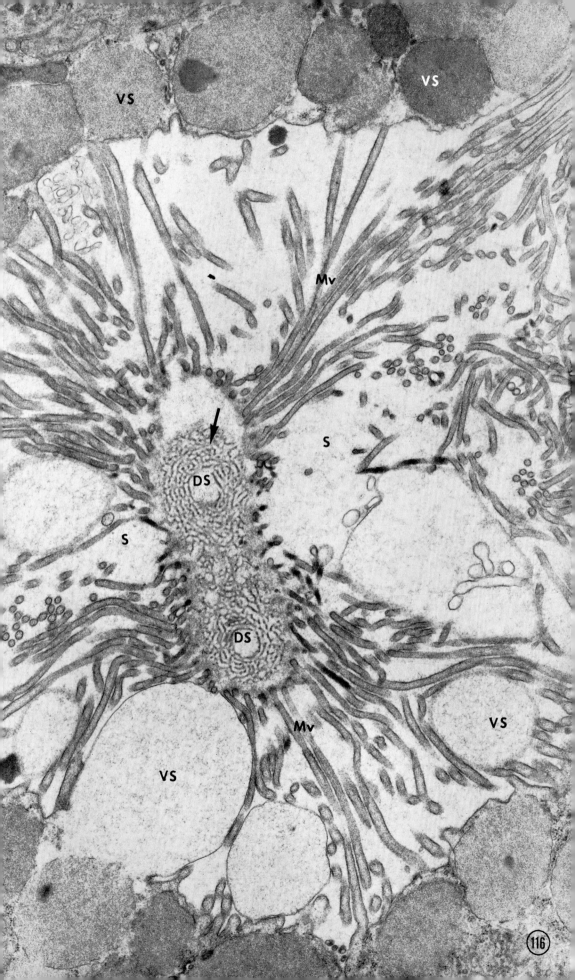

Plate 117 ▷

The fine structure of the extracellular ducts of the epithelial cells in the spermatheca is quite different from that of the gland cell ducts, illustrated in Plates 115 and 116. In place of the 'porous' fibrillar walls of the latter, the epithelial ducts are compact, and as shown by this transverse section, are built up of alternating concentric light and dark layers [black asterisk] surrounding an opaque inner zone [white asterisk]. The diameters of the duct and its lumen are respectively *ca.* 3·5–4 micra and 1 micron, and the laminar duct wall shows a spacing of about 280 Å. The duct is secreted within a cylinder invaginated from the epithelial cell membrane [arrows], and is an extracellular structure. The epithelial cells lack the secretory vesicles present within the adjoining gland cells; few organelles are present within their cytoplasm, but close to their apical surface adjoining the cuticle lining the spermathecal lumen are found many microtubules and clustered mitochondria [M].

These ducts pass through the cuticular lining of the organ and empty into the main lumen. The epithelial cells of the spermatheca are ectodermal in origin, and secrete this lining. The epithelial ducts are also probably composed of cuticle, but clearly of a very specialised type.

(× 31,000.)

(Philips EM 200. From Gupta and Smith (1968). Micrograph reproduced by courtesy of Oliver & Boyd.)

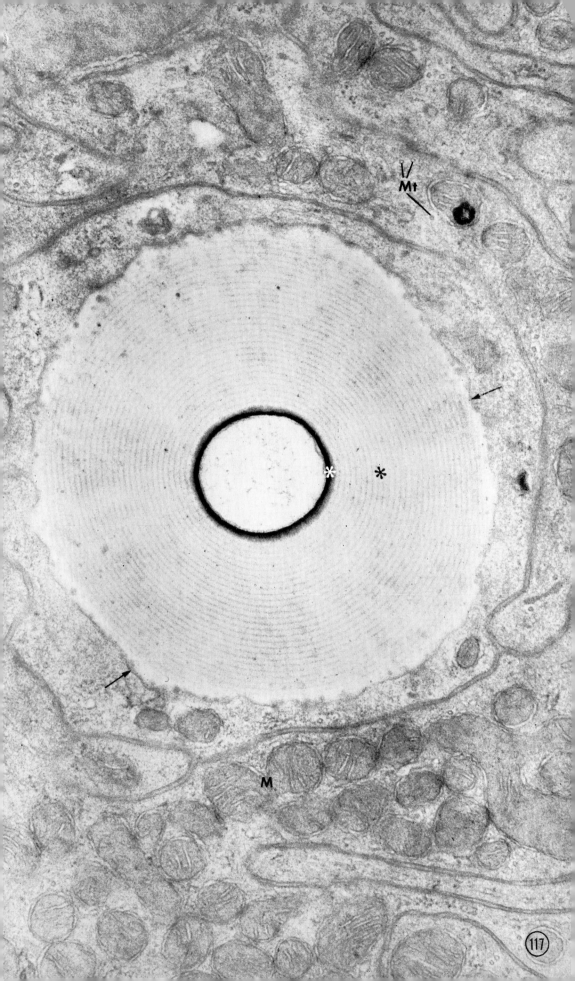

Supplementary References

The following studies on the fine structure of insect cells and their products came to the author's attention or were published after completion of the manuscript. Other recent references have been included in the text.

INTEGUMENT AND INTEGUMENTARY GLANDS

BARBIER, R. 1967. Mise en évidence d'espaces intercellulaires importants dans l'hypoderme et de formations paracristallines dans le liquide exuvial chez les larves de *Galleria mellonella* L. (Lépidoptère, Pyralidae) lors de la mise en place de la cuticuline. *C.r. hebd. Séanc. Acad. Sci., Paris*, **264**, 2337–2340.

BORDEREAU, C. 1967. Cuticle intersegmentaire des images de termites supérieurs (Isoptera, Termitidae): dimorphisme sexuel, ultrastructure, relations avec la physogastrie de la reine. *C.r. hebd. Séanc. Acad. Sci., Paris*, **264**, 1997–2000.

BUCK, R. C. 1967. Mitosis and meiosis in *Rhodnius prolixus*: the fine structure of the spindle and diffuse kinetochore. *J. Ultrastruct. Res.*, **18**, 489–501.

CLEMENTS, A. N., and POTTER, S. A. 1967. The fine structure of the spermathecae and their ducts in the mosquito *Aëdes aegypti*. *J. Insect Physiol.*, **13**, 1825–1836.

CROSSLEY, A. C. S., and WATERHOUSE, D. F. 1968a. The ultrastructure of a pheromone-secreting gland in the male scorpion-fly *Harpobittacus australis* (Bittacidae: Mecoptera). *Tissue & Cell*, **1**, in press.

CROSSLEY, A. C. S., and WATERHOUSE, D. F. 1968b. The fine-structure and chemistry of the osmeterium of *Papilio* larvae. *Tissue & Cell*, **1**, in press.

DELACHAMBRE, J. 1967. Origine et nature de la membrane exuviale chez la nymphe de *Tenebrio molitor* L. (Ins. Coleoptera). *Z. Zellforsch. mikrosk. Anat.*, **81**, 114–134.

EVANS, J. J. T. 1967a. The integument of the Queensland fruit fly, *Dacus tryoni* (Frogg.). I. The tergal glands. *Z. Zellforsch. mikrosk. Anat.*, **81**, 18–33.

EVANS, J. J. T. 1967b. The integument of the Queensland fruit fly, *Dacus tryoni* (Frogg.). II. Development and ultrastructure of the abdominal integument and bristles. *Z. Zellforsch. mikrosk. Anat.*, **81**, 34–48.

FILSHIE, B. K., and WATERHOUSE, D. F. 1968. The structure and development of a surface pattern on the cuticle of the green vegetable bug *Nezara viridula*. *Tissue & Cell*, **1**, in press.

HAYES, T. L., PEASE, R. F. W., and CAMP, A. S. 1967. Stereoscopic scanning electron microscopy of living *Tribolium confusum*. *J. Insect Physiol.*, **13**, 1143–1145.

LAI-FOOK, J. 1968. The fine structure of wound repair in an insect (*Rhodnius prolixus*). *J. Morph.*, **124**, 37–78.

OVERTON, J. 1967. The fine structure of developing bristles in wild type and mutant *Drosophila melanogaster*. *J. Morph.*, **122**, 367–380.

STUART, A. M., and SATIR, P. 1968. Morphological and functional aspects of an insect epidermal gland. *J. Cell Biol.*, **36**, 527–549.

MUSCLE AND NEUROMUSCULAR JUNCTIONS

ANDERSON, W. A., and ELLIS, R. A. 1967. A comparative electron microscope study of visceral muscle fibers in *Cambarus, Drosophila* and *Lumbricus*. *Z. Zellforsch. mikrosk. Anat.*, **79**, 581–591.

AUBER, J. 1967. Distribution of two kinds of myofilaments in insect muscles. *Am. Zool.*, **7**, 451–456.

AUBER-THOMAY, M. 1967. Modifications ultrastructurales au cours de la dégénérescence et de la croissance de fibres musculaires chez un insecte. *J. Micros.*, **6**, 627–638.

CROSSLEY, A. C. S. 1968. The fine-structure, and mechanism of breakdown, of larval intersegmental muscles in the blue blow-fly *Calliphora erythrocephala*. *J. Insect Physiol.*, in press.

HAGOPIAN, M. 1967. Three shapes of mitochondria in femoral muscle of the cockroach, *Leucophaea maderae* Fabricius. *J. Morph.*, **122**, 147–168.

HAGOPIAN, M., and SPIRO, D. 1968. The filament lattice of cockroach thoracic muscle. *J. Cell Biol.*, **36**, 433–442.

363

SUPPLEMENTARY REFERENCES

HEHN, G. 1967. Die Muskulatur des Eileiters von *Carausius morosus*. I. Mitteilung. Histologische Untersuchungen. *Z. Zellforsch. mikrosk. Anat.*, **78**, 511–545.

LAI-FOOK, J. 1967. The structure of developing muscle insertions in insects. *J. Morph.*, **123**, 503–528.

LENNIE, R. W., GREGORY, D. W., and BIRT, L. M. 1967. Changes in the nucleic acid content and structure of thoracic mitochondria during development of the blowfly, *Lucilia cuprina*. *J. Insect Physiol.*, **13**, 1745–1756.

MCNEILL, P. A., and HOYLE, G. 1967. Evidence for superthin filaments. *Am. Zool.*, **7**, 483–498.

OSBORNE, M. P. 1967. The fine structure of neuromuscular junctions in the segmental muscles of the blowfly larva. *J. Insect Physiol.*, **13**, 827–833.

OSBORNE, M. P. 1967. Supercontraction in the muscles of the blowfly larva: an ultrastructural study. *J. Insect Physiol.*, **13**, 1471–1482.

REEDY, M. K. 1967. Cross-bridges and periods in insect flight muscle. *Am. Zool.*, **7**, 465–481.

REGER, J. F. 1967. A comparative study on sub-filament organization in primary myofilaments of basalar direct flight and tibial extensor muscles of the lepidopteran, *Achalarus lyciades*. *Z. Zellforsch. mikrosk. Anat.*, **81**, 361–365.

SANDBORN, E. B., DUCLOS, S., MESSIER, P.-E., and ROBERGE, J.-J. 1967. Atypical intestinal striated muscle in *Drosophila melanogaster*. *J. Ultrastruct. Res.*, **18**, 695–702.

SCHAEFER, C. W., VANDERBERG, J. P., and RHODIN, J. 1967. The fine structure of mosquito midgut muscle. *J. Cell Biol.*, **34**, 905–910.

SMIT, W. A., BECHT, G., and BEENAKKERS, A. M. T. 1967. Structure, fatigue, and enzyme activities in 'fast' insect muscles. *J. Insect Physiol.*, **13**, 1857–1868.

STEVENSON, E. 1968. Carbohydrate metabolism in the flight muscle of the southern armyworm moth, *Prodenia eridania*. *J. Insect Physiol.*, **14**, 179–198.

TICE, L. W. 1968. A comparison of the distribution of enzymatically and non-enzymatically produced lead phosphate in insect flight muscle. *Tissue & Cell*, **1**, 97–101.

TOSELLI, P. A., and PEPE, F. A. 1968a. The fine structure of the ventral intersegmental abdominal muscles of the insect *Rhodnius prolixus* during the molting cycle. I. Muscle structure at molting. *J. Cell Biol.*, **37**, 445–461.

TOSELLI, P. A., and PEPE, F. A. 1968b. The fine structure of the ventral intersegmental abdominal muscles of the insect *Rhodnius prolixus* during the molting cycle. II. Muscle changes in preparation for molting. *J. Cell Biol.*, **37**, 462–481.

USHERWOOD, P. N. R. 1967. Insect neuromuscular mechanisms. *Am. Zool.*, **7**, 553–582.

NERVOUS SYSTEM

BOULTON, P. S., and ROWELL, C. H. F. 1968. Structure and function of the extraneural sheath in insects. *Nature, Lond.*, **217**, 379–380.

BUCHHOLTZ, C. 1967. Neuroethologische Untersuchungen an *Calopteryx splendens* Harr. (Odonata) nach Röntgenbestrahlungen des Zentralnervensystems. *Z. Zellforsch. mikrosk. Anat.*, **82**, 282–306.

GIRARDIE, A., and GIRARDIE, J. 1967. Étude histologique, histochimique, et ultrastructurale de la pars intercerebralis chez *Locusta migratoria* L. (Orthoptère). *Z. Zellforsch. mikrosk. Anat.*, **78**, 54–75.

LAMPARTER, H. E. 1967. Intrazelluläre symbiontische Bakterien im Zentralnervensystem der Ameise. *Z. Zellforsch. mikrosk. Anat.*, **81**, 1–11.

LANE, N. J. 1968a. Distribution of phosphatases in the Golgi region and associated structures of the thoracic ganglionic neurons in the grasshopper, *Melanoplus differentialis*. *J. Cell Biol.*, **37**, 89–104.

LANE, N. J. 1968b. The thoracic ganglia of the grasshopper, *Melanoplus differentialis*: fine structure of the perineurium and neuroglia with special reference to the intracellular distribution of phosphatases. *Z. Zellforsch. mikrosk. Anat.*, **86**, 293–312.

MANCINI, G., and FRONTALI, N. 1967. Fine structure of the mushroom body neuropile of the brain of the roach, *Periplaneta americana*. *Z. Zellforsch. mikrosk. Anat.*, **83**, 334–343.

SCHARRER, B. 1967. The neurosecretory neuron in neuroendocrine regulatory mechanisms. *Am. Zool.*, **7**, 161–169.

STEIGER, U. 1967. Über den Feinbau des Neuropils im Corpus pedunculatum der Waldameise. Elekronenoptische Untersuchungen. *Z. Zellforsch. mikrosk. Anat.*, **81**, 511–536.

TREHERNE, J. E., and MADDRELL, S. H. P. 1967. Axonal function and ionic regulation in the central nervous system of a phytophagous insect (*Carausius morosus*). *J. exp. Biol.*, **47**, 235–247.

CORPUS CARDIACUM

BEAULATON, J. 1967. Sur la localisation ultrastructurale d'une activité cholinestérasique dans le corps cardiaque de *Rhodnius prolixus* Stål. (Hétéroptère, Reduvidae) aux quatrième et cinquième stades larvaires. *J. Micros.*, **6**, 65–80.

PROTHORACIC GLAND

BEAULATON, J. 1967a. Localisation d'activités lytiques dans la glande prothoracique du ver à soie du chêne (*Antheraea pernyi* Guér.) au stade prénymphal. I. Structures lysosomiques, appareil de Golgi et ergastoplasme. *J. Micros.*, **6**, 179–200.

BEAULATON, J. 1967b. Localisation d'activités lytiques dans la glande prothoracique du ver à soie du chêne (*Antheraea pernyi* Guér.) au stade prénymphal. II. Les vacuoles autolytiques (cytolysomes). *J. Micros.*, **6**, 349–370.

SENSE ORGANS

FUGE, H. 1967. Die Pigmentbildung im Auge von *Drosophila melanogaster* und ihre Beeinflussung durch den *white*+-Locus. *Z. Zellforsch. mikrosk. Anat.*, **83**, 468–507.

MELAMED, J., and TRUJILLO-CENÓZ, O. 1967. The fine structure of the central cells in the ommatidia of dipterans. *J. Ultrastruct. Res.*, **21**, 313–334.

MOULINS, M. 1967. Les cellules sensorielles de l'organe hypopharyngien de *Blabera craniifer* (Insecta, Dictyoptera). Étude du segment ciliaire et des structures associées. *C.r. hebd. Séanc. Acad. Sci.*, Paris, **265**, 44–47.

MOULINS, M. 1967. Les sensilles de l'organe hypopharyngien de *Blabera craniifer* Burm. (Insecta, Dictyoptera). *J. Ultrastruct. Res.*, **21**, 474–513.

SLIFER, E. H. 1967. Sense organs on the antennal flagella of earwigs (Dermaptera) with special reference to those of *Forficula auricularia*. *J. Morph.*, **122**, 63–80.

WHITE, R. H., and SUNDEEN, C. D. 1967. The effect of light and light deprivation upon the ultrastructure of the larval mosquito eye. I. Polyribosomes and endoplasmic reticulum. *J. Exp. Zool.*, **164**, 461–478.

WHITE, R. H. 1967. The effect of light and light deprivation upon the ultrastructure of the larval mosquito eye. II. The rhabdom. *J. Exp. Zool.*, **166**, 405–426.

DORSAL VESSEL AND HAEMOCYTES

CASSIER, P., and FAIN-MAUREL, M.-A. 1968. Sur la présence de microtubules dans l'ergastoplasme et l'espace périnucléaire des œnocytoïdes du criquet migrateur, *Locusta migratoria migratorioides* (R. et F.). *C.r. hebd. Séanc. Acad. Sci.*, Paris, **266**, 686–689.

HOFFMANN, J. A., STOEKEL, M.-E., PORTE, A., and JOLY, P. 1968. Ultrastructure des hémocytes de *Locusta migratoria* (Orthoptère). *C.r. hebd. Séanc. Acad. Sci.*, Paris, **266**, 503–505.

SALT, G. 1967. Cellular defense mechanisms in insects. *Fedn Proc. Fedn Am. Socs exp. Biol.*, **26**, 1671–1674.

PERICARDIAL CELLS

AGGARWAL, S. K., and KING, R. C. 1967. The ultrastructure of the wreath cells of *Drosophila melanogaster* larvae. *Protoplasma*, **63**, 343–352.

CROSSLEY, A. C. S. 1968. The fine-structure of pericardial cells in the blue blow-fly *Calliphora erythrocephala*. *J. Morph.*, in press.

FAT BODY AND MYCETOCYTES

ARNOTT, H. J., and SMITH, K. M. 1967. An ultrastructural study of the development of a granulosis virus in the cells of the moth *Plodia interpunctella* (Hbn.). *J. Ultrastruct. Res.*, **21**, 251–268. (Viral multiplication principally in fat body cells.)

EVANS, J. J. T. 1967. The integument of the Queensland fruit fly, *Dacus tryoni* (Frogg.). III. Development and ultrastructure of the fat body cells and oenocytes of the Queensland fruit fly, *Dacus tryoni* (Frogg.). *Z. Zellforsch. mikrosk. Anat.*, **81**, 49–61.

GHARAGOZLOU, I. D. 1967. Existence d'inclusions d'ultrastructure lamellaire dans le noyau de certains bactériocytes du tissu adipeux de *Periplaneta americana* (Insecte Blattidae). *C.r. hebd. Séanc. Acad. Sci.*, Paris, **264**, 1056–1057.

LOCKE, M., and COLLINS, J. V. 1968. Protein uptake into multivesicular bodies and storage granules in the fat body of an insect. *J. Cell Biol.*, **36**, 453–483.

LOUIS, C. 1967. Cytologie et cytochimie du mycétome de *Pseudococcus maritimus* (Ehrhorn) (Homoptera, Coccidae). *C.r. hebd. Séanc. Acad. Sci.*, Paris, **265**, 437–440.

MUSGRAVE, A. J., and GRINYER, I. 1968. Membranes associated with the disintegration of mycetomal micro-organisms in *Sitophilus zea-mais* (Mots.) (Coleoptera). *J. Cell Sci.*, **3**, 65–70.

SUPPLEMENTARY REFERENCES

ODHIAMBO, T. R. 1967. The fine structure and histochemistry of the fat body in the locust, *Schistocerca gregaria. J. Cell Sci.*, **2**, 235–242.

WIGGLESWORTH, V. B. 1967. Cytological changes in the fat body of *Rhodnius* during starvation, feeding and oxygen want. *J. Cell Sci.*, **2**, 243–256.

SALIVARY GLANDS AND SILK GLANDS

FLOWER, N. E., and KENCHINGTON, W. 1967. Studies on insect fibrous proteins : the larval silk of *Apis, Bombus* and *Vespa* (Hymenoptera: Aculeata). *Jl R. microsc. Soc.*, **86**, 297–310.

GAUDECKER, B. 1967. RNA synthesis in the nucleolus of *Chironomus thummi*, as studied by high resolution autoradiography. *Z. Zellforsch. mikrosk. Anat.*, **82**, 536–557.

JURAND, A., SIMÕES, L. C. G., and PAVAN, C. 1967. Changes in the ultrastructure of salivary gland cytoplasm in *Sciara ocellaris* (Comstock, 1882) due to microsporidian infection. *J. Insect Physiol.*, **13**, 795–803.

SCHIN, K. S., and CLEVER, U. 1968a. Ferritin-uptake by salivary glands of *Chironomus tentans* and its intracellular localization. *Expl Cell Res.*, **49**, 208–211.

SCHIN, K. S., and CLEVER, U. 1968b. Ultrastructural and cytochemical studies of salivary gland regression in *Chironomus tentans. Z. Zellforsch. mikrosk. Anat.*, **85**, 262–279.

INTESTINAL TRACT

ARNOTT, H. K., and SMITH, D. M. 1967. Intracellular inclusions in the gut epithelial cells of *Piesma cinereum* Say. *J. Cell Biol.*, **34**, 639–646.

COUCH, E. F., and MILLS, R. R. 1968. The midgut epithelium of the American cockroach: acid phosphomonoesterase activity during the formation of autophagic vacuoles. *J. Insect Physiol.*, **14**, 55–62.

GOURANTON, J. 1967a. Élaboration d'une mucoprotéine acide dans l'appareil de Golgi des cellules d'une portion de l'intestin moyen de divers Cercopidae. *C.r. hebd. Séanc. Acad. Sci., Paris*, **264**, 2584–2587.

GOURANTON, J. 1967b. Accumulation de ferritine dans les noyaux et le cytoplasme de certaines cellules du mésentéron chez des Homoptères Cercopides âgés. *C.r. hebd. Séanc. Acad. Sci., Paris*, **264**, 2657–2660.

GOURANTON, J. 1968a. Composition, structure, et mode de formation des concrétions minérales dans l'intestin moyen des Homoptères Cercopides. *J. Cell Biol.*, **37**, 316–328.

GOURANTON, J. 1968b. Présence d'une zone cytoplasmique différenciée autour des noyaux dans les cellules de l'intestin moyen de *Cixius nervosus* L. (Homoptera, Fulgoroïdea). *C.r. hebd. Séanc. Acad. Sci., Paris*, **266**, 818–819.

GOURANTON, J., and FOLLIOT, R. 1968. Présence de cristaux de ferritine de grande taille dans les cellules de l'intestin moyen de *Campylenchia latipes* Say. (Homoptera, Membracidae). *Revue can. Biol.*, **27**, 77–81.

HOPKINS, C. R. 1967. The fine-structural changes observed in the rectal papillae of the mosquito *Aëdes aegypti*, L. and their relation to the epithelial transport of water and inorganic ions. *Jl R. microsc. Sci.*, **86**, 235–252.

NOIROT, C., NOIROT-TIMOTHÉE, C., and KOVOOR, J. 1967. Revêtement particulaire de la membrane plasmatique en rapport avec l'excrétion dans une région spécialisée de l'intestin moyen des termites supérieurs. *C.r. hebd. Séanc. Acad. Sci., Paris*, **264**, 722–725.

NOIROT-TIMOTHÉE, C., and NOIROT, C. 1967. Liaison de mitochondries avec des zones d'adhésion intercellulaires. *J. Micros.*, **6**, 87–90.

TERZAKIS, J. A. 1967. Substructure in an epithelial basal lamina (basement membrane). *J. Cell Biol.*, **35**, 273–278.

MALPIGHIAN TUBULES

BERRIDGE, M. J., and OSCHMAN, J. L. 1968. A structural basis for fluid secretion by Malpighian tubules. *Tissue & Cell*, **1**, in press.

GRIMSTONE, A. V., MULLINGER, A. M., and RAMSAY, J. A. 1968. Further studies on the rectal complex of the mealworm *Tenebrio molitor*, L. (Coleoptera, Tenebrionidae). *Phil. Trans. R. Soc. B*, **253**, 343–382.

MALE REPRODUCTIVE SYSTEM

KESSEL, R. G. 1967. An electron microscope study of spermiogenesis in the grasshopper with particular reference to the development of microtubular systems during differentiation. *J. Ultrastruct. Res.*, **18**, 677–694.

MAILLET, P.-L., and FOLLIOT, R. 1967. Nouvelles observations sur le transport de microorganismes intranucléaires, appelés particules Phi, par les spermatozoïdes chez des insectes Homoptères. *C.r. hebd. Séanc. Acad. Sci., Paris*, **264**, 965–968.

MEYER, G. F. 1968. Spermiogenese in normalen und Y-defizienten Männchen von *Drosophila melanogaster* und *D. hydei. Z. Zellforsch. mikrosk. Anat.*, **84**, 141–175.

ODHIAMBO, T. 1968. The architecture of the accessory reproductive glands of the male desert locust. II. Microtubular structures. *Tissue & Cell*, **1**, 155–182.

TAHMISIAN, T. N., DEVINE, R. L., and WRIGHT, B. J. 1967. The ultrastructure of the plasma membrane at the division furrow of grasshopper germ cells. *Z. Zellforsch. mikrosk. Anat.*, **77**, 316–324.

FEMALE REPRODUCTIVE SYSTEM

BACCETTI, B. 1967. L'ultrastruttura delle ghiandole della ooteca in ortotteri acridoidei, blattoide e mantoidei. *Z. Zellforsch. mikrosk. Anat.*, **77**, 64–79.

HINTON, H. E. 1968. Structure and protective devices of the egg of the mosquito *Culex pipiens. J. Insect Physiol.* **14**, 145–161.

KOCH, E. A., SMITH, P. A., and KING, R. C. 1967. The division and differentiation of *Drosophila* cystocytes. *J. Morph.*, **121**, 55–70.

ROTHERAM, S. 1967. Immune surface of eggs of a parasitic insect. *Nature, Lond.*, **214**, 700.

CONNECTIVE TISSUES

ASHHURST, D. E. 1968. The connective tissues of insects. *Ann. Rev. Entomol.*, **13**, 45–74.

CELL JUNCTIONS

BULLIVANT, S., and LOEWENSTEIN, W. R. 1968. Structure of coupled and uncoupled cell junctions. *J. Cell Biol.*, **37**, 621–632.

GOURANTON, J. 1967. Structure des 'desmosomes septaux'. *J. Micros.*, **6**, 505–508.

MESSIER, P.-E., and SANDBORN, E. B. 1967. Filaments as a possible substructure of septate desmosome and membrane. *Revue can. Biol.*, **26**, 23–34.

NOIROT, C., and NOIROT-TIMOTHÉE, C. 1967. Un nouveau type de jonction intracellulaire (zonula continua) dans l'intestin moyen des insectes. *C.r. hebd. Séanc. Acad. Sci., Paris*, **264**, 2796–2798.